Catholicism and Fundamentalism

*The Attack on "Romanism"
by "Bible Christians"*

Karl Keating

Catholicism and Fundamentalism

*The Attack on "Romanism"
by "Bible Christians"*

Ignatius Press   San Francisco

Nihil Obstat: Rev. Msgr. Joseph Pollard, S.T.D.
                  Censor Librorum

Imprimatur: + Most Reverend Roger Mahony
                  Archbishop of Los Angeles
                  January 28, 1988

Cover design by Marcia Ryan

© 1988 Ignatius Press, San Francisco
All rights reserved
ISBN 0-89870-177-5 (SB)
ISBN 0-89870-195-3 (HB)
Library of Congress catalogue number 87-82939
Printed in the United States of America

Do not be afraid, speak out, and refuse to be silenced;
I am with thee, and none shall come near to do thee harm;
I have a great following in this city.
(Acts 18:9–10)

Contents

Preface 9
1. Background to Controversy 13
2. The Anti-Catholic's Sourcebook 27
3. A Mission to Catholics 51
4. Old-Time Religion, Old-Time Tactics 68
5. Bringing Catholics to Real Christianity 78
6. "I Have Literally Bent over Backwards" 86
7. Appealing to the Young 99
8. At the Fringe 107
9. Inspiration of the Bible 121
10. Tradition versus "Traditions of Men" 134
11. Development of Doctrine 142
12. Fanciful Histories of Catholicism 154
13. Salvation 164
14. Baptism of Infants 177
15. The Forgiveness of Sins 182
16. Purgatory 190
17. Peter and the Papacy 198
18. Infallibility of the Pope 215
19. The Eucharist 232
20. The Mass 246
21. Honoring the Saints 259
22. Marian Beliefs 268
23. The Inquisition 290
24. Practical Apologetics 301
25. Food for the Mind 320
26. Afterword 340
    Appendix 345
    Bibliography 347
    Index 351

Preface

Few orthodox Catholics can imagine themselves leaving their religion for another. If, in the disorientation that comes between sleep and wakefulness, they imagine changing their spiritual allegiance, they see themselves waving a fond farewell to Rome ("Well, it was almost what we were looking for") and walking but a short distance to something Romelike.

They may see themselves turning to Eastern Orthodoxy, perceived as a haven from modern religious travails, or to Anglo-Catholicism, still a lure for the romantic and for readers of Pusey, Keble, and the early Newman. Or they may see themselves withdrawing from the active practice of religion, remaining "culturally Catholic," honoring the faith of their upbringing in the breach and the perhaps twice-yearly observance (to placate spouse and children). To convert to mainline Protestantism, or to collapse into agnosticism, does not occur to them even in nightmares, and outright atheism is for crackpots and sour old men. They can contemplate only a slight shift—that, or a life of undistinguished lapsarianism.

What few practicing Catholics can imagine is that they might chuck Catholicism for something like fundamentalism, to which they are not drawn at all. Still, they know that people of their acquaintance, people from their own parishes, have made the transition, and are seemingly none the worse for wear. These former Catholics function the same way on the job, cavort with their children at the same parks, and shop at the same malls. They seem largely unchanged by their newfound faith.

Despite that, their conversion is taken as a betrayal because it is a denial. A change to Eastern Orthodoxy or Anglo-Catholicism is more an adjustment than a real switch; even becoming a lapsed Catholic makes sense, since it is a matter of letting spiritual indolence take control. But fundamentalism? To embrace it is to reject Catholicism outright, because fundamentalism does not just modify, but discards, the sacramental and liturgical core of Catholicism. One might as well subscribe to an obscure Eastern cult. To most Catholics, that would be just as sensible.

This lack of sympathy with the bare possibility of conversion to fundamentalism may be one reason the fundamentalist problem is misunderstood by Catholics. After all, it is hard to understand something that is not taken seriously. But the allure of fundamentalism *should* be taken seriously, if for no other reason than that hundreds of thousands of Catholics have taken it so seriously in the last few years that they have joined "Bible-believing" churches. Many of them have become not just non-Catholics, but anti-Catholics, because such an attitude is the natural result of the logic of their position. They perceive a duty to bring into "real Christianity" the family and friends they left at Mass, and bring them in they have. In this they have not been left to their own devices. Hundreds of organizations and thousands of individuals work to introduce Catholics to fundamentalism, and each year they distribute millions of books, tracts, and recordings. They have been remarkably successful, and their techniques and arguments are worth examining.

First, though, a few words about what not to expect. What follows will be no thorough review of fundamentalism as a whole and still less of Protestantism. The focus is on that part of fundamentalism actively engaged in anti-Catholic work and on the issues brought up in that work. Just as fundamentalists form a subset of all Protestants, so actively anti-Catholic fundamentalists are a subset of all fundamentalists. It is the tireless workers in the anti-Catholic fields who are profiled here, and even then there is room to consider only representatives of the movement and only some of their charges.

Do not expect this book to discuss what it is not meant to discuss. (There is little more frustrating for a writer than to be accused of badly handling a topic he had no intention of discussing anyway.) The focus is on those fundamentalists, whether blessed with notoriety or with anonymity, who try to convince Catholics to forsake Rome and on the arguments they make against Catholicism. Many of the best-known fundamentalists do not fall within this purview because they act irenically, making common cause with Catholics on social and political matters and never using terms such as "papist", or "Romish", or "jesuitical"—terms that are giveaways for active anti-Catholics.

Keep in mind that when we try to locate fundamentalism on the religious spectrum, we run into all sorts of terminological confusions. What popularly goes by the name may be considered one wing of evangelicalism. In fact, the theology attributed to fundamentalists in this book can be attributed to many self-described evangelicals who are put off by fundamentalism's reaction to the Catholic Church. It is easy to find people who call themselves evangelicals, who disdain fundamentalists, who are reasonably friendly with Catholics (even allowing us the title Christian), yet whose theological beliefs are indistinguishable from those of strict fundamentalists. Millions who shun the label are theologically fundamentalists.

For convenience—or out of discomfort in being bracketed with people who get a bad press—they choose a looser label. And loose it is. Evangelicalism is a spectrum. At one end it merges, even coincides, with strict fundamentalism; at the other it fades into mainline Protestantism, which is to say, religious liberalism. It is a matter of convenience that the term fundamentalist is used in these pages. There appears to be no adequate alternative. "Evangelical" is too broad; "conservative evangelical" is too awkward; "Bible Christian" implies that no other Christians base their faith on the Bible.

In covering anti-Catholic activity among fundamentalists, a writer cannot please everyone, Catholic or fundamentalist. Sometimes he cannot please anyone. Each reader will lament that something was left out, something was given too much attention, or something was given the wrong emphasis. "Why did he skip *the* one important point?" people will ask. "Why is *this* group omitted?"

The United States boasts (if that is the proper word) hundreds of anti-Catholic organizations. Only a few can be profiled here. Little-known organizations headed by little-known anti-Catholics have been given as much space as their well-known counterparts because most anti-Catholic groups are small, though their cumulative effect is large. Even then, it is not so much the groups that are examined as their arguments. The selection of arguments has not been entirely arbitrary, although it may appear so to the reader unable to find a consideration of the one that most interests him. Opponents of "Romanism" throw countless accusations against the Church. There is hardly space to list them all, let alone space to refute them. Far better, surely, to look at a sampling, stating the anti-Catholics' positions, so far as possible, in their own words and leaving room for what are intended to be adequate, although not complete, Catholic rejoinders.

The first part of this book deals with "professional anti-Catholics", fundamentalists who earn their livelihoods by attacking the "Whore of Babylon". In the second part representative issues are dissected. The final chapters give advice in practical apologetics (what to do, what not to do) and in the intellectual preparation necessary for fruitful apologetics work.

Chapter 1

Background to Controversy

The story of fundamentalism may be viewed in three main phases.[1] The first lasted a generation, from the 1890s to the Scopes Trial of 1925. Fundamentalism emerged as a reaction to liberalizing trends in American Protestantism. Under a separatist impulse and influenced by millennialism and dispensationalism,[2] it broke off, but never completely, from evangelicalism, of which it may be considered one wing. In its second phase, after what many considered a crushing defeat at Dayton, Tennessee, it passed from view but never disappeared and never even lost ground. Finally, fundamentalism came to the nation's attention again a generation ago, and it has enjoyed remarkable growth since.

Not counting quasi-Christian sects such as the Mormons and Jehovah's Witnesses, fundamentalism has experienced the greatest growth, in percentage terms, of any type of Christianity. Converts have included the previously unchurched and dropouts from other denominations. What has been surprising is that Catholics comprise a disproportionate share of the new recruits. The Catholic Church in America claims about a quarter of the country's inhabitants, so one might expect about a quarter of the converts to fundamentalism to have been Catholics at one time. Indeed, a reasonable expectation might be for an even smaller share, since people already in a church tend to remain through in-

---

[1] Standard works on fundamentalism include James Barr, *Fundamentalism* (Philadelphia: Westminster, 1977); Gabriel Hebert, *Fundamentalism and the Church* (Philadelphia: Westminster, 1957); George Marsden, ed., *Evangelicalism and Modern America* (Grand Rapids: Eerdmans, 1984); Jerry Falwell, *The Fundamentalist Phenomenon* (New York: Doubleday, 1981); Ernest R. Sandeen, *The Roots of Fundamentalism* (Chicago: University of Chicago Press, 1970).

[2] See p. 19, below.

13

ertia, while the unchurched have fewer ties to keep them from conversion. Yet in many fundamentalist congregations a third, a half, or even a majority of the members once gave allegiance to Rome.[3] This varies around the country, of course.

Fundamentalist churches in the South claim few converts from Catholicism because there never have been many Catholics there anyway. In parts of the Northeast and Midwest, where Catholics are more numerous, one finds former Catholics making up a majority of some fundamentalist congregations. In the Southwest, with a high Hispanic population, whole congregations consist of former Catholics. As many as one out of six Hispanics in this country is now a fundamentalist. So great and so rapid has the exodus been that only twenty years ago one could find almost no Hispanic fundamentalists.

Although present-day fundamentalism is mainly American[4] and is, as a movement within or alongside evangelicalism, rather new, many of its leaders speak as though it has been a well-formed, if often hidden, whole since the days of Christ. At the least, many people, both inside and outside fundamentalism, think it is unalloyed Reformation religion. This impression is bolstered by professional anti-Catholics, who speak and write like the Reformers they admire. They have steeped themselves in Calvin's *Institutes* or Luther's *Works,* and they use the diction of the sixteenth century. Writings of their opponents are called "epistles of straw" (Luther's label for the Epistle of James). They throw around the term "Antichrist" with abandon, as though it were a talisman. Whatever they dislike is "blasphemous", even if the matter at hand has nothing to do with blasphemy. And the histrionics of their pulpit orations give unhappy credence to stere-

---

[3] Many "professional anti-Catholics" converted from Catholicism, a fact that leads some critics of fundamentalism to conclude, wrongly, that anti-Catholicism is a manifestation not of doctrinal differences, but of emotional traumas in the converted.

[4] Fundamentalism is restricted mainly to English-speaking countries but it is spreading rapidly elsewhere.

otypes. (Yes, some fundamentalist preachers really do thump Bibles.)

Despite such appearances, fundamentalism's connection to the Reformation is not as clear as nonfundamentalists might think or as fundamentalists might hope. The direct historical link is not only obscure, but nearly absent. In recent years fundamentalism has received a considerable press, and people realize it is resurgent, but many also think it has been around for centuries and has only recently achieved notoriety. Not so.

True, there long have been people who have been, say, strict Calvinists, and fundamentalism is nothing if not Calvinistic. Yet until a lifetime ago fundamentalism as we know it was not a separate movement within Protestantism, and the word itself was unknown. People who today would be called fundamentalists were then just Baptists or Presbyterians or whatever; they did not perceive themselves as belonging to a religious faction within Protestantism, a faction that transcended denominational lines. In the last decade of the nineteenth century there arose issues that made them start to withdraw from mainline Protestantism, so that today, while their descendants may still be Baptists or Presbyterians or whatever, they are first fundamentalists, even if they shy away from that term and adopt one that has not been so abused by the secular media.

The issues that first divided fundamentalism from the remainder of Protestantism were the Social Gospel, a liberalizing and secularizing trend within Protestantism; the embrace of Darwinism, which seemed to call into question the reliability of Scripture; and the higher criticism of the Bible that came out of Germany. New thinkers attempted to synthesize secularism and Christianity and did so by giving up Christianity, or so the conservatives thought. In reaction to these trends early fundamentalist leaders united around several basic principles, but it was not until the publication of the series of twelve volumes called *The Fundamentals*[5] that the movement received its name.

---

[5] Hebert, *Fundamentalism*, 17.

The basic elements of fundamentalism were formulated almost exactly a century ago at the Princeton Theological Seminary in Princeton, New Jersey, by Benjamin B. Warfield, Charles Hodge, and their associates.[6] What they produced became known as Princeton theology, and it appealed to conservative Protestants who were concerned with the Social Gospel movement.

Between 1909 and 1915 the brothers Milton and Lyman Stewart, whose wealth came from oil, underwrote *The Fundamentals,* a series of twelve paperback books. The preface to the volumes explained their purpose: "In 1909 God moved two Christian laymen to set aside a large sum of money [$300,000] for issuing twelve volumes that would set forth the fundamentals of the Christian faith, and which were to be sent free to ministers of the gospel, missionaries, Sunday school superintendents, and others engaged in aggressive Christian work throughout the English-speaking world." Three million copies were distributed. Each volume contained seven or eight essays. Aside from studies of strictly doctrinal matters, there were attacks on modern biblical criticism, critiques of scientific theories, personal testimonies, commentaries on missionary work and evangelization, and accounts of heresies. The last category included essays on "Catholicism: Is It Christian?" and "Rome, the Antagonist of the Nation".[7]

There were sixty-four contributors, including scholars such as C. I. Scofield, compiler of the *Scofield Reference Bible*; W. J. Eerdman and his son, Charles; H. C. G. Moule, Anglican bishop of Durham; James M. Gray, dean of the Moody Bible Institute; and Warfield himself. They included Presbyterian ministers, Methodist evangelists, editors of religious periodicals, professors, even an Egyptologist.[8] As Edward Dobson, an associate pastor at Jerry Falwell's Thomas Road Baptist Church, put it, "They were

---

[6] Hebert, *Fundamentalism,* 17.
[7] Hebert, *Fundamentalism,* 19.
[8] Hebert, *Fundamentalism,* 17.

certainly not anti-intellectual, snakehandling, cultic, obscurantist fanatics."[9]

The fundamentals identified in the series have been tallied variously, some listing as many as fourteen points. Most commentators agree on at least these five: (1) the inspiration and infallibility of Scripture; (2) the deity of Christ, including his Virgin Birth; (3) the substitutionary atonement of his death; (4) his literal resurrection from the dead; and (5) his literal return in the Second Coming. Dobson writes, "Although some have expanded this list to include such issues as a literal heaven and hell, soulwinning, a personal Satan, and the local church, nevertheless the doctrinal character of fundamentalism still centers around the five fundamentals listed."[10]

The books were noticed by many who were unsympathetic to the views expressed in them. On May 22, 1922, Harry Emerson Fosdick, himself a theological liberal, preached on the subject "Shall the Fundamentalists Win?" He used the title of the books to designate the people he was opposing, and the label stuck. He was not, though, the coiner of the word. That honor goes to Curtis Lee Law, who, in an editorial for the New York *Watchman-Examiner* of July 1, 1920, defined "fundamentalists" as those "who mean to do battle for the fundamentals".[11]

This at least explains how the name of the movement came into being. The movement itself has a more confused origin. It had no one founder, nor was there a single event that precipitated its advent. Fundamentalist writers—especially those who write against the Catholic Church—insist that fundamentalism is nothing but a continuation of Christian orthodoxy, which prevailed for three centuries after Christ, went underground for twelve hundred years, surfaced with the Reformation, took its knocks from vari-

---

[9] Edward Dobson, "Fundamentalism—Its Roots", *New Catholic World*, January/February 1985, 5.

[10] Dobson, "Fundamentalism", 9.

[11] Hebert, *Fundamentalism*, 9.

ous sources, and was alternately influential and diminished in visibility. According to its partisans, fundamentalism is what remains after the rest of Christianity, if it can be granted the title, has fallen into apostasy.

The real history of fundamentalism is more prosaic. It is mainly an American phenomenon influenced by British evangelicalism, and it would be difficult to trace its antecedents beyond the Great Awakening of the 1720s, by the end of which, two decades later, perhaps a third of the adults in the Colonies had undergone a religious conversion. The Great Awakening might be credited with making the larger number of Americans consciously religious, and a widely spread religious sense meant a fertile ground for what would come to be called fundamentalism.

Most commentators look to the nineteenth century for fundamentalism's origin. That century saw the steady dividing of American Protestantism, as first one disaffected group split from its denomination, then another. For example, the Methodist revival of 1866, held on the centenary of the establishment of Methodism in America, culminated in the Holiness Camp Meeting of Vineland, New Jersey, a year later, and *that* culminated in schism, with the Holiness Churches splitting off from Methodism, which itself had split off from Anglicanism.

It was the nineteenth century that saw the rise of millennialism and dispensationalism, closely allied beliefs. The former refers to the literal thousand-year reign of Christ on earth (see Rev 20) and is usually accompanied by a propensity for interpreting scriptural prophecies as referring to present or imminent historical events—in recent years, the Cold War and the status of Israel. The varieties of millennialism are numerous, there being no party line on the matter among fundamentalists. There is little agreement about when the Second Coming will occur—will it be before or after the millennium?—and less agreement on how to understand what many acknowledge to be predictions about the immediate future. A century ago, millennialism was chiefly known for the frequency with which its proponents gave precise, but unfailingly wrong, dates for the end of the world. Millennialists are more circumspect today.

Dispensationalism was a theory developed by John Nelson Darby (1800–1882), founder of the Plymouth Brethren. Darby divided history into dispensations, or eras, in which God dwells in different ways with different people. Dispensationalists distinguished between Israel and the Church—one God's earthly people, the other his heavenly people. The distinctive phrase of their movement was "dividing the word of truth". This referred to deciding which parts of the Bible refer to Israel and which to the Church.

The present era was considered the "time of the Gentiles", in which Israel suffers as it awaits the fulfillment of biblical prophecies. These prophecies are to be fulfilled beginning at the Rapture, when the "saints" will be taken alive to heaven. The Rapture immediately precedes the Tribulation, which cleanses the world in anticipation of Christ's reign. Darby's writings influenced C. I. Scofield, and today many fundamentalists receive their instruction in dispensationalism from *The Scofield Reference Bible*.

Neither millennialism nor dispensationalism figures much in disputes between Catholics and fundamentalists, although many of the latter, along with many evangelicals, are preoccupied with such notions, as evidenced by the popularity of books such as Hal Lindsey's *Late Great Planet Earth*. Complaints about Catholicism seldom refer to peculiarly fundamentalist or evangelical doctrines; the focus is almost always on peculiarly Catholic doctrines. For their part, Catholics take little interest in millennialism, although it intrigued their ancestors at the turn of the eleventh century, and even less in dispensationalism, which has never intrigued any of them.

Fundamentalists regard the Bible as the keystone of their faith. Their understanding of inspiration and inerrancy comes from Benjamin Warfield's notion of plenary-verbal inspiration, meaning that in the autographs all of the Bible is inspired and the inspiration extends not just to the message God wished to convey, but

to the very words chosen by the sacred writers. For many fundamentalists, particularly those not of an intellectual bent, this
reduces to the dictation theory of inspiration—the human authors
were mere stenographers, their only task being to record what the
Voice said. This, of course, implies not only a Bible free from
error, which is also the orthodox Catholic position, but also a Bible free from ambiguity and, often, symbolism, one in which the
words are taken in the plainest sense, which often means the sense
they would have if taken out of context. (An exception is John 6,
where the Eucharist is promised. This chapter is never taken literally by fundamentalists, but is by Catholics.)

The key problem with fundamentalists' understanding of the
Bible is that they have no rational grounds for what they believe.
That sounds harsh, but it is true, and fundamentalists admit it. As
E. J. Young says, "If the Bible is not a trustworthy witness of its
own character, we have no assurance that our Christian faith is
founded upon Truth." He argues that refusing to make the Bible
alone normative is to embrace "results which are hostile to supernatural Christianity".[12] The Bible must be accepted as the sole
rule of faith because any other position leads to the abandonment
of Christianity, and that, as Churchill might say, is something up
with which we will not put. We believe the Bible to be true, say
fundamentalists, because to adopt any other position is to deny
the truths in which we otherwise believe. It is not hard to see that
this position has seldom appealed to the intellectually demanding,
since the implication is that it would be salutary to accept even a
wrong understanding of the Bible so long as basic Christian
truths, whatever one thinks they might be, are protected.

Although the doctrines of the inspiration and inerrancy of the
Bible come first to the tongue of most fundamentalists, the logically prior doctrine is the deity of Christ. For the Catholic, his deity is accepted either on the word of the authoritative and infallible
Church or because a dispassionate examination of the Bible and
early Christian history shows that he must have been just what he

---

[12] Dobson, "Fundamentalism", 7.

claimed to be, God. Most Catholics, as a practical matter, use the first method; many—the apologist Arnold Lunn[13] was a good example—use the second while not denying the first. In either case, there is a certain reasoning involved. For the fundamentalist the assurance of Christ's divinity comes not through reason, or even through faith in the Catholic meaning of the word, but in a different way.

As Warfield put it, "The supreme proof to every Christian of the deity of his Lord is in his own inner experience of the transforming power of his Lord upon the heart and life."[14] One consequence of this has become painfully clear to many fundamentalists. When one falls into sin, or when the ardor that was present at conversion fades, the transforming power of Christ seems to go, and so might one's belief in his deity. It is one thing to say that belief should so manifest itself in Christians that people will say, "See how they love one another." It is something else to posit the truth of Christ's divinity on the constancy of human holiness and spiritual consolations. This accounts for many defections from fundamentalism. The dark night of the soul, which visits many, results in jettisoning the fundamentalist position, and often what is embraced is not another brand of Christianity, but a vague agnosticism.

As an appendage to the doctrine of the deity of Christ, and considered equally important in *The Fundamentals,* is the Virgin Birth. (Some fundamentalists list this separately, making six basic doctrines instead of five.) One might expect the reality of heaven and hell or the existence of the Trinity to be next, but the Virgin Birth is taken as a vital belief, since it protects belief in Christ's deity. One should keep in mind, though, that when fundamentalists speak of Christ's birth from a virgin, they mean a virgin only until his birth. Their common understanding is that Mary

---

[13] As an example of the Catholic apologetic, see Arnold Lunn, *The Third Day* (London: Burns Oates, 1945).

[14] A. C. Dixon et al., eds., *The Fundamentals* (Los Angeles: Bible Institute of Los Angeles, 1909), 2:239.

had later children, all those disciples referred to as Christ's "brethren".

In reaction to the Social Gospel advocates, who said Christ gave nothing more than a good moral example, the early fundamentalists insisted on their third point, that he died a substitutionary death. He not only took on our sins; he received the penalty that would have been ours. He was actually *punished* by the Father in our stead.

On the matter of the Resurrection fundamentalists do not differ from orthodox Catholics. Christ rose physically from the dead, not just symbolically. His Resurrection was not a collective hallucination of his followers or something invented by pious writers of later years. It really happened, and to deny its actuality is to deny Scripture's reliability.

The most disputed topic, among fundamentalists themselves, is the Second Coming. If there is agreement, it is only on the point that Christ will physically return to Earth. When that will be is up for grabs. Premillennialists say it will be before the millennium, the thousand-year reign. Postmillennialists say it will be after. There is little consensus on just what the millennium itself will be. There are also disputes about the Rapture and the Tribulation. With respect to the latter, there is widespread disagreement on its nature and its timing with respect to the millennium. Some think it is around the corner, with the Russians playing the role assigned to the northern power in Daniel.[15] Others say it is in the distant future. If Catholics may be called partial to St. Malachy's prophecies about the Popes and to the three secrets of Fatima, fundamentalists may be termed absorbed in chronicling the Last Days, the only difficulty being that no two major commentators agree on what will happen or when.

---

[15] There are innumerable variations on the theme, with many fundamentalists coming close to mimicking William Miller both in his penchant for setting dates for the Second Coming (he guessed 1843, later 1844) and in his accuracy as a prognosticator.

Such are the five or six main points discussed in the books that gave fundamentalism its name. They are not necessarily the points that most distinguish fundamentalism today. One rarely hears much discussion about the Virgin Birth, for instance. Of course, there is no question about fundamentalists believing that doctrine (but not the perpetual virginity of Mary), but to the general public, and to most fundamentalists themselves, fundamentalism has today a somewhat different emphasis.

First to catch one's eye is the fundamentalists' reliance on the Bible to the complete exclusion of any authority wielded by the Church. The second is their insistence in a faith in Christ as personal Lord and Savior. "Do you accept Christ as your personal Lord and Savior?" they ask. "Have you been saved?" This is unalloyed Christian individualism. The individual is saved without real regard to a church, the congregation, or anyone else. It is a one-to-one relationship, with no mediators, no sacraments, just the individual Christian and his Lord. The Christian *knows* when he has been saved, down to the hour and minute of his salvation, because his salvation came when he "accepted" Christ. It came like a flash, never to be forgotten, the way it came to Paul on the Damascus Road.

In that instant, the fundamentalist's salvation was assured. There is now nothing that can undo it. Without that instant, he would be doomed. That is why the third most visible thing about fundamentalists is their evangelism. If sinners do not undergo the same kind of salvation experience fundamentalists have undergone, they will go to hell. Fundamentalists perceive a duty to spread their faith—what can be more charitable than to give others a chance for escaping hell?—and in that they have been successful.

Their success is partly due to their discipline. For all their talk about the Catholic Church being "rule-laden", there are perhaps no Christians who operate today in a more regimented manner. Their rules—mainly nonbiblical, one might add—extend not just to religion and religious practices proper but to facets of everyday life. (Strictures on drinking, gambling, dancing, and smoking come to mind.)[16] What is more, fundamentalists are intensely involved in their local congregations.

Many people returning to the Catholic Church from fundamentalism complain that as fundamentalists they had no time or room for themselves; everything centered around the church. All their friends were members; all their social activities were staged by it. Not to attend Wednesday evening services in addition to one or two services on Sunday, not to participate in Bible studies and youth groups, not to dress and act like everyone else in the congregation—these immediately put one beyond the pale, and in a small church (few fundamentalist churches have more than a hundred members) this meant ostracism, a silent invitation to worship elsewhere.

Many of the influences that have given rise to fundamentalism, including the fissiparousness of nineteenth-century Protestantism, have been signs of underlying puritanism—not, of course, the puritanism of the seventeenth-century Puritans, but the attitude that is at the core of every offshoot from traditional Christianity, the desire to return to the purity of the early Church. This kind of puritanism remains the motivating force of fundamentalism, as demonstrated by one of the key charges against the Catholic Church, that it has obscured the original purity of Christianity with centuries of unscriptural encrustations. For the fundamentalist, one of the first duties is to grasp the essence, the pith, of Christianity as it left the mouth of its Founder—and then to admit no "inventions".

Many Catholics who have written about fundamentalism misunderstand it. They psychologize it into a mass of emotional contradictions. They accept the view of the popular press that fundamentalism is not a matter of theology but of pathology. A man subscribes to the fundamentalist position, it is said, because he is ashamed of being poor, or because he is ill educated, or be-

[16] Some fundamentalists read others right out of Christianity for occasionally throwing the dice or bending the arm, although the Bible nowhere condemns gambling with one's superfluous wealth or drinking spirits in moderation.

cause the priest or minister at his previous church mistreated him and he is out for revenge or for consoling pats on the back. He does not accept fundamentalism the way an enlightened liberal accepts liberalism, with consideration and forethought. Some critics come perilously close to concluding that any fundamentalist is a loon. Granted, some are—but so are some Catholics and more than a few secularists.

Peggy L. Shriver, assistant general secretary of the National Council of Churches of Christ in the United States, says that "because an insecure ego can be supported by the scaffolding of a fundamentalist faith, it is not surprising that many people who are 'marginal' to society are drawn to fundamentalism. Various studies have shown that there are fewer wealthy and well-educated people who count themselves fundamentalists and a greater number of low-income and less educated people than the population at large."[17] This gentle put-down is imprudently echoed by Catholic writers, who might be surprised to learn that fundamentalists, such as Loraine Boettner in his *Roman Catholicism,* make the same charge against the Catholic religion, saying Catholic societies are backward compared to Protestant—after all, just look at Spain and Ireland, then at England and the United States. The Catholic Church finds its numbers among the poorer classes, they say, a sign that Catholicism is not blessed by God, since divine election manifests itself through material prosperity.[18]

Whatever forces might have steered a man to fundamentalism in the first place—and it must be granted that emotional factors play a part, as they do in most conversions, no matter the direction—he remains a fundamentalist for doctrinal reasons. He might have left his previous church out of anger or frustration, and he might have been attracted to the fundamentalist congregation down the road because the pastor is a fine preacher or because the church members befriended him.

---

[17] Peggy L. Shriver, "Guardians of Fundamentalism's Fortress", *New Catholic World,* January/February 1985, 15.

[18] Loraine Boettner, *Roman Catholicism* (Philadelphia: Presbyterian and Reformed, 1962), 13–18.

These emotional pushes and pulls are short-lived, and in most cases they merely help the convert do what he wanted to do anyway. He could have found ministers as eloquent or congregants as kind in one of the mainline Protestant churches or even in some eccentric cult, but, as important as those factors might be, they were not the reason he converted. His conversion had to do with doctrines. The doctrines to which he adheres are not ones he discovered for himself, furtively reading the Bible late at night while his wife and children slept. The doctrines he was taught first, and the Bible has been used to justify them.

Fundamentalists use the Bible to protect beliefs that are, in fact, antecedent to the Bible, which is interpreted so it justifies what they already hold, although most fundamentalists think what they believe comes straight out of the sacred text and that they are merely acknowledging its plain meaning. This confusion on their part is matched by one on the part of most nonfundamentalists, who think fundamentalists interpret Scripture in a strictly literal manner. This is incorrect. Fundamentalists do not take each word of the Bible in its surface sense, although it is commonly thought they do. To justify some of their doctrines, fundamentalists must discover in a metaphor a new "literal" interpretation of Scripture, and they not uncommonly find themselves arguing that what is really the plain, surface meaning is nothing but dangerous symbolism. They do not hesitate to read between the lines if such reading is needed to preserve their position—a position that precedes their scriptural interpretation.

In an analogous fashion, fundamentalists engaged in anti-Catholic work will interpret not just the Bible, but Christian history and Catholic creedal and apologetic works, in whatever way is required for them to prove their main point, that the Catholic religion bears only superficial resemblance to the religion founded by Christ, that it is mainly a religion of men, not of God. Their technique can be demonstrated by scrutinizing representative anti-Catholic publications, groups, and individuals.

Chapter 2

The Anti-Catholic's Sourcebook

We all like a good argument. We like the give-and-take, and we enjoy watching one party score a point and the second return the favor. A good argument, particularly on an important theme, stimulates our minds and helps us draw our own conclusions. We do not demand that each participant give both sides—each needs to give only his own, as well as he can—but we do insist on fair play. We do not want one participant to misrepresent what the other thinks or to make points by using cheap shots. Ridicule, misrepresentation, taking quotations out of context, bending the truth, leaving out important facts—these violate the rules of the game. We feel cheated if one side tries to gain an unfair advantage. If all this is true when the participants meet face to face before an audience, it is even truer when the argument is conducted in writing, when all we have is one side's version tucked between the covers of a book. Nowhere, perhaps, are these rules of fair play violated with greater regularity than in the writings of fundamentalists who attack the Catholic religion.

It is no secret that in recent years fundamentalist churches have been gaining members at a surprising rate. Many of the new recruits are former Catholics. In fact, in many fundamentalist churches, more than half the members converted from Catholicism. The reasons for the conversions are many, but most converts have been influenced by arguments attacking "Romanism". Some fundamentalists who seek out Catholics as converts are not merely profundamentalist; they are also decidedly anti-Catholic. They expend more effort on abusing the Catholic religion than on justifying their own. They are more interested in showing Catholicism is wrong, no matter what it takes to "prove" that, than they are in showing their position is right.

Just a few years ago people were saying anti-Catholicism was going the way of the dinosaur. If so, it seems the dinosaur has made an unexpected comeback, because anti-Catholicism is healthier now than it has been for years. New organizations dedicated to undermining the Church keep cropping up, and old ones are revivified, and together they turn out more tracts, magazines, and books than ever before—millions of copies each year.

After reading enough of this material one becomes aware that the same points tend to be made in the same way, even in the same words. Who is borrowing from whom? It does not seem that any of these groups relies heavily on any other. Instead, they all seem to fall back on one source, Loraine Boettner's *Roman Catholicism,* which might be called the "Bible" of the anti-Catholic movement within fundamentalism. It is in this book that the anti-Catholic position is most extensively expressed. *Roman Catholicism* is worth examining, because what credibility the anti-Catholic movement has depends largely on the credibility of this one volume.

First, a few words about the author. Loraine Boettner has to his name a dozen books, several of them still in print. His first, *The Reformed Doctrine of Predestination,* was published in 1932. Other titles include *The Christian Attitude toward War, The Atonement,* and *Immortality.* In 1962 Boettner saw through the presses the book for which he is best known, *Roman Catholicism.* It was published by the Presbyterian and Reformed Publishing Company and has been reprinted numerous times. Well over a hundred thousand copies of *Roman Catholicism* have been sold, most of them in the last few years. After a career of teaching at Protestant schools of divinity, Boettner retired to Rock Port, Missouri, from which he still issues occasional salvos against Catholics, but for the most part he is retired from the fray and gives encouragement to younger people who have taken up his fight.

When *Roman Catholicism* was first published, the book and its author gained instant notoriety. Today there are many persons, organizations, and publications that are better known as promoters of anti-Catholicism, but none is more influential. Few people realize that most professional anti-Catholics are deeply indebted to Loraine Boettner's work. Pick up an anti-Catholic tract, then turn to the same subject in *Roman Catholicism*. As likely as not, the words will be the same, simple plagiarism. In the world of religious bigotry, it seems all roads lead to *Roman Catholicism*. That is not surprising, since this fat book is full of juicy tidbits. Its 466 pages are packed with countless accusations against Catholics and their religion. It was meant to be the definitive anti-Catholic work, something that would give intellectual substance to an attitude unwelcome in most circles.

Roman Catholicism operates at two levels. On the first and more important, it is an attack on the Catholic religion, its charges ranging across doctrines, ecclesiastical and secular history, and Catholic customs. On the other level the book is a defense of Boettner's own beliefs. As he puts it, "The primary purpose of this work is to set forth in strong contrast the differences between the evangelical Protestant and the Roman Catholic churches, both in regard to doctrine and in regard to practical effects where these two systems have been effective in the lives of the people."[1] Nowadays the term fundamentalist would more commonly be used for the position Boettner espouses, and it is, indeed, mainly fundamentalists who use his text as their source of ammunition against the Catholic Church.

There is no room here to discuss each point Boettner brings up—the refutation of a one-sentence charge may take a page, and his tome would require a small library as an adequate reply—but the style of *Roman Catholicism* can be conveyed, and the reader can see there are serious deficiencies in the book, which forms the basis of the anti-Catholic movement.

The main problem with Boettner's *magnum opus* is that it suffers from a real lack of intellectual rigor. For example, he shows virtually no familiarity with the writings of the first several centuries of

---

[1] Boettner, *Catholicism*, x.

the Christian era. He skips from the Bible to nineteenth- and twentieth-century anti-Catholic works. Even if he would not go to original sources, he could have examined Johannes Quasten's *Patrology*, the first three volumes of which were composed in the decade before *Roman Catholicism* was written, or Joseph Tixeront's *History of Dogmas,* an older but standard work. A casual reading of these should have demonstrated to him that from the earliest years distinctive Catholic doctrines were present—belief in the Real Presence, the hierarchy of bishops and priests, papal supremacy, suffrages for the dead—and he should have seen there is little support for the fundamentalist position. Even if he refused to draw the ordinary conclusions from Quasten and Tixeront, he at least would have been put on notice that he had more to consider. He just takes too much for granted.

There is no indication that he has made use of any hardheaded apologetic works by Catholics or that he has tested his arguments against a knowledgeable opponent before reducing them to print. His major sources are people who do not just disagree with Catholicism but who openly oppose it, often for what the reader suspects to be base motives. Boettner accepts at face value any claim made by an enemy of the Church. Even when verification of a charge is easy, he does not bother to check up. If he finds something unflattering, he prints it.

Take as an example his reliance on William Cave, chaplain to King Charles II, who wrote in *The Lives of the Apostles* that in the Greek original of Eusebius Pamphilius' *Ecclesiastical History,* completed about 325, there is no reference to Peter being Bishop of Rome. Boettner accepts this as sufficient proof that the apostle was never in the capital of the Empire, a fact he wishes to use in debunking the papacy.[2] He could have checked Cave's assertion easily. Had he looked at the two-volume edition of the *Ecclesiastical History* in the Loeb Classical Library, he would have found on pages 144 and 190 of volume one and page 48 of volume two just what Cave said was not there.

[2] Boettner, *Catholicism,* 118.

Despite the reliance of so many pamphleteers on Boettner's book, the only thing that makes it seem substantial is its weight in pounds. Its weight in scholarly attainment is nil. It has an index of authors and an index of subjects, each only a page and a half long. In the whole book there are only two dozen footnotes, all of them added to reflect minor changes in the Catholic Church since Vatican II. Within the text biblical passages are properly cited, but references to Catholic works are usually so vague as to discourage checking. A certain Pope is alleged to have said something, but there is no citation. A Catholic author of the seventeenth century supposedly claimed such-and-so, but again no reference. A quotation might be given, but no hint as to its source. Or there might be mention of a book, but no page number. Most statements that in other books would deserve footnotes get nothing at all here. Sources that include both title and page number (and they are rare) are generally to non-Catholic works. Indeed, if this were a book on science or economics, and if it were put out by an academic press, the publisher would have insisted on literally hundreds of notes to back up the equally large number of citations, claims, and interpretations. But we get none of that here.

The lack of citations would not be important if Boettner were merely expounding his own position, but they are crucial when he dredges up what seem to be self-condemnatory admissions by Catholics. He would be under no obligation to burden his book with references if he were only stating what fundamentalism is. But more must be expected of an author who accuses the opposition of knavery and deception.

Although not all works referred to in the body of the text are listed in the bibliography, most are—yet the bibliography names only twenty-three books and three magazines. Only seven of the books, and none of the magazines, are by Catholics.[3] One book,

---

[3] The books by Catholics include James Gibbons, *Faith of Our Fathers* (Baltimore: John Murphy, 1876); John A. O'Brien, *The Faith of Millions* (Huntington, Ind.: Our Sunday Visitor, 1938); John A. Ryan and Francis J. Boland, *Catholic Principles of Politics* (New York: Macmillan, 1949); Philip Hughes, *A Popular History of the Catholic Church* (Garden City, N.Y.: Doubleday, 1949); Glenn D. Kitt-

by Fulton Sheen, is an "inspirational" text and, while enjoyable reading, has little to do with the matters discussed in *Roman Catholicism*. A second book is a look at the lives of a few Popes; another is on Catholic principles of politics, a topic hardly touched on by Boettner. Three others are overviews of the Catholic faith written for laymen, not one of which was designed to answer the kinds of attacks Boettner launches.[4] The seventh book is Philip Hughes' *A Popular History of the Catholic Church*, an abridgment of his three-volume work *A History of the Church*. As it turns out, Boettner refers to only a few lines from Hughes' book, and those are taken out of context.[5]

Of the sixteen books by non-Catholics, six are by former Catholic priests: Emmett McLoughlin; L. H. Lehmann; Joseph Zacchello; and Charles Chiniquy, the famous nineteenth-century sensationalist.[6] There is also an exposé by a former nun. To round out the picture, Boettner lists a book by Paul Blanshard, perhaps the best-known professional anti-Catholic of a generation ago. These are the books—written by disaffected ex-Catholics or by people who never have been Catholic but who have made their mark in the world by pushing unadorned bigotry—from which Boettner gets his juiciest information. Relying on them for the straight story on the Catholic Church is like relying on a political

---

ler, *The Papal Princes* (New York: Funk & Wagnalls, 1960); Martin J. Scott, *Things Catholics Are Asked About* (New York: Kenedy, 1927); Fulton J. Sheen, *Peace of Soul* (New York: McGraw-Hill, 1940).

[4] Most works that present the Catholic Faith accurately do not anticipate fundamentalist attacks and so hardly can be faulted for not answering questions they were not intended to answer.

[5] Boettner, *Catholicism*, 127. Hughes is quoted as saying that Gregory the Great "is the founder of the papal monarchy", and Boettner says Hughes is admitting that Gregory was the first Pope, which is the standard fundamentalist position. Actually, Hughes is referring to the establishment of the papal political monarchy, not to the establishment of the papacy—something clear if the few sentences quoted from him are read in context.

[6] Some of his books, such as *The Priest, the Woman, and the Confessional*, seem never to have gone out of print. There is always a market for the lurid.

candidate to tell you all the good points about his opponent. Surely Boettner would object to an attack on Martin Luther's theology that made use of works by disgruntled ex-Lutherans but ignored Luther's own writings. He would say, and rightly so, that such an attack was unbalanced, and that is just the kind of thing a reader might say of *Roman Catholicism* when he discovers how much it relies on tales from angry ex-Catholics.

Now it may well be that a man leaving one religion for another can write fairly, without bitterness, about the one he left behind. After all, John Henry Newman did just that in his autobiography, *Apologia Pro Vita Sua*. But it stands to reason that most people who suddenly think they have an urge to write about their change of beliefs just want to vent their frustrations or justify their actions. Their books should be read and used with discretion, and they should not be used at all as explanations of the beliefs of their old religion if the books betray the least hint of rancor. Unfortunately, Boettner cannot keep away from such books.

Because of his reliance on disgruntled former Catholics, Boettner has absolutely no appreciation of the Catholic religion from the inside. He has made little effort to learn what the Catholic Church says about itself and how Catholics answer the objections he makes. What "inside information" he has comes from people who can hardly be trusted to tell the Catholic side of the story. In case after case, no matter what the topic, Boettner provides only a statement of the fundamentalist position, which he then juxtaposes to a caricature of the Catholic position as set out by one of the ex-priests. Without fail, whenever the Catholic position looks foolish, as it often does in his book, it is because it has been entirely misstated. Boettner is not content with honestly giving the Catholic view and then explaining why he considers it wrong; he must give a parody of the Catholic view, and then he refutes *that*.

But that is not all. There are literally hundreds of errors of fact in this book. In any ten consecutive pages one can find ten palpable blunders. These are real mistakes, not innocent things such as typographical errors. There are major errors, and there are minor ones, and they lead one to ask at what point does sloppiness become more than mere negligence? When does it show actual bad faith, a deliberate unwillingness to do one's homework?

Consider the case of Bishop Josip Strossmayer. First take the story as given by Boettner in his chapter on the infallibility of the Pope. This doctrine was formally defined at the First Vatican Council in 1870. Before the definition was voted on by the assembled prelates, some spoke against ratifying it. One who did so was Strossmayer. Here is how Boettner recounts the story:

> Among those who opposed the decree was the scholarly archbishop [actually, bishop] Strossmayer, who made a famous speech in which he declared boldly: "I have set myself to study with the most serious attention the Old and New Testaments, and I have asked these venerable monuments of truth to make known to me if the holy pontiff, who presides here, is the true successor of St. Peter, vicar of Christ, and the infallible doctor of the church. I find in the apostolic days no question of a pope, successor to St. Peter, the vicar of Jesus Christ, any more than a Mohammed who did not then exist. Now having read the whole New Testament, I declare before God, with my hand raised to that great crucifix, that I have found no trace of the papacy as it exists at this moment."

Immediately after that long quotation, Boettner gives what he says is the end of the speech. The last sentence reads: "I conclude victoriously, with history, with reason, with logic, with good sense, and with a Christian conscience, that Jesus Christ did not confer any supremacy on St. Peter, and that the bishops of Rome did not become sovereigns of the church, but only by confiscating one by one all the rights of the episcopate."[7]

Strong language, eh? Boettner gives no source for these words attributed to Strossmayer, and with good reason. Their source was not Strossmayer. Had Boettner turned to the *Catholic Encyclopedia*, he would have discovered half a page on "the scholarly archbishop", and he would have discovered that the speech is a well-known forgery, composed by a former Augustinian priest named José Augustín de Escudero.[8]

---

[7] Boettner, *Catholicism*, 244–45.
[8] *Catholic Encyclopedia*, s.v. "Strossmayer, Joseph Georg", 14:316.

What was Strossmayer's real position on infallibility? Did he oppose the promulgation of the dogma? Yes, he did. He opposed it for ecumenical reasons. He was the bishop of Diakovar, in what is now Yugoslavia. For years he had been working for a reunification of the Eastern Orthodox churches with the Catholic Church. He thought such a reunification was a real possibility and that the formal promulgation of the doctrine of papal infallibility would be an obstacle.

Boettner explains none of this, but the facts were easily accessible to him. Read again the words attributed to Strossmayer. Do they read like the words of a European who obtained a doctorate in philosophy at twenty and a doctorate in theology at twenty-seven, who taught canon law at the University of Vienna, who was praised for his "remarkably good Latin" by the Pope? No, they read like the words of a longtime Protestant. Note, too, the sloppy way the forgery was drawn up. This "scholarly archbishop" prefaces his declaration with the clause "now having read the whole New Testament", which apparently means he had never gone through the sacred text before. At the time of Vatican I Strossmayer was fifty-five. Are we to believe this learned and mature man had never read the New Testament before the convening of the Council?

Boettner's great failing with respect to this incident is that he took no pains at all to investigate the Catholic version of the story. It would have taken ten minutes at a library to discover that the speech was not what it purported to be. He did not have to believe the *Catholic Encyclopedia* or the numerous ecclesiastical histories written by Catholics, yet he should have become suspicious when they said the speech is a forgery. He should have done further homework. But he was not as interested in accuracy as in sensationalism, which is always the enemy of truth. This story is such a great blow against the Catholic Church—why spoil it with the facts?

This gaffe about Strossmayer's speech is bad enough, but it is prefaced by a worse one. The beginning of the chapter on the infallibility of the Pope presents the reader with Boettner's explanation of what Vatican I decreed. First he accurately quotes *Pastor*

Aeternus, which states that the Pope is infallible when "he speaks *ex cathedra,* that is, when in discharge of the office of pastor and doctor of all Christians, by virtue of his supreme Apostolic authority, he defines a doctrine regarding faith and morals to be held by the universal Church."[9]

Then comes the blooper. Boettner says, "Infallibility is not claimed for every statement made by the pope [true enough], but only for those made when he is speaking *ex cathedra,* that is, seated in his papal chair, the chair of St. Peter, and speaking in his official capacity as head of the church."[10] At the end of the sentence is an asterisk, which takes the reader to this footnote: "A scientific commission appointed by pope Paul VI in July, 1968, to investigate the antiquity of the 'Chair of St. Peter' . . . reported early in 1969 that the chair dates from the late ninth century. . . ." The point is that Peter's real chair does not exist, so a Pope cannot sit in it. Since, by official decree of Vatican I, he is infallible only when sitting in Peter's chair, he cannot issue infallible definitions at all. The Catholic Church is refuted by its own archaeology!

Boettner entirely misconstrues the meaning of *ex cathedra.* It indeed translates as "from the throne" or "from the chair", but it does not mean the Pope has to be sitting in the chair Peter owned for his definition to be infallible. To speak "from the chair" is to speak in an official capacity, as when we say a judge speaks "from the bench", even if he makes his ruling while standing in the courthouse hallway. This is another mistake Boettner could have avoided had he turned to a dictionary or encyclopedia.

Although he says infallibility extends only to matters of faith and morals, and then only when a Pope makes an official pronouncement addressed to all Christians, Boettner does not understand the principles he quotes. He apparently does not realize that a Pope is not claimed to be infallible when he tries to predict tomorrow's weather or solve today's arithmetic problem. This

[9] Boettner, *Catholicism,* 235.
[10] Boettner, *Catholicism,* 235.

should be apparent to Boettner, but it is not, as shown by the following example. He relates that

> in the year 1590 Sixtus V issued an edition of the Vulgate which he declared to be final, and prohibited under an anathema the publication of any new editions thereafter unless they should be exactly like that one. However, he died soon after, and scholars found numerous errors in his edition. Two years later a new edition was published under pope Clement VIII, and that is the one in general use today. Clearly Sixtus V was in error—another example of the absurdity of that doctrine which holds that the pope is infallible in matters of faith and morals.[11]

But a Pope's order that no one should publish a version of the Vulgate differing from the official version has nothing to do with faith and morals. It is not a matter of faith that any particular edition of the Bible is without printing errors or that it has been translated accurately. The order by Sixtus V was merely a matter of discipline; it did not define a point of doctrine or of morals, a distinction Boettner does not appreciate.

One of his key points in *Roman Catholicism* is that "Romanism" must be untrue because in so many particulars it differs from the Christianity of the New Testament. Over the centuries, he says, the Catholic Church has added beliefs, rituals, and customs that contradict what is found in the Bible. He calls this "the melancholy evidence of Rome's steadily increasing departure from the simplicity of the Gospel", and he claims "human inventions have been substituted for Bible truth and practice".[12]

His point is that Catholicism cannot be the religion established by Christ because it has all these "extras", forty-five of which he lists under the title "Some Roman Catholic Heresies and Inventions".[13] A few he examines at greater length later in the book, but most are mentioned once here and then conveniently forgotten.

---

[11] Boettner, *Catholicism*, 88.
[12] Boettner, *Catholicism*, 88.
[13] Boettner, *Catholicism*, 7–9.

Although his listing takes up little space, its tone is representative of that of the book as a whole. Consider a few of the "inventions".

Item: "Making the sign of the cross . . .[A.D.] 300".[14] That's it. That's the whole charge, that the sign of the Cross was not "invented" until well into the Christian era. Actually, Christians began making the sign of the Cross at a very early date. The theologian Tertullian, writing in 211, said, "We furrow our forehead with the sign [of the Cross]."[15] Making the sign was already an old custom when he wrote. It may have been common even while some of the apostles were alive. But the mistake Boettner makes in the antiquity of the practice is not the important thing. The real question is: Why does he include this point at all? The answer: because the sign of the Cross is something not found in the pages of the New Testament. The reader is to conclude that it must be contrary to Christianity, yet that makes little sense. In fact, such a principle undermines even Boettner's own fundamentalism.

After all, fundamentalists meet for worship on Sunday, yet there is no evidence in the Bible that corporate worship was to be made on Sundays. The Jewish Sabbath, or day of rest, was, of course, Saturday. It was the Catholic Church that decided Sunday should be the day of worship for Christians, in honor of the Resurrection. And what about the form of fundamentalist services: hymns, readings, preaching? No mention is made in the New Testament of the form of worship (other than that set out at the Last Supper, which gives the outline of the Mass). If Catholicism has changed matters of practice or customs over the centuries, fundamentalism has done the same. The proper question is not whether the Church founded by Christ looks today exactly as it did then (if that is the criterion, then his Church cannot be found anywhere), but whether what purports to be his Church has kept all the same beliefs, while understanding them better and drawing

---

[14] The ellipses appear in Boettner's list of "inventions".
[15] Tertullian, *De corona* 3, 2.

out their implications more deeply, even if in external practices the Church has developed and changed over the years.

Item: "Priests began to dress differently from laymen . . . 500". So what? The same charge can be brought against fundamentalist preachers who conduct services while dressed in choir robes. Boettner's statement happens to be true, but it proves nothing. The main vestment worn by priests during Mass is the chasuble. It is really nothing more than a stylized Roman overcoat. In the sixth century, while fashions changed around them, for liturgical purposes priests kept to the clothing they had used for some time. They did not adopt special dress for Mass, but, as everyday fashions changed over time, their dress began to stand out.

On very formal occasions today, such as a presidential inauguration, the principal players wear top hats and tails. You do not otherwise see that kind of clothing anymore, but remember that Abraham Lincoln wore the equivalent as his regular attire. The present-day use of top hats and tails is another example of dress for a special occasion being frozen in a particular style. It just so happens that priests' vestments are much older than top hats.

Item: "Extreme unction . . . 526". This single line is no doubt intended to make the reader believe the Catholic Church invented this sacrament, which is also known as the anointing of the sick, five centuries after Christ. Notice that Boettner makes no effort to give the Church's explanation of the sacrament's origin. Why? Because the origin is found in the New Testament itself: "Is one of you sick? Let him send for the presbyters of the Church, and let them pray over him, anointing him with oil in the Lord's name. Prayer offered in faith will restore the sick man, and the Lord will give him relief; if he is guilty of sins, they will be pardoned" (James 5:14–15). This scriptural injunction was followed from the earliest days of the Church. If Boettner wanted to say this sacrament was "invented", he should have said it was "invented" while the apostles were still alive, but that, of course, would give the sacrament legitimacy.

Item: "Latin language, used in prayer and worship, imposed by [Pope] Gregory I . . . 600". Now it is true that Latin was used in worship in the year 600. The Church spread from the Greek-speaking East to the Latin-speaking West in apostolic times. One of Paul's epistles was written to the Christians in Latin-speaking Rome. It should cause no raised eyebrows to learn that worship was undertaken in the vernacular, which was Greek in much of the East and Latin in the West. What is Boettner's point? Maybe his complaint is that the Pope "imposed" Latin, forbidding other languages to be used. In the West, Latin did come to be used in the Mass to the exclusion of vernacular languages (such as French, German, and English) that developed centuries later because Latin became the official language of the Catholic Church—something it still is. (Vatican documents of importance are still issued in authoritative Latin versions.) Are we to conclude that there is some mystery about it? Well, there probably is, to people who do not read Latin, just as there is mystery in French to those who know only English.

So what is Boettner trying to say with this "invention"? Perhaps he wants to suggest that, until recently, priests used Latin, even after the people had turned to vernacular tongues, in order to keep secret such things as what was happening during Mass. That theory does not hold up, since even Catholics who knew no Latin knew what was going on at Mass—all they had to do was look on the right-hand pages of their missals to see the translation of the Latin that was on the facing pages. If Church authorities were trying to keep laymen ignorant about the Mass, by encouraging the use of missals they approached their task in a self-defeating way.

Item: "Worship of the cross, images, and relics authorized in . . . 786". Do Catholics give slivers of wood, carvings of marble, and pieces of bone the kind of adoration they give God? That is what Boettner seems to say. What if a Catholic were to say to him, "I saw you kneeling with your Bible in your hands. Why do you worship a book?" He would rightly answer that he does not worship a book. He uses the Bible as an aid to prayer. Likewise, Catholics do not worship the Cross or images or relics. They use these physical objects to remind themselves of Christ and his special friends, the saints in heaven. The man who keeps a picture of his family in his wallet does not worship his wife and children, but he honors them. The woman who keeps her parents' picture on the mantel does not subscribe to ancestor worship; the picture just reminds her of them so she can honor them. (Recall Ex 20:12: "Honor thy father and thy mother.") No one really thinks the pictures are themselves the objects of worship.

The origin of Boettner's story is this. In the Byzantine Empire there developed what was known as the Iconoclastic heresy, which held that all images (statues, paintings, mosaics) of saints and of God must be destroyed on the theory that they were meant to be worshiped. Eventually, around 786, this heresy was defeated, and the old custom, going back to the first century, of permitting artistic representations was again allowed. Boettner has the date right; he just does not understand the story.

Item: "Baptism of bells instituted by Pope John XIII . . . 965". What is the reader supposed to make of this? Most non-Catholics realize that Catholics baptize infants, but bells? If Catholics think they can baptize bells, why not baptize automobiles or any other inanimate object? The charge, if true, does make the Church look silly—and in a sense it really is true. There was indeed a "baptism of bells", but it was not a baptism. When a church received new bells for its tower, the bells were blessed, usually by the local bishop. Any object can be blessed, a blessing being a dedication to a sacred purpose. The ceremony used in the blessing of bells was reminiscent in some ways of the ceremony used in baptism (the bells were even given nicknames), so in popular usage it came to be called the "baptism of bells", although no Catholic thought the bells actually received a sacrament. The phrase is therefore wholly innocent, but when anti-Catholics refer to it in just a few words it looks suspicious.

Item: "Celibacy of the priesthood, decreed by pope Gregory VII (Hildebrand) . . . 1079". Anti-Catholics take considerable delight in noting that some of the apostles, including Peter, were married and that for centuries Catholic priests were allowed to marry. Catholics do not deny that some early Popes were married and that celibacy, for priests in the Latin (Western) Rite, did not become mandatory until the early Middle Ages. Anti-Catholic writers generally fail to note that all along married men have been eligible for ordination in the Eastern rites. Celibacy has never been mandatory in those rites, but in the Latin Rite it has been, as a matter of discipline. It came to be thought in the West that priests could more perfectly fulfill their duties if they remained unmarried. This follows Paul's advice.

After saying he wished those to whom he was writing were, like himself, unmarried (1 Cor 7:7–9), Paul said he thought celibacy was the best state in which to be (1 Cor 7:26), noting that "he who is unmarried is concerned with God's claim, asking how he is to please God; whereas the married man is concerned with the world's claim, asking how he is to please his wife" (1 Cor 7:32–33). When a man becomes a priest in the Latin Rite, he knows that he will not be able to marry. Marriage is a good thing (in fact, Catholics acknowledge Christ elevated marriage to a sacrament), but it is something priests are willing to forgo for the sake of being better priests. No one is forced to be a priest (or a nun, for that matter; nuns also do not marry) so no Catholic is forced to be celibate. Those who want to take the vows of the religious life should not object to having to follow the rules. That does not mean that the rules, as found at any one time, are ideal or cannot be modified—celibacy is a disciplinary, not a doctrinal, injunction—but it does mean that it is unfair to imply from the rules, as Boettner has, that the Catholic religion scorns marriage.

Item: "Transubstantiation proclaimed by Pope Innocent III . . . 1215". The implication is that transubstantiation was not believed until 1215—that it was, indeed, an "invention". The facts are otherwise. Transubstantiation is just the technical term used to describe what happens when the bread and wine used at Mass are turned into the actual Body and Blood of Christ. The belief that this occurs has been held from the earliest times. It stems from the sixth chapter of John's Gospel, the eleventh chapter of First Corinthians, and the several accounts of the Last Supper. As centuries passed, theologians exercised their reason on the belief to understand more completely how such a thing could happen and what its happening would imply. Because some of them, in trying to explain the Real Presence, developed unsound theories,[16] it became evident that more precise terminology was needed to ensure the integrity of the belief. The word transubstantiation was finally chosen because it eliminated certain unorthodox interpretations of the doctrine, and the term was formally imposed at the Fourth Lateran Council in 1215. So the use of the technical term was new, but not the doctrine. Similarly, although the term Trinity was first used by Theophilus of Antioch about 181, Christians certainly believed in the doctrine from apostolic times. They may not have understood its ramifications as they are understood today, but they believed in the Trinity. The doctrine was not invented when the official term was coined.

Item: "Auricular confession of sins to a priest instead of to God, instituted by pope Innocent III, in Lateran Council . . . 1215". It is charges such as this that make one doubt the good faith of professional anti-Catholics. It would have taken little to discover the antiquity of auricular confession—and even less to learn that Catholics do not tell their sins to a priest "instead of to God", but to God *through* a priest, appointed by our Lord as an *alter Christus,* or "other Christ", an official stand-in for Christ.

Origen, writing around 244, referred to the sinner who "does not shrink from declaring his sin to a priest of the Lord".[17] Cyprian of Carthage, writing seven years later, said, "Finally, of how much greater faith and more salutary fear are they who . . . confess to the priests of God in a straightforward manner and in sorrow, making an open declaration of conscience."[18] In the fourth century Aphraates gave this advice to priests: "If anyone uncovers his wound before you, give him the remedy of repentance. And he that is ashamed to make known his weakness, en-

---

[16] The first theologian of note to oppose the doctrine of transubstantiation was Berengarius of Tours (c. 1000–1088).

[17] Origen, *In Leviticum homiliae* 2, 4.

[18] Cyprian, *De lapsis* 28.

courage him so that he will not hide it from you. And when he has revealed it to you, do not make it public."[19]

These men, writing as much as a thousand years before the Lateran Council of 1215, were referring to a practice that was already old and well established, a practice stemming from apostolic times. Christ commissioned the apostles this way: "When you forgive men's sins, they are forgiven, when you hold them bound, they are held bound" (Jn 20:23). Clearly, no priest can forgive sins on Christ's behalf unless first told the sins by the penitent. Auricular confession is implied in the very institution of the sacrament. The Lateran Council did not "invent" the practice; it merely reaffirmed it while emphasizing the importance of penance.

Item: "Adoration of the wafer (host), decreed by pope Honorius III . . . 1220". What the reader is supposed to think, apparently, is that Catholics worship the bread used at Mass. They do not. What they worship is Christ, and they believe the bread and the wine are turned into his actual Body and Blood, including not only his human nature, but also his divine nature. If Catholics are right about that, then surely the host deserves to be worshiped, since it really is God. This matter was properly dealt with in 1769 by Samuel Johnson, who was an Anglican, not a Catholic. His biographer, James Boswell, asked him about "the idolatry of the Mass". "Sir," replied Dr. Johnson, "there is no idolatry in the Mass. [Catholics] believe God to be there, and they worship him."[20] So, if Catholics are right, then a Pope would be correct in decreeing that the host should be worshiped, just as he would be right to say Jesus should be worshiped if he were to walk into the room. Boettner should direct his complaint not at some nonexistent worship of ordinary bread, but at Catholics' notion that the bread becomes something other than bread.

Item: "Bible forbidden to laymen, placed on the Index of Forbidden Books by the Council of Valencia . . . 1229". This looks

---

[19] Aphraates, *Demonstrationes* 7, 3.

[20] James Boswell, *The Life of Samuel Johnson* (Everyman's Library), 1:376.

damaging, but the first thing to note is that there are several errors here. The first is that the Index was established in 1543, so a council held in 1229 hardly could have listed a book on it. Second, there apparently never has been a Church council held in Valencia, Spain. Even if there had been, it could not have been held in 1229 because the city was then controlled by the Moors. It is inconceivable that Moslems, who were at war with Spanish Christians and had been off and on for five centuries, would allow Catholic bishops to hold a council in one of their chief cities. The Christian armies did not liberate Valencia from Moorish rule until nine years later, in 1238. So Valencia is out. But there is another possibility, and that is Toulouse, France, where a council (but not an ecumenical council) was indeed held in 1229. And, yes, that council dealt with the Bible, yet here again Boettner errs. He says the Bible was forbidden to laymen; the implication is that no layman anywhere was permitted from that point on to read any Bible. Not so.

The council held in Toulouse dealt with the Albigensian heresy, a variety of Manichaeanism, which maintained that marriage is evil because the flesh is evil. From this the heretics concluded that fornication could be no sin because what happens to flesh is of no importance. They even encouraged ritualistic suicide among their members because self-murder, which affected only an evil body, could not be immoral. They opposed the taking of oaths, and this undermined the social order, since feudalism rested on oaths of loyalty to one's superior, much the way our society rests on the security of contracts.

In order to promulgate their views, the Albigensians used vernacular versions of the Bible to "substantiate" their theories. The Church had no complaint about mere translations of the Bible; vernacular versions had been appearing for centuries. But the Albigensians were twisting the Bible to support an immoral moral system. So the bishops at Toulouse restricted the use of the Bible until the heresy was ended. They were trying to stop the heresy's spread because it was the cause of civil unrest and considerable suffering. Their action was a local one, and when the Albigensian problem disappeared, so did the force of their order, which never affected more than southern France. This is hardly the across-the-board prohibition of the Bible that Boettner, for debating purposes, would like to see but that never existed.

Item: "Cup forbidden to the people at communion by Council of Constance . . . 1414". The implication is that bishops and priests were trying to keep from laymen something they should have had by rights. The real situation is not hard to understand. The Catholic position has always been that after the Consecration the actual Body and Blood of Christ are contained in the smallest particle of the host or the tiniest drop from the cup. One does not receive only the Body in the host and only the Blood from the cup. If that were so, then for a complete Communion one indeed would need to partake of both. But if both the Body and Blood are contained in each, then the communicant needs to receive only one, if there are good reasons for imposing such a restriction. In 1414 there seemed to be. The first reason was that some people misunderstood the Eucharist and thought it had to be received under both forms because one form contained only the Body and the other only the Blood. By restricting communicants to the host alone the Church emphasized the true doctrine. The other reason was a practical one. In giving the cup to the laity there was a chance the contents would be spilled, so, out of respect, the restriction was imposed.

Item: "Apocryphal books added to the Bible by the Council of Trent . . . 1546". This is reminiscent of the remark made in *1066 and All That* that at the English Reformation "the pope and his followers seceded from the Church of England"—the difference being that Boettner is serious. The fact is that the Council of Trent did not add to the Bible what Protestants call the apocryphal books. Instead, the Reformers dropped from the Bible books that had been in common use for centuries. The Council of Trent, convened to reaffirm Catholic doctrines and to revitalize the Church, proclaimed that these books always had belonged to the Bible and had to remain in it. After all, it was the Catholic Church, in the fourth century, that officially decided which books composed the canon of the Bible and which did not. The Council of Trent came on the scene about twelve centuries later and merely restated the ancient position.

These "inventions" are representative of the forty-five listed by Boettner. No effort is made to give sources for his charges, and little effort is made to say what the significance of the "inventions" might be. That task is left to innuendo. What Boettner implies is that any belief or practice not found in the pages of the New Testament in plain words must be spurious and must have been instituted for some nefarious purpose.

What he does not point out is that fundamentalism has doctrines and customs that are not found in the Bible either. Many fundamentalist churches, for example, forbid the drinking of wine as sinful, yet Christ not only drank wine—he was even accused of being a drunkard (Lk 7:34)—but he made wine out of water, hardly something he would have done had he disapproved of drinking it. The examples could be multiplied. The fact is that no church looks exactly the same as that of the New Testament era, and, since Christ founded a living Church, one should expect it, like any living thing, to grow and mature, changing somewhat in appearance while maintaining the same identity and substance, holding on to the original deposit of faith while coming to understand it more deeply. The real question is not why Catholicism has produced "inventions" but why one thinks Christ's Church should not have.

The imaginativeness displayed in Boettner's "inventions" is representative of the writing one finds throughout *Roman Catholicism*. Consider some of his other comments. He calls All Souls' Day, November 2, "Purgatory Day",[21] a term never used by Catholics because the feast is not in commemoration of purgatory but of the souls there. He thinks the sacrament of orders involves not just the ordination of priests, but the "consecration of nuns".[22] He believes Our Lady of Guadalupe was really "a god-

---

[21] Boettner, *Catholicism*, 185.
[22] Boettner, *Catholicism*, 189.

dess worshipped by the Indians in Mexico".[23] As an argument against monasticism, he says Christ "did not withdraw himself from the world, nor did he teach his disciples to do so".[24] Boettner forgets that Christ spent forty days in the desert in preparation for his public ministry (Mt 4:1–11; Lk 4:1–13), and if that is not withdrawing oneself from the world, what is?

More common than these silly mistakes are Boettner's appeals to sensationalism. He says "the feeling of fear and dread of the priest, so characteristic of people in Romanist lands, is comparable only to the fear and dread that pagan people have for the witch doctor",[25] which demonstrates how little he knows of either. He argues against the Real Presence by saying the Catholic understanding of the Eucharist amounts to "cannibalism".[26] He suggests the Church encourages devotion to Mary because pilgrimages made in her honor bring "huge revenues to the Vatican".[27] What is more, Mary is thought of by Catholics "as a kind of fourth person of the Blessed Trinity".[28] He believes a "large number of gangsters and crooked politicians in the big cities . . . have maintained their standing in the church while continuing uninterruptedly their evil practices. . . . It is generally accepted that Romanists, having been to Mass, especially on Sunday, can do about as they please the remainder of the day."[29]

Boettner approves of the opinion of another writer that "the intellectual and moral level of priests is not nearly as high as, for instance, that of teachers and doctors, and . . . only a minority have any exceptional ability or deep religious feeling".[30] He asks, "Why is it . . . that the Roman Catholics of Southern Ireland are so inferior to their Protestant neighbors in Northern Ireland?"

---

[23] Boettner, *Catholicism*, 136.
[24] Boettner, *Catholicism*, 302.
[25] Boettner, *Catholicism*, 53.
[26] Boettner, *Catholicism*, 176.
[27] Boettner, *Catholicism*, 163.
[28] Boettner, *Catholicism*, 151.
[29] Boettner, *Catholicism*, 184.
[30] Boettner, *Catholicism*, 59.

His answer is a quotation from Charles Chiniquy, who said "the principal cause of the degradation of Ireland is the enslavement of the Irish women by means of the confessional".[31] And, according to a book Boettner cites, young women who enter the convent are taught to hate their parents.[32] The list could go on, but why bother?

Bishop Fulton Sheen said that few people in America hate the Catholic religion, but many people hate what they mistakenly believe is the Catholic religion—and that if what is hated really were the Catholic religion, Catholics would hate it, too. Confusing lists—lists intended to cause confusion, such as the one published in *Roman Catholicism*—and gratuitous slurs have done much to foster this hatred and confusion. What is more, they have discouraged fundamentalists from finding out what the Catholic religion really is, and that is a disservice to both fundamentalists and Catholics.

A reader can forgive an author a few mistakes. Perhaps the publication schedule did not allow all the checking and rechecking he might have wanted. Maybe the book's editor was incompetent. The typesetter may have erred. But when the mistakes are so gross and so frequent as Boettner's, when there is almost no effort to present the other side's point of view, when the "authorities" one relies on to state the Catholic position are mainly professional Catholic baiters—when all this happens, can the reader be blamed for thinking the book was composed in bad faith?

Like others before him, Loraine Boettner has found an enemy of his own fashioning. He castigates it, misrepresents it, ridicules it, but it is not the Catholic religion as Catholics know it, and the "history" he presents is not the history of the Catholic Church. He has given the public what may be fundamentalism's most sustained attack on "Romanism". It is an attack that has enjoyed, so far, a certain success, but its manifest inadequacy suggests that it, too, will pass. *Roman Catholicism* has been an effective propaganda

---

[31] Boettner, *Catholicism,* 215.

[32] Boettner, *Catholicism,* 323.

tool only because its arguments were not challenged early enough by Catholics. Now that is changing. Eventually Boettner's book and the anti-Catholic movement relying on it will be widely appreciated to be the embarrassments they are. Toward that end, it may be profitable to examine some of the groups and persons that have drawn their inspiration from Boettner.

Chapter 3

A Mission to Catholics

Outside the Baptist church where the head of Mission to Catholics International was to speak there was a large table filled with Catholic artifacts. It was set up for the titillation of the congregants. People were shaking their heads over what they saw, wondering how these pagan trinkets could be used by folks who called themselves Christians. Bartholomew F. ("Bart") Brewer, a former Discalced Carmelite priest, was going to tell these California Baptists the dark secrets of the Catholic Church. He had been to this church before, but they were anxious to hear more stories about the people trapped in Romanism. Next week he would be halfway across the country, telling the same things to others, some old friends, some new listeners.

Ruth Brewer, Bart's wife, stood behind the table and explained what these peculiar items were. She pointed out holy cards, rosaries, medals, scapulars, crucifixes. The main attractions were a chalice filled with small hosts and a large priest's host, all presumably unconsecrated. They were brittle with age, but quite serviceable—"Cookie Christs", as some opponents of the Church call them. To one side were some of the dozens of tracts published by Mission to Catholics, each attacking some facet of Catholicism, and books and cassette tapes that the Brewers' ministry made available. It was a festive occasion.[1]

The service began with the customary hymns, a few homiletic words from the minister, and announcements from Brother This and Sister That. Then Bart Brewer was introduced, and he told

[1] The pastor of the church told a visitor, "We bought this place from the Jews at a good price", beating them at their own game, he apparently thought.

them what he had told them before, and they loved it. "Amen, brother!" someone shouted, and he was echoed by others in the small church. "Amen, amen!" Heads nodded in agreement at each revelation of Catholic iniquity and shook in despair as the listeners were told of the doom awaiting Romanists if they did not convert to Christianity.

The talk was part anatomical, part autobiographical. Brewer dissected Catholicism, using quotations from the Bible to show how it strayed from the New Testament. The treatments of Catholic doctrine and history were cursory and, unsurprisingly, skewed; there was no effort to suggest what the Catholic rejoinders might be. He mentioned experiences as a priest, how his reading the Bible convinced him the Catholic Church was not the Church established by Christ. He spoke about his ministry, which started small but, although still small in terms of personnel (his wife, at least one paid assistant, and several volunteers to handle the mail), had grown so that he regularly crisscrossed the country and mailed out hundreds of thousands of tracts and thousands of books[2] and cassettes each year.[3]

He ended his talk the way he ends them all, with an appeal for action. If Catholics do not leave the Church of Rome, he said, they will be damned. Like the Moslems, like the Jews, they will go to hell, and their pious actions will not help them in the least. They must be saved, and it is up to real Christians to take the gospel to them. The way to do that is to wean them from the Catholic Church, showing them its errors, how it contradicts the Bible, how it has been built on paganism.

---

[2] The books include titles by Avro Manhattan, an inveterate anti-Catholic and author of *The Vatican-Moscow-Washington Alliance, The Vatican Billions, Catholic Power Today, Murder in the Vatican,* and *Vatican Imperialism in the 20th Century.*

[3] The last year for which Mission to Catholics International published figures was 1979. In its January 1980 newsletter, it reported that during the previous year more than 250,000 books, tracts, and tapes were distributed. At that time most of the organization's work was restricted to the seven westernmost states. It has since expanded throughout the continental United States and into Europe.

A good way to start, he said, is by forming a committee for evangelization. The members pray together and then head for the front, the lines of battle being drawn outside Catholic churches. There, as people leave Mass on Sunday morning, Mission to Catholics tracts are distributed. (The most zealous evangelists might, after the last Mass and despite treading on pagan ground, enter the churches and, going even further than Brewer advises, slip tracts into missalettes. That way Catholics would read the truth about the Mass during the Mass itself.)[4]

Of course, distributing tracts implies fielding questions, so the committee members would have to do more than just pray in preparation for their ministry. They would have to study. First would come Scripture. Already avid Bible readers, they would have to redouble their efforts to anticipate any Catholic rebuttals. Then, of course, they would review the Mission to Catholics materials, including its tracts; monthly newsletter, *Challenger*; and Bart Brewer's autobiography, *Pilgrimage from Rome*.[5] Next, they could turn to literature put out by other anti-Catholic organizations. There would be much to learn, but much to learn from. Indeed, there is no shortage of anti-Catholic materials and no shortage of anti-Catholic organizations. This is a boom industry, and Bart Brewer is on the cutting edge. But his is not the only group convincing people to leave St. Miscellanius' for Good Book Baptist, and Mission to Catholics was not even first on the scene, nor has it received the most press.

At the fringe, and therefore garnering the most publicity, are Tony Alamo and Jack Chick. Alamo's is the ministry that distributes posters claiming that the Catholic Church owns all the major media—which, if true, would at least demonstrate that the Church is the worst-managed organization in the world, since it

---

[4] Although leaders of anti-Catholic groups regularly deny any advocacy of trespassing, harassment, or vandalism, their rhetoric is so strident that their more zealous followers draw the necessary inferences.

[5] Bartholomew F. Brewer, *Pilgrimage from Rome* (Greenville, S.C.: Bob Jones University Press, 1982).

cannot even instruct its employees to write good copy about itself. Chick's is the outfit that publishes the *Alberto* comic books and pocket-sized booklets, also illustrated, that reveal secrets hidden even from Maria Monk. These two groups account for many column inches, but few conversions. They are the perfect bogeymen: frightening in visage, but essentially harmless. To be converted by them, one already has to be, mentally, a lost cause, the kind of person who would as likely support flat-Earthism or preach a diet of yak milk and powdered sparrow eggs.

More responsible, if that is the word, and certainly more effective, are groups such as the Conversion Center, Jimmy Swaggart Ministries, Christians Evangelizing Catholics, and Mission to Catholics International. Some have been around for decades and have seen themselves revivified by the renewed interest in anti-Catholicism. Others rely on television and rake in a bundle, part of it, ironically enough, from Catholics. But most anti-Catholic organizations are small, confining their work to a single state or even to a single city. Of all the groups, large or small, Mission to Catholics has the greatest variety of literature for sale and is surely one of the most effective in producing conversions.

Bart Brewer's account of his conversion to fundamentalism appeared first in a tract, *The Conversion of a Catholic Priest*. It was expanded into *Pilgrimage from Rome,* published in 1982 by what is perhaps the leading anti-Catholic publisher, Bob Jones University Press. The book, although more complete than the tract, is less a self-revelation than a course in anti-Catholicism set in the first person.

Most people think Catholics convert to fundamentalism because they conclude the Church is too "liberal" dogmatically and that they convert to modernist religions or no religion because the Church is perceived to be too "conservative". Bart Brewer's conversion throws these notions for a loop. His conversion to a more "conservative" Christianity came about through what is generally regarded as a "liberal" motive: dislike of celibacy.

He was ordained in 1957, at age twenty-eight, at the Shrine of the Immaculate Conception in Washington, D.C. for the Discalced Carmelites. Shortly thereafter he was assigned to the Philippines. There he promptly got involved romantically with a high school girl, and his bishop as promptly sent him packing for home. He left the Carmelites and became a secular priest, working in a parish in San Diego. "My psychological motivation for celibacy was decreasing rapidly", he wrote.[6] "I was not at all hesitant then [when Pope John XXIII convened the Second Vatican Council] to be outspoken in my anticipation that the law of celibacy would be removed." When it was not, "for the first time I doubted the authority of my church, not in religious pride, but in true sincerity".

He admitted recognizing that "celibacy was not dogma but tradition and church law", and he said that throughout his religious schooling ("four years of the prep, two years of the novitiate, three years of philosophy, and four years of theology"), "never once did I question one iota of Roman Catholic teaching". It is a little hard to see how the Church's refusal to change a mere disciplinary rule could result in Brewer's doubting the authority of the Church—the wisdom of the Church's leadership, perhaps, but its authority?

Sounding like a modernist shedding his Catholic past, Brewer "soon realized that to think and to reason on one's own, without the help of Mother Church, was not sin", although nowhere has he cited a Catholic authority that suggests thinking on one's own is sinful. He found himself working in Long Beach as a Navy chaplain, going home each night to his mother's apartment, where the two of them would listen to fundamentalist radio preachers. They "began to question teachings such as purgatory, the immaculate conception of Mary, the assumption of Mary, and the seven sacraments in the light of Scripture. The very last sacrament we were willing to relinquish in the light of Scripture was the Holy Eucharist", which seems particularly odd since Fulton Sheen, no slouch on matters of conversion and unconver-

---

[6] In a tract titled *The Conversion of a Catholic Priest.*

sion, once remarked that, as a rule, the first thing to go is one's belief in the Real Presence.

Brewer's mother, then in her sixties, was secretly baptized in a Protestant church, not telling him so he would not rush his decision. But when his stint with the Navy was up shortly thereafter, they packed their bags and took off for San Francisco, with hardly a fare-thee-well to his bishop. His next task, he said, was to determine what the ultimate religious authority might be. He found his authority in the Bible.

It was in the Seventh-Day Adventist Church, which he joined because his mother already had, that Brewer met his future wife. Only after he and Ruth were married and he had served as pastor of an Adventist church for some time did he discover that the writings of Ellen G. White, the founder of the sect, were to be considered as inspired as the Bible. That, he said, was too much to take, so he resigned his pastorship. (He did not explain how he could have been an Adventist minister and not have known the status of Mrs. White's writings, just as it must be the rare Mormon elder who does not know the Book of Mormon is placed on a par with Scripture.)

He and Ruth, with their young son, returned to San Diego, where he decided to begin an organization that would help Catholics convert to fundamentalism. "I felt there was a real need for a church that would bridge the gap between Catholicism and Protestantism. Many felt uncomfortable or afraid of Protestant churches, but being a former priest, I believed, would help them feel more comfortable in leaving their church. I understood their frustration, I had faced their questions, I had experienced the same difficult decision to leave." He never did establish his own church; Mission to Catholics is a traveling ministry. Each weekend Brewer speaks at one or more Protestant churches, almost all of them Baptist, and solicits both financial aid and recruits. The recruits are trained in the techniques of distributing tracts and adroitly avoiding tough questions. (They routinely fall back on the line "let me ask my pastor".) Each week thousands of tracts are mailed out.

Most are written by Brewer himself. Others bear the names of other former priests, such as Mark Pena; Anthony Pezzotta; and L. H. Lehmann, author of *Out of the Labyrinth*. Bob Jones, chancellor of Bob Jones University, has his name on one Mission to Catholics tract, *The Church of Rome in Perspective*. It is a reprint of an article he wrote for a magazine, *Faith for the Family*, distributed by his school, and is perhaps the most ill-tempered tract published by Mission to Catholics. Its invective, only occasionally matched in Brewer's own writings, which are pointed enough, makes one wonder about the temptations one must undergo in a ministry such as this.

Jones begins by saying, "Pope Paul VI, archpriest of Satan, a deceiver and an antichrist, has, like Judas, gone to his own place." The tract goes downhill from there. At one point Jones attempts to raise the level of discussion, if only momentarily, by citing a diary kept by Bernard Berenson, the famous art collector and critic (who was, by the way, an Episcopalian). Here is what Jones says:

A pope must be an opportunist, a tyrant, a hypocrite, and a deceiver or he cannot be a pope. Bernard Berenson, in his *Rumor and Reflection* (a sort of notebook which he kept while hiding from the Germans in the hills above Florence during the Second World War), tells about the death of an early twentieth-century pope as described by his personal physician. When they came to give him the last rites, the pope ordered the priest and acolytes from the room, crying, "Get out of here. The comedy is over."

The gist, then, is that some unidentified Pope, knowing his end was at hand, acknowledged that his office and religion were jokes and that he had lived a lie.

Compare what Jones gives with what Berenson actually wrote:

Yesterday a friend was here, a Roman of good family, closely related to the late Cardinal Vannutelli and thus in touch with the Vatican. He told me that soon after the death of Pope Benedict XV, his own father was dying. A priest was called in, but the father refused to see him. Thinking to comfort the son, the priest said: "Don't take it hard. Such things will happen nowadays. Why, the late Holy Father on his deathbed sent away the priests with: 'Off with you, the play is over' " (*la commedia e finita*). His Holiness surely meant *commedia* as *divina*, *Divine Comedy* like the title of Dante's masterpiece.[7]

The problem is not just that Jones did not report the words accurately or that he attributed the story to the Pope's physician. The problem is that he did not know (or care) what the Pope was referring to when he said *la commedia e finita*. If Jones were to read the *Divine Comedy*, he would be sorely disappointed to find in it no guffaws or rib-tickling jokes, and the reason is that the word "comedy" is used in a much older sense than the one having to do with humor. Berenson was right to translate *la commedia e finita* as "the play is over". Another way to put it might be "the drama of my life is over", which is hardly the confession of duplicity Jones wishes us to think the Pope made.

To what extent has Bart Brewer allowed himself to become like some of the people with whom he rubs shoulders? In private discussions he is invariably polite, and in his writings and in public talks he professes love for individual Catholics, yet he collaborates with people such as Bob Jones, who is unable to make the same claim with a straight face. The influence of such people shows. *Challenger* contains innumerable misrepresentations of Catholic doctrines and history, and Brewer's penchant for them no doubt comes from his imprudence in his choice of accomplices, who care little about accuracy. Apparently he works on the principle that the enemy of my enemy is my friend, but that is courting danger. He should keep in mind C. S. Lewis' remark that when supping with the devil, one needs to use a long spoon.[8]

Brewer has made the same mistake Loraine Boettner made when he wrote *Roman Catholicism*. Boettner relied heavily on professional anti-Catholics such as Lehmann, Charles Chiniquy (a

---

[7] Bernard Berenson, *Rumor and Reflection* (New York: Simon and Shuster, 1952), 43.

[8] C. S. Lewis, *The Weight of Glory* (Grand Rapids: Eerdmans, 1949), 56.

nineteenth-century sensationalist every bit as reliable as Maria Monk), and Paul Blanshard. Now Blanshard, the chief anti-Catholic writer of a generation ago, was not even a Christian—in fact, he was a secular humanist—yet Boettner had no qualms about quarrying his work for rocks to throw at the Church. The claim of leading fundamentalists that their attacks on the Catholic religion are made out of love for individual Catholics loses much of its credibility because they are unwilling to decline the use of unfair tactics. One might say they are unwilling to wage a just war; they want to do battle, and they do not hesitate to use any weapon at hand, no matter how foul.

In a way, of course, this is good, since much of what they write unintentionally repels. It is difficult for an informed Catholic who studies anti-Catholic literature to refrain from saying, "Here, let *me* do it! I can present your case more convincingly than you can." Still, there are the numbers. However ineptly the fundamentalist position may be expressed, it draws each year thousands of Catholics out of the Church, and it makes that many more workers for the anti-Catholic movement. No matter how many people shut their minds to fundamentalism because of excesses by fundamentalist writers, countless others embrace that form of Christianity because what they read convinces them of its truth. At the least, they find anti-Catholics writing about issues that seem to matter, that affect their salvation—issues usually ignored by Catholic writers and the diocesan press.

This may account for the popularity of *Challenger*. Typeset on a microcomputer, it is printed on a single sheet of paper folded once to make a four-page self-mailer. It carries no illustrations, other than an occasional reproduction of the cover of *Pilgrimage from Rome*. The front page is usually written by Brewer and features essays on topics such as "Catholics and the Bible", "The Wealth of Rome", "Biblical Christians Will Leave Romanism", and "Is There a Mediatrix?" This is the preachy page.

The second page is always a testimonial from "another ex-Catholic for biblical Christianity". Stories are given by men and women, young and old. They speak of rather sudden conversions—not generally as quick as the one on the Damascus Road, perhaps, but nothing remotely like the drawn-out process undergone by converts to Catholicism such as John Henry Newman, Arnold Lunn, or, more recently, Sheldon Vanauken and Thomas Howard. Consider representative examples.

Joanne Diriam[9] said she had visited the Shrine of the Immaculate Conception in Washington, D.C. "I had been reading about the Pope being in South America. . . . All of a sudden, I could not understand why the 'poor people' had to support a church that was obviously extremely rich! . . . I knew that I could no longer be Catholic." Her explanation makes one think of a story told by Fulton Sheen.[10] He had been giving a retreat to priests, and one of the younger priests asked him during one of his talks why the Church did not liquidate its holdings, sell off the ornaments and artwork, and give everything to the poor. The young man was rather insistent, and he came up to Sheen later and made the same point. Sheen looked at him closely and asked, "How much did you steal?" "What?" was the reply. "How much did you steal?" repeated Sheen. Then the young priest told the truth. He had been stealing from the collection basket, and he justified his acts by saying the Church was too wealthy anyway and could afford the loss.

Joanne Diriam let the cat out of her bag in an aside, noting that when the Pope was in South America, "he had reprimanded those very poor people regarding birth control". If Sheen were here, he would probably trace her conversion to her dislike of the Church's position on contraception, her concern being not so much the foreign poor's access to the pill, but her own. No one, he might say, could be so ignorant of the Church's temporal condition that the discovery of the existence of a finely ornamented church would trigger an instantaneous conversion. Complaints about the alleged wealth of the Church are always excuses for something else.

---

[9] *Challenger* (San Diego: Mission to Catholics International), June 1985.
[10] Given in conferences at a retreat for the priests of the Archdiocese of Washington in 1974.

Like the others who have decided to "tell all", Norman Nichols[11] was raised a Catholic. When he was about thirty, his "born-again" Baptist roommate convinced him to visit a Baptist church. His landlady, also a Baptist, had been pushing him to go for some time, and he regularly told her no, but he felt he could not refuse his friend. He went and was so moved that he responded to the altar call. "I never did go back to the Roman Catholic Church." This was a man who claimed to have been well instructed as a Catholic and who said he regularly practiced his religion.

Larry Wise[12] was twenty-eight when he converted. As a Catholic, he had never once read the Bible, but he did read Hal Lindsey's *Late Great Planet Earth*, and he watched Jack Van Impe on television. He decided to go on one of Van Impe's Holy Land tours and while on it received an anti-Catholic tract. When he returned home and went to Mass, "I saw the statues, I remembered the verses: 'Thou shalt not make unto thee any graven images' (Ex. 20:4). Then I thought of the Rosary and remembered another verse: 'For there is one God, and one mediator between God and men, the man Christ Jesus' (I Tim. 2:5). As I sat watching the priest I remembered other verses: 'A bishop (pastor) must be blameless, the husband of one wife. . . .' (I Tim. 3:1–5); 'Call no man your father upon the earth; for one is your Father, which is in heaven' (Matt. 23:9)." More verses came to mind (his short tour of the Holy Land apparently having been a cram course in New Testament memorization), and he quickly concluded that he "could no longer participate in a church where the teachings are so contrary to what the Bible teaches". Like the others, he unpoped.

The third page of each *Challenger*, the correspondence page, is devoted to short testimonials and notes of thanks.[13] No names are given for the writers, only the states of residence. One writer

---

[11] *Challenger*, April 1985.

[12] *Challenger*, February 1985.

[13] Complaints from Catholics are printed occasionally, most of them badly reasoned or entirely unreasoned; they serve as useful straw men.

complained that "this area has many wicked ways of life like drinking, dancing, and gambling. The priest usually takes part in these things and doesn't tell the poor, uninformed people the truth." Another said, "I have already won my boss and hopefully my brother in St. Louis with the tracts you sent." A New Yorker wrote, "As of today I am no longer a Catholic. I have been reading the Bible for the last three years, and then a friend gave me *Scriptural Truths for Roman Catholics,* [a tract] from your organization. I would like as many as possible to pass along." Many people write about trying to convince their spouses or children to convert. One man, reporting success, said, "I was a Catholic for 45 years. My wife and five children have all been saved." Another reported that "I am an ex-Catholic, now newly born-again, and am encountering much hostility from my family. I need a lot of prayers and help in ministering and witnessing to them." Some report even bringing their aged parents into fundamentalism.

The fourth page of *Challenger* often sports an ad for *Pilgrimage from Rome* ("one copy: $6.50; ten copies: $44.00") and a list of Brewer's scheduled talks—one or two each weekend, others during the week, generally at Baptist churches. The list demonstrates that Brewer's ministry extends across the country, even across the Atlantic—he undertook his first, extensive speaking tour of Europe in 1986. He is constantly on the move, preaching, for instance, at thirteen churches in New York State in one month.[14]

This last page of the newsletter also includes requests for prayers, usually for financial assistance or for the conversion of some straggler. Not all the prayers have been answered in the way desired. In 1981 Mission to Catholics started a daily, fifteen-minute radio program called "Contend for the Faith", with Brewer as the principal speaker. It was aired first on a station in San Diego, and there were plans to expand into other markets. In a much-ballyhooed campaign, subscribers to *Challenger* anted up ten

---

[14] Including a talk, appropriately enough, in West Babylon, New York. *Challenger,* March 1985.

thousand dollars to get the program started and were asked to pray for its expansion. But contributions from listeners could not meet costs, and the original kitty was quickly depleted. In short order the schedule was cut to Saturdays only. Even that was too expensive, and the program was finally, and quietly, canceled.

Challenger goes out, of course, mainly to committed fundamentalists, some of whom are themselves converts from Catholicism, some of whom are hereditary anti-Catholics. The publication keeps people informed about the work of the organization and provides them, over a period of years, with a fairly complete apologetics course, at least regarding anti-Catholicism.

It is not the newsletter, though, that convinces people to jump ship, to leave the Barque of Peter at fundamentalism's siren call. That task is left to Mission to Catholics' books and tapes, but mainly to its many tracts, dozens of them. They are divided into four groups: testimonies of former priests (including one by Brewer himself and one by Charles Chiniquy); testimonies of former nuns (such as *Ex-Nun Finds Peace with God*); testimonies of former Catholic laymen (the Bible being one woman's *Passport to Freedom*); and miscellaneous tracts, most of them on particular Catholic doctrines or practices. Far and away the most popular tract, if encomiums printed in *Challenger* are any indication, is Brewer's *Scriptural Truths for Roman Catholics*. Nearly four thousand words of small type, it is the kind of screed that can confuse Catholics right out of the Church—and it has been quite successful in doing just that.

The first section is titled "The True Church". It tries to demonstrate that it was not Peter but Christ who was the rock mentioned in Matthew 16:18. Brewer rests his argument on an examination of the Greek, a tactic that usually works when his Catholic reader knows no Greek and is not aware the first Gospel was composed in Aramaic, the language Christ spoke. In fact, the argument Brewer makes, if applied to the Aramaic and not just the Greek, actually backfires against him, but he does not let the reader in on that secret. The question of "what the Greek says" is frequently brought up by fundamentalists. Anti-Catholics, who often know little Greek themselves, are able to make hay with it only because most Catholics know still less.

The next section is on the papacy. Brewer cites some titles given to the Pope, such as "Holy Father", and, without giving any sources, some claims allegedly made by recent Popes, claims that, taken out of historical context and only a few words at a time, seem rather suspicious to those new to ecclesiastical history. He then lists a few verses of Scripture, such as "Call no one on earth your father" (Mt 23:9) and "Is there a God besides me?" (Is 44:8), the latter given to show, apparently, that the Pope is not divine.

Following this is a short consideration of the priesthood, consisting mainly of highly selective quotations from the Bible. The gist is that only Christ is a priest under the New Dispensation; the Catholic priesthood was foisted on the Church by Cyprian of Carthage and "was part of the merger of paganism with Christianity". Naturally enough, no look at the priesthood is complete without an excoriation of the Mass.

The fundamentalist understanding, or misunderstanding, is that Catholics believe Christ dies anew at each Mass. This violates Hebrews 7:27, "He died once for all", and half a dozen other verses in that book, says Brewer. Then he turns to the Real Presence, which he considers to be at best a real symbolism. Again the reader is given a short course in Greek. "When Jesus said, 'This is my body' or 'blood', He did not 'change' the substance, but was explaining that He is the one 'represented' by the passover bread and wine. Jesus did not say *touto gignetai,* this has become or is turned into, but *touto esti,* which can only mean this represents or stands for."

This is a blunder. True, *touto gignetai* means "this has become", and, true, the sacred text does not read *touto gignetai,* but which Catholic claimed it does? When it comes to the meaning of *touto esti,* which is indeed found in the text, Brewer has things backward. As any Greek dictionary will show, *esti* is simply the verb "to be". It means "is". It means "represents" only secondarily, just as "is" in English can mean "represents", but usually does not. The plain, the literal, reading of *touto esti* is "this is".[15]

Scriptural Truths for Roman Catholics, having misapplied elementary Greek, then looks at confession, the sacrament of penance, and justification. The reader discovers that no man has been empowered by Christ to forgive sins: "Who can forgive sins, but only God?" (Mk 2:7). He also learns not to confess to a priest: "Repent . . . and pray to god" (Acts 8:22). Deprecated is the Church's appeal to John 20:22–23: "Receive the Holy Spirit; when you forgive men's sins, they are forgiven, when you hold them bound, they are held bound." Brewer makes the standard argument that this was not a grant of a power to forgive sins, but to preach repentance, even though that flies in the face of the plain words of the text and the understanding of all the early Fathers of the Church. When considering justification, he argues salvation by faith alone and quotes fourteen biblical verses to buttress his case, but conveniently makes no reference to James 2:24: "You see, then, that it takes deeds as well as faith if a man is to be justified." This tract makes no effort, on this or any other topic, to present the Catholic side or to deal with the weaknesses in its own argument.

Then comes the juiciest part of the tract, a section labelled "Roman Catholic Inventions", a list of forty-four beliefs or customs supposedly borrowed from paganism or created *ex nihilo*. Each item includes an approximate date of first belief or use. The list was taken, without attribution, from the first chapter of Loraine Boettner's *Roman Catholicism*. Almost none of the forty-four items are mentioned in other tracts from Mission to Catholics. What the reader thus is left with, in most cases, is a short statement consisting of no more than eight or ten words—and, of course, an uneasy feeling. These "inventions" are given not to present the reader with a complete syllogism, but to leave him

---

[15] When a verse's plain or primary sense argues in favor of the Catholic position, anti-Catholics ignore that sense and base their attack on a less-likely sense, often not admitting that their case is not open and shut.

with suspicions. Pile up enough innuendos, and one has what appears to be a convincing case against the Church.

This list is partly reincarnated in another Mission to Catholics tract, *Can a Christian Remain a Roman Catholic?* The author, John Phillips, claims that "Rome did not arrive at its dogmatic positions hastily or lightly. She is the product of many centuries of gradual departure from the true faith of the Church found in the word of God." More than thirty of the other tract's "Catholic Inventions" are then reproduced. "This is Rome", says Phillips. "These are the dogmas we associate with Rome. They are unscriptural. All of them are the very antithesis of New Testament doctrine."

One blind spot that afflicts all professional anti-Catholics is the difference between doctrines and practices. That Christ rose from the dead is a doctrine; that Catholics are to abstain from meat on Good Friday is a practice, a disciplinary measure only. There is nothing doctrinal about the latter: it is not a belief, but a custom, and it can be altered as circumstances warrant. It is one thing to allege that some of Christianity's original doctrines have been dropped and non-Christian doctrines adopted. That, if demonstrated, would show the Catholic Church is defectible, that it is not really the institution founded by Christ. But to argue that the Catholic Church cannot be the one founded by him because, say, "priests began to assume distinctive robes in A.D. 500" is to rest one's apologetics on a basic confusion. No one, not even a fundamentalist, can argue rationally that the Church today should appear, even in all outward respects, just like the Church of apostolic times. If fundamentalists were clear in their own minds about the distinction between doctrines and practices, they would not bother arguing about the latter, because they would realize the knife cuts both ways.

Even when it comes to purely doctrinal matters, they are confused. On the one hand they seem to think there could be no proper development of doctrines as Catholics understand the term, no deeper understanding of them as centuries pass. Frank Sheed noted that one cannot stop people from drawing true inferences from true doctrines.[16] If "This is my body", for instance, then certain things logically follow regarding the Eucharist. On the other hand, fundamentalists are not averse to their own brand of doctrinal development; they too believe things that are not found on the face of Scripture. There are peculiarly fundamentalist doctrines that find no warrant in Scripture and that should, by the fundamentalists' own rationale, be thrown out. Such difficulties are never discussed in literature from organizations such as Mission to Catholics because they are not perceived to exist. Professional anti-Catholics take the fundamentalist position as a given, the Catholic position as a usurpation, and their chief concern is to undermine the latter, not to justify the former.

---

[16] Frank Sheed and Maisie Ward, *Catholic Evidence Training Outlines*, 4th ed. (London: Sheed and Ward, 1948), 252.

Chapter 4

Old-Time Religion, Old-Time Tactics

One might surmise a religious tract titled *From Voodooism and Roman Catholicism to the Living Saviour* would be written by George Bush, popularizer of voodoo economics. Not so. The author, Clarence Ismey, is a Haitian, a onetime Catholic and (simultaneously, he says) voodooist who was converted to fundamentalism through the persistence of an illiterate man who had memorized dozens of Bible verses and recited them, one after another, until Ismey's defenses were breached. It took only one day.

Ismey claims he was promptly ostracized by his family and moved to Port-Au-Prince, where he was befriended by other Protestants. He attended a fundamentalist seminary, where he decided he was called to minister to the hundred thousand Haitians living in New York City. There he works as an associate of the Conversion Center, one of the oldest anti-Catholic groups in the country.

The name of this organization is wonderfully neutral, giving no hint what people are supposed to convert from or to, but it does not take long to see that the sole purpose of the group is to transform Catholics into fundamentalists. This is clear from an examination of its price list. The three dozen tracts available for purchase have titles such as *The Confusion of the Popes, The Roman Catholic Bible Says, Roman Catholic Articles of Faith, Transubstantiation,* and *The Mass—Sacrifice or Sacrilege?* Books for sale include *Catholicism against Itself, You Can Lead Roman Catholics to Christ, Secrets of Romanism,* and *Letters to a Roman Catholic Priest.* Also on the list are perennial favorites such as *Fifty Years in the Church of Rome,* by Charles Chiniquy, whose nineteenth-century horror stories still sell; *The Two Babylons,* written in 1853 by Alexander

Hislop, who claimed Catholicism arose from ancient Babylonian cults; and *Roman Catholicism,* by Loraine Boettner, godfather of the modern anti-Catholic movement.

The Conversion Center, which had its "international head-quarters" (in fact, its only office) in Havertown, Pennsylvania, and is now located in Newtown Square, was founded by the late Alex O. Dunlap, who, with four other onetime trustees, is said to be "at home with the Lord—Rev. 14:13". The present head of the group is the Rev. Donald F. Maconaghie, who lists himself as acting director. A pithy description of the group is given on the masthead of each issue of its newsletter: "A fundamental Faith Mission, Home & Foreign, offering spiritual and temporal help to Roman Catholic priests, nuns, and 'whosoever will' ". The ostensible targets of the Conversion Center's ministrations are thus priests and religious, but most of the tracts and books end up being thrust into the hands of Catholic laymen.

On the whole, the Conversion Center seems to be a smaller operation than Mission to Catholics, but a reasonably influential one, since it makes some effort to concentrate its energies toward a subset of Catholics. Its principals must have some concern about continuity, though. Photographs of the annual meeting show a modest crowd in a small Baptist church, and the leaders of the organization, like a disproportionate number of people in the pews, are mainly elderly.

The Conversion Center's newsletter, which appears irregularly and carries less copy than Mission to Catholics' *Challenger,* offers some interesting viewpoints. The March 1984 issue, for instance, was devoted to the topic "Is Mary the 'Mother of God'?" The author, as is usually the case, was Maconaghie. He starts this way: "After being practically beaten to death in the Republic of Ireland for preaching the Gospel,[1] I was made very sick in the hospital by being forced to listen to 'prayers' said by the nursing sister. Most of these prayers were to Mary, 'the Mother of God' ".

---

[1] One naturally would like to see how local newspapers characterized the incident.

Maconaghie says Mary cannot be the Mother of God because that
would make her mother, Anne, the grandmother of God. "Likewise, James, the brother of our Lord, would be the brother of
God. David would be the forefather of God." The promoter of
the notion of *Theotokos* (God-bearer) "was an unscrupulous
bishop of Egypt, Cyril, who was promptly anathematized for his
new and idolatrous doctrine by the most prominent bishop of his
day, Nestorius, Patriarch of Constantinople". At the Council of
Ephesus, "Cyril ganged up on Nestorius, and by blackmail and
bribery (fairly admitted in the *Catholic Encyclopedia*) the 'Mother
of God' controversy was settled in favor of Cyril. Consequently
Cyril has been pronounced a 'saint' and Nestorius a 'heretic'."

So where did this notion of *Theotokos* come from? asks
Maconaghie. From Egypt, of course, where Isis, "the Egyptian ma-
donna", carried "her little 'sun-god', Horus, in her arms" and
where "the worship of Seb, 'the father of the gods,' was supplanted by this 'mother-goddess' ". Get it? Isis was worshiped instead of Seb; Mary is worshiped instead of the Father.

(This issue of the newsletter ends, by the way, with a paragraph
in praise of Bart Brewer, head of Mission to Catholics International, with whom Maconaghie "had the joy of visiting Mexico
and sharing the Gospel with the people there". In fact, several of
the Conversion Center's tracts have been reprinted by Mission to
Catholics under its own name.)

There are interesting reports given by Maconaghie in the following issue. Under a large headline reading "CONVERSION
CENTER LEADER DEBATES THEOLOGIAN IN VATICAN" is a short article,
most of which concerns a 1963 visit by Maconaghie to Rome.
Then he says, "A few weeks ago I again visited Rome. This time I
was invited by a high member of the Vatican Hierarchy. I entered
with an official pass, duly issued by the Vatican bureaucracy.
There in the 'Holy' See I debated point by point the doctrines of
our precious Lord for four solid hours with a Vatican theologian."

That's it. From the headline one might imagine Maconaghie
squaring off against Joseph Cardinal Ratzinger, but he gives no

hint concerning the identities of the "high member of the Vatican Hierarchy" who invited him or of the "Vatican theologian" with whom he "debated". He does say later that he had a long discussion with an archbishop. Is this the man who invited him, or the man he debated with, or did he merely exchange the usual courtesies with a visiting American prelate? The impression given the fundamentalist reader, no doubt, is that Maconaghie was in Rome doing what Hus or Luther did, putting the Vatican know-nothings in their places.

The August/September 1986 issue of the Conversion Center's newsletter features a peculiar "Dear Friend" letter from Maconaghie. It begins this way:

> Cardinal Newman came perhaps the nearest of anyone in explaining how the Roman Catholic Church has so completely betrayed the message of the Christian Gospel. I think he was endeavouring to be as charitable as possible when he attributed the great betrayal to actual possession of the Church of Rome by an evil spirit. In his book *[An Essay on] The Development of Christian Doctrine* (page 6) he says, "The spirit of Rome has risen again in its former place, and has evidenced its identity by its works. It has possessed the church there planted as an evil spirit might seize the demoniacs of primitive times, and makes her speak words which are not her own. In the corrupt Papal System we have the very cruelty, the craft and the ambition of the Roman Republic, its cruelty in its unsparing sacrifice of the happiness and virtue of individuals to a phantom of public expediency, in its forced celibacy within, and its persecutions without; its craft in its falsehoods, its deceitful deeds and lying wonders; and its grasping ambition in the very structure of its policy, in its assumption of universal dominion: but it still claims the sovereignty under pretense. The Roman Catholic Church I will not blame, but pity—she is in thraldom."

Maconaghie continues by saying of Newman,

> He masterfully enumerates the perversions that have resulted from this demoniacal possession very concisely as follows: "She virtually substitutes an external ritual for moral obedience, penance for penitence, confession for sorrow, profession for faith, the lips for the

heart." Cardinal Newman was, of course, only one of many religious leaders who has warned us of this evil which has possessed the corrupt Papal System. Among them are the founders of the Methodist, the Presbyterian and the Lutheran churches [that is, John Wesley, John Knox, and Martin Luther].

The impression given by Maconaghie is that Newman, when a prince of the Church, condemned the "papal system"—and this in his most important book.

There are several things wrong with these quotations. For one thing, without letting the reader in on it, Maconaghie has dropped some phrases, added one word, and changed another word.[2] The meaning of the passages is changed slightly from what Newman actually wrote. His words are made to seem harsher than they were. This sleight of hand can be overlooked because it is minor compared to the real problem.

The real problem is that these words from Newman, which appear at the beginning of his book in what he labels an "Advertisement", do *not* give his views at the time of writing. Quite the contrary. They are quotations from earlier writings, and he here specifically *retracts* them. He is saying these judgments, made when he was a Protestant, were *wrong*. Yet Maconaghie would have us think these are "Cardinal" Newman's present opinions, the notions with which he went to his grave.

---

[2] The passage actually reads this way: "The spirit of old Rome has risen again in its former place, and has evidenced its identity by its works. It has possessed the Church there planted, as an evil spirit might seize the demoniacs of primitive times, and makes her speak words which are not her own. In the corrupt Papal system we have the very cruelty, the craft, and the ambition of the Republic; its cruelty in its unsparing sacrifice of the happiness and virtue of individuals to a phantom of public expediency, in its forced celibacy within, and its persecutions without; its craft in its falsehoods, its deceitful deeds and lying wonders; and its grasping ambition in the very structure of its polity, in its assumption of universal dominion: old Rome is still alive; no where have its eagles lighted, but it still claims the sovereignty under another pretence. The Roman Church I will not blame, but pity—she is, as I have said, spellbound, as if by an evil spirit; she is in thraldom." John Henry Newman, *An Essay on the Development of Christian Doctrine* (Baltimore: Penguin, 1974), 60.

The passages being retracted were written in 1834, when Newman was thirty-three. As a young Anglican minister, he had been anti-Roman, as most in his circle were. But he learned much over the next eleven years, and when he wrote the "Advertisement", which is dated October 6, 1845, he was convinced his earlier views were incorrect, that he had been operating from mere prejudice. In fact, just after Newman completed *An Essay on the Development of Christian Doctrine,* he became a Catholic. He was, at his conversion, a layman—not a priest, certainly not a cardinal. He was not raised to the cardinalate until 1879, thirty-four years later.

So Maconaghie is triply wrong—wrong in the quotations, which he adulterates; wrong in their import, which he misrepresents; wrong in Newman's status, which he misunderstands.

This is a good example of the way fundamentalist opponents of the Church bend facts to the snapping point. Little printed by professional anti-Catholics—those who make their living by attacking "Romanism"—can be taken at face value. The reader cannot assume blithely all is on the up and up. Nearly every paragraph requires an investigation, but who has time for that? Worse, how many suspect an investigation is even needed? Not many, of course, which is why writings like Maconaghie's do so much harm and, for the most part, go unchallenged.

A curious thing about the Conversion Center's newsletters is that most of the photographs of things Catholic are at least forty years old. Shown have been a priest giving an anointing in a hospital room where the patient's bed might have been used for those wounded at Verdun; another priest, in a grainy photo, celebrating a Tridentine Mass; Communion being given to servicemen wearing World War II uniforms; and a seminarian using a typewriter that Barry Fitzgerald might have brought to the set of his movies with Bing Crosby.[3]

---

[3] The disinclination of the Conversion Center to locate more recent photographs parallels its disinclination to discover what the Catholic Church really believes. It is more convenient to use photographs on hand, as it is more convenient to use anti-Catholic arguments handed down from father to son.

The picture of the seminarian appears with the title "Seminarians Need Help!" The help needed, of course, is not the kind the Vatican might desire. Maconaghie prints portions of a letter from a young man studying—God knows why—for the priesthood: "Within a year I can be ordained a priest . . . but my convictions are against the Catholic church. In fact, I've come to know of the falsehood of the R.C. church. There are a lot of practices and beliefs in the R.C. church which are irrational, absurd, and unbiblical. To mention a few: infallibility of the pope, immaculate conception, Marian devotion and devotion to saints. . . . I feel that the Spirit of the Lord is leading me out of the Catholic church. I have been reading your esteemed publication and am convinced that the Baptist church is the true church of the Lord. Can I too become a Baptist pastor?"

In a sidebar is another letter. The name of the writer and his seminary have been deleted. He says, "I have been praying for the success of all your works for the propagation of the Gospel message. I feel that the Lord is calling me too, to join you and render humble service." He then asks Maconaghie's help in getting admitted to a fundamentalist school of theology.

These letters sound so bizarre that they might be no more authentic than the Hitler diaries, but they are probably legitimate. Considering the state of seminaries today, there is no reason why incipient fundamentalists cannot be found in them alongside incipient agnostics, though it does seem odd that young men convinced the Catholic Church is the Whore of Babylon, as the Conversion Center regularly states, would not leap from the fire at the first opportunity.

The newsletters are not the only bizarre things distributed by the Conversion Center. Some of its tracts are a bit odd. Consider one called *10 Reasons Why I Am Not a Roman Catholic*. The first point, given in full, reads like this:

1. THE PAPACY IS A HOAX. Peter never claimed to be pope. He was never in Rome. He knew that Jesus Christ, not himself, was the "Rock". It is written, "Call no one on earth your Father; for one is your Father, who is in heaven" Mt 23:9.

How does one answer this? The effort required to respond to these four sentences is so disproportionate to their length—it would take several pages to give a complete answer[4]—that even people who know why these remarks are wrong would be tempted to find refuge in T. S. Eliot's line: "What have we to do but stand with empty hands and palms turned upwards?"[5] The temptation is to do nothing, to make no response, but that lets anti-Catholics win the skirmish by default. It must be admitted they enjoy a certain tactical (if short-term) advantage in that they can get away with presenting bare-bones claims such as these; they wear out Catholicism's defenders by inundating them with short remarks that demand long explanations.

Other points in this tract are similarly terse. The next two are:

2. MARYOLATRY [sic] IS A HOAX. It is written of Christ, "Neither is there salvation in any other name. For there is no other name under heaven given to men by which we must be saved" Acts 4:12.

3. PURGATORY IS A HOAX. It is a money-making scheme. It is written, "The blood of Jesus Christ, his Son, cleanses us from ALL SIN" 1 JOHN 1:7.

The penultimate point reveals that the tract is outdated:

9. I AM AN AMERICAN CITIZEN, and refuse to be the subject of a deluded Italian Prince. It is written, "No man can serve two masters" Mt 6:24.

The Conversion Center also distributes a card titled *10 Reasons Why I Drink*. It is the kind of thing one pulls out of a shirt pocket and offers along with a business card. The first of the ten reasons is, "I love to vomit." The last reads, "It's my way of obeying God, Who says, 'Wine is a mocker, strong drink is raging; and whosoever is deceived thereby is not wise.' Proverbs 20:1." The

---

[4] The great advantage possessed by anti-Catholics is that so few of their targets have the stamina to compose the necessary replies, and thus many charges go unanswered. The claims made about the papacy will be answered in later chapters of this book.

[5] T. S. Eliot, "Choruses from 'The Rock' ", *The Complete Poems and Plays 1909–1950* (New York: Harcourt, Brace & World, 1971), 108.

Conversion Center, like most fundamentalist groups, opposes the drinking of wine, no exceptions. No search of anti-Catholic writings, no matter how thorough, will reveal any discussion of the use of wine versus the misuse of wine. The drink Hilaire Belloc praised in his most famous poem is off limits for fundamentalists.[6] This stricture puts even the casual reader of the Bible in an awkward spot, since Christ first displayed his miraculous powers by turning water into wine at Cana, and he used wine at the Last Supper. Surely he did not disapprove of its use, as distinguished from its abuse. Some fundamentalists try to explain away such awkwardness (by saying, for example, that the drink at the Last Supper was unfermented grape juice, not wine), but most simply ignore the problem. Far better to turn to more more profitable endeavors—such as American history.

The Conversion Center publishes a small leaflet bearing Abraham Lincoln's likeness. It is called *Lincoln's Warning*. Credit is given to Charles Chiniquy's *Fifty Years in the Church of Rome*. The reader learns that Lincoln said: "The priests, the nuns and monks, who daily land on our shores under the pretext of teaching their religion . . . are nothing else than emissaries of the pope, to undermine our institutions . . . and prepare a reign of anarchy here as they have done in Ireland, in Spain, and wherever there are people that want to be free."

Those who do not realize it was the Catholics of Ireland, rather than the English colonizers of Ireland, who initiated the trouble there can learn the sixteenth president thought "papists" a positive danger to the Republic: "Till lately I was in favor of the unlimited liberty of conscience, as our Constitution gives it to the Roman Catholics. But now it seems to me that, sooner or later, the people will be forced to put an amendment to that clause toward the papists. Is it right to give the privilege of citizenship to men who are the sworn and public enemies (No. 1) of our Constitution, our laws, our liberties, and our lives? . . . I am for liberty

---

[6] Hilaire Belloc, "Heroic Poem in Praise of Wine", *Complete Verse*, ed. W. N. Roughead (London: Duckworth, 1970), 80.

of conscience in its noblest, broadest, highest sense. But I cannot give liberty of conscience to the pope or his followers, the papists, so long as they tell me that their conscience orders them to burn my wife, strangle my children, and cut my throat when they find* the opportunity." The asterisk refers to a footnote, which says "Lincoln was finally assassinated April 14, 1865, by Roman Catholics."

If an experiment in historiography is in order, one might ask the people at the Conversion Center, who apparently believe Lincoln wrote these lines, just where in his collected letters, speeches, or official documents they can be found. Lincoln was not one to make idle charges; if Catholics told him they were bound in conscience to burn his wife, strangle his children, and cut his throat, he no doubt left posterity details of just who informed him of this curious obligation. Searching his writings might be fruitless, though; the clue is that the expression "public enemy" came into vogue only in the 1920s.

Chapter 5

Bringing Catholics to Real Christianity

Although Bill Jackson's ministry, Christians Evangelizing Catholics, is small, he is in considerable demand on the fundamentalist lecture circuit, and the reports of his tours in his newsletter show that he puts on plenty of miles. He may speak in several states in a month, and in 1985 he even took his message to Ireland, where he spent seventeen years as a minister, and to England. The newsletter is sent from his San Jose, California, home to about eight hundred names, but the number belies Jackson's influence. Many of the names are of ministers or of leaders of similar organizations. Through one name might come a talk to hundreds of people, or a single acquaintance might arrange for Jackson to speak at several churches, multiplying his effectiveness.

Jackson shares with his readers news about his children and their spiritual maturation, asking, in one issue,[1] for prayers for his son Dave, who "has come back to the Lord" and who thinks "the Lord has other things He wants him to do with his life" than lay carpets, which Dave finds "physically difficult to continue". The other children are more established. Bill, Jr., and his wife live in New York City; Colleen and her family are in the San Joaquin Valley; and Mark is in Chicago, studying at the Moody Bible Institute, perhaps to join his father in convincing Catholics to leave the Church while there is still time. Also studying, readers are told, are "four Roman Catholics who have been saved through taking the 'Treasures in Your Catholic Bible' study course. . . . I met one of them recently, and he needs your prayer for his Roman Catholic wife." The study course is printed by Tabernacle Press

---

[1] January 1985 issue.

78

of Louisville, Kentucky, the firm that prints Jackson's tracts (twelve so far, soon more) and booklets (four), which he distributes "on a free will offering basis".

In his newsletter Jackson does more than recount his family's version of the Pilgrim's Progress, of course. He gives practical examples of what can be done by one person to bring Catholics into real Christianity. He called one article "Use Your Local Priest".[2] In it he explained that he at one time worked with a telephone ministry organized by a Baptist church in San Francisco. "We used a business directory and made random calls to certain areas." One night he called St. Mary's Catholic Church. A layman answered, and Jackson asked him about "the assurance of salvation". The layman, stumped, went for the priest. "Needless to say," said Jackson, "the priest didn't know anything more about salvation than the layman had, but, during our conversation, he specifically told me he did not have assurance of salvation. From that time on, whenever I telephoned a person who identified themselves [sic] as a Roman Catholic, I could say, 'I talked to one of your priests the other day. He said he wasn't sure of going to heaven, but my Bible says that we can know.' I would then quote 1 John 5:13 and found this a very good way to initiate a gospel presentation."

This can, indeed, be a good means to effect conversions. Another way is to march right up and accost a priest. "You might visit the priest and find him unwilling to talk, as a Baptist pastor and I experienced recently. When we knocked on his door and introduced ourselves, he said, 'I am a busy person. No one gets to see me without an appointment. This is one of the rudest things I ever saw, your just coming here and expecting to talk to me.' (These are not his verbatim words, but the jest [sic] of what he said to us.) If you run across this, excuse yourself politely and then call to make an appointment with him."

Appointments can be revelatory; good use can be made of priestly ignorance thus exposed. "Sometimes the very lack of

2 November 1984 issue.

positive doctrinal standing by a priest can be used in evangelism. We often quote the priest we met last year in Dayton who was very difficult to corner, but who finally joined a conversation we were having with a Catholic lady theologian. We asked him if the Bible was the word of God, if he was sure of salvation, if the Mass was a sacrifice—and all he could do was to uneasily shift from one foot to another and say, 'I don't know.' " Is it any wonder, with examples like these, that Jackson writes that "it has been said that an educated Catholic must cut off his head and leave it outside when he goes to church?" An irresolute priest invites precisely this kind of abuse.

Jackson calls himself not prolife but pro-eternal life. One of his tracts[3] advises fundamentalist prolife workers to "realize your responsibility to the child you saved from abortion" by converting the parents to fundamentalism. "The greatest thing that can happen is for the mother to be evangelized and saved. Recently I met a young lady who, when unsaved, was planning an abortion. She was contacted by Christians who persuaded her to keep her baby and who led her to the Lord. Later, the father was also saved. So instead of three lives—one wrecked, one murdered, and one unsaved—we have a Christian family with a positive testimony of God's grace." It is hard to fault Jackson's logic here; he has, in this regard, a better appreciation of what is needed than do many Catholic prolifers who are satisfied just to halt abortions. However great a triumph it is to have one more life spared, stopping there is not enough. To do so is to ignore the deeper causes of the abortion mentality, which is necessarily a secularist and irreligious mentality.

Catholics, who for so many years carried on the prolife battle seemingly alone, now sometimes express annoyance that fundamentalists, who have more recently become active in the movement, seem unable to restrain themselves from evangelizing during strategy sessions. It is one thing, these Catholics think, to save babies, quite another to seek conversions among movement

[3] *Pro (Eternal) Life.*

members. They would not be so annoyed if they perceived that the fundamentalists are perhaps being more consistent than they are and perhaps have a keener appreciation that abortion is as much a problem of the soul as a problem of the scalpel.

Aside from the newsletter, which preaches to the converted, Jackson produces tracts. One is titled *Is Roman Catholicism a Cult?* When Catholics think of cults, they think of the Hare Krishnas, the Moonies, the Scientologists. They find it hard to imagine that some Protestants think of the Catholic religion as a cult. But among fundamentalists, this is taken for granted and is a matter of keen concern. "Very likely", Jackson writes, "this is the most often asked question when I minister regarding Roman Catholic evangelism." Catholics are naturally offended at being called cultists, at least in the sense the fundamentalists mean to use the term.[4]

As in so many matters, fundamentalists and Catholics are at loggerheads because they define terms differently. Jackson explains fundamentalists' peculiar definition: "The word, as generally used by the Lord's people today, means some kind of false religion, especially one that denies the basic truths of Christianity. We may get a consensus of opinion [among fundamentalists] that would state a cult is a religion that does not believe in basic Christian truths and is always characterized by a denial of the uniqueness of biblical revelation and a salvation at least partially dependent on the works and merits of its adherents." In other words, a cult is any religion that is not fundamentalism.

Granted, this is not a particularly helpful definition, but there is some sense to it. For the man who believes in fundamentalism, any other religion is necessarily erroneous. The Catholic Church adopts a similar perspective in acknowledging that every religion other than the Catholic is to some extent erroneous. But the Church differs in approach from fundamentalism in that it always (and not just since Vatican II) has been willing to acknowledge

---

[4] Ironically, many ex-fundamentalists depict fundamentalism as a cult, complete with "brainwashing", but it is difficult to locate ex-Catholics who consider Catholicism a cult in the same sense.

that other religions contain greater or lesser degrees of truth, depending on how much they mirror Catholicism. Eastern Orthodoxy is truer than, say, high-church Anglicanism, which is truer than Presbyterianism, which is truer than Unitarianism. Few fundamentalists are willing to be so generous. One is either a fundamentalist or damned, and, if damned, it does not much matter how close to heaven's gate one might be, because outside is still outside.

Jackson lumps the Catholic Church with the cults because "Roman Catholics have added to the Bible. They have no means of solid interpretation. Their present attitude toward its inerrancy is thoroughly liberal, and they have through the years been vocal in condemning God's Word. The Bible was placed on the Index of Forbidden Books—they will now tell you that was only because of erroneous Protestant translations—but it was first placed there in 1229, over 100 years before Wycliffe's first translation."

These sentences contain some of the chief fundamentalist objections to Catholicism. Note that Jackson says the Church provides no means for "solid interpretation". At first this seems laughable coming from someone who dismisses any authority other than himself in interpreting Scripture. The individual is the least solid of all interpreters, which is precisely why Protestantism has been fissiparous. Jackson is more on target in saying the Catholic attitude toward inerrancy is "thoroughly liberal". This is his perception of the disarray in Catholic exegesis over the last twenty years. To him it appears the historico-critical method and its "assured results" are fully indicative of the official Catholic position on the Bible. Then he claims the Church had been "vocal in condemning God's Word" by placing the Bible on the Index of Forbidden Books in 1229. Of course, the Index was first printed in 1543, more than three centuries after that, but no matter. The gaffe is not entirely Jackson's fault. Here he was relying on Bart Brewer of Mission to Catholics, who made the same claim in one of his tracts, and Brewer in turn got the date from Loraine Boettner's *Roman Catholicism,* which gives no source for it.

Note the last phrase, "over 100 years before Wycliffe's first translation". This is not a gratuitous line, no idle reference or mere name dropping. Wycliffe is understood by most fundamentalists to have been the first to put Scripture into English.[5] For them, the culmination of what Wycliffe is understood to have started is the King James Version. One will find in the case of many fundamentalists a reverence for that translation that approaches idolatry. There have been many fallings-out among fundamentalists because some will use only the King James Version, claiming that no other version is accurate, while others will adopt newer translations.

Jackson's tract has other complaints about the Catholic Church. While attempting to suppress the Bible, the Church foists on Christianity things of its own fashioning, such as the doctrine of the Assumption. "The addition of blasphemous Tradition and changeable Papal teaching is as bad as looking for inspiration in [Mary Baker Eddy's] *Science and Health . . .* or *The Book of Mormon*. It is difficult to come up with any modern definition of what is a cult and include Jehovah's Witnesses, Mormons, and a host of others and omit the largest false religious system of all—Roman Catholicism." Jackson says that "only as we see the system for what it really is can we fulfill our evangelistic resposibilities to the millions of souls lost therein—blinded by Satan and believing a lie. May we clearly define the system and truly love the people, and may God use us in Roman Catholic evangelism."

Is Roman Catholicism a Cult? is a tract that appeals mainly to committed fundamentalists. It will sway few Catholics because its title is alienating, and its few paragraphs try to cover so many points that none is covered well. More effective, no doubt, has been Jackson's tract *Charismatic Catholics*. It has been printed by Tabernacle Press for Jackson and reprinted by the Conversion Center and Mission to Catholics; it is a good example of the way anti-Catholics cooperate.

[5] Even John Foxe, author of the decidedly anti-Catholic *Book of Martyrs* (1563), denied this. He wrote, "If histories be well examined we shall find both before the Conquest and after, as well before John Wickliffe was born as since, the whole body of the Scriptures was by sundry men translated into our country tongue." Hugh Pope, *English Versions of the Bible* (St. Louis: Herder, 1952), 63.

Catholic charismatics are a prime target for fundamentalists because they already have a keen appreciation of the Bible. They actually read it, which many "mainline" Catholics do not; non-charismatics are often immune to appeals to the Bible because they know little about it. Those familiar with Scripture, on the other hand, sometimes find themselves unable to counter arguments posed by fundamentalists, since their study of apologetics and theology has not kept pace with their study of the Bible. They accept the premise that any Christian truth should be demonstrable by appealing to the plain words of the text, and they are dismayed to discover there is no clear mention of auricular confession, infant baptism, or the Immaculate Conception in any book from Matthew to Revelation. Thus many charismatics (non-Catholic as well as Catholic, of course) fall prey to fundamentalist blandishments, each blandishment coming in the form of a quotation from Scripture.

"A person who claims to be a born again Christian and remains in the Roman Catholic Church is ignorant, disobedient, or hypocritical", concludes Jackson. One cannot stay in the Catholic Church and evangelize from within. God "told his people to come out of paganism and idolatry" (2 Cor 6:14–18). The answer? "It is essential that every true born again child of God separate from the church of Rome or any false system of religion and unite with a Bible believing fundamental Christian local church so that they [sic] can serve God in true obedience." To the person impressed by concatenated biblical quotations (examples of which will be omitted here), this kind of argument is persuasive. Charismatics see that syllogisms of a sort can be constructed from Bible passages, and they surprisingly often act on the syllogisms—as do thousands of Catholics who disdain the charismatic approach to religion but who, like some of their charismatic brethren, have no ready intellectual defenses against fundamentalism. Most Catholics, of whatever stripe, are vulnerable to fundamentalist attacks.

Just as some of Jackson's tracts are aimed at a wide audience, others are aimed at a select few. One is aimed directly at seminarians. It is entitled *Think: Should You Become a Priest?* This pocket-sized leaflet first quotes Pius XII and John XXIII about the paucity of vocations. The reader is told that "St. Alphonsus Liguori wrote eloquently about the duties and dignity of a priest." Then focus shifts. To answer the question on the cover, "we must go to the Word of God and to your innermost heart". This passage is given: "And every priest standeth daily ministering and offering oftentimes the same sacrifices, which can never take away sins, but this man (Jesus), after he had offered one sacrifice for sins forever, sat down on the right hand of God. . . . For by one offering he hath perfected forever them that are sanctified" (Heb 10:11–12, 14). A sacrificing priesthood is therefore a superfluity, says Jackson. The Bible clearly says so. "Ceasing to trust a human priesthood for propitiation and absolution, and placing our trust in Jesus' perfect work—this is salvation!" He makes no attempt, of course, to consider how the Catholic Chruch understands the verses he quotes.

One problem with fundamentalists is that they think the points they bring up have never been considered by the Church. It does not occur to them to find out what informed Catholics understand by a particular passage of Scripture. They find it incomprehensible that someone could have a conclusion that differs from theirs. In this regard their minds lack subtlety.

They generally admit that Catholics hold their beliefs in good faith, but they think they hold them in unalloyed ignorance, having no rational grounds for them at all. When mention is made of someone believing in "blind faith", most people immediately think of stereotypic Bible thumpers, but Bible thumpers, as often as not, think immediately of Catholics. They think Catholics believe what they do either out of habit, having been brought up that way, or because they are under the influence of rapacious clerics, who keep them in intellectual bondage the better to mulct them. The Catholic religion is the opium of the people, say fundamentalists.

Chapter 6

"I Have Literally Bent over Backwards"

A generation ago the only one in the family who was well-known was Jerry Lee Lewis, who, with hits such as "Great Balls of Fire", was at the top of the rock-and-roll charts. Jerry Lee long since disappeared from celebrity status, but the family still has someone at the top of the charts—the television rating charts, this time. It is Jerry Lee's cousin, Jimmy Lee, better known as evangelist Jimmy Lee Swaggart.

"The Jimmy Swaggart Telecast" is seen by as many as three million Americans weekly. The ministry's monthly magazine, *The Evangelist,* has about a million readers. Jimmy Swaggart is now as popular a television evangelist as Robert Schuller (of "Crystal Cathedral" fame), Oral Roberts, or Jerry Falwell, each of whom had a head start on him. Of the many television evangelists, great and small, it is Swaggart who is known for forthright anti-Catholicism.

An Assemblies of God minister, Swaggart bases his operations in Baton Rouge, Louisiana (which is "67% Catholic" and, he explains, "a little more superstitious, a little 'more Catholic' " than the rest of the country).[1] There he has a $30 million World Ministry Center, which includes the Jimmy Swaggart Bible College. It is in Baton Rouge that he tapes his programs and plans his crusades.[2]

For most of his career Swaggart has been indistinguishable from other television preachers. Only in the last few years has his

---

[1] Jimmy Swaggart, "Startling Incidents and Amazing Answers to Prayer", *The Evangelist,* July 1985, 45.

[2] Swaggart is also a singer and claims that his income comes strictly from record sales.

anti-Catholicism become painfully noticeable, no doubt because anti-Catholicism has become fashionable. Like other trends, it has come out of the closet.

At first the objectionable comments were given over the air as infrequent *obiter dicta*. Listeners were told, for instance, that the Catholic Church killed fifty to sixty million people during the Dark Ages because they would not convert. "They cut your head off. They shot you through with an arrow. They tortured you to death", Swaggart explained on one of his broadcasts. He said the Church had a law passed in 416 that made membership mandatory under penalty of death, and he noted that "priests are just leading people to hell". He decried "liturgical religious monstrosities" such as the Mass. Despite such remarks, much of his audience consists of Catholics.[3]

Things came to a head when Swaggart published "A Letter to My Catholic Friends" in the January 1983 issue of *The Evangelist*. The resulting brouhaha eventually died down, but Swaggart decided to stir things up once more after discovering that he had not lost all his support from Catholics and that many non-Catholics were pleased at what he had said. In July 1985 *The Evangelist* carried "the first in a series of articles [by Swaggart] which will, I hope, lay a scriptural foundation illuminating 'the faith which was once delivered unto the saints' (Jude 3)—and this same faith as interpreted within Roman Catholic teaching". This series was in part a revision of the "Letter", which had run to about a dozen pages, and the series was, in turn, revised into a book, *Catholicism & Christianity*.[4]

The Evangelist is a curious magazine, clearly centered about one man. Major articles are written by Swaggart or his wife, Frances. There are contributions by others, but they are usually secondary.

---

[3] Jerry Falwell reports that thirty percent of *his* support comes from Catholics, but Swaggart's is probably less. Falwell projects a more refined, urban image—most Catholics in America have urban backgrounds, not rural—and does not collapse into anti-Catholicism the way Swaggart does.

[4] Jimmy Swaggart, *Catholicism & Christianity* (Baton Rouge: Jimmy Swaggart Ministries, 1986).

In some issues, more pages are by the Swaggarts than by all other contributors combined. Consider the issue that inaugurated Swaggart's series on Catholicism. The cover story was on "The New Evangelists: What Do They Preach?" In seven pages promoters of secular humanism were examined, including Bob Guccione, Hugh Hefner, Larry Flynt, Norman Lear, and Phil Donahue. The author: Jimmy Swaggart. Next was a question-and-answer column titled "Brother Swaggart, Here's My Question". ("Question: Is the Bible filled with inconsistencies, contradictions, and errors as some claim?")

Next were some non-Swaggart pieces: one on prophecy, by Willard Cantelon, who "has met with world leaders in private and spent hours in personal interviews"; one on the afterlife, by David Wilkerson, author of *The Cross and the Switchblade*; an obituary; and two pages of news shorts. Then came the "Letters from Our Viewers" column, hosted by Frances Swaggart, and this was followed by a report on the Jimmy Swaggart Ministries' charitable distributions overseas.

Jimmy Swaggart returned as author with "Christianity and Catholicism"; the accompanying photograph was of a gold crucifix at the end of a rosary. There followed a full-page advertisement encouraging readers to attend a Swaggart crusade; two pages on faith by C. M. Ward, a radio preacher for the Assemblies of God; and then another piece by Swaggart, "Startling Incidents and Amazing Answers to Prayer". (It is here one learned that "one of the nation's major newspapers [unidentified] said just the other day, 'Any time you see a Catholic church in Louisiana, you will also see a bar very close by.' I think they were intending it as a compliment—which it certainly is not—but, basically, it is the truth.")

Then came a request that the Jimmy Swaggart Ministries be mentioned in one's will; a column on dating by the youth minister at the World Ministry Center; a first-person account of conversion by a Crow Indian; a two-page pitch for money by Frances Swaggart, who penned across the page, "Please let me bear [*sic*] my heart to you"; an advertisement for the *Jimmy Swaggart Giant Print Commentary Bible* ("The Best $60 Investment You Could

Ever Make!"); an open letter by Swaggart to the Assemblies of God on the eve of that denomination's general council; and "From Me to You", in which Swaggart prefaced his comments with "I believe God has spoken these words to me". The last few pages of the magazine hawked cassettes, records, and booklets by Swaggart, the latter having titles such as *The Council of Jerusalem, Questions and Answers: Volume 4,* and *The Unpardonable Sin.*

No doubt about it: this is not a small operation. It is so large now, so successful, so moneyed, that Swaggart can chance alienating his Catholic viewers and readers by moving from the hard sell to the harder sell. In "A Letter to My Catholic Friends", he put it this way: "I try never to pull any punches. I believe that if we are to truly serve our Lord, we must face all issues honestly and up-front. There have been times when I've made Catholics angry through statements I've made, but what I've said has always been said in love. Because I love them, I will tell them the truth." Swaggart accepts that many Catholics have been born again; he thinks they fail to act on their rebirth if they remain in the Catholic Church. His "Letter" was intended to give them reasons to leave.

The "Letter" begins by noting that the Church "basically teaches that only those who are *in* the Catholic church will be saved". This is of course true, although not in the Feeneyite sense. Fundamentalists do not object to such a claim—which amounts to saying that the Catholic Church is the only one founded by Christ—merely because it is some religion other than theirs that claims to be the Way. Their objection is that Catholics say an institution, a "system", is necessary for salvation.

"Bible Christians" often use the term religion in a derogatory, not in a theological or sociological, sense. Their meaning is not the dictionary's, which defines religion as the recognition on the part of man of a superhuman, controlling power deserving obedience and worship. By religion fundamentalists mean a complex, rule-laden, man-made, even casuistical scheme for effecting salvation on one's own.

Swaggart continues by saying that "Catholic tradition [which he nowhere defines] suggests that . . . Mary—not Jesus—is the mediator between God and man. There is little clear-cut distinction between God the Father and Jesus in the mind of most Catholics; hence, their tendency to think of *either* the Father or the Son as 'the Christ'." Catholics are thus Modalists—or perhaps Patripassians who think the Father suffered on the Cross.

The reader learns, for instance, that "It was not long ago that the Catholic church *burned people at the stake*—by the tens of thousands—for *reading the Bible!* Only a generation ago Catholics were *forbidden* to read the Bible, the position being that if there were anything important in there the priest would tell the common people about it." The emphasis is Swaggart's, as is the notion that priests could not tell their parishioners much about the Bible because they read only a truncated version of it known as the breviary. "The Catholic church's doctrines are made up basically of legendary, mythical, apocryphal, human traditions—rather than being based on the Word of God." In fact, Catholicism is "a *false religion*. It is not a Christian religion, and it is *emphatically* not the 'church of Christ on earth' as it claims to be."

From generalities to specifics. The next topic is the papacy. Swaggart makes the same argument other fundamentalists make. He looks to the Greek text of Matthew 16:18–19 and argues that since Peter and the rock are referred to by two slightly different Greek words, the rock cannot be Peter but must be Christ. He makes no reference to the gender of Greek nouns or to the Aramaic language, which Christ spoke, which uses the word *kepha* in each place, so the passage reads: "Thou art *Kepha,* and upon this *kepha* I will build my church", just as in modern French the phrasing would be: "Thou art *Pierre,* and upon this *pierre* I will build my church." Reference to the Greek text is regularly made by fundamentalists when arguing with Catholics; it will be considered in a later chapter. For now it is enough to note this is an argument every Catholic needs to master, because every Catholic will find himself facing fundamentalists who try to impress him with their superficial, and largely mistaken, knowledge of Greek.[5]

---

[5] Although many fundamentalists study Greek, in order to read the New Testament in the language of its composition, leading anti-Catholics are, as a rule,

After explaining that the power of the keys was nothing more than the power, or "right", to be the first to preach the Resurrection on Pentecost, not the wider power believed by Catholics to be held by the papacy, Swaggart notes that "Peter would have been ineligible to be a Pope as he was married".

Surprisingly enough—or perhaps not so surprisingly, considering their lack of familiarity with the Bible—many Catholics are upset by this revelation. They think it is a telling point against the legitimacy of the papacy, since they have never heard that Popes or bishops or priests might at one time have been permitted to be married, just as few of them know that even today priests in the Eastern rites may be married. Swaggart himself might be disappointed to learn that a good number of early Popes, not just Peter, were not celibate. He might be especially disappointed to learn that this has always been acknowledged by Catholic historians and that no Catholic apologist has ever thought the fact argued against the existence of the papacy, for the very good reason that clerical celibacy, at whatever level, is a discipline, not a doctrine.

If Swaggart's argument regarding Peter's marital status does not clinch the matter, the next point does. He says "there isn't a shred of literary, historical, archaeological, or scriptural evidence that Peter went to Rome or was ever in Rome. The Bible makes no mention of Peter being in Rome, and Paul, in his letter *from* Rome, never mentioned Peter being there. . . .There isn't one word in secular history supporting the Catholic contention that Peter lived in Rome." Swaggart is not just wrong here, but ignorant.

If it is archaeological evidence he wants, he can turn to John Evangelist Walsh's *The Bones of St. Peter*,[6] which recounts in detail the excavations under the high altar of St. Peter's Basilica. If he wants literary or historical proof, he can turn to a reference

---

remarkably deficient in Greek and often base their arguments on elementary misunderstandings of the language.

[6] John Evangelist Walsh, *The Bones of St. Peter* (Garden City, N.Y.: Doubleday, 1982).

work such as William A. Jurgens' *The Faith of the Early Fathers,*[7] which quotes sixteen passages from early Christian writers attesting to Peter's being in Rome and dying there. In fact, we have more sources citing Peter's presence in Rome than we have affirming Caesar's crossing of the Rubicon.

Apparently Swaggart has never read the Fathers of the Church or any historian such as Eusebius, and there is scant evidence of any familiarity with archaeology or ancient literature. He knows little about the "literary, historical, or archaeological evidence" in the matter. The only evidence he has is the fourth on his list, scriptural evidence, and that is the only evidence most fundamentalists will consider in a matter such as this, even when the Bible is incompetent to decide the issue.

Fundamentalists' reverence for the word of God is often so extreme that it becomes distorted, and they think the Bible should be the last word on any matter occurring between the start of Christ's public ministry and the close of the first century. It does not occur to them that other works may shed light on happenings of the period. What is more, they do not perceive that we can gain considerable insight regarding the proper interpretation of the Bible if we discover how the earliest Christians understood it.

Swaggart ends his discourse on the nonexistence of the papacy by saying, "Catholic tradition says that Peter was the first Pope. Who, then, was the second one?" Granted, one will not find the second Pope named as such in the Bible, but his name is listed in any encyclopedia. He was Linus, as a few moments' research would have shown Swaggart, who made no effort to look at even plainly secular sources (forget Catholic sources) in developing his critique of Catholicism. His main source was, as it is for most anti-Catholic fundamentalists, Loraine Boettner's *Roman Catholicism.*

From the papacy Swaggart moves on to the standard objection that the Church violates 1 Timothy 4:1–3 because priestly celi-

---

[7] William A. Jurgens, *The Faith of the Early Fathers* (Collegeville, Minn.: Liturgical Press, 1970).

bacy amounts to the "forbidding to marry" that Paul complains about, and from there he goes to Matthew 23:9 ("call no man on earth your father") to demonstrate that the priesthood does not really exist because priests are called "Father". Then it is to the Mass, where the reader is told that "it is *barbaric* to even insinuate that He has to be crucified again and again". Of course, it is Swaggart who does the insinuating, since no Catholic thinks Christ dies anew at each Mass.

In peroration, it is back to Mary, who turns out to have had other children since Jesus was called her "first-born" (Mt 1:25)— Swaggart being wholly ignorant of the meaning of the term under the Mosaic law—and whose own mother cannot have been named Anne since "there is no hint, either in secular history or the Bible" of such a person, an example of Swaggart's unfamiliarity with the apocryphal gospels.

Swaggart's end is in his beginning. "As I close I want to say, as I've said previously in this article, that the Catholic organization is not a Christian organization. Its claims are false; it is a false religion. It is not the Christian plan of salvation, nor the Christian way. Whosoever follows its errant doctrines will be deceived and end up eternally lost." He reassures the annoyed by saying that "every statement in this article is *fact* based on Scripture and historical record. It is not the ranting of someone blindly opposed to something as a matter of *opinion*." And he really believes that. As uninformed and misinformed as Swaggart is, he is no Jack Chick or Tony Alamo. He does not try to deceive. He thinks he is giving the whole story, and his facts, such as they are, are taken mainly from sources he trusts.

Encouraged by the response to his articles in *The Evangelist*, Swaggart published in 1986 *Catholicism & Christianity*, an attractively bound hardback described on the dust jacket as a "powerful new book [that] examines each of the basic tenets of Catholicism and compares them against the standards and precepts of the Word of God". In fact, it is not as complete as Loraine Boettner's *Roman Catholicism* (it has half as many pages and a third as much text). This is not to say that Boettner's book is complete in the sense of being scholarly or of taking into account Catholic rejoinders to his claims, but Boettner considers more topics, and always at greater length, than does Swaggart. No, *Catholicism & Christianity* will not replace *Roman Catholicism* as the main handbook for professional anti-Catholics, but it may reach more folks in the pews and have a greater effect in the long run.

Swaggart's book recapitulates his magazine series; indeed, much of it is lifted word for word from *The Evangelist*. Since the book had, in a way, a trial run, the ubiquity of its blunders, non sequiturs, and contradictions is surprising. If criticisms of the magazine series were proffered, whether by Catholics or fundamentalists, they apparently were not incorporated into the manuscript of the book.

Start with a modest error. On the dust jacket and in the introduction,[8] Swaggart says there are "over 600 million Roman Catholics" in the world. But in his concluding chapter he says "there are nearly 800 million nominal Catholics in the world".[9] Feeling charitable, one might say this is just an example of poor proofreading, but the next error cannot be.

In referring to the Assumption, Swaggart says: "Oddly enough, this mystical belief had been a peripheral precept [*sic*] within the Catholic church since the Middle Ages, but was only given official certification in 1950."[10] In other words, the doctrine had been believed, even if not officially defined, for maybe eight hundred years. Elsewhere he refers to "Mary being *suddenly* taken bodily into heaven. (We say 'suddenly' because no one knew about Mary's physical 'translation' before it was unexpectedly announced by the Vatican in 1950.)"[11]

Swaggart asserts that transubstantiation "is, without question, one of the most absurd doctrines ever imposed on a trusting public",[12] though he does not venture to say how such an absurdity

---

[8] Swaggart, *Catholicism*, viii.
[9] Swaggart, *Catholicism*, 206.
[10] Swaggart, *Catholicism*, 103.
[11] Swaggart, *Catholicism*, 12.
[12] Swaggart, *Catholicism*, 60.

can be believed by millions of people who, demonstrably, are neither fools nor knaves. He repeats the common notion that the doctrine "was first formulated by Paschasius Radbertus, Abbot of Corbey, at the beginning of the ninth century".[13] His confusion about the Eucharist is exemplified by his belief that the chief eucharistic feast is "Holy Thursday, or the Feast of Corpus Christi".[14]

Discussing the duty to confess at least once annually, which only applies to those in mortal sin, Swaggart claims that "even though a person had not sinned during the year, he would still be consigned to eternal hellfire—simply because he had not 'reported in' to the priest during the year."[15] He asks, "How many political figures, public servants, judges, and men of high and important positions are held in bondage because of intimate secrets revealed to their priests? The most personal facts of every Catholic family, of every Catholic heart (which should be known only to God) are known by priests in their most intimate details."[16]

Swaggart thinks the title "pope" means "universal bishop", that "inquisition" translates as "torture", that an indulgence is "a permit for indulging in sin", that Paul said bishops had to be married (did they cease being bishops when they became widowers?), that the Rosary was "copied from the Hindus and Muhammadans [sic]", that "by tradition was meant human opinions", that the Bible was placed on the Index of Forbidden Books in 1229 (the Index was instituted in 1543, and no authentic Bible was ever put on it). These are just a few of the blunders appearing on only five pages.[17]

Swaggart notes that "in this book on Catholic tradition, I have literally bent over backwards to ensure that every statement is true".[18] His contortions do not seem to have helped much, per-

13 Swaggart, *Catholicism*, 61.
14 Swaggart, *Catholicism*, 64.
15 Swaggart, *Catholicism*, 83.
16 Swaggart, *Catholicism*, 88.
17 Swaggart, *Catholicism*, 159–163.
18 Swaggart, *Catholicism*, 200.

haps because he relied on few sources other than his imagination and bitter ex-Catholics. His bibliography consists of only fifteen works, some of which he apparently did not use at all in writing his book.[19] In *Catholicism & Christianity* there are dozens of quotations—largely from anti-Catholics, but also from ancient Catholic writers, even from papal encyclicals—yet page numbers are given only twice,[20] and usually the titles of books from which quotations are taken are not given. Often the writer's name is withheld (or not known), as when Swaggart introduces a quotation with the words "one Catholic stated".[21]

The truth is that Swaggart does not know what pages or books or authors the quotations he uses came from (presuming they are legitimate quotations in the first place), because he never read the quoted works. He lifted the quotations from the writings of other anti-Catholics, who failed to give citations in *their* books. "My information has come primarily from former Catholic priests", he admits.[22] He refers to Bart Brewer's *Pilgrimage from Rome* and Clark Butterfield's *Night Journey from Rome to the New Jerusalem,* hardly books from which one could expect to learn much about Catholic beliefs or history. (It may give one a feel for the reliability of these works to know that Brewer's was published by Bob Jones University Press and Butterfield's is distributed by the Antichrist Information Center, which is run by Alberto Rivera, the hero of Jack Chick's comic book *Alberto*.)

If Swaggart "bent over backwards", literally or otherwise, there is scant evidence of it. His book is a fine example of the danger of mixing a little knowledge with considerable prejudice. If he were less prejudiced—that is, less inclined to accept blindly every unflattering thing said about the Catholic Church—and more

---

[19] Swaggart, *Catholicism,* 221. One such book is Peter M. J. Stravinskas, *The Catholic Response* (Huntington, Ind.: Our Sunday Visitor, 1985), which Swaggart lists as a newspaper article.

[20] One such page citation is to Newman, *Essay,* which is called in the text *The Development of the Christian Religion*. Swaggart, *Catholicism,* 164.

[21] Swaggart, *Catholicism,* 36.

[22] Swaggart, *Catholicism,* 200.

knowledgeable, Jimmy Swaggart would be embarrassed that his name is on such a travesty, because he is not really a bad man, just a man badly misinformed.

No one would mistake him for an academician; he does not lie awake at night wondering whether he did his homework. What he is is famous, influential, and effective. He is even, according to Barbara Nauer, who heads the Catholic Writer and Artist Guild, a nice man—and she has some grounds to say that, since she considers Jimmy and Frances Swaggart her friends and once spent three hours "yelling at and pounding the table" with the man. (She is mentioned, but not by name, in *Catholicism & Christianity*.)[23] "Swaggart's irk with Catholicism seems to rise from thoroughly honorable motives", she says. "Swaggart's bias against Catholicism, given his fervid Protestantism, is in no way unreasonable. Swaggart seems ready to like *Catholics*." The task for Catholics is to "stop wringing their hands about Swaggart and start educating him about the true Church". The same should be done for less-famous fundamentalists. If Catholics will not do that, "we *deserve* to live with his horsewhippings".[24]

Bill Jackson's Christians Evangelizing Catholics is a one-man ministry unknown to most Catholics, even to most fundamentalists. By contrast, Jimmy Swaggart's name is recognized even by people who have never watched his program. Where Jackson works with at most thousands of dollars, Swaggart has tens of millions. In a year Jackson might speak to a few thousand people; on any Sunday Swaggart speaks to thousands of thousands.

Yet there are few Jimmy Swaggarts. The number of television evangelists is small, and there are few radio preachers who have syndicated programs. But there are hundreds of fundamentalists who host radio or television programs that are broadcast over just one station, and there are thousands who have ministries along the lines of Jackson's. While most of these operations are restricted to one town or one section of a town (Jackson's is

[23] Swaggart, *Catholicism*, 53–54.
[24] Barbara Nauer, "Catholic Calls Swaggart 'Holy Scourge' ", *Baton Rouge Morning Advocate*, 15 February 1985, 10A.

geographically large as such things go), they have a cumulative impact far greater than Swaggart's because there are so many of them.

The demographics are unavailable, but of Swaggart's three million American viewers, surely only a few hundred thousand are Catholics. (Other stars of religious television would enjoy higher proportions since their anti-Catholicism is muted.) Even Swaggart's Catholic viewers will be more influenced by the evangelist that comes to the door than by the evangelist heard on television. Most Catholics who meet fundamentalism meet it at the local level, and, if they are convinced by its arguments, they are convinced because they have spoken directly with local fundamentalists who have taken them through the Bible and various tracts.

The most important thing about Swaggart's ministry so far as Catholics are concerned—what makes it as influential as it is—is that it legitimizes anti-Catholicism and emboldens local fundamentalists to knock on Catholic doors. They normally would not take such a step without considerable prodding. On the whole, fundamentalists are reserved, wary of talking about religion outside their own circles, and until recent years they largely kept to themselves. But Swaggart and the other media preachers are exemplars. Their apparent success in taking on the Roman institution (which gives no audible answer to their charges) encourages the people who gather for Bible study each week at Good Book Baptist.

Chapter 7

Appealing to the Young

Anti-Catholic fundamentalists are not necessarily old fogies. Exhibit number one: the late Keith Green, popular religious singer who was killed in a plane crash. His *Last Days Newsletter,* published by his Last Days Ministries of Lindale, Texas, carried four installments of the *Catholic Chronicles,* each "edited and compiled by Keith Green". These issues of the newsletter were so well received that they were reprinted in 1980 and 1981 in the form of tracts. The tracts found a wide audience. Though no longer available from Last Days Ministries,[1] they remain influential and deserve mention.

Give them their due. They are simply the best-looking tracts put out by either side in the fundamentalist-Catholic squabble. The typography is clean, almost booklike (italics, bold, reduced footnotes), there is original artwork, and the printing is in two colors, making for black text, red headlines, and a pink background. Not unjustifiably, the outfit that ran the presses is called Pretty Good Printing.

Somewhat surprisingly, the first tract is on the Holy Eucharist; it is subtitled "Eating the Flesh of Deity". Green explains to his readers why he avoids "the more obvious departures from biblical foundation—such as the worship of and prayers to the Virgin Mary, the infallibility of the pope, purgatory and prayers for the dead. . . ." They will be discussed later, he says. "But for this

---

[1] Last Days Ministries sends to inquirers a statement issued by Melody Green, Keith Green's widow. She explains the *Catholic Chronicles* have been withdrawn from distribution because "[w]e are aware of Catholics who have been wounded by these tracts. We are also aware of others who have adopted a critical, self-righteous attitude toward Catholics."

first article I believe that we should get right to the root" of Catholic worship, and that is the Eucharist. He at least knows what the opposition's core devotional belief is.

There follows a reasonably fair explication of Catholic doctrines, although it is laced with smart asides and an abundance of exclamation points. Green gives extensive quotations from the canons of Trent, getting in his jabs by prefacing his account with biblical verses such as "Thou shalt not make unto thee any graven image" (Ex 20:4), the point being, of course, that the host is a graven image. He then comments on those scriptural passages Catholics use in proof of the Eucharist, and he makes the standard argument that the Greek in Mt 26:26 ("This is my body . . .") can only mean the bread "represents", "signifies", or "stands for" Christ. He admits the Greek phrase is *touto esti,* and he says it means "this is" (which is true), but he insists, contrary to any Greek grammar book, that the verb can only be taken in the symbolic sense.

Regarding this and all the other topics he considers, his arguments are unoriginal. He even concludes this tract with a few paragraphs on the "real" origin of the Eucharist. Like Ralph Woodrow—perhaps because he read Woodrow's *Babylon Mystery Religion*—Green finds the Eucharist prefigured in the worship of Osiris and in Mithraism.

The attack is stepped up in the second of the *Catholic Chronicles.* This one is on the Mass and is subtitled *Jesus Dies Again.* Those with good eyesight will catch the footnote on the first page, where credit is given to one of Bart Brewer's tracts, another example of the way anti-Catholic fundamentalists rely on and quote one another.

On the inside is a reproduction of a Gustav Doré drawing of the Crucifixion. The text is again unoriginal so far as Green's arguments are concerned, but he differs from other fundamentalist writers in that he quotes Catholic sources. Canons of Trent are given, as are passages from Vatican II and some lines from a booklet distributed by the Knights of Columbus' Catholic Information Service.

Green sees the falsity of the Mass in its apparent violation of Christ's words that "It is finished" (Jn 19:30). Not distinguishing between Christ's death and his sacrifice, he says in the Mass Christ dies anew, and thus Catholics think his task was not finished at all. Green is unable to perceive that the sacrifice can be perpetuated (presented again) even though the death occurred once. There follow four selections from Hebrews, each, to Green, attesting to the contradiction between what the Mass purports to be and what the Bible says. "Once for all" (Heb 10:10) is the banner fundamentalists wave. Christ died once, so Catholics, who think he dies again at each Mass, aren't really Christians, but cultists.

To establish the Catholic Church as nothing but a cult, Green presents the third tract in his series, *Salvation According to Rome*. The largest tract (11 by 17 inches, folded to make four pages) and the longest (about 4,000 words), it was surely not the work of a single evening at the typewriter. It is a formidable piece of paper—not in the sense of the soundness of the arguments, but in their intensity, their seeming thoroughness, their ability to impress the theologically uneducated (which is to say just about everyone in the pews, whether fundamentalist or Catholic).

Green's comparison is between "salvation by grace", which implies an absolute assurance of salvation, and the Catholic sacramental system. He begins by deriding the Catholic distinction between mortal and venial sins, saying "there is in fact no such thing as a venial sin. ALL SIN IS MORTAL! It is true that some sins are worse than others, but it is also true that all sins if not forgiven bring death to the soul." He talismanically quotes Scripture: "The wages of sin is death" (Rom 6:23); "The soul that sinneth, it shall die" (Ezek 18:4); but overlooks 1 John 5:17: "Not all sin is fatal."

This is a good example of a common failing among fundamentalists, and not just those who are actively anti-Catholic. They memorize their lessons well, but they memorize selectively because they are taught only certain things. Although they read the entire Bible, with, naturally enough, special emphasis on the New Testament, verses that do not mesh with what their pastors have told them are either skipped or just not perceived as being trouble spots. On any one topic, they learn verses that, concatenated, seem to prove conclusively their position, and it is on these that they concentrate their apologetics. Few of them seriously ponder the meaning of those large chunks of the Bible that are pushed into the background. It is the rare fundamentalist who will go verse by verse through Scripture, seeing if he can piece together a coherent whole. In fact, most ex-fundamentalists say their first doubts about fundamentalism came when they read a biblical passage for the hundredth time and suddenly realized that it did not square with what they'd been taught at Sunday school.

Convinced, in the first place, that the Bible is easy to understand, and convinced that all its parts admit but one interpretation and that anyone interpreting differently must be acting in bad faith, they had given no thought to the possibility that the Catholic position might have something in its favor. The Bible must, unless the reader is not a Christian at all, lead him to but one interpretation, which happens to be identical with that of his fundamentalist pastor. There is no point in looking elsewhere.

Though they held this view, these onetime fundamentalists could not entirely escape the plain words of the text. First this, then that verse would bother them. They would read that "not all sin is fatal" and wonder, not whether sin is to be divided between mortal and venial (even ex-Catholic fundamentalists generally have no feel for those terms), but, more simply, how that verse could be reconciled with apparently contradictory ones. Their teachers' technique of selective quotation (which they believed was not selective, but exhaustive) kept them in line, but the number of these discomfiting passages grew, and eventually a critical mass was reached.

In *Witness*, Whittaker Chambers explained that the communist, before his break with that ideology, one night wakes up in a cold sweat, convinced he is hearing screams. What he hears is his subconscious—and perhaps his conscience—finally piecing together stray fragments, and he realizes what communism really is. He can taste its reality. On one level he in fact always has known, or at least for a long time known, what it is, but his prejudice has kept the implications of that knowledge submerged. Then he hears screams.[2]

It is somewhat the same with the fundamentalist before his conversion to another brand of Christianity. For a long time he has gathered these ill-fitting verses, "pondering them in his heart". From their existence he has drawn no conclusion, trusting that at length he will be shown just how they fit into his creed, until, seemingly out of the blue, it occurs to him that fundamentalism may be fundamentally wrong.

But this is getting ahead of the story. It is enough to note here that Keith Green's tracts are fine examples of the best small-compass, anti-Catholic writing by fundamentalists. He uses all the standard techniques, all the pat phrases, and he uses them convincingly—or so it must seem, since the tracts have enjoyed a considerable success, particularly among the young who used to listen to his songs.

The fourth of the *Catholic Chronicles* asks, *What Did Vatican II Really Change?* The answer: nothing. It is a favorite ploy of fundamentalists to say that the Church made a big production out of changing itself, bringing things up to date, telling the world it was sloughing off its old prejudices and needless doctrinal encumbrances, when in fact all the essentials remain the same. It was all a public relations gambit, designed to elicit sympathy for a Church in decline. And it worked. Most people have been fooled, but not the fundamentalists.

Some of this, of course, is quite true. There have been changes since the Council, but there has been no alteration at all in basic doctrines or in principles of operation. The Catholic Church is still the sole true Church (it is in the Catholic Church that Christ's Church "subsists", according to Vatican II),[3] and, while Friday

---

[2] Whittaker Chambers, *Witness* (New York: Random House, 1952), 14.

[3] *Lumen Gentium*, 8.

abstinence may no longer be required, the Church has not abandoned the principle that religious authority may legislate on matters of discipline and devotion.

Green quotes at length from Loraine Boettner's *Roman Catholicism*. Boettner, called by Green a "noted Evangelical authority on Roman Catholic doctrine", looks at Vatican II and sadly concludes that "an infallible church simply cannot repent". Rome will always be Rome, and Vatican II changed nothing of importance. The Catholic Church has scraped off its barnacles and is ready to take to the seas again. This enemy of truth may be more seaworthy now than it was a generation ago. "The agelong danger that Protestantism has faced from the Roman Church has not diminished", cautions Boettner; "in fact, it may well have increased."[4] Like Queen Victoria, he is not amused, nor is Keith Green, nor, one supposes, are the impressionable readers of the *Catholic Chronicles*.

From Texas and the home of Last Days Ministries the focus shifts to New York, where we find another organization that appeals largely to the young, Solid Rock Ministries. It mails out, at irregular intervals, a newsletter that carries, below the mailing label, the line "Jesus is coming back soon. . . . Are you ready?" According to the head of the organization, Donald Spitz, among those who should not feel comfortable in answering that question are Catholics, for the simple reason that Catholics, if they remain Catholics, are damned.

One issue of the newsletter opens with two revelations granted Spitz (they read like the pedestrian stuff some Catholic visionaries claim to have been told), then it goes on to warn of one of Satan's favorite tricks, religion. "Another of his favorite lies is to make you 'religious'. He'll keep you entangled in rituals, sacraments, ceremonies, and other 'traditions of men' that have been manufactured into doctrines."

The reader is not surprised to discover, a few pages further along, a letter from a young woman who explains, as an ex-

---

[4] Boettner, *Catholicism*, xii.

Catholic, that she knows Solid Rock Ministries is "persecuted and maligned because of the stand [it has] taken opposing the false doctrines of Catholicism". She then recounts her childhood up-bringing and the discovery, as a teenager, that "despite my fear of God and my strongly held moral beliefs, I was more prone to do evil than good. Countless penances did not improve my sinful disposition", and she says she ended near despair. She was invited repeatedly to a Bible study, but regularly declined. At last, her resistance gone, she decided to go. "I intended to teach those 'born again fanatics', those 'Jesus freaks', a lesson in Catholi-cism." She was surprised to discover they were studying not a catechism, but the Gospel according to John. (What did she ex-pect at a Protestant Bible study?)

"As the sweetness of the Word of God gently rolled over my 'sin tired' senses, I found that I was unable to criticize the teaching of the Word"—perhaps because, as a Catholic, she had never been introduced to the study of the Bible and was in no position to raise even the simplest objections to odd interpretations of it. In six months, after attending the classes weekly, she was "born again". She tried attending Mass at St. Patrick's Cathedral, and her soul "was filled with rage when I realized the damnable crime that was being committed against God and against millions of sincere, yet spiritually blinded people". It is these people, these Catholics, that she and the people at Solid Rock Ministries mean to reach. They aim mainly at the young.

Her letter is followed by an article on "Cults and More Cults". The author is Spitz. After perfunctory mention of the Jehovah's Witnesses and the Mormons, he gets right to the point. The real enemy is the Catholic Church. His arguments are unexceptional and are not worth reproducing at length. One story of his must suffice. "One day at Mass [this was before he unpoped] I remem-ber the priest reading from the Gospel of Matthew, about not us-ing vain repetitions in prayer. I thought to myself, 'That's very beautiful, and also really makes sense.' No sooner was the reading completed when the service continued on with some 'canned prayers' repeated numerous times, followed by a sermon on the

'Joys of the Rosary' ". He closes by noting, with Loraine Boettner and others, that Vatican II really changed nothing of substance. Indeed, he even refers to *Unam Sanctam* and says it is still a fair indicator of the Catholic position (true enough, if understood properly). As Spitz puts it, the bull, issued by Boniface VIII, said "submission to the authority of the Pope is a requirement for salvation". The Catholic Church is out to get us all.

Chapter 8

At the Fringe

"There has been a multi-million dollar campaign made through the media to convince people that I am a bigoted, anti-Catholic, hate-literature publisher", wrote Jack Chick in the introduction to *Smokescreens*.[1] "And do you know something? They have been very effective in convincing people that this is what I am."

Apparently they have, whoever "they" are, because Jack Chick is generally regarded as the king of the anti-Catholic publishers. He has received more attention in the Catholic press since 1980 than all other professional anti-Catholics combined, and his rantings against the Church have inspired even Protestant publications, such as *Christianity Today,* to investigate his operation. His ideas are so perverse, his hate mongering so outlandish, that even some anti-Catholics shun him. If the average Catholic has heard anything about the recent revival of anti-Catholic prejudice, he has heard about Jack Chick.

Because of all the publicity, two things have happened. Chick and his chief assistant, Alberto Rivera (who claims to be a one-time Jesuit and bishop), have been given a prominence in the anti-Catholic movement they in fact do not have, their writings seeming to be more influential than they really are, and other anti-Catholic organizations—the ones that produce the converts to fundamentalism—have been ignored. It may be that in some Catholic publications Chick and Rivera have received more column inches than anyone other than the Pope. And they simply have not been worth it, because their barks are far out of proportion to their bites. They make good copy but few converts and

---

[1] Jack Chick, *Smokescreens* (Chino, Calif.: Chick Publications, 1983), 5.

nowhere near the converts one would expect from all the fire-works.

The other problem is that coverage of them has meant coverage of other anti-Catholic organizations has been shallow. While full-page articles have been devoted to Chick Publications' comics, in most Catholic papers only passing comments have been given to the organizations that really have been dragging Catholics out of the Church and into fundamentalism. Chick and Rivera have thrown something of a shadow across the fundamentalist land-scape, and it is sometimes hard to realize there are other groups lurking in the bushes. One reason for this is that Chick has sought publicity as though he were running for office, while most profes-sional anti-Catholics quietly go about their work, making no ef-fort to grab headlines. They want converts, not notoriety. To seek the public eye is to put oneself on the spot.

It is one thing to make strange claims about the Catholic reli-gion, but something else to find yourself having to support the claims with facts and rational arguments, which you might have to do if you shout too loudly. So most fundamentalists are re-served. They push their ideas, but avoid confrontations that force them to debate. Only when they think they are up against ill-informed papists (and no one else) do they open their satchels, drag out a Bible, and ask, "How does *this* square with what the Catholic Church says?" But Chick does not worry about having his arguments fall flat because he does not argue. He just, well, pontificates and then ignores challenges to fight.

None of this means Chick is not worth covering. He is. His colorful comic books and pocket-sized tracts have been widely distributed, and some Catholics, particularly impressionable teenagers and young adults, have accepted his notions and left the Barque of Peter at the first port of call. But most people influenced by Chick have been opposed to Catholicism all along and never gave any allegiance to Rome. Chick's materials merely heighten their native bigotry and give them the satisfaction of knowing that their prejudices are, in some circles, socially acceptable. After all, here is someone much more prejudiced than they, someone who has achieved a measure of notoriety, someone who has put the enemy on the defensive, and he seems to be doing quite well, thank you.

Chick's literature would be unimportant, quite unworthy of the sustained treatment it has received in the Catholic press, if his were the only anti-Catholic organization in the nation. There are few flat-Earthers, and no one pays them much heed. They would be worth examining, perhaps, if there were societies of oval-Earthers who received legitimacy because they could separate themselves in the public mind from those who think the world is shaped like a fat dish. Chick's very existence makes all the other anti-Catholic groups look moderate, and they are therefore more influential than they otherwise would be. Fundamentalists who are squeamish about supporting all of Chick's theories owe him a vote of thanks; he makes them look good.

It is similar to the big lie technique. Most people, even most with an ingrained prejudice against the Church, realize the comic books are grotesqueries. They seem to say, "We acknowledge Jack Chick is overzealous; we admit that. But his zealotry only demonstrates that what Mission to Catholics, the Conversion Center, and Jimmy Swaggart say must be accurate. These other evangelists have eliminated Chick's infelicities, and what we are left with is the unvarnished truth." It is this kind of thinking that makes Chick's work important.

He first gained notoriety with the publication of the comic book *Alberto* in 1979. This is Alberto Rivera's story—or so it is claimed. The thirty-two pages are well illustrated, in the style of Marvel Comics. The drawings are detailed, even explicit, making no effort to leave the reader wondering. The story begins in Spain in 1942. The first few pages recount the last hours of Alberto's mother. The young Alberto is shown at her deathbed. The priest in attendance tells him "your mother has not only received the sacraments, but special indulgences by the pope, our Holy Father". It thus should be an easy death, but not so. The next box shows her last moments. She sees "horrible monsters coming at me!!" Hands raised to keep the visions at bay, she cries, "Don't you see them? They want to put me in fire! They want to get me, Alberto! I don't want to die and go there!" But, of course, she does die, and she does go there, even though we are told her family knew she was a saint. "To my knowledge," said her husband, "she never missed going to Mass." Alberto, not comforted by the priest, thinks that "It's all a lie! The sacraments didn't help my mother. . . . The Church didn't help her when she needed help and comfort." Despite his disillusionment, Alberto becomes a priest.

We next see him, now "Dr." Alberto Rivera, in San Diego in 1979. Mysteriously run off the freeway by some enemy, he finds temporary refuge through a friend and begins to recount his story, beginning with the true nature of the Church. The tale is familiar to anyone who has read Maria Monk's revelations. In Spain, for instance, convents and monasteries are connected by tunnels; along the passages are chambers where the bodies of illicitly conceived (and quickly murdered) infants are buried. The Pope does not actually run the Church; the real ruler is the Jesuit General. The tortures of the Inquisition are recounted in glorious, dripping color. And so forth.

Rivera was trained from youth, he says, to infiltrate and subvert Protestantism. The denominations assigned to him were the Plymouth Brethren, Pentecostal, Baptist, and United Evangelical. He was fabulously successful and was rewarded by secretly being made a bishop. His credentials are demonstrated through a photograph of what purports to be an identification card issued him by the Spanish government. His photograph (he is wearing a Roman collar) seems to have been superimposed over the card. The reader is also shown "a copy of the last official certification given to me just before I left Spain in 1967". Investigations by *Christianity Today*[2] and the Catholic League for Religious and Civil Rights[3] confirmed that neither the Diocese of Madrid, where Rivera claims to have been a priest, nor the Jesuits have any record of him, but what can one expect from papist conspirators?

---

[2] Gary Metz, "Jack Chick's Anti-Catholic Comic Book Is Exposed as a Fraud", *Christianity Today*, 13 March 1981.

[3] Information on Rivera is available from the Catholic League, 1100 West Wells Street, Milwaukee, Wisconsin 53233.

Alberto was followed by *Double-Cross,* a recounting of Rivera's further exploits, particularly the rescue of his sister from the clutches of rapacious nuns (her escape from the convent seems to have been modeled closely on Maria Monk's) and Rivera's flight from hit squads sent after him by the Vatican. The reader is regaled with a photograph of Kathryn Kuhlman meeting Paul VI and a drawing of Jimmy Carter meeting John Paul II. These well-known Christians were in cahoots with Rome. And so was someone else—Jim Jones turns out to have been a Jesuit who did himself in, along with his followers, in fulfillment of his Jesuit oath.

Later additions to the Chick Publications library include *The Godfathers,* which demonstrates that the Catholic Church is the "Mother of Abominations" referred to in Revelation 17; *The Force,* "a prophetical study revealing the occult side of the Whore of Revelation"; and *The Big Betrayal,* based on Charles Chiniquy's *50 Years in the Church of Rome,* which demonstrates that the Church arranged Abraham Lincoln's assassination. If something meatier than comics is wanted, the reader can turn to Chick Publications' illustrated catalogue and order books such as *The Two Babylons,* another nineteenth-century potboiler; *Night Journey from Rome to the New Jerusalem,* by Clark Butterfield, allegedly an ex-priest; *The Vatican-Moscow-Washington Alliance,* by longtime Catholic-baiter Avro Manhattan; or even *The Secret History of the Jesuits,* which "boldly exposes the Vatican's involvement in world politics, intrigues, and the fomenting of wars throughout history".

Then there is *Smokescreens.* This ninety-three-pager is actually a transcript of a cassette the author made. He markets it by saying that the reader gets not only the words of the cassette, but revealing photographs as well. "What you are going to read in this book is absolutely devastating." He explains that "we believe at Chick Publications that the Whore of Revelation is the Roman Catholic Institution",[4] and he names such Protestant lights as Luther,

---

[4] Chick, *Smokescreens,* 4–5.

Calvin, Knox, and, in more recent years, Moody and Spurgeon as agreeing with this conclusion. The title of the book comes from the smokescreens the Jesuits have set to make people think the Whore of Revelation is something that will come in the distant future, not something that is present today and headquartered in the Vatican.

There follow several short chapters: one on "The Wafer-God", another looking at the St. Bartholomew's Day Massacre, a third on the way Croatian Catholics supposedly backed the Nazis. Then come chapters on the application of Revelation 17 to the Church, the way Catholics have secretly gained influence through the television shows of supposedly Protestant evangelists, and the Vatican's long-term plans for conquest.

Next comes self-congratulation. Chick explains how brave he was to publish Alberto Rivera's story. "When it finally dawned on me that we were being set up for another inquisition, I realized what a mess I'd be in if I sounded the alarm and the Christians wouldn't believe it. I could lose our business, our reputation and friends. If I printed Alberto's story, I would be going into a battle that would jeopardize my family and my own life." But he knew what to do. "I went before the Lord in prayer and the thing I dreaded came to pass. I asked the Lord if I should attack the mother of harlots and abominations of the earth. Should I attack the Vatican? The Lord said yes. And so we published *Alberto*." Although he followed the Lord's explicit directions, Chick didn't get the backing he expected from other fundamentalists. He said of one, "Here is a man I used to pray for. But no longer. The Lord stopped me"—the same Lord, apparently, who instructed his followers to love their enemies, even their former accomplices. "When the heat came on Chick Publications for what we were doing, I was amazed. It all came through the same group. There seemed to be a link between all these men who are promoting the story that Alberto is a fraud." He cites the stories in *Christianity Today, Cornerstone* (a magazine appealing to young evangelicals), and *Our Sunday Visitor*.[5]

[5] Chick, *Smokescreens*, 64.

Then he demonstrates there is no honor among professional anti-Catholics. He attacks Bill Jackson of Christians Evangelizing Catholics and Bart Brewer, head of Mission to Catholics. "Both of these men are supposed to be operating ministries to Catholics. And yet, they're going around to churches trying to destroy our credibility." Well, not quite. Brewer, for instance, noted in his newsletter, *Challenger,* that he has been asked often about Alberto Rivera's credibility, and he would neither support nor disavow either Rivera or Jack Chick. On this matter he took the agnostic position.

After Jack Chick got the publicity he so ardently sought, he had to go it alone. Not entirely alone, perhaps, for he still had Alberto Rivera, who could tell him about the "blueprint for Catholic America", something he was briefed on when a Jesuit. It went all the way back to the time of the Pilgrims. Remember those people leaving Europe for America in the seventeenth and eighteenth centuries, seeking religious freedom, people such as the Pilgrims? All Protestants? Hardly. Among them were numerous papists from England, Ireland, and France. "These were plants", Rivera told Chick. "The Jesuits made sure this part of our history was erased and removed." Once the fifth column was in place, its task was to "destroy or control all the Christian schools across America. Throughout the years, Jesuits, working undercover, have gotten into special committees on school boards to remove the emphasis on the Bible and replace it with psychology as found in the Spiritual Exercises of Ignatius of Loyola." They transformed public schools into Ignatian retreats. After the schools came the judiciary, then politics, then the military and newspapers. "Even back in the time of Lincoln over half the newspapers in the United States were controlled by the Vatican."[6]

Chick asked Rivera, "How Catholic is our military position?"

"Horrifying", said Rivera.

"I then asked about the political picture."

"It is even worse."

---

[6] Tony Alamo, going Chick and Rivera one better, claims the Vatican controls all the major news media.

"Then I said: What about the Catholic structure of the judiciary?"

"It is very painful because of the heavy Jesuit penetration of this area", said Rivera.

"Is this preparing the way for the coming inquisition?" asked Chick.

"That's correct", replied Rivera. "First for anarchy. We were briefed that after all these years of penetration and infiltration, what was needed was riots and anarchy in order to finally take over. By the time the Roman Catholic Institution is ready to take over politically, militarily, educationally, and religiously, that means they will have some legal basis to do so."

Is there any hope? wondered Chick. Yes, said Rivera, but only if Chick Publications' materials are distributed even more widely. The United States, conveniently enough, is where the prophecies of the Last Days will be fulfilled, and the ground has to be prepared. "If it were not for the publications we printed, we would be in a different situation today."[7]

Time grows short. Protestant pastors have to be on guard; all the worst things they have heard about Catholics are true. Those are Catholic eyes staring at them in the night. "I was recently told", recounts Chick, "that in 1949 an ex-Jesuit priest told a Rev. Eubanks in California that when the Vatican takes control of the United States, every pastor and his family will be shot in the head."[8] And if that is not convincing, what is? What further proof is needed, save perhaps the name of the ex-Jesuit, the full name of Rev. Eubanks, and the name of the man who recently told all this to Chick? It should be enough to know that "the Jesuits, the Illuminati, the Opus Dei, and the Masons"[9] are the real makers of smokescreens. One need only keep his eyes open.

Many Catholics have been doing just that, keeping them open and on Jack Chick and Alberto Rivera. The Catholic League for Religious and Civil Rights has reported on Chick Publications

---

[7] Chick, *Smokescreens*, 76–79.
[8] Chick, *Smokescreens*, 88.
[9] Chick, *Smokescreens*, 92.

since at least 1981, and *Our Sunday Visitor* and *The National Catholic Register* have run articles, short and long, about the duo. Chick no doubt has made a tidy sum in distributing his dozens of comics, books, and tracts. Rivera is in some small demand as a speaker and no doubt finds it profitable to play on fears of uninformed Protestants. He operates what he calls the Antichrist Information Center and is available for public talks.

Although most anti-Catholic organizations will not have anything to do with Jack Chick, Chick Publications, or Alberto Rivera, there is one that will. End Time Books, part of the Holy Alamo Christian Church, Consecrated, offers for sale the cassette version of *Smokescreens*. Also for sale are other books advertised by Chick: Edmond Paris' *The Secret History of the Jesuits*, Avro Manhattan's *The Vatican-Moscow-Washington Alliance*, and Charles Chiniquy's *The Priest, the Woman, and the Confessional*.

Tony Alamo is best known for distributing a poster claiming all the major news media "are secretly owned by the Vatican". At the top of the poster is a large-print "Warning!" It is revealed that in Romanist hands are *Life, People, Time, Newsweek,* three television networks, the Hearst newspaper chain, *The New York Times, The Los Angeles Times,* "and many other other local newspapers, T.V. and radio stations". It seems the Vatican uses these media "to exonerate themselves [*sic*] from crimes they [*sic*] have done and are doing . . . and to smear and malign who they [*sic*] will". At the bottom of the poster is a big "Watch out!!"

The poster and the considerable publicity it received were the first most people had heard about what was originally called the Tony & Susan Alamo Christian Foundation, which began as a Christian street ministry in Southern California. It was established by Tony Alamo, a former pop singer, and his wife, Susan. The Alamos moved their operation to Alma, Arkansas, where they built an empire of unrelated businesses. Their holdings even included the largest country-and-western clothing store in Nashville. Members of the Alamo cult worked in its enterprises as "volunteers", thereby allowing Alamo to amass millions.

Susan Alamo died in 1982. Tony was convinced she would be resurrected in short order, and faithful cultists kept round-the-clock vigils, convinced their prayers would bring her back. Just about the time his followers might have begun doubting the likelihood of his wife's imminent return, Alamo hit on a new angle, anti-Catholicism. It was in early 1984 that his posters appeared in at least fifty cities around the country, and not long after came *The Pope's Secrets*, an eight-page, closely spaced explanation of the Vatican's shenanigans. In that booklet the reader learns that a conveniently dead Australian archbishop said "the demands of the holy father (the Pope) are that the public services should be 100% Roman Catholic soon. Care must be taken that no suspicion may be raised when Roman Catholics are secretly given more government jobs than Protestants, Jews, and other heretics." This revelation is followed by quotations from Chick Publications' books.

Next comes a history lesson. After World War II, explains Alamo, the Vatican set up the John Birch Society so the American public would become concerned about communism and would overlook the Vatican's encroachments. The Vatican likewise underwrote "every major terrorist group in the world. The reason for this is to keep people's thoughts on unexplainable, insane tragedies that their [sic] terrorist groups are committing while the Vatican is busy undermining all the governments of the world so they [sic] can have world dominion (papal power). When terrorist news hits, it is so shocking that it minimizes the news of the Vatican taking away the U.S. Constitution and of people being deprived of their religious freedoms." Alamo does not explain how there can be any news of these Catholic usurpations if the Vatican controls the media—but that is a quibble.

There is no reason to recount each of the tales in this flyer. The author demonstrates an active imagination, one that takes him far beyond what even Alberto Rivera has been able to concoct. Rivera, for instance, was unable to discover the "liquor and wine slave labor camps" run by the Christian Brothers and other religious orders that "unlawfully use free labor (thousands of Roman Catholic monks)".

In 1985 Tony Alamo remarried. Since it would have been inappropriate for his organization to have continued carrying his former wife's name, the group is now known as the Holy Alamo Christian Church, Consecrated. (Its literature does not make clear whether the adjective "Holy" is meant to modify "Alamo" or "Church".)

In a tract called *It Was All a Lie!* the second Mrs. Alamo, Elizabeth, assures the reader that "you can find out all about 'them': the Roman Catholic cult, the harlot of Revelation . . . and about how God has told throughout the entirety of the King James Version of the Holy Bible about her, *as well as her falling,* immediately before the Lord Jesus Christ returns to this earth."

She explains that "I understand *now* why the Inquisitions and the Crusades were minimized in history classes, why propaganda was supposedly only a 'Russian tactic' and why Latin was the mandatory language in junior high school. The conversations I had overheard about Catholicism as a child were absolute truth. The Catholic motto of Satan is obvious—confuse, convince, convert."

If there is any anti-Catholic propaganda that needs to be ignored rather than opposed, it is Tony Alamo's. His efforts are so extreme they make extremists look moderate. So why not ignore him entirely? Because, like Alberto Rivera and his comic books, this is another example of a fanatic making run-of-the-mill anti-Catholics look good. The public is always willing to accept someone or some organization that appeals to its unrespectable prejudices if it can, at the same time, reject propagandists at the fringe. Alamo may have hornswoggled enough people to work for him for free that he is now a wealthy man, but he really has no substantial following, nor do his ideas.

The work of Chick, Rivera, and Alamo as point men of fundamentalist anti-Catholicism legitimizes Mission to Catholics, the Conversion Center, and the other "moderate" anti-Catholic organizations. The three have allowed the groups that effect conversions to appear reasonable and respectable by distancing themselves from their foolishness. "Moderate" anti-Catholics are seen as making the necessary distinctions, as thinking the questions through carefully—which is nonsense, but convenient nonsense.

With the election of John F. Kennedy, pundits said nativism was on the wane. The anti-Catholicism that had been a part of America's heritage from the first—and that at times suppurated into political movements such as the Know-Nothings in the 1850s and the Ku Klux Klan in the 1920s—was gone, done in by the wisdom of the electorate, and it would not return. But it has returned, in a more virulent strain than has been seen in more than two generations. There have been at least two main causes.

First, fundamentalism itself is having an upsurge. Largely dormant since the Scopes Trial, it has grown rapidly in the last twenty years, partly as a reaction to liberal Protestantism. If liberal Protestantism, as represented by the "mainline" churches, has as its symbol the question mark, fundamentalism has as its symbol the exclamation point. It is attractive because it stands for something, and that something is definite.

The apparent weakness of Catholicism is the second reason the anti-Catholic element in fundamentalism is growing. When Kennedy was elected, few thought of the Church as anything but monolithic. It had come through the milder anti-Catholic movement of the 1920s with nary a scratch, and in doing so it had confirmed the status of Catholics, who as recently as fifty years before that were, mainly, unwelcome newcomers to America. But the attack on the Church in the 1920s, spearheaded by the Klan (which concentrated its efforts on the Church as represented by immigrants, not on blacks), fizzled because the Church was perceived as being too strong; it seemed to be a fight not worth entering. Not so in recent years. Even fundamentalists who may touch no literature other than the Bible sense the Catholic Church has had problems, and many of them have been led to believe the problems are insurmountable and, in fact, are indicative of its ultimate collapse. They think Catholicism's true nature is finally catching up with it. Like wild dogs that attack only injured prey, professional anti-Catholics have gone after the Church because they sense irresolution. The old Church too easily survived attacks such as theirs. They think they can get away with something now, and they are running hard.

Examples of fundamentalism's darkest side could be repeated without end. There is no need to examine dusty books or yellowed leaflets to find them. They exist in numbers that were unimaginable only a few years ago. For the most part, Catholics have little notion of the depth of anti-Catholic sentiment. The most fanatic of the anti-Catholics—people such as Chick, Rivera, and Alamo—work on a different level than do garden-variety fundamentalists. The latter do what they do because they seek the truth. They are willing to follow syllogisms to their conclusions, even though they have uncritically followed some badly premised syllogisms to get where they are. They think they have discovered religious truth, and what they have discovered impels them to share it with others and to do whatever is necessary to make others see what they see. Often they take liberties with the facts, although usually they are unconscious of doing so. To them, their arguments seem conclusive. They can discover no weaknesses—although, to be sure, they have not searched particularly hard for any.

They are like political radicals. They have isolated a problem (their own sinfulness, in the case of fundamentalists; society's, in the case of radicals) and are determined to effect a solution. In doing that they will have to remove obstacles that stand in their way. For radicals, the main obstacle has been America itself; for fundamentalists, it is the Catholic Church, an even tougher nut to crack. Radicals willingly put aside other concerns and devote their time to the Cause; it is expected of them. They are defined by their pursuit of what they perceive to be justice. Fundamentalists are equally committed, but they often find themselves doing what others would expect them not to do. Everything about them speaks of reticence, yet they attack what they believe to be the most nefarious institution in the world, certainly the longest lived. Those who cannot fight Rome publicly read about, listen to, and send contributions to those who can.

Few fundamentalists are up in arms about Methodism, Episcopalianism, or Lutheranism, but every fundamentalist is worried about the Catholic Church. His interest first might be piqued by one or more of the fanatics, or he might become aware of the problem by hearing a more respectable fundamentalist preacher or by being given a newsletter from a ministry devoted to saving Catholics from certain doom. He comes to understand it is the Catholic Church that is the embodiment of eschatological evil. His attitude might be one of unadorned hatred—this seems to be ever more popular, or at least ever more public—or it might be a quiet, gentlemanly dislike. In either case, he has put the Catholic Church in a category no other religion or movement can occupy.

If he is a former Catholic, he brings with him all the intellectual and emotional baggage that implies. That often means he will be a fiercer anti-Catholic than the person brought up as a fundamentalist, perhaps because he feels he has more to atone for, perhaps because he blames the Church for his own failings. Regardless, he fears it as a tool of powers the average Catholic is only dimly aware of, and he considers himself duty bound to help those still in the clutches of Rome.

Chapter 9

Inspiration of the Bible

The Reformers said the Bible is the sole source of religious truth, and its understanding must be found by looking only at the words of the text. No outside authority may impose an interpretation, and no outside authority, such as the Church, has been established by Christ as an arbiter.[1] As heirs of the Reformers, fundamentalists work on the basis of *sola scriptura*,[2] and they advance this notion at every opportunity. One might think it would be easy for them to explain why they believe this principle.

Yet there is perhaps no greater frustration, in dealing with fundamentalists, than in trying to pin them down on why the Bible should be taken as a rule of faith at all, let alone as the sole rule of faith. It all reduces to the question of why fundamentalists accept the Bible as inspired, because the Bible can be taken as a rule of faith only if it is first held to be inspired and thus inerrant.

Now this is a problem that does not keep most Christians awake at night. Most have never given it any serious thought. To the extent they believe in the Bible, they believe in it because they operate in a milieu that is, if post-Christian in many ways, still steeped in Christian ways of thought and presuppositions. A lukewarm Christian who would not give the slightest credence to the Koran would think twice about casting aspersions on the Bible. It has a certain official status for him, even if he cannot explain it. One might say he accepts the Bible as inspired (whatever that

---

[1] See Paul Cardinal Taguchi, "The Study of Sacred Scripture", reprinted in John Steinmueller, *The Sword of the Spirit* (Waco, Tex.: Stella Maris, 1978), 87–108.

[2] Curiously enough, so do exegetes of the historico-critical school, many of whom refuse to consider evidence extrinsic to the Bible when developing their theories.

may mean for him) for some "cultural" reason, but that, of course, is hardly a sufficient reason, since on such a basis the Koran rightly would be considered inspired in a Moslem country.

Similarly, it is hardly enough to say that one's family has always believed in the Bible, "and that's good enough for me". It may indeed be good enough for the person disinclined to think, and one should not disparage a simple faith, even if held for an ultimately weak reason, but mere custom cannot establish the inspiration of the Bible.

Some fundamentalists say they believe the Bible is inspired because it is "inspirational", but that is a word with a double meaning. On the one hand, if used in the strict theological sense, it clearly begs the question, which is: How do we know the Bible is inspired, that is, "written" by God, but through human authors? And if "inspirational" means nothing more than "inspiring" or "moving", then someone with a deficient poetic sense might think the works of a poetaster are inspired.

Parts of the Bible, including several whole books of the Old Testament, cannot be called "inspirational" in this sense in the least, unless one works on the principle of the elderly woman who was soothed every time she heard "the blessed word Mesopotamia".[3] One betrays no disrespect in admitting that some parts of the Bible are as dry as military statistics—indeed, some parts *are* nothing but military statistics—and there is little there that can move the emotions.

So, it is not enough to believe in the inspiration of the Bible merely out of culture or habit, nor is it enough to believe in its inspiration because it is a beautifully written or emotion-stirring book. There are other religious books, and even some plainly secular ones, that outscore most of the Bible when it comes to fine prose or poetry.

What about the Bible's own claim to inspiration? There are not many places where such a claim is made even tangentially, and most books in the Old and New Testaments make no such claim

[3] Ronald Knox, *In Soft Garments* (New York: Sheed and Ward, 1942), 138.

at all. In fact, no New Testament writer seemed to be aware that he was writing under the impulse of the Holy Spirit, with the exception of the author of Revelation. Besides, even if every biblical book began with the phrase "the following is an inspired book", such phrases would prove nothing. The Koran claims to be inspired, as does the Book of Mormon, as do the holy books of various Eastern religions. Even the writings of Mary Baker Eddy, founder of Christian Science, claim inspiration. The mere claim of inspiration is insufficient to establish a book's bona fides.

These tests failing, most fundamentalists fall back on the notion that "the Holy Spirit tells me the Bible is inspired", an exercise in subjectivism that is akin to their claim that the Holy Spirit guides them in interpreting the text. For example, the anonymous author of *How Can I Understand the Bible?* a booklet distributed by the Radio Bible Class, lists twelve rules for Bible study. The first is "seek the help of the Holy Spirit. The Spirit has been given to illumine the Scriptures and make them alive to you as you study them. Yield to his enlightenment." If one takes this as meaning that anyone asking for a proper interpretation will be given one by God—and that is exactly how many fundamentalists understand the assistance of the Holy Spirit to work—then the multiplicity of interpretations, even among fundamentalists, should give people a gnawing sense that the Holy Spirit has not been doing his job very effectively.

Most fundamentalists do not say, in so many words, that the Holy Spirit has spoken to them directly, assuring them of the inspiration of the Bible. They do not phrase it like that. Rather, in reading the Bible they are "convicted" that it is the word of God, they get a positive "feeling" that it is inspired, and that's that— which often reduces their acceptance of the Bible to culture or habit. No matter how it is looked at, the fundamentalist's position is not one that is rigorously reasoned to. It must be the rare fundamentalist who, even for sake of argument, first approaches the Bible as though it is not inspired and then, on reading it, syllogistically concludes it is. In fact, fundamentalists begin with the fact of inspiration—just as they take the other doctrines of fundamentalism as givens, not as deductions—and then they find things in the Bible that seem to support inspiration, claiming, with circular reasoning, that the Bible confirms its inspiration, which they knew all along.

The man who wrestles with the fundamentalist approach to inspiration at length is unsatisfied because he knows he has no good grounds for his belief. The Catholic position is the only one, ultimately, that can satisfy the intellect. The Catholic method of finding the Bible to be inspired begins this way. The Bible is approached as any other ancient work. It is not, at first, presumed to be inspired. From textual criticism we are able to conclude that we have a text the accuracy of which is more certain than the accuracy of any other ancient work.

Sir Frederic Kenyon notes that

> [f]or all the works of classical antiquity we have to depend on manuscripts written long after their original composition. The author who is the best case in this respect is Virgil, yet the earliest manuscript of Virgil that we now possess was written some 350 years after his death. For all other classical writers, the interval between the date of the author and the earliest extant manuscript of his works is much greater. For Livy it is about 500 years, for Horace 900, for most of Plato 1,300, for Euripides 1,600.[4]

Yet no one seriously disputes that we have accurate copies of the works of these writers. Not only are the biblical manuscripts we have older than those for classical authors, we have in absolute numbers far more manuscripts to work from. Some are whole books of the Bible, others fragments of just a few words, but there are thousands of manuscripts in Hebrew, Greek, Latin, Coptic, Syriac, and other languages. What this means is that we can be sure we have an accurate text, and we can work from it in confidence.

Next we take a look at what the Bible, considered merely as a history, tells us, particularly the New Testament, and particularly

---

[4] Quoted in Lunn, *Third Day*, 28.

the Gospels. We examine the account of Jesus' life and death and his reported Resurrection. Using what is in the Gospels themselves, what we find in extrabiblical writings from the early centuries, and what we know of human nature (and what we can otherwise, from natural theology, know of divine nature), we conclude that Jesus either was just what he claimed to be, God, or was a madman. (The one thing we know he could not have been was merely a good man who was not God, because no merely good man would make the claims he made.)

We are able to eliminate his being a madman not just from what he said—no madman ever spoke as he did; for that matter, no sane man ever did either—but from what his followers did after his death. A hoax (the supposedly empty tomb) is one thing, but one does not find people dying for a hoax, at least not one from which they have no prospect of advantage. The result of this line of reasoning is that we must conclude that Jesus indeed rose from the dead and that he was therefore God and, being God, meant what he said and did what he said he would do.

One thing he said he would do was found a Church, and from both the Bible (still taken as merely a historical book, not at this point in the argument as an inspired one) and other ancient works, we see that Christ established a Church with the rudiments of all we see in the Catholic Church today—papacy, hierarchy, priesthood, sacraments, teaching authority, and, as a consequence of the last, infallibility. Christ's Church, to do what he said it would do, had to have the note of infallibility.

We thus have taken purely historical material and concluded that there exists a Church, which is the Catholic Church, divinely protected against teaching error. Now we are at the last part of the argument. That Church tells us the Bible is inspired, and we can take the Church's word for it precisely because the Church is infallible. Only after having been told by a properly constituted authority (that is, one set up by God to assure us of the truth of matters of faith) that the Bible is inspired do we begin to use it as an inspired book.

Here is how Arnold Lunn put it in a 1932 letter to C. E. M. Joad:

> We now approach the Bible, and approach it in the same spirit as that in which we should approach any other human document. We do not believe the Bible merely because it is the Bible, but because we are convinced of its veracity by rational inferences similar in kind to those which convince us of other historical facts. We do not, for instance, accept the fact that Christ rose from the dead merely because we find the Resurrection recorded in the Gospels; we accept the Resurrection because, of all theories which have been put forward to explain the origin of Christianity, the only theory which fits all the facts is the theory that Jesus of Nazareth claimed to be God and proved his claim by rising from the dead. . . . The Roman Catholic, then, claims to prove from the Bible, which he is still treating as a purely human document, that Christ intended to found an infallible Church. Where, then, is this Church? The Roman Catholic Church alone possesses, so the Catholic believes, all the "notes" which enable us to distinguish between the Church which Christ founded and its heretical rivals. The Catholic claims to prove by pure reason that Christ was God, that Christ founded an infallible Church, and that the Roman Catholic Church is the church in question. Having travelled thus far by reason unaided by authority, it is not irrational to trust the authority, whose credentials have been proved by reason, to interpret difficult passages in the Bible.[5]

Note that this is not a circular argument. We are not basing the inspiration of the Bible on the Church's infallibility and the Church's infallibility on the word of an inspired Bible. That indeed would be a circular argument.

What we have is really a spiral argument. On the first level we argue to the reliability of the Bible as history. From that we conclude an infallible Church was founded. Then we take the word of that infallible Church that the Bible is inspired. It reduces to the proposition that, without the existence of the Church, we could not tell if the Bible were inspired. As Augustine said, "I would

---

[5] Arnold Lunn and C. E. M. Joad, *Is Christianity True?* (Philadelphia: Lippincott, 1933), 33–34.

not believe in the Gospel if the authority of the Catholic Church did not move me to do so."[6]

What has just been discussed is not, obviously, the kind of mental exercise people go through before putting trust in the Bible, but it is the only truly reasonable way to do so. Every other way is inferior—psychologically adequate, perhaps, but actually inferior. In mathematics we accept on "faith" that one and one make two and that one, when added to any integer, will produce the next-highest integer. These truths seem elementary to us, and we are satisfied to take such things at face value, but apprentice mathematicians must go through a semester's course the whole of which is taken up demonstrating such "obvious" truths. Fundamentalists are quite right in believing the Bible is inspired, but their *reasons* for so believing are inadequate because knowledge of the inspiration of the Bible can be based only on an authority established by God to tell us the Bible is inspired, and that authority is the Church.

Here a more serious problem enters. It seems to some that it makes little difference why one believes in the Bible's inspiration, just so one believes in it. But the basis for one's belief in its inspiration directly affects how one goes about interpreting the Bible. The Catholic believes in inspiration because the Church tells him so—that is putting it bluntly—and that same Church has the authority to interpret the inspired text. Fundamentalists believe in inspiration, although on weak grounds, but they have no interpreting authority other than themselves.

Newman put it this way in an essay on inspiration published in 1884:

> Surely then, if the revelations and lessons in Scripture are addressed to us personally and practically, the presence among us of a formal judge and standing expositor of its words, is imperative. It is antecedently unreasonable to suppose that a book so complex, so unsystematic, in parts so obscure, the outcome of so many minds, times,

[6] See John Henry Newman's discussion of this point in his *Discussions and Arguments on Various Subjects* (London, 1891), 366.

and places, should be given us from above without the safeguard of some authority; as if it could possibly, from the nature of the case, interpret itself. Its inspiration does but guarantee its truth, not its interpretation. How are private readers satisfactorily to distinguish what is didactic and what is historical, what is fact and what is vision, what is allegorical and what is literal, what is idiomatic and what is grammatical, what is enunciated formally and what occurs *obiter,* what is only of temporary and what is of lasting obligation? Such is our natural anticipation, and it is only too exactly justified in the events of the last three centuries, in the many countries where private judgment on the text of Scripture has prevailed. The gift of inspiration requires as its complement the gift of infallibility.[7]

J. Derek Holmes emphasizes that

> [t]hroughout his argument Newman never ignored the main point, that since the writing was irregular, inconsistent, or incomplete, it was antecedently highly improbable that it would contain the whole of the revealed Word of God. The Bible did not contain a complete secular history, and there was no reason why it should contain a complete account of religious truth. It was unreasonable to demand an adequate scriptural foundation for Church doctrines, if the impression gained from the Bible was of writers who took solemn and sacred truths for granted and who did not give a complete or full treatment of the sense of revelation. The writings did not reflect all the beliefs of the writer and events were often presented without comment or moral implication.[8]

Fundamentalists' understanding of inspiration directly affects the way they interpret the Bible and the doctrines they discover in it. Many—not all those writing treatises, but some of them and certainly many in the pews—subscribe to what reduces to a dictation theory of inspiration. This is unfortunate, because "a 'dictation' theory may seem a natural account of some experiences of the prophets, but it is psychologically incredible when applied to

---

[7] John Henry Newman, *On the Inspiration of Scripture,* ed. J. Derek Holmes and Robert Murray (Washington: Corpus Books, 1967), 111.

[8] Newman, *Inspiration,* 10–11.

St. Luke writing his prologue or St. Paul writing to Philemon."[9]
A suggestion of the troubles faced by fundamentalists who subscribe to the dictation theory or its practical equivalents comes in
passages such as 1 Corinthians 1:14–16. Here is what Paul writes:
"Thank God that I did not baptize any of you except Crispus and
Gaius; so that no one can say it was in my name you were baptized. (Yes, and I did baptize the household of Stephanas; I do not
know that I baptized anyone else.)" Under the dictation theory,
with Paul simply transcribing what God whispered in his ear, one
would have to conclude God temporarily forgot who it was Paul
baptized. Other examples could be given to show that inspiration
is more subtle than many people suspect.

Here is another problem. How does one, on fundamentalist
terms, decide when more than one interpretation of a particular
passage is allowable and when only one can be admitted? The
Catholic Church is silent on the proper interpretation of many
biblical passages, readers being allowed to accept one of several
understandings.

Take, as an example, Jonah's escapade at sea, which readers often find disturbing. Ronald Knox said "no defender of the sense
of Scripture ever pretended, surely, that this was a natural event.
If it happened, it was certainly a miracle; and not to my mind a
more startling miracle than the raising of Lazarus, in which I take
it Catholics are certainly bound to believe. Surely what puts one
off the story of Jonah is the element of the *grotesque* which is
present in it."[10] Actually, what happened to Jonah can be looked
at three ways, one of which relies on nothing miraculous occurring at all.

The most common interpretation nowadays, and one that is
held by indubitably orthodox exegetes, is that the story of the
prophet being swallowed and then disgorged by a "great fish" is

---

[9] Newman, *Inspiration,* 51.
[10] Ronald Knox and Arnold Lunn, *Difficulties* (London: Eyre & Spottiswoode,
1952), 109.

merely didactic fiction, a grand tale told to establish a religious point. Catholics are perfectly free to take this or a more literal view, but one seldom will find a fundamentalist who thinks of Jonah as allegory or anything of that sort, although he really has no *authority* for opting for one interpretation over another.

Strictly literal interpretations of what happened to Jonah actually come in two forms. One relies on the fact that people apparently have been swallowed by whales and lived to talk about it. In 1891 a seaman, James Bartley, from a ship named the *Star of the East,* was found missing after an eighty-foot sperm whale had been caught. He was presumed drowned. The next day, when the crew cut up the whale, Bartley was discovered alive inside.[11] If Jonah's three days in the whale were counted like Christ's three days in the tomb, after the Semitic fashion—that is, parts of three distinct days, but perhaps only slightly more than twenty-four hours total—then it is possible that Jonah could have been coughed up by that great fish just as his story says. This would be a purely natural explanation of the episode.

The other literal interpretation is that Jonah indeed underwent what the story, read as straight history, says he did, but survived only because of a positive miracle, and several different sorts of miracles have been suggested, such as suspended animation on Jonah's part or a fish with a remarkably large air supply and decidedly mild gastric juices.

Related to the problem of inspiration is the problem of the canon of Scripture. What books constitute the Bible? Catholics can repair to the decisions of the Church, most clearly formalized at Trent and at the fourth-century councils at Hippo and Carthage; these produced lists of books that are to be accepted as inspired on the authority of the infallible Church. Inspired books, taken together, form the Bible. That is the Catholic way to answer the question. What does a fundamentalist fall back on?

[11] Amy Wallace, David Wallechinsky, and Irving Wallace, *People's Almanac* (Garden City, N.Y.: Doubleday, 1975), 1339.

William G. Most discusses the rather surprising comments made in 1910 by Gerald Birney Smith, professor at the University of Chicago and speaker at that year's Baptist Congress. As Most says, "Smith's frankness was really remarkable. He reviewed every way he knew to determine which books are or are not inspired" and thus to be included in the canon.

Smith explained that "Luther proposed a practical test. . . . The distinction which he actually had in mind was between those writings which have the power to bring men the assurance of forgiveness through Christ and those which have no such power." Luther was of course relying on his doctrine of salvation by faith alone (not, as Paul would have it, salvation by faith, which is a different thing, implying faith is a prerequisite for salvation but by itself insufficient). "Luther thought a book that intensely preaches this doctrine was inspired", explains Most, "otherwise not. Of course, he never provided proof for such a standard. Nor could it be a standard, for Luther, or any other writer, could compose a book that would preach according to Luther's requirements; yet that book need not on that account be inspired."

Smith, continuing his analysis of the Protestant basis for determining the canon, noted that John Calvin, in his *Institutes,* offered a different test: "The word will never gain credit in the hearts of men till it be confirmed by the internal testimony of the Spirit." This claim, too—relying on subjective "feelings"—was useless, Smith said, referring to the assaults on the Bible that were prevalent even a long lifetime ago. "The application of this test . . . would eliminate the existing distinction between canonical and non-canonical writings more completely than would the most radical conclusions of biblical criticism." After all, many parts of Scripture do not seem uplifting at all, such as 1 and 2 Chronicles, also known as 1 and 2 Paralipomenon, which, like much of Numbers and Deuteronomy, are dull—not the style of writing that shouts, "I'm inspired!" And some clearly noncanonical and thus noninspired books such as Thomas à Kempis' *Imitation of Christ* are more moving than many whole books of the Bible.

Most notes that "what Professor Smith demonstrates is that for a Protestant there simply is no way to know which books are inspired. That means, in practice, that a Protestant, if he is logical, should not appeal to Scripture to prove anything; he has no sure means of knowing which books are part of Scripture!"[12]

One consequence of this inability to ascertain the canon has been that the Protestant Bible is an incomplete Bible. Missing are the books of Tobit, Judith, Wisdom, Ecclesiasticus, Baruch, and the two books of Maccabees, as well as sections of Esther (10:4 to 16:24) and Daniel (3:24–90 and chapters 13 and 14). These are known to Catholics as the deutero-canonical works. They are just as much a part of the Bible as the rest of the Old Testament, the proto-canonical books. Luther rejected the deutero-canonical books and passages largely because they conflicted with his theological theories. In 2 Maccabees 12:46, for instance, it is said that "it is a holy and wholesome thought to pray for the dead that they may be loosed from their sins"—a reference to purgatory. Such a book had to go—it did not mesh with the Reformer's doctrines. (Luther even spoke disparagingly about some New Testament books, such as James, but he was unable to find a rationale for removing them from the canon.)

However easy it may have been for the Reformers to say that some books are inspired and thus in the canon, while others are not, they in fact had no solid grounds for making such determinations. Ultimately, an infallible authority is needed if we are to know what belongs in the Bible and what does not. Without such an authority, we are left to our own prejudices, and we cannot tell if our prejudices lead us in the right direction.

The advantages of the Catholic approach to proving inspiration are two. First, the inspiration is really proved, not just "felt". Second, the main fact behind the proof—the fact of an infallible, teaching Church—leads one naturally to an answer to the prob-

[12] William G. Most, *Free from All Error* (Libertyville, Ill.: Franciscan Marytown Press, 1985), 9–11.

lem that troubled the Ethiopian eunuch (Acts 8:31): How is one to know what interpretations are right? The same Church that authenticates the Bible, that establishes its inspiration, is the authority set up by Christ to interpret his word.

Chapter 10

Tradition versus "Traditions of Men"

Fundamentalists say the Bible is the sole rule of faith. Everything one needs to believe to be saved is in the Bible, and nothing needs to be added to the Bible. The whole of Christian truth is found within its pages. Anything extraneous to the Bible is simply wrong or hinders rather than helps one toward salvation.

Catholics, on the other hand, say the Bible is not the sole rule of faith and that nothing in the Bible suggests it was meant to be. In fact, the Bible indicates it is not to be taken by itself. The true rule of faith is Scripture and Tradition, as manifested in the living teaching authority of the Catholic Church, to which were entrusted the oral teachings of Jesus and the apostles plus the authority to interpret Scripture rightly.

Vatican II explained the relationship between Tradition and Scripture this way:

Hence there exist a close connection and communication between sacred Tradition and sacred Scripture. For both of them, flowing from the same divine wellspring, in a certain way merge into a unity and tend toward the same end. For sacred Scripture is the word of God inasmuch as it is consigned to writing under the inspiration of the divine Spirit. To the successors of the apostles, sacred Tradition hands on in its full purity God's word, which was entrusted to the apostles by Christ the Lord and the Holy Spirit. Thus, by the light of the Spirit of truth, these successors can in their preaching preserve this word of God faithfully, explain it, and make it more widely known. Consequently it is not from sacred Scripture alone that the Church draws her certainty about everything which has been revealed. Therefore both sacred Tradition and sacred

Scripture are to be accepted and venerated with the same devotion and reverence.[1]

The fundamentalist side usually begins its argument by citing two verses. The first is this: "So much has been written down, that you may learn to believe Jesus is the Christ, the Son of God, and so believing find life through his name" (Jn 20:31). The other is this: "Everything in the scripture has been divinely inspired, and it has its uses; to instruct us, to expose our errors, to correct our faults, to educate in holy living" (2 Tim 3:17). Fundamentalists say these verses demonstrate the reality of *sola scriptura*.

Not so, reply Catholics. The verse from John's Gospel tells us only that the Bible was composed so we can be helped to believe Jesus is the Messiah. It does not say the Bible is all we need for salvation, nor does it say the Bible is actually needed to believe in Christ. After all, the earliest Christians had no New Testament to appeal to; they learned from oral, not written, instruction. Until relatively recent times, the Bible was inaccessible to most people, either because they could not read or because printing had not yet been invented. All these people learned from oral instruction, passed down, generation to generation, by the Church. Granted, it would have been advantageous for them to have the Bible at hand also, but it was not necessary for their salvation.

Much the same can be said about 2 Timothy 3:17. To say that all inspired writing "has its uses" is one thing; to say that such a remark means that only inspired *writing* need be followed is something else. Besides, there is a telling argument against the fundamentalists' claim. It is the contradiction that arises out of their own interpretation of this verse. John Henry Newman explained it this way:

> It is quite evident that this passage furnishes no argument whatever that the Sacred Scripture, without Tradition, is the *sole rule of faith*; for, although Sacred Scripture is *profitable* for these four ends, still it

---

[1] *Dei Verbum*, 9.

is not said to be *sufficient*. The Apostle requires the aid of Tradition (2 Thess. 2:15). Moreover, the Apostle here refers to the Scriptures which Timothy was taught in his infancy. Now, a good part of the New Testament was not written in his boyhood: some of the Catholic Epistles were not written even when St. Paul wrote this, and none of the Books of the New Testament were then placed on the canon of the Scripture books. He refers, then, to the Scriptures of the Old Testament, and if the argument from this passage proved anything, it would prove too much, viz., that the Scriptures of the New Testament were not necessary for a rule of faith.[2]

The Bible actually denies that it is the complete rule of faith. John tells us that not everything concerning Christ's work is in Scripture (Jn 21:25), and Paul says that much Christian teaching is to be found in the tradition that is handed down by word of mouth (2 Tim 2:2). He instructs us to "stand fast, and hold the traditions which you have learned, whether by word or by our epistle" (2 Th 2:15). We are told that the first Christians "were persevering in the doctrine of the apostles" (Acts 2:42), which was the oral teaching that was given long before the New Testament was written—and centuries before the canon of the New Testament was settled.

This oral teaching must be accepted by Christians as they accepted the written teaching that at length came to them. "He who listens to you, listens to me; he who despises you, despises me" (Lk 10:16). The Church, in the persons of the apostles, was given the authority to teach by Christ; the Church would be his stand-in. "Go, therefore, making disciples of all nations" (Mt 28:19). How was this to be done? By preaching, by oral instruction: "See how faith comes from hearing, and hearing through Christ's word" (Rom 10:17). The Church would always be available as the living teacher. It is a mistake to limit Christ's word to the written word only or to suggest that all his teachings were reduced to writing. The Bible nowhere supports either notion.

---

[2] Newman, *Inspiration,* 131n.

After all, God, speaking through Isaiah, promised a living voice in the Church that Christ would establish: "This is my covenant with them, says the Lord: My spirit that is upon you, and my words that I have put in your mouth, shall not depart out of your mouth, nor out of the mouth of your children, nor out of the mouth of your children's children, says the Lord, from now until forever" (Is 59:21). This prophecy must refer to a living Church, the culmination of Israel, and not to a book because no book, not even the Bible, is a living teacher.

The oral teaching would last until the end of time. "But the word of the Lord lasts forever. And this word is nothing other than the Gospel which has been preached to you" (1 Pet 1:25). Note that the word has been "preached"—that is, it was oral. This would endure. It would not be supplanted by a written record like the Bible (supplemented, yes, but not supplanted), but would continue to have its own authority.

In this discussion it is important to keep in mind what the Catholic Church means by Tradition. The term does not mean legends or mythological accounts, nor does it mean transitory customs or practices that come and go as circumstances warrant, such as styles of priestly dress, particular forms of devotion to saints, or even liturgical rubrics. Tradition means the teachings and teaching authority of Jesus and, derivatively, the apostles. These have been handed down and entrusted to the Church (which means to its official teachers, the bishops in union with the Pope). It is necessary that Christians believe in and follow this Tradition as well as the Bible (Lk 10:16). The truth of the faith has been given primarily to the leaders of the Church (Eph 3:5), who, with Christ, form the foundation of the Church (Eph 2:20). The Church has been guided by the Holy Spirit, who protects this teaching from corruption (Jn 14:16).

Paul illustrated what Tradition is: "The chief message I handed on to you, as it was handed on to me, was that Christ, as the scriptures foretold, died for our sins. . . . That is our preaching, mine or theirs as you will; that is the faith that has come to you" (1 Cor

15:3, 11). He said also, to Timothy, who was a bishop, "Thou hast learned, from many who can witness to it, the doctrine which I hand down; give it into the keeping of men thou canst trust, men who will know how to teach it to others besides themselves" (2 Tim 2:2). In other words, Timothy, one of the successors to the apostles, was to teach what he had learned from his predecessor, Paul. The apostle praised those who followed Tradition: "I must praise you for your constant memory of me, for upholding your traditions just as I handed them on to you" (1 Cor 11:2).

The first Christians "occupied themselves continually with the apostles' teaching" (Acts 2:42) long before there was a Bible. The fullness of Christian teaching was found, right from the first, in the Church as the living embodiment of Christ, not in a book. The teaching Church, with its oral traditions, was authoritative. Paul himself gives a quotation from Jesus that was handed down orally to him: "It is more blessed to give than to receive" (Acts 20:35). This saying is not found in the Gospels and must have been passed on to Paul. Indeed, even the Gospels themselves are oral Tradition that has been written down (Lk 1:1–4). What is more, Paul does not quote Jesus only. He also quotes from early Christian hymns, as in Ephesians 5:14. These and other things have been given to Christians "by the command of the Lord Jesus" (1 Th 4:2).

Fundamentalists have objections to all of this, of course. They say Jesus condemned Tradition. They note that Jesus said, "Why is it that you yourselves violate the commandment of God with your traditions?" (Mt 15:3). Paul warned, "Take care not to let anyone cheat you with his philosophizings, with empty phantasies drawn from human tradition, from worldly principles; they were never Christ's teaching" (Col 2:8). But these verses merely condemn erroneous human traditions, not truths that were handed down orally and entrusted to the Church. These truths are part of what is known as Tradition (with an upper-case "T", to distinguish it from lower-case human traditions or customs).

Consider Matthew 15:6–9, which fundamentalists often bring up: "So by these traditions of yours you have made God's laws ineffectual. You hypocrites, it was a true prophecy that Isaiah made of you, when he said, This people does me honor with its lips, but its heart is far from me. Their worship is in vain, for the doctrines they teach are the commandments of men." At first glance, this seems to undercut the Catholic position, but look at the context. Jesus was not here condemning all traditions. He condemned only those that made God's word void. In this case, it was a matter of the Pharisees making a pretended dedication of their goods to the Temple so they could avoid using them to support their aged parents. By doing this, they dodged the commandment to "Honor thy father and thy mother" (Ex 20:12).

Elsewhere, Jesus instructed his followers to abide by traditions that are not contrary to God's commandments. "The scribes and the Pharisees, he said, have established themselves in the place from which Moses used to teach; do what they tell you, then, continue to observe what they tell you, but do not imitate their actions, for they tell you one thing and do another" (Mt 23:2–3).

He told the Pharisees that they were hypocrites who "will award to God his tithe, though it be of mint or dill or cumin, and have forgotten the weightier commandments of the law, justice, mercy, and honor; you did ill to forget one duty while you performed the other" (Mt 23:23). In short, Jesus insisted we should follow all legitimate traditions. In all these cases he was referring to traditions in the sense of customs (lower-case tradition), not to Tradition in the sense of the Church's teaching authority (upper-case). The latter is wider than the former and includes it.

The big problem, no doubt, is determining what constitutes authentic Tradition. How do we know that what had been handed down by the Catholic Church is correct doctrine and practice? We know it is correct because Christ promised that the gates of hell would not prevail against the Church (Mt 16:18). The Church would be indefectible; its official teaching would be infal-

lible. To it, through Peter, Christ gave his own teaching authority (Mt 16:19; 28:18–20).

Under the Old Covenant, it was said, "The lips of the priest
shall keep knowledge, and they shall seek the law at this mouth"
(Malachi 2:7). Under the New Covenant, Christ sent his Church
to teach men and transferred to it the authority the priests of the
Old Covenant had. We find Philip the deacon asking the Ethiopian, who was reading Scripture, "Canst thou understand what
thou art reading?" The Ethiopian replied, "How could I
. . .without someone to guide me?" (Acts 8:30–31). We are reminded that "no prophecy in Scripture is the subject of private
interpretation" (2 Pet 1:20). The Bible, while meant to be read by
individual Christians, indicates that a divinely appointed guide is
needed to get through treacherous passages, of which there are
many.

"But the Bible itself says it is the sole rule of faith!" insist fundamentalists. They quote John 5:39, in which it is said, "search the
scriptures", but they do not take the phrase in context. They
imagine it to be a command to the reader: "Get your Bible and
verify that all Christian truths can be discovered in the plain sense
of the text." That is not what Jesus was saying. He was rebuking
disbelieving Jews, not claiming that the Bible is the sole rule of
faith. Jesus was pointing out to the Pharisees that the messianic
prophecies were fulfilled in him. "If you read Scripture, you can
verify this for yourselves!" He was referring to a single theme.
This verse cannot be stretched to mean that all religious truth can
be found on the surface of the Bible.

Fundamentalists also cite Acts 17:11, which refers to the Be-
reans, who "welcomed the word with all eagerness, and examined the scriptures, day after day, to find out whether all this was
true". Again, here is a verse taken out of context. What really
happened is that these people first had been taught Christianity
orally and now checked to see if its claims matched the Old Testament prophecies. The verse does not at all mean one uses the Bible
as a checklist for all Christian doctrines. (If it meant that, there
would be, again, the problem Newman brought up, that the Old

Testament *alone* would be sufficient as a rule of faith, the New Testament unnecessary.)

What fundamentalists often do, unfortunately, is see the word "tradition" in Matthew 15:3 or Colossians 2:8 or elsewhere and conclude that anything termed a "tradition" is to be rejected. They forget that the term is used in a different sense, as in 2 Thessalonians 2:15, to describe what *should* be believed. Jesus did not condemn all traditions; he condemned only erroneous traditions, whether doctrines or practices, that undercut Christian truths. The rest, as the apostles taught, were to be adhered to.

The notion of *sola scriptura* arose when the Reformers rejected the papacy. In doing that they also rejected the teaching authority of the Church. They looked elsewhere for the rule of faith and thought they found it in the Bible. Really, they had no place else to look. By default, the interpretation of the Bible would be left to the individual, as guided by the Holy Spirit.

In theory this may sound fine, but it has not worked well in practice, and that argues against the truth of the theory. Actually, both reason and experience tell us the Bible could not have been intended as each man's private guide to the truth. If individual guidance by the Holy Spirit were a reality, each Christian would understand the same thing from any particular verse since God cannot teach error. Yet Christians have understood contradictory things from Scripture—even Christians whose "born-again" experiences cannot be doubted. Indeed, fundamentalists often differ among themselves on what the Bible means. They may agree on most major points, but the frequency and vehemence of their squabbles on lesser matters, which should be just as clear if the Holy Spirit is enlightening them, prove the sacred text cannot explain itself.

Chapter 11

Development of Doctrine

The opening verse of Hebrews reminds us that "in the old days, God spoke to our fathers in many ways and by many means". This was done, the Greek implies, fragmentarily and under various figures. Man was not handed religious truth as though from a Scholastic theologian, neatly laid out and indexed. There was no antediluvian equivalent of the *Baltimore Catechism*. Doctrines had to be thought out, lived out, even pieced together, over centuries, the great leaps coming through new revelations.

Most fundamentalists will acknowledge that much. They admit there was a real development in doctrine: an initial message, which became clouded, nearly lost, at the Fall, and then progressively fuller explications as God prepared Israel for the Messiah, until finally the apostles were instructed by the Messiah himself. Gregory the Great put it like this: "With the progress of the times the knowledge of the spiritual fathers increased; for, in the science of God, Moses was more instructed than Abraham, the prophets more than Moses, the apostles more than the prophets."[1]

With Christ and the apostles general revelation ended. The clear teaching of the Bible is that after the death of the last apostle no further revelation is to be made.[2] Christ was the fulfillment of the law of the Old Testament (Mt 5:17) and the ultimate teacher of humanity: "You have one teacher, Christ" (Mt 23:10). The apostles recognized that their task was to pass on, perfectly intact, the

---

[1] Gregory I (the Great), *In Ezechielem homiliae* 2, 4, 12.

[2] This refers to general revelation, which is to be believed by all. Private revelations have been given since apostolic times—Fatima is a modern example—but belief in particular private revelations is not necessary for salvation and is not incumbent on the faithful.

faith given to them by the Master: "Thou hast learned, from many who can witness to it, the doctrine which I hand down; give it into the keeping of men thou canst trust, men who will know how to teach it to others besides themselves" (2 Tim 2:2); "It is for thee to hold fast to the doctrine handed on to thee, the charge committed to thee" (2 Tim 3:14).

Keeping to the teaching of the apostles, the Fathers rejected the claims of heretics, such as the Gnostics, to possess secret doctrines or a new revelation. Irenaeus and Tertullian stressed that the fullness of revelation is contained in the doctrines of the apostles, doctrines that are preserved unfalsified through the succession of bishops. This is not to say that there is not a true progress in the understanding of what has been entrusted to the Church. One cannot prevent men from drawing true inferences from true doctrines. Anyone with a serious interest in Christianity will ask, What does this doctrine imply? How does it relate to that doctrine? How can it be squared with this other belief? How does it relate to changed conditions in the world, to things that were not even dreamt of when the last of the Twelve died? In short, how is any doctrine to be understood, what does a true understanding imply, and what does it exclude?

In answering these questions, the Church develops—we perhaps can say "matures"—doctrines, but it does not alter their essence. It is not a matter of inventing new beliefs, but of clearing up obscurities regarding old ones. Vincent of Lerins, in about 450, explained it this way: "But perhaps someone is saying, Will there then be no progress of religion in the Church of Christ? Certainly there is, and the greatest. . . . But it is truly progress and not a change of faith. What is meant by progress is that something is brought to an advancement within itself; by change, that something is transformed from one thing into another."[3]

The fathers of Vatican II explained development in this fashion:

The tradition which comes from the apostles develops in the Church with the help of the Holy Spirit. For there is a growth in the

---

[3] Vincent of Lerins, *Commonitoria* 23, 28.

understanding of the realities and the words which have been handed down. This happens through the contemplation and study made by believers, who treasure these things in their hearts (Luke 2:19, 51), through the intimate understanding of spiritual things they experience, and through the preaching of those who have received through episcopal succession the sure gift of truth. For, as the centuries succeed one another, the Church constantly moves forward toward the fullness of divine truth until the words of God reach their complete fulfillment in her.[4]

Thomas Aquinas noted that truths that were at one time only implicitly believed are later expressly proposed for belief.[5] An example of this—an example to which he could not, of course, have had recourse—is the doctrine of the Immaculate Conception. It was talked about for centuries and then, at what seemed the opportune moment, formally defined. At any one time, the student of theological history will find, there were more articles to be believed than there had been at any earlier time, but fewer than there were to be later. Clarity is added, but never subtracted. As the world grows old, we have the comfort of more doctrinal security (if we but ask for it) than did our ancestors. This growth in doctrine comes about in various ways. Sometimes it arises from the prayerful thinking of theologians and appears as the result of obscure disputations or forgotten essays in forgotten journals. More usually it is a matter of old truths being made clearer to avoid misunderstanding or heresies being headed off at the pass.

Consider the doctrine of the Trinity. It is not present on the face of Scripture, not just in the sense that the word Trinity is never used—its first use was by Theophilus of Antioch in 181[6]—but also in the sense that it is by no means obvious, from the surface meaning of the text, that the Holy Spirit is a divine Person. We naturally read back into the Bible the beliefs we already hold, each of us having been instructed in the Faith before ever picking up the

---

[4] *Dei verbum*, 8.

[5] Thomas Aquinas, *Summa theologiae* II, 1, 7.

[6] Theophilus of Antioch, *Ad Autolycum*, 2, 15.

Bible. References to the Holy Spirit's divinity seem to jump out at us. If we imagine ourselves as ancient pagans or as present-day non-Christians, coming across the Bible for the first time, we realize that the status of the Holy Spirit is by no means clear. If we think of ourselves as having no recourse to divine Tradition and to the Magisterium of the Church, we can appreciate how easy it must have been for the early pneumatological heresies to arise.

Another example is transubstantiation. In the sixth chapter of John's Gospel the Eucharist is promised. If this chapter is read in conjunction with the accounts of the Last Supper, it is easy to see that the first Christians knew, from the very start, that the bread and wine were transformed into Christ's actual Body and Blood. Though attesting that such a transformation happens, the Bible is silent about *how* it happens. Little wonder, then, that in later years disputes arose concerning the way this mysterious change took place. (Perhaps the greatest wonder is that there was no serious opposition to the Real Presence at all until the writings of Berengarius of Tours, who lived in the eleventh century.)

Not until 1215, at the Fourth Lateran Council, was the term transubstantiation imposed, the imposition being not so much the addition of something new as the exclusion of various false explanations. This tongue twister was the only term that eliminated wrong (but seemingly right) explanations of the mystery, that gave equivocating opponents of it no room to hide. From the Gospels Christians knew that the Real Presence was real, and, had they given no thought at all to the matter for the succeeding twelve centuries, no definition would have been required at Lateran IV for the simple reason that no disputes would have arisen regarding what the doctrine really meant. But because people did put their minds to the matter, because they did try to draw true inferences from true doctrines, and because not all of them were adept at that, disputes did arise, and a formal definition was necessary.

Another example. The Council of Nicaea responded to the most damaging ancient heresy, Arianism, by adopting the non-scriptural word *homoousios* ("same substance") and contrasting it with *homoiousios* ("like substance").[7] Christ was of the same substance as the Father, not merely of a like substance—that is, he was himself divine, not just the most favored of creatures. The Church had come, finally, to a full, or at least a sufficiently full, understanding of Christology and was able to say authoritatively, "On this subject, the Bible and Tradition mean *this*."

As these cases and innumerable others demonstrate, doctrinal questions can remain in a state of suspense for years. The Church has never felt the need to define formally what there has been no particular pressure to define. This strikes many, particularly non-Catholics, as odd. Why were things not cleared up in, say, the year 100 so folks could know what to believe? Why did Rome issue no laundry list of definitions in the early days and let it go at that? Why was no end run made around all these troubles that plagued Christianity precisely because things were unclear? The remote reason is that God has had his own timetable and an excellent rationale (to which we are not privy) for keeping to it. A more immediate reason is that Rome, meaning the Magisterium of the Church, could not define what it did not know. This returns us to the subjects of infallibility and inspiration. The Pope and the bishops, when teaching in union with him, are infallible in defining dogmas, but infallibility works only negatively. Papal *ex cathedra* pronouncements and ecumenical councils are, through the intervention of the Holy Spirit, prevented from teaching what is untrue, but they are not forced to teach what *is* true.

The Pope and the bishops are not inspired the way the authors of Scripture or the prophets were. To make a new definition, to clear up some dogmatic confusion, they first must use reason, operating on what is known to date, to be able to teach more precisely what is to be held as true. They cannot teach what they do not know, and they have no access to oracular shortcuts. The one

---

[7] The Semi-Arians having argued there was no important distinction between the two terms, which differ in spelling by only the smallest Greek letter, we have had preserved for us the saying that "there isn't an iota of difference" between two closely related things. In fact, the distinction between *homoousios* and *homoiousios* was crucial.

great advantage they have over their ancient predecessors in the papacy and episcopacy, over theologians such as Augustine and Aquinas, is that they begin with a more clearly defined body of doctrine. Augustine did not have the advantage of a conciliar decree on transubstantiation; Aquinas could not refer to one on papal infallibility. They could not very well reason *from* such formalized doctrines to the doctrines' natural implications, at least not in the way now possible. One cannot reach a legitimate conclusion unless the premises are first safe in hand, and if the premises are relatively few, conclusions, no matter how excellent, will also be few.

This chapter has gotten this far with hardly a word about charges by fundamentalists, but there has been a purpose in the delay. Fundamentalists' confusion can be perceived most readily if the Catholic position on doctrinal development is discussed first. Consider what Bill Jackson, head of Christians Evangelizing Catholics, says: "The Roman Catholic Church likens itself to a flower box in which many seeds have been planted. They are God's revelations to men; some have just come up, others are blossoming, etc. They claim these seeds were all planted by Christ, but that they develop at different times depending on the need of the Church." He argues that "the first error is saying Christ planted the seeds. Many important Roman Catholic doctrines have no scriptural basis—Immaculate Conception, Assumption, Purgatory, etc. The next error is to suppose that any need was not provided for the infant church. Paul said he preached the whole counsel of God (Acts 20:27). How could he, if some of God's truths were in seed form buried beneath the earth? Scripture was given by inspiration of God (2 Tim 3:16). He never changes; God's Truth never changes. Any development of doctrine is of human or satanic origin."[8]

Jackson thinks the Catholic Church believes in time-delayed revelation. Entirely new religious beliefs are just waiting to

<hr />

[8] Bill Jackson, *A Christian's Guide to Roman Catholicism* (Manteca, Calif.: Christians Evangelizing Catholics, n.d.), sec. 88.

sprout—and will, as soon as Rome is properly watered. It is his flower-box analogy that leads Jackson astray. This analogy fundamentalists picked up from Catholic apologists. Catholics thought that by using it they were making doctrinal development clearer, but fundamentalists thought the analogy was an admission of something the Church does not in fact believe. The analogy, despite its seeming clarity, can lead one astray. It is, in fact, simply inadequate to explain doctrinal development.

Joseph Tixeront, referring to Catholic apologists in his *History of Dogmas,* put it like this: "Generally scholars have been too easily satisfied with vague formulas and mere comparisons, which are not precise enough (the child who becomes a man, the kernel that becomes a tree, etc.). For the question to be answered in a technical and adequate manner is this: When is an idea or a doctrine a mere development of another idea or doctrine, and when is it to be considered a substantial alteration or transformation of it?"[9] Frank Sheed had a similar thought when he wrote against using the shamrock as an explanation of the Trinity.[10] The shamrock does not help us understand the doctrine, he said; it just helps us swallow it. And the analogy of seeds too easily permits fundamentalists to imagine the Catholic Church teaches that entirely new doctrines, unrelated to existing ones, are going to pop up at any time.

If Jackson misconstrues the Catholic position, at least he looks for it, which is more than can be said for most fundamentalists. He makes some effort to give the Catholic view. Like all fundamentalists, he finally falls back on the standard line, which is that what Catholics call doctrinal development is nothing more than a centuries-old accumulation of pagan beliefs and rites. The Catholic Church has not really refined the original deposit of faith; instead, it has added to it from the outside. In its hurry, particularly in the early centuries, to enlarge the membership rolls, it let just

---

[9] Joseph Tixeront, *History of Dogmas* (Westminster, Md.: Christian Classics, 1984), 1:7.

[10] Frank Sheed, *Theology and Sanity* (Huntington, Ind.: Our Sunday Visitor, 1978), 12.

about anybody in the door—and when existing inducements were not enough, it adopted pagan ways to get pagans to "convert". Each time the Church did this it moved further away from real Christianity.

As an example of this thinking, consider Christmas. Strict fundamentalists do not observe Christmas, and not only because the name of the feast is inescapably "Christ Mass". Some say they disapprove of it because there is no proof Christ was born on December 25; they say he could not have been born then because the shepherds, who were in the fields with their sheep, did not put sheep into the fields during winter. Still others note the Bible is silent about the Feast of Christmas. But these are all prolegomena. The real reasons are that Christmas was established, quite indisputably, by the Catholic Church (which is bad enough) and that the Church superimposed this holy day on a pagan festival (which is worse). Connections are made to Chaldean and Babylonian worship, Zoroastrianism, even Anglo-Saxon rites. Santa Claus is unmasked as nothing but a commercialized version of Catholicism's St. Nicholas. As Donald F. Maconaghie of the Conversion Center writes in a tract distributed to his mailing list, "No one who acknowledges the supreme authority of the Holy Scriptures to direct in all questions of doctrine and practice will have any fellowship in Xmas [sic] celebrations after his attention has been called to the matter, unless he does it deliberately in selfwill."[11]

Fundamentalists complain that the Church transformed pagan festivals into Christian feasts, and such an association with paganism, they think, is conclusive proof of Rome's compromising. They quote with relish John Henry Newman's seemingly damaging admission:

> We are told in various ways by Eusebius, that Constantine, in order to recommend the new religion to the heathen, transferred to it the outward ornaments to which they had been accustomed in their own. It is not necessary to go into a subject which the diligence of

---

[11] From his tract *What about Christmas?*

Protestant writers has made familiar to most of us. The use of temples, and these dedicated to particular saints, and ornamented on occasions with branches of trees; incense, lamps, and candles; votive offerings on recovery from illness; holy water; asylums; holydays and seasons, use of calendars, processions, blessings on the fields; sacerdotal vestments, the tonsure, the ring in marriage, turning to the East, images at a later date, perhaps the ecclesiastical chant, and the Kyrie Eleison, are all of pagan origin, and sanctified by their adoption into the Church.[12]

Fundamentalists forget that even paganism had some truth mixed in with its error. Christianity took those elements of truth, removed erroneous associations so that they ceased to be pagan, and made use of the purified truth the better to express Christian notions. Christianity gave new meanings to old things, and in the process the pagan connections ceased. It was a matter of outright replacement, not compromise.

Another good, although strained, example of the fundamentalist attitude may be found in a sermon by the Rev. D. Martyn Lloyd-Jones, who says the problem with Rome "is not so much a matter of 'denial' of the truth, but rather such an addition to the truth that eventually it becomes a departure from it". To admittedly orthodox teachings "she 'adds,' with a damnable plus, things which are utterly unscriptural and which, indeed, become a denial of the Scripture". There follows a litany more hysterical than usual for fundamentalists, Lloyd-Jones going so far as to insist the Church "teaches her people to worship images" (most fundamentalists just say this is the natural result, although perhaps not the intent, of Church teachings). With respect to beliefs that are peculiarly Catholic, Lloyd-Jones says that "there is not a word about [them] in the New Testament". Part of his problem is that he thinks the Catholic Church teaches that "she has received 'continuing revelation' "—Bill Jackson's seeds again. "She does

---

[12] Newman, *Essay,* 369. Few fundamentalists complain that the Jewish Feast of Tabernacles coincided with a Canaanite vintage festival, much as Christmas did with the festival of Sol Invictus. Consistency has never been fundamentalism's strong suit.

not believe, as true Protestants do, that revelation ended with what we have in the New Testament."[13]

Give him partial points. It is true that Catholics do not think revelation ended with what is in the New Testament. They believe, though, that it ended with the death of the last apostle. The part of revelation that was not committed to writing—the part that is outside the New Testament and is the oral teaching that is the basis of Tradition—*that* part of revelation Catholics also accept, and in this they follow the apostle Paul's injunction: "Stand firm, then, brethren, and hold by the traditions you have learned, in word or in writing, from us" (2 Th 2:14). If Lloyd-Jones thinks the Church believes in a continuing revelation, he has not bothered to study the first chapter of any elementary theological work by a Catholic. Every discussion of revelation notes that revelation ended when the last apostle died. Lloyd-Jones' trouble, the trouble of all fundamentalists, is that he labors under the misconception that Scripture has the last word and that the Tradition built on oral teaching counts for nothing.

One of the keenest arguments against the fundamentalists' "Bible only" position was given by Newman in *Tract 85*, written while he was still an Anglican. This is the way J. M. Cameron summarizes Newman's argument in his introduction to Newman's *An Essay on the Development of Christian Doctrine*:

> The argument is directed towards the Protestant critic of Tractarianism and in a simplified form goes like this. You criticize the Tractarians for teaching such doctrines as, for example, the Apostolic Succession of bishops or that the Eucharist is a sacrifice, and your criticism rests on the contention that these doctrines are not plainly and unambiguously contained in Scripture and may not indeed be in the Bible at all. I concede, goes the reply, that these doctrines are not to be found in the letter of Scripture or on its surface. But this is just as true of other doctrines you as an orthodox Protestant believe quite firmly; such doctrines as, let us say, the Godhead of the Holy

[13] From the March/April 1985 issue of *The Trinity Review*, the newsletter of the Trinity Foundation.

Spirit or that Holy Scripture contains all that is sufficient for salvation. Neither of these doctrines is contained on the surface of Scripture, and there would even be logical difficulties in supposing that Scripture contained the latter doctrine. It seems to me that you ought in consistency to believe less than you do or more than you do. If you confine yourself to what is contained in Scripture then the content of your belief will be thin and even incoherent and you will have no rationale for giving the Bible this supreme position. What you do, inconsistently, believe (for you are not, thank God, a Unitarian) is a warrant for your going further and adopting as your criterion the tradition of the first few centuries and using this tradition, embodied in the formularies of the Church, as that in the light of which Scripture is to be read and understood. You must either move upwards into Catholicism or downwards into unbelief. There is no midway point of rest.[14]

Newman noted that, in any century, what was believed by the Catholic Church can be seen to be the logical and necessary outgrowth and the deeper understanding of what was believed the century before. Going backward, from the nineteenth century to the very early Middle Ages, is easy. No one really doubts that what was called the Catholic Church in 1845, when Newman wrote, was the same institution that took that name in, say, 845. (Newman wrote, of course, before the definitions of the Immaculate Conception, papal infallibility, and the Assumption, three of the main "unscriptural" doctrines pointed at by fundamentalists, but his argument is just as valid, just as useful, today.)

The hard part concerns the early centuries, but, if one examines these in sequence, he sees a natural progression, a true growth in doctrine. There is no change of course, but a continuation along a single road. Something is clarified in one century, and in the next that clarification is investigated and built on so that a further clarification is produced. On and on it goes. What was determined with finality in the past is kept—there is no jettisoning of old doctrines for new—but fuller understandings are added. Thus, the few biblical references to Mary result in the splendid devotion to

---

[14] Newman, *Essay*, 27–28.

the Mother of God that was a hallmark of the medieval Church, best exemplified, perhaps, by the monument that is Notre Dame Cathedral.

Newman's is not the final word on the development of doctrine, not by any means, but his is a tour de force that should be savored by anyone who wants to be able to give more than just a pat answer to fundamentalists who say today's peculiarly Catholic doctrines have nothing to do with the beliefs of the early Church. His argument is too refined and too large to be used in regular apologetic work, but at least the book can be recommended to fundamentalists who are serious about learning how the Catholic Church views doctrinal development and to Catholics who want to savor fine prose and finer theological thinking. As in so many matters, there is no better teacher than Newman.

Chapter 12

Fanciful Histories of Catholicism

If few fundamentalists know the history of their own religion—
and distressingly few do—even fewer have any appreciation for
the history of the Catholic Church. They become easy prey for
purveyors of fanciful histories that claim to account for the origin
and advance of Catholicism. These histories take two basic
forms. One makes the legalization of Christianity during the
reign of the Emperor Constantine the determining fact; the other
looks to the influence of the ancient mystery religions. Both conclude Catholicism is part Christian, part pagan, and wholly to be
rejected.

The first version seems more like real history and is generally
the more convincing, at least to readers with some schooling,
while the second plays better to people who look for sensationalism and depends for its effect on superficial similarities between
Catholicism and pagan cults.

The first, which might be called the "pagan convert" theory,
begins, most commonly, with a listing of Catholic "inventions".
These are doctrines or practices that the Church allegedly adopted
for the most part from paganism long after apostolic times. The
first thing to notice is that in any list of "inventions" doctrines are
mixed up with practices, fundamentalist writers apparently not
understanding the difference.

A doctrine is a fixed belief, a dogma, such as (to limit it to peculiarly "Catholic" doctrines) the Immaculate Conception, the Assumption, purgatory, the sacraments, transubstantiation. Practices, on the other hand, are changeable. They are customs, ways
of doing things. They include, for instance, rituals or dress or
habits of prayer that may change over the years: the language of

the Mass, the style of priestly vestments, the use or nonuse of incense during Mass, making the sign of the Cross. Of course, these practices are connected with doctrines, but they are not themselves doctrines. It is immaterial that many practices are present neither in the Bible nor in early Christian history. Practices are not the subject of revelation, the way doctrines are; they are adopted as present needs require and are dropped for the same reason.

To continue with the first kind of "history": Fundamentalist writers begin by listing "inventions", mixing doctrines and practices indiscriminately. They then assign dates of origin to them. They generally claim the "inventions" postdate the Edict of Milan, which was issued in 313 and made Christianity legal in the Roman Empire. This is the cutoff date, all the bad things in Catholicism supposedly arising after that point. In fact, the dating of the "inventions" is often grossly wrong or, where right, irrelevant to the point in question, which is: When did Catholicism begin?

For instance, transubstantiation is usually assigned to the Fourth Lateran Council, held in 1215. This, say fundamentalists, was when the doctrine was "invented". Wrong. This was when the technical term "transubstantiation" was settled on as the right term to use to describe the doctrine of the Real Presence, which, in the writings of the Fathers of the Church, can be shown to antedate Constantine's reign. In fact, the doctrine can be proved from John 6. So, the year 1215 *does* concern transubstantiation, but it is not the date when the doctrine underlying the term was first believed.

After presenting a list of "inventions", anti-Catholic writers cite John Henry Newman's admission, quoted in the previous chapter, that many Catholic customs are of pagan origin.[1] What Newman said is quite true, naturally, and merely demonstrates that some kinds of Catholic practices are common to many liturgical religions. By the way, it is worth pointing out that funda-

---

[1] Newman, *Essay*, 369.

mentalist writers usually misquote this passage from Newman; for instance, they tend to leave out "the ring in marriage". After all, giving rings in marriage is something they do in their own churches, and they do not want to be reminded that the practice is pagan in origin, as are other elements of their wedding ceremonies.

After listing the "inventions" and quoting Newman, the fundamentalist writers get to history proper. They say that until the reign of Constantine, all was well with Christianity. It remained essentially intact, although there were a few minor heresies in the three centuries following Pentecost. The early Christians, they say, took the Bible alone as their guide. They were not Protestants, and they were certainly not Catholics. They were just Christians. They faced persecution, first from the Jews, later from the Roman Empire. The persecution ended when, through the Edict of Milan, Constantine legalized Christianity.

It was either then or, decades later, when Christianity was made the official religion of the Empire that, as Loraine Boettner phrased it,

> thousands of people who still were pagans pressed into the church in order to gain special advantages and favors that went with such membership. They came in in far greater numbers than could be instructed or assimilated. Having been used to the more elaborate pagan rituals, they were not satisfied with the simple Christian worship but began to introduce their heathen beliefs and practices. Gradually, through the neglect of the Bible and the ignorance of the people, more and more heathen ideas were introduced until the church became more heathen than Christian.[2]

But there were still "real" Christians, few in number, often in hiding, who kept the Faith through the centuries, until, at the Reformation, they gained a certain ascendancy. The spiritual heirs of these people are today's fundamentalists.

This outline of ecclesiastical history, as given by Boettner and others, depends for its support on several things. The most im-

---

[2] Boettner, *Catholicism*, 11.

portant is dating. The theory is that all was well with the Church until Constantine gave it political preference. Yet if all was well with Christianity prior to 313—if it had not yet transmogrified into Catholicism—we should expect to find all the peculiarly Catholic doctrines and practices arising only after that date. Before that, the historical record should show us a Christianity undistinguishable from present-day fundamentalism. This is what fundamentalist commentators imply is the case, as they list dozens of Catholic "inventions", each allegedly arising after 313.

Now it would have to be conceded that fundamentalists would have at least a superficial case if all the "inventions" they list *did* first develop after Christianity was legalized. If, in the first three centuries of Christian history, we could find no distinctively Catholic beliefs or practices, that would be an argument in favor of fundamentalism. When we look at ecclesiastical history, what do we really find? We see many of these peculiarly Catholic practices, and virtually all of the peculiarly Catholic doctrines, are mentioned in works written during the first, second, and third centuries. Some of the references are, admittedly, sparse, but others are surprisingly full, referring to these doctrines and practices as already being old. We find mention of a sacrificing priesthood, a hierarchy of bishops, prayers for the dead, the veneration of saints, and much more—enough, at any rate, to demolish the fundamentalists' attempt at history.

This story about Constantine and the supposed influx of paganism into the Church might be called the standard fundamentalist history: bare bones, not backed up with facts, ignorant of when the doctrines and practices really came into existence. Still, it is not an unreasonable theory, just a wrong one. If the datings were right, there would be merit to it.

There is a more exotic history that often is seen as a supplement to the standard one. It might be called the "Whore of Babylon" theory. Its best-known proponent is Ralph Woodrow, author of *Babylon Mystery Religion*. Instead of attributing the existence of Catholicism to Christianity's legalization by Constantine, Woodrow and authors of like-minded works concentrate on superficial similarities between Catholicism and the ancient mystery religions, particularly the Babylonian cults. They make the logically false argument that similarity implies descent, and they pile up hundreds of examples, not one of which, in isolation, proves anything, but which, taken all together, persuade the ignorant by sheer volume.

To understand how wrong these fundamentalist writers are, one needs to understand a little about the religions that predated Christianity. There were, of course, the religions of Rome and Greece, which were unable to satisfy men's hunger for God. The Roman religion was moralistic, concerned largely with inculcating civic virtue, but it lacked anything that could capture the imagination. The Greek religion was nonmoral (indeed, the Greek gods were often quite immoral), but it left more room for the imagination. The Greek religion was rejected by the best minds of Greece, who turned from it to philosophy, which, while taking many wrong turns, did at last make some progress, declaring the supremacy of the spiritual while adopting a false view of matter.

Then came the mystery religions, which promised to rescue men from the puerility of the traditional Greco-Roman cults. These religions, coming into the Empire from the East beginning about three centuries before Christ, included the cults of Isis from Egypt, Adonis from Babylonia, Attis from Phrygia, and Mithra from Persia. They seem to have arisen through personifications of nature, particularly birth and death as seen in the cycles of the seasons. Commonly, the resurrected gods had been sent from heaven, or the abode of the gods, to "save" humanity. These cults were clothed in luxurious rituals and impressed people brought up on the desiccated religions of Rome and Greece or on philosophy, which seemed to have run into a dead end. What made the mystery cults particularly attractive was that they offered the two things people in the Empire most wanted, the assurance of personal immortality and union with God, what could be called salvation. This salvation was achieved by being initiated into the mysteries, or secret teachings, of a cult. After the initiation, which usually came through a kind of baptism, the new converts participated in a ceremony that reenacted the death and rebirth of the god.

These cults bore marked, though superficial, resemblance to Catholicism, which is what fundamentalist writers have played on. They also bore marked resemblance to fundamentalism, at least in things that Catholicism and fundamentalism hold in common, and this is something always overlooked in anti-Catholic writings. If the truth of Catholicism is undercut by similarities to mystery religions, so is the truth of fundamentalism. If Catholicism happens to have more points of similarity with paganism, it is not because it is more likely to have grown from these cults, but because it is a broader religion. Looked at another way, Catholicism is full-blown Christianity, while fundamentalism is truncated Christianity, so there exist more aspects in Catholicism to which there could be parallels in paganism. If the existence of similarities means Catholicism is false, the same conclusion must be drawn about fundamentalism; in this regard they sink or swim together.

That, anyway, is an overview of the pagan religions in the Roman Empire of the first century. It is from them, particularly from the mystery cults, that Woodrow insists Catholicism sprang. Most of his proofs are laughable; all of them are unworthy of serious consideration. Yet he can claim to have sold a quarter of a million copies of his book since it appeared in 1966—no mean feat and one that demonstrates that anti-Catholic sentiment is not only alive and well among fundamentalists and evangelicals, but that many of our separated brethren are concerned enough about the Catholic Church to turn to books that purport to deal with its origins. They want to learn how this strange growth developed.

A thirst for scholarship is not the only reason, not even the main reason, people buy this book. The main attraction is a kind of prurience. *Babylon Mystery Religion* does not have much to say about sex; it is not prurient in the most common connotation of the word. It is prurient according to the other dictionary definition in that it satisfies restless cravings many people have. They want to believe there is a dark secret to Catholicism, and they want to be let in on the secret. They want to luxuriate in horror stories, and they want their worst suspicions confirmed. Woodrow's book shows that Catholicism's success has been due not to its merits, but to influence-peddling, fortuitous events, and underhanded dealings, even violence. It demonstrates that Catholicism is really something dark and alien to Christianity— something, in fact, connected with Christianity only tangentially, not essentially. Woodrow's thesis, which is not new to him, is that Catholicism's distinctive elements have not been derived from authentic Christianity. They are not legitimate developments, but wholesale borrowings from pre-Christian cults. This is how the back cover of the book explains it:

> *Babylon Mystery Religion* is a detailed Biblical and historical account of how, when, why, and where ancient paganism was mixed with Christianity. From the early days of Babylon and the legends surrounding Nimrod, Semiramis, and Tammuz, certain rites and rituals are traced in their various developments, thus providing clues whereby the "mystery" is solved! The apostles had predicted that there would come a "falling away" and the proof of their prediction is now evident in history. With such evidence in hand, all true believers should seek, as never before, the simplicity found in Christ himself and to earnestly contend for that original faith which was once delivered unto the saints.

Babylon Mystery Religion is indebted to Alexander Hislop's *The Two Babylons,* first published in 1853 and reprinted innumerable times since. In fact, Woodrow's book would not be described wrongly as a revised version of Hislop's. The argument is that things that distinguish Catholicism from Protestantism—such as the papacy, intercession of the saints, and purgatory—are really borrowings from ancient pagan religions. With sketches, photographs, woodcuts, and a host of one-liners, Woodrow attempts to show this. From Egyptian devotion to Isis, the reader is told, comes Catholic devotion to Mary, and from Buddhism comes the sign of the Cross. St. Bridget never existed, but was merely a replacement for a fertility goddess. Lent was derived from festivals in honor of the death and resurrection of Tammuz.

Woodrow searched for coincidences, found some, and concludes that similarity implies descent. That, of course, is simply illogical. His demonstration that distinctive Catholic beliefs were taken from Egyptian, Babylonian, or Roman religions will convince no one acquainted with ancient or ecclesiastical history. His proofs are nothing more than a listing of similarities, and even then the similarities are often strained. He unconsciously sums up his technique as he decries the Catholic tendency to erect magnificent churches with bell towers. Wanting to show the use of towers comes from the Babylonians and the Tower of Babel, he begins by saying, "If the reader will permit us a certain liberty at this point. . . ."[3] But by "this point", already a quarter of the way through the text, the book is nothing but a concatenation of liberties, and Woodrow has taken them about as far as they can go.

Here is an example. In the chapter on the Mass, there is a photograph of the interior of St. Peter's. As the text explains, it "shows the altar of St. Peter's and [the] huge canopy (the baldachinum [sic])—ninety-five feet high—which is supported by four columns, twisted and slightly covered by branches. At the top of the columns—'on high above' the most important altar in Catholicism—are sun-images like those that were used in pagan worship."[4]

Here the reader glances to the opposing page. The photograph has superimposed on it three arrows. Two point to these "sun-images" at the top of the columns. The "sun-images" are so indistinct that Woodrow has penned in, next to the arrows, little "happy face" suns so the reader will understand what is supposed

---

[3] Ralph Woodrow, *Babylon Mystery Religion* (Riverside, Calif.: Ralph Woodrow Evangelistic Association, 1966), 44.

[4] Woodrow, *Babylon,* 130. Woodrow forgets that Scripture uses the sun image for the Lord: "But unto you that fear my name, the Sun of justice shall arise, and health in his wings: and you shall go forth, and shall leap like calves of the herd. And you shall trample down the wicked when they shall be ashes under the sole of your feet in the day that I do this, saith the Lord of hosts" (Malachi 3:20–21).

to be present. The third arrow points to the apse. There, "high on the wall, as the photograph also shows, is a huge and elaborate golden sunburst image which, from the entrance of the church, also appears 'above' the altar. . . . Interestingly enough, the great temple at Babylon also featured a golden sun-image."[5]

This is his proof: he sees what he thinks is a "sunburst" and promptly deduces that Catholicism borrowed from the Babylonian cults. It is safe to say that Woodrow has never been to the Vatican and has never examined a clear photograph of the interior of the basilica. If he had, he would not have committed such a blunder. What he thinks is an "elaborate golden sunburst" on the far wall of St. Peter's is nothing less than a representation of the Holy Spirit, in the form of a dove exuding rays of light. (Even fundamentalists use the dove motif in artwork.) The dove hovers over the reliquary said to contain St. Peter's chair. This is perhaps the most famous piece of art in the church—certainly the most eye-catching after the baldachin—and this blunder is representative of Woodrow's book. All in all, his contribution to the religious debate is a sorry example of "a detailed and historical account of how, when, why, and where ancient paganism was mixed with Christianity".

There is no need to refute each claim or explain each comparison made by Woodrow. His method is crude, and his book is unworthy of a point-by-point reply. A Catholic, if so inclined, could find in the mystery religions enough similarities to fundamentalism to prove that fundamentalism is really an offshoot of the cults, but the proof would be worthless. He could demonstrate that some mystery religions venerated a holy book as containing all religious truth (their version of *sola scriptura*), just like fundamentalism. He could illustrate how the mystery religions claimed to give an "assurance of salvation", just like fundamentalism. Such similarities would establish nothing. They would not imply descent.

[5] Woodrow, *Babylon*, 130–131.

When they look at the mystery religions, writers such as Woodrow think that by using Catholic terms as labels for pagan practices they have shown Catholicism's origin. That simply is not logical, but, no matter how weak these arguments may be in the abstract, they influence people. Should they? No, because we should expect the true religion to be a fulfillment of, but not a complete contradiction of, mankind's earlier stabs at religious truth. After all, each ancient religion had something true in it, even if what was true was buried under much that was false and even pernicious. On the positive side, ancient religions were remote preparations for Christ's coming, which occurred in the "fullness of time", when mankind had taken itself about as far as it could go on its own.

We should expect that the religion that is the fullness of truth, coming in the "fullness of time", would incorporate the good points of earlier religions while rejecting their errors. Conversely, a religion that rejected not only the errors, but also the good points, of earlier religions would seem to be incomplete, as though it went too far in trying to remain pure, as though it threw out more than just the bathwater.

Chapter 13

Salvation

There is no more confusing topic, when fundamentalists and Catholics sit down to talk, than salvation. It goes beyond the standard question posed by fundamentalists: "Have you been saved?" It also means "don't you wish you had an assurance of salvation?" Fundamentalists, along with most evangelicals, think they do. They are absolutely sure they will go to heaven immediately after death, and their assurance is no less lively than is the assurance of the Moslem participant in a jihad, who thinks he will be translated to seventh heaven (with all its houris) if he dies in battle.

Catholics are prone to label this presumption, but that really is not what it is. In Catholic theology, presumption is the attitude that one can gain heaven by his own merits or can gain pardon without repentance. It often manifests itself in a belief that one will be given an opportunity, at the last moment, to make amends—to get to confession, to say a perfect act of contrition—all based on the idea that one has led a reasonably good life. It is a kind of gambling, with the last throw of the dice guaranteed to come up right, and it is a sin because there is no reason to think things will happen that way, and to presume on one's salvation is to play fast and loose with one's soul. It is the most terminal form of Russian roulette.

Fundamentalists do not look at the matter as though they were playing a game. They conclude from the Bible that Christ actually promised that heaven is theirs in exchange for a remarkably simple act. All they have to do, at just one point in their lives, is "accept Christ as their personal Savior". Then it is done. They may live exemplary lives thereafter, but living well is not crucial. It does not affect their salvation.

No matter what happens later, no matter how evilly they might live the remainder of their days, their salvation is assured. Granted, the Holy Spirit might punish them in this life for their sins (here fundamentalists take a rather Old Testament view on why one ought to be good—to avoid temporal evils, not to gain heaven, which is guaranteed no matter what). But in no way can they undo their salvation, because it has nothing at all to do with the intrinsic worth of their souls or with what Catholics term actual sins.

It comes down to Galatians 2:20: "The Son of God, who loved me and gave himself for me". Christ is seen as one's *personal* Savior, and that is why these words are a favorite with fundamentalists. For them, everything depends on an inner conviction that Christ died for them personally, and this verse is the ideal expression of it. Curiously, though, it stands alone in the apostle's writings. Everywhere else he insists that Christ gave himself for *us,* and that he died for *us.* Paul was a churchman and sought salvation through the Church.

Kenneth E. Hagin, a Protestant evangelist, notes that this assurance of salvation comes through being "born again": "Except a man be born again, he cannot see the kingdom of God" (Jn 3:3). "The new birth", says Hagin, "is a necessity to being saved. Through the new birth you come into the right relationship with God." There are many things that this new birth is not.

> The new birth is not: confirmation—church membership—water baptism—the taking of sacraments—observing religious duties—an intellectual reception of Christianity—orthodoxy of faith—going to church—saying prayers—reading the Bible—being moral—being cultured or refined—doing good deeds—doing your best—nor any of the many other things some men are trusting in to save them.

Those who have obtained the new birth "did the one thing necessary—they accepted Jesus Christ as personal Savior by repenting and turning to God with the whole heart as a little child".[1] And that was all they needed to do.

For Catholics, salvation depends on the state of the soul at death. Christ has already redeemed us, unlocked the gates of heaven, as it were. (Note that redemption is not the same as salvation but is a necessary prelude.) He did his part, and now we have to cooperate by doing ours. If we are to pass through those gates, we have to be in the right spiritual state. We have to be spiritually alive. If a soul is merely in a natural state, without sanctifying grace, which is the grace that gives it supernatural life, then it is dead supernaturally and incapable of enjoying heaven. It will not be allowed through the gates. But if it has sanctifying grace, then heaven is guaranteed even if a detour through purgatorial purification is required first. The Church teaches that only souls that are objectively good and objectively pleasing to God merit heaven, and such souls are ones filled with sanctifying grace.

The saint who never committed a mortal sin and the lifelong sinner who did not stop sinning until he repented on his deathbed will each gain heaven, although the one will have to be cleansed in the anteroom of purgatory. When they get to heaven, the one with the greater capacity for love will enjoy greater blessedness there, although each will enjoy it as fully as he is capable. As Catholics see it, anyone can achieve heaven, and anyone can lose it. The lifelong sinner can remain that to the very end—and he then becomes an eternally lost sinner. The apparent saint can throw away salvation at the last moment and end up no better off than the man who never did a good deed in his life. It all depends on how one enters death, which is why dying is by far one's most important act.

To some it seems arbitrary that God would put the main emphasis on one's last moments, which may come entirely by surprise, but this reality is tempered by the fact that everyone is given a chance to repent—and not just a chance, but a succession of

[1] Kenneth E. Hagin, *The New Birth* (Tulsa, Okla.: Kenneth Hagin Ministries, 1983), 2–3.

chances. Grace abounds and can always be grabbed if only reached for. God does everything short of getting down on his knees in front of us and begging us to repent.

That, anyway, is the way the Catholic Church looks at the matter. For fundamentalists it makes no difference how one lives or ends his life. One could be another Mother Teresa, yet still be damned by not accepting Christ in the fundamentalists' sense—and there have been more than a few fundamentalist writers who have remarked that Mother Teresa is doomed, her (to them false) faith and earthly good works notwithstanding. On the other hand, one can sober up Sunday morning, go to church, heed the altar call, announce to the congregants an acceptance of Jesus as personal Lord and Savior, and, so long as that is really believed, all is well. Nothing can be done, no sin can be committed, no matter how heinous, that will forfeit salvation.

The reason is that "accepting Jesus" has nothing to do with turning a spiritually dead soul into a soul alive with sanctifying grace. The soul remains the same. Whether one has led a good life or a clearly wicked one, the soul is depraved, worthless, unable to stand on its own before God; it is a bottomless pit of sin, and a few more sins thrown in will not change its nature, just as taking a cleaning compound to it will not make it shine in the least. For the fundamentalist, sanctifying grace is a figment of Catholics' imaginations. Accepting Christ accomplishes one thing and one thing only. It makes God cover one's sinfulness. It makes him turn a blind eye to it. It is as though he hides the soul under a cloak. Any soul under this cloak is admitted to heaven, no matter how putrescent the reality beneath; no one without the cloak, no matter how pristine, can enter the pearly gates.

The Reformers saw justification as a mere legal act by which God declares the sinner to be meriting heaven even though he remains in fact unjust and sinful. It is not a real eradication of sin, but a covering or nonimputation. It is not an inner renewal and a real sanctification, only an external application of Christ's justice. The Catholic Church, not surprisingly, understands justification differently. It sees it as a true eradication of sin and a true sancti-

fication and renewal. The soul becomes objectively pleasing to
God and so merits heaven. It merits heaven because now it is actually good. Scripture conceives of the forgiveness of sins as a real
and complete removal of them. The words used are "blot out"
(Ps 50:3), "clears away" (Ps 102:12), "blotting out" (Is 43:25),
"takes away" (Jn 1:29). The few times the Bible mentions "covering" sins refer not to the forgiveness of sins by God, but to the
forgiveness of one man's sins by another. Since we cannot actually forgive one another's sins (that is up to God), the best we can
do is overlook them or "cover" them. Fundamentalism's notion
that God "covers" our sins, but does not actually remove them, is
an unfortunate misreading of the Bible that found its origin in
Luther.

On the positive side, the Bible shows that justification is a rebirth. It is a generation of a supernatural life in a former sinner (Jn
3:5; Titus 3:5), a thorough inner renewal (Eph 4:23), and a real
sanctification (1 Cor 6:11). The soul itself becomes beautiful and
holy. It is not just an ugly soul hidden under a beautiful cloak.
Because it is beautiful and holy, it can be admitted to heaven,
where nothing unclean is allowed.

The assurance of salvation is perhaps the most enticing tenet of
fundamentalism, particularly for people steeped, justly, in the
guilt of their former lives.[2] There is no need for true reformation
of character, although to some extent that follows because of the
joy of being saved and the very real desire to live the kind of life
one's fellow fundamentalists lead. Being "born again" can be so
easy, and in that sense it is a relief. There is, at least, no need for an
embarrassing confession of faults, whether to a congregation or
to a priest in a dark cubicle or, sometimes worse, to oneself. One
can avoid all particularities, admitting transgressions in general,
forgetting them in particular. There is no need for a true examination of conscience. Once one accepts Christ as his personal Lord
and Savior, the past ceases to exist; more precisely, it exists, but it

[2] This seems to hold true for prisoners. Catholic inmates report that many of
their fellows are attracted to fundamentalism because the "born-again" experience
lets them avoid atoning for their sins.

does not at all matter. It does not have to be made up for or atoned for, and it does not even have to be built on.

Does this sound too good to be true? Take a look at what fundamentalists say. Wilson Ewin, the author of a booklet called *There Is Therefore Now No Condemnation*,[3] says that "the person who places his faith in the Lord Jesus Christ and His Blood shed at Calvary is eternally secure. He can never lose his salvation. No personal breaking of God's or man's laws or commandments can nullify that status." Ewin cites Hebrews 9:12, which states: "nor by the blood of goats and calves, but by his own blood he entered the most holy place once and for all, having obtained eternal redemption." "To deny the assurance of salvation would be to deny Christ's perfect redemption", argues Ewin, and this is something he can say only because he confuses redemption and salvation. The truth is that we are all redeemed—Christians, Jews, Moslems, animists in the darkest forests—but our salvation is conditional.

Ewin says that "no wrong act or sinful deed can ever affect the believer's salvation. The sinner did nothing to merit God's grace and likewise he can do nothing to demerit grace. True, sinful conduct always lessens one's fellowship with Christ, limits his contribution to God's work and can result in serious disciplinary action by the Holy Spirit." (But how serious can this disciplinary action be, since the loss of heaven is not part of it?) "However," Ewin continues, "none of the numerous examples of sin involving God's people in the Bible ever teach or suggest a loss of salvation. The reason? Salvation is by grace from the moment of the new birth until physical death occurs." He cites Romans 5:15: "But the free gift is not like the offense. For if by the one man's offense many died, much more is the grace of God and the gift by the grace of the one man, Jesus Christ, abounded to many."

What this means, explains Ewin, is that

the sinner must be declared righteous in order to be saved. The righteousness is imputed (credited) to the sinner who repents and

[3] Distributed by the Bible Baptist Church of Nashua, New Hampshire.

trusts only in Christ and His shed Blood for salvation. The sinner never becomes righteous. He is simply declared righteous. The righteousness of Christ is credited to the sinner who trusts. This wonderful truth is expressed in these words, "But to him who does not work but believes on him who justifies the ungodly, his faith is accounted for righteousness, just as David also described the blessedness of the man to whom God imputes righteousness apart from works: Blessed are those whose lawless deeds are forgiven, and whose sins are covered; blessed is the man to whom the Lord shall not impute sin (Rom 4:5–8).

Ewin says that

absolute assurance of salvation through imputed righteousness can never be broken by sin. The reason is simple—this righteousness has nothing to do with the keeping of God's commandments or moral law. The Bible says, "But now the righteousness of God apart from the Law is revealed, being witnessed by the Law and the Prophets, even the righteousness of God which is through faith in Jesus Christ to all and on all who believe" (Rom 3:21–22). God's law or commandments were given to point out the fact of sin. The law shows the unregenerated man how wicked and lost he is before a Holy God. Keeping them or breaking them has no part in the believer's possession of credited or imputed righteousness.

Ewin is particularly candid. Most fundamentalist writers state the assurance of salvation in a slightly different way. They do not emphasize the logical consequence of their position, that later sin, no matter how great, cannot undo one's salvation. They agree with Ewin that assurance can be absolute, but instead of arguing that "no personal breaking of God's or man's laws or commandments can nullify" that assurance, they emphasize that someone who has been saved will not, in fact, sin as frequently as he did before accepting Christ as his personal Savior. (They do not say he will not sin at all.) Good works, for them as for Ewin, still have nothing to do with obtaining salvation, but they are a sign of election. Keith Green put it this way in his tract *Salvation According to Rome*:

Good works, of course, are pleasing to God and they have an important and necessary place in the life of the Christian. They naturally follow if one has true faith, and they are performed out of love and gratitude to God for the great salvation that He has bestowed. Good works, in other words, are not the cause and basis of salvation, but rather the fruits and *proof* of salvation. . . . [The Christian] performs them not to *get* saved, but because he *is* saved.

Some fundamentalists, perhaps uncomfortable with the cold logic of Ewin's position and even with the softer version given by Green, go so far as to say that one can indeed lose salvation through later sin. They see the assurance of salvation as conditional and not absolute; it is dependent on the sinner keeping his part of a bargain. If the sinner continues to sin as before, he loses salvation, which is assured only so long as his repentance manifests itself outwardly in a reformed life. This is perilously close to the Catholic position and is grounded on Hebrews 10:26: "If we go on sinning wilfully, when once the full knowledge of truth has been granted to us, we have no further sacrifice for sin to look forward to; nothing but a terrible expectation of judgment, a fire that will eagerly consume the rebellious." But this appears to be a minority position among fundamentalists, since most see it as no assurance at all and as making salvation a consequence of man's works. The majority view is that salvation, if once achieved, simply cannot be lost, most fundamentalists being satisfied to say that the saved man either will not sin or will not sin grievously. They may not carry their principles to their end and assert, with Ewin, that no sin can undo salvation; they just affirm that the saved man will not, in fact, commit any great sin. They avoid the charge of antinomianism by never admitting the saved man is, in a way, free to sin as he wishes, because they insist he will not wish to sin as he once did. (They seem disinclined to make an empirical investigation of the matter. They take no surveys to learn if there can be found a saved man who sins just as avidly as before, perhaps on the theory that any such continuation in sin would prove that he was never saved in the first place.)

From all this fundamentalists conclude that the New Testament, when speaking of living people as saints, means not that they will *become* saints in heaven *if* they follow God's commandments (this is the way Catholics understand Paul to have written), but that they are already, right now, saints, just like the saints in heaven. They have no more chance of not being allowed into heaven than have heaven's present residents of being thrown out. "You are no longer exiles, then, or aliens; the saints are your fellow citizens, you belong to God's household" (Eph 2:19).

Catholics look at such verses as merely Paul's expectations for his disciples; fundamentalists look at them as his acknowledgment of their existing status. Ronald Knox noted that there is no need "to suppose that all these high-sounding phrases which St. Paul uses about the Church refer to a collection of Saints already made perfect. To be sure, he calls all Christian folk 'saints'; it is his way; he sees us not as we are but as we ought to be. These 'saints' had to be warned against fornication, against thieving, against bitter schisms; it is the Church we know."[4]

The anonymous author of *Can Anyone Really Know for Sure?*[5] says the "Lord Jesus wanted His followers to be so sure of their salvation that they would rejoice more in the expectation of heaven than in victories on earth. 'These things I have written to you who believe in the name of the Son of God, that you may know that you have eternal life, and that you may continue to believe in the name of the Son of God (1 John 5:13).' " The author admits, though, that there can be a false assurance: "The New Testament teaches us that genuine assurance is possible and desirable, but it also warns us that we can be deceived through a false assurance. Jesus declared: 'Not everyone who says to me, "Lord, Lord" shall enter the kingdom of heaven' (Mt 7:21)." But one can find true assurance. "First, you must accept the fact of the finished work of Christ. Acknowledging your sin (Rom 3:23, 6:23) and inability to save yourself (Eph 2:8, 9), place your trust in Jesus Christ as your personal Savior (Acts 16:13). Having done that, you can know your salvation is real. That's true assurance!"

---

[4] Ronald Knox, *St. Paul's Gospel* (New York: Sheed and Ward, 1950), 60.
[5] *Can Anyone Really Know for Sure?* (Grand Rapids, Mich.: Radio Bible Class, 1985), 4, 20–21.

Is it really? Consider the case of a fundamentalist minister convicted of a heinous crime. What must the man in the pew conclude from his sin? That the pastor was just as saved as his congregants, who would have been embarrassed to attend a movie rated less than PG? Logically they would have to say precisely that, if the man had been saved according to the fundamentalist scheme of things, even if his experience of salvation had come years before, even if his last years had been ones of perversity. From the fundamentalists' perspective, one can do nothing to lose salvation.

Putting aside the question whether this is a positive invitation to antinomianism—after all, if one is guaranteed heaven, why not have fun here below while the having's good?—the congregants naturally wonder whether their pastor was ever saved at all. No matter what the theory might be, it rankles to think a saved person would do such a thing or that a saved person would sin at all. One might call it the fundamentalist equivalent of Catholics wondering whether the man in the chasuble was ever validly ordained. A man never validly ordained as a priest cannot confect the sacraments, even if he goes through the motions perfectly. A fundamentalist pastor who himself was never saved—well, that is a disturbing thought.

It is a thought that leads to one of two conclusions. Either this pastor was never saved in the first place, although everyone thought he was—this implies one can never tell from outward actions who is saved and who is not—or he was indeed saved but can now sin with impunity. But that is repugnant to common moral convictions. A pastor known for years by his congregants would be presumed saved; if they could be fooled, couldn't the man have fooled himself? If he, with some formal religious training, thought he was born again when he was not, how is the average fundamentalist to know whether his conversion "took"?

How can any fundamentalist know his salvation experience was real, that it "worked"? He cannot. Leading a good life immediately after being born again proves nothing, since one might sin grievously at a later time. Leading a bad life right after apparently being saved does not disprove it, since one's sins are immaterial.

Either way, the doctrine seems nearly useless because, when reflected on seriously, it seems to make impossible the very assurance it is supposed to give.

Besides, there are verses that call the whole notion of the assurance of salvation into question. "I buffet my own body, and make it my slave; or I, who have preached to others, may myself be rejected as worthless", says Paul (1 Cor 9:27). This follows the well-known verses that speak of running a race, and the race, of course, is the race of life, the finish line being entrance into heaven. The author of the Radio Bible Class booklet says that Paul "did not want to lose the reward for service through failing to satisfy his Lord; he was not afraid of losing his salvation". While that interpretation seems to strain the passage a bit, it is not entirely unreasonable, but 1 Corinthians 9:27 should not be read in isolation.

Compare it to Philippians 2:12: "Beloved, you have always shown yourselves obedient; and now that I am at a distance, not less but much more than when I am present, you must work to earn your salvation, in anxious fear." Other translations say "work out your own salvation in fear and trembling". This is not the language of self-confident assurance. What is more, Paul tells us, "All of us have a scrutiny to undergo before Christ's judgement-seat, for each to reap what his mortal life has earned, good or ill, according to his deeds" (2 Cor 5:10), and God "will award to every man what his acts have deserved" (Rom 2:6). But if the only act of consequence is the born-again experience, what difference do the other acts make? The apostle notes that "there is graciousness, then, in God, and there is also severity. His severity is for those who have fallen away, his graciousness is for thee, only so long as thou dost continue in his grace; if not, thou too shalt be pruned away" (Rom 11:22). Paul wrote this to people who were already "saved", in a state of grace—a grace they could lose, becoming "unsaved".

These verses demonstrate that we indeed will be judged by what we do and not just by the one act of whether we accept Jesus as our personal Lord and Savior. Yet it is not to be thought that being do-gooders is sufficient. The Bible is quite clear that we are saved by faith. The Reformers were quite right in saying this, and to this extent they merely repeated the constant teaching of the Church. Where they erred was in saying that we are saved by faith alone. If it is true that we are judged by our acts (presuming first we have faith), then it is not enough to say that faith alone, in the traditional Protestant sense of fiduciary faith—trust in Christ's promises—can be enough. If it were, we would not have to worry about our other acts.

Recall that Nicodemus was told by Christ that he must be reborn by water and the Holy Spirit (Jn 3:5). In the fundamentalist scheme of things, despite their protestations, the water reduces to nothing at all. For Catholics the whole phrase "water and the Holy Spirit" is one; it means baptism. For fundamentalists only the second part of the phrase is operative. The Holy Spirit does his job by convicting us of sin and showing us we need to put our faith in Christ. The water is forgotten. If one dies after being born again, but before being baptized, one gets to heaven anyway. Although fundamentalists look at baptism as an ordinance, it is not necessary for salvation. There is no real connection between baptism and salvation because baptism as such does nothing. It is the intellectual acceptance of Christ that does it all.

Just as baptism, then, is not actually needed for salvation, the acceptance of Christ as personal Lord and Savior being enough, so no other act, no matter how good, can assist salvation. This flies in the face of the passages from Paul. Another way to look at it is this. Consider Romans 5:2: "We are confident in the hope of attaining glory as the sons of God." If we, having been born again in fundamentalism's sense, are now sure of heaven, and if we know nothing can deprive us of it, then we have no reason to hope because we *know* that heaven is ours. But "our salvation is founded upon the hope of something", says Paul. "Hope would not be hope at all if its object were in view; how could man still hope for something which he sees?" (Rom 8:24). We hope for heaven, however well disposed we might be spiritually, because we know we still have a chance to lose it.

"Are you saved?" asks the fundamentalist. "I am redeemed," answers the Catholic, "and like the apostle Paul I am working out my salvation in fear and trembling, with hopeful confidence—but not with a false assurance—and I do all this as the Church has taught, unchanged, from the time of Christ."

Chapter 14

Baptism of Infants

Fundamentalists say the Catholic Church errs in baptizing infants. Baptism, they say, is for adults only, and it is to be administered only after an adult has undergone a "born-again" experience—that is, after he has "accepted Jesus Christ as his personal Lord and Savior". At the instant of acceptance, when he is "born again", the adult becomes a Christian, one of the elect, and his salvation is assured. Baptism follows, although it actually does nothing itself to secure salvation; one who dies before being baptized, but after "being saved", goes to heaven anyway.

Baptism, for fundamentalists, is not a sacrament, but an ordinance. It does not produce the grace it symbolizes; it is merely a symbol, a public manifestation of the adult's conversion. Since only an adult can be converted, baptism is not appropriate for infants or for young children below the age of reason. Most fundamentalists say infants and young children are automatically saved, no matter what. Only once a person reaches the age of reason and has sinned does he need to "accept Jesus" in order to reach heaven.

The Catholic Church has always understood baptism differently, of course, understanding it as a sacrament that accomplishes several things, the first of which is the remission of sin, both original sin and actual sin: in the case of infants and young children, only original sin, since they are incapable of actual sin; in the case of older persons, both. "Repent, Peter said to them, and be baptized, every one of you, in the name of Jesus Christ, to have your sins forgiven; then you will receive the gift of the Holy Spirit. This promise is for you and your children, and for all those, however far away, whom the Lord our God calls to himself " (Acts 2:38–39). We also read: "Rise up, and receive baptism, washing away your sins at the invocation of his name" (Acts 22:16). These commands are universal, not restricted to adults.

Along with this forgiveness of sins comes an infusion of grace. It is this grace that makes the soul spiritually alive and capable of enjoying heaven. There are other benefits, too, such as the elimination of punishment due for sins and the right to special graces necessary to enable the baptized to fulfill his baptismal promises.

In the Middle Ages, some groups, such as the Waldenses and Catharists, rejected infant baptism. Later, the Anabaptists ("rebaptizers") echoed them in saying infants are incapable of being baptized validly. But the Catholic Church has always held that Christ's law applies to infants as well as adults. Jesus said that no one can enter heaven unless he has been born again of water and the Holy Spirit (Jn 3:5). His words can be taken to apply to anyone capable of having a right to his Kingdom. He asserted such a right even for children: "Let the children be, do not keep them back from me; the Kingdom of heaven belongs to such as these" (Mt 19:14).

Fundamentalists say this verse does not apply to young children or infants since it implies the persons being referred to are able to approach Christ on their own. (Older translations have "Suffer the little children to come unto me", which seems to suggest they can do so under their own power.) Fundamentalists conclude the passage refers only to older, ambulatory children, those capable of sin. But the parallel text says, "Then they brought little children to him" (Lk 18:15), and following this are the same words as in Matthew 19:14. What is more, some translations even use the term "infants". Indeed, in the Greek the words refer to infants in arms, little children who are unable to approach Christ on their own. Besides, Paul notes that baptism has replaced circumcision (Col 2:11–12). Of course, it was mainly infants who were circumcised under the Old Law; circumcision of adults was rare, there being few converts to Judaism. If Paul, in making this parallel, meant to exclude infants from baptism, it is strange that he did not say so.

It is not often admitted by fundamentalists that nowhere does the Bible actually say baptism is to be restricted to adults. They just conclude that is what it should be taken as meaning, even if the text does not explicitly support such a view. Naturally enough, the people whose baptisms we read about in Scripture are adults because they were converted as adults. This makes sense, because Christianity was just starting out and there were no "cradle Christians", no people brought up from childhood in Christian homes.

One might ask, Does the Bible ever say that infants or young children *can* be baptized? The indications are fairly clear. Lydia was converted by Paul's preaching. "She was baptized, with all her household" (Acts 16:15). The jailer of Paul and Silas, who was about to commit suicide when they were miraculously freed from their imprisonment, was converted by them. We are told that "without delay he and all his were baptized" (Acts 16:33). And in his greetings to the Corinthians, Paul recalled that, "Yes, and I did baptize the household of Stephanas" (1 Cor 1:16).

In all these cases, whole households or families were baptized. Presumably this means more than just the spouse: at least the children, probably also servants, if the household had any. But would an impoverished jailer, about to kill himself for what he took to be malfeasance, have servants at all, being, as he was, near the bottom of the social ladder? Not likely. "He and all his" must refer to himself plus at least two others; if it referred to just himself and his wife, we would expect to read "without delay he and his wife were baptized", but we read "without delay he and all his were baptized".

The natural implication is that the jailer had at least one child who was baptized, too. A similar argument can be made in the other cases. Granted, we cannot tell the age of the children; they may have been past the age of reason, not infants. Then again, they could have been babes in arms. More probably, there were both younger and older children. Even though the scriptural evidence is not absolutely conclusive on the issue, it leans in favor of infant baptism. At any rate, there is nothing in the New Testament that says infants and young children are unsuited to baptism.

The present Catholic attitude accords perfectly with early Christian practices. Origen, for instance, wrote in the third century that "the Church received from the apostles the tradition of giving baptism also to infants."[1] John Chrysostom said, "For this reason we baptize even infants, though they do not have sins [of their own]: so that there may be given to them holiness, righteousness, adoption, inheritance, brotherhood with Christ, and that they may be his members."[2] The Council of Carthage, in 252, condemned the opinion that infants should be withheld from baptism until the eighth day after birth.[3]

Now these citations—they could be multiplied—do not themselves prove, beyond doubt, that baptism of infants was authorized by Christ, but they do refer to a practice that was already old at an early date. After all, the Council of Carthage was not adjudicating a dispute about infant baptism as such, but was deciding at what point infants should be baptized. No one, apparently, was claiming the practice was contrary to Scripture or Tradition. It was as though they were saying, "We all agree infants can be baptized and that infant baptism was practiced from the first, but exactly *when* should they be baptized?" Another telling point: If infant baptism was opposed to the religious practices of the first believers, why do we have no record of early Christian writers condemning it?

Fundamentalists do not pay much attention to the historical situation. They deflect appeals to history by saying baptism requires faith and children are incapable of having faith. Thus, no baptism for them. It is true that Christ prescribed instruction and actual faith for adult converts (Mt 28:19–20), but his general law on the absolute necessity of baptism for salvation (Jn 3:5) puts no restriction on the subject of baptism. Although infants are included in

---

[1] Origen, *Commentarii in Romanos* 5, 9.
[2] John Chrysostom, *Catecheses ad illuminandos* Apud Aug., Contra Iul. 1, 6, 21.
[3] Cyprian, *Epistulae* 64 (59), 2.

the law, they cannot be expected to meet requirements that cannot be met because of their age. They cannot be expected to be instructed and have faith when they are incapable of receiving instruction or manifesting faith.

The fundamentalist position on infant baptism is a consequence not of the Bible's strictures, but of the logic of fundamentalism's notion of salvation. Although the Bible is not as clear on the issue as we might wish, certainly what it says leans toward the Catholic position, which is seconded by early Christian practice and writings. Fundamentalists ignore all that because they must preserve their concept of how salvation is obtained. They see salvation as coming not through an infusion of grace, which is the Catholic position, but through an acceptance of Jesus as one's personal Lord and Savior. Since only an adult can be saved in this way, they conclude baptism is wasted on infants and young children—thus their opposition to the Catholic position.

Chapter 15

The Forgiveness of Sins

All pardon for sins comes, ultimately, from Calvary, but how is this pardon to be received by individuals? How are people who sin today to obtain forgiveness? Did Christ leave us any means within the Church to take away sin? The Bible says he gave us two means. Baptism was given to take away the sin inherited from Adam (original sin) and any sins (called actual sins, because they come from our own acts) committed before baptism. For sins committed after baptism, a different sacrament is needed. It has been called penance, confession, and reconciliation, each word emphasizing one of its aspects.

During his life, Christ forgave sins, as in the case of the woman taken in adultery (Jn 8:1–11) and the woman who anointed his feet (Lk 7:48). He exercised this power as *man,* "to convince you that the Son of Man has authority to forgive sins while he is on earth" (Mk 2:10). Since he would not always be with the Church visibly, Christ gave this power to other men so the Church, which is the continuation of his presence throughout time, would be able to offer forgiveness to future generations. He gave his power to the apostles, and it was necessarily a communicable power, one that could be passed on to their successors and agents, since, obviously, the apostles would not always be on earth either. "He breathed on them, and said to them, Receive the Holy Spirit; when you forgive men's sins, they are forgiven, when you hold them bound, they are held bound" (Jn 20:22–23).[1]

---

[1] This was one of only two times we are told that God breathed on man, the other being when he made man a living soul (Gen 2:7). It emphasizes how important the establishment of the sacrament of penance was.

Christ told the apostles to follow his example: "As the Father sent me, so am I sending you" (Jn 20:21). What he did, they were to do. Just as the apostles were to carry Christ's message to the whole world, so were they to carry his forgiveness: "I promise you, all that you bind on earth shall be bound in heaven, and all that you loose on earth shall be loosed in heaven" (Mt 18:18). This power was not to be used as being from themselves, but as being from God: "This, as always, is God's doing; it is he who, through Christ, has reconciled us to himself, and allowed us to minister this reconciliation of his to others" (2 Cor 5:18). Indeed, confirms Paul, "We are Christ's ambassadors" (2 Cor 5:20).

It is said by some that any power given to the apostles died with them. Not so. Some powers, certainly, must have, such as universal jurisdiction. But the powers absolutely necessary to maintain the Church as a living, spiritual society had to be passed down, generation to generation. If they ceased, the Church would cease, except as a quaint abstraction. Christ ordered the apostles to "make disciples of all nations". It would take time, much time. He promised his assistance: "And behold I am with you all days, even to the consummation of the world" (Mt 28:19–20).

If the apostles and disciples believed that Christ instituted a priesthood that included the power to forgive sins in his stead, we would expect the successors of the apostles—that is, the bishops—and Christians of later years to act as though such power was legitimately and habitually exercised. On the other hand, if the priestly forgiveness of sins was what fundamentalists term it, an "invention", and if it was something foisted on the young Church by ecclesiastical or political leaders, we would expect to find records of protest. In fact, in early Christian writings we find no sign of protests concerning priestly forgiveness of sins. Quite the contrary. We find confession to a priest was accepted as consistent with the original deposit of faith.

If the Church itself instituted confession (or "auricular confession", as some like to emphasize: private confession "to the ear" of a priest), and if the sacrament did not stem directly from Christ, it should be possible to point to a date for its "invention". Some opponents of the Catholic position think they can do that. Loraine Boettner claims "auricular confession to a priest instead of to God" was instituted in 1215 at the Fourth Lateran Council.[2] This is an extreme example, even for a committed anti-Catholic. There are not many people with the gumption to place the "invention" of confession so late, since there is so much early Christian writing—a good portion of it a thousand and more years before that Council—that refers to the practice of confession as something already long established. One cannot very well "invent" something that has been around a millennium and more.

Actually, the Fourth Lateran Council did not introduce confession, although it did discuss it. To combat the lax morals of the time (morals are always more lax than they should be, at any time in history; that is one consequence of original sin), the Council more specifically defined the already-existing duty to confess one's sins by saying Catholics should confess at least once a year. To issue an official decree about a sacrament is hardly the same as "inventing" that sacrament.

The earliest Christian writings, such as the first-century *Didache,* are indefinite on the procedure to be used for the forgiveness of sins, but a self-accusation is listed as a part of the Church's requirement by the time of Irenaeus.[3] The sacrament of penance is clearly in use, but it is not yet clear from Irenaeus just how, or to whom, confession is to be made. Is it privately, to the priest, or before the whole congregation with the priest presiding? The one thing we can say for sure is that the sacrament is understood by Irenaeus to go back to the beginning of the Church.

Slightly later Christian writers, such as Origen,[4] Cyprian,[5] and Aphraates,[6] are quite clear in saying confession is to be made to a

---

[2] Boettner, *Catholicism,* 8.
[3] Irenaeus, *Adversus haereses* 1, 13, 5.
[4] Origen, *In Psalmos homiliae* 2, 6.
[5] Cyprian, *De lapsis* 28.
[6] Aphraates, *Demonstrationes* 7, 3.

priest. (In fact, in their writings the whole process of penance is termed *exhomologesis,* which simply means confession: the confession was seen as the main part of the sacrament.) Cyprian writes that the forgiving of sins can take place only "through the priests".[7] Ambrose makes things clear, saying, "this right is given to priests only".[8] Pope Leo I says absolution can be obtained only through the prayers of the priests.[9] These utterances are not taken as anything novel, but as reminders of accepted belief. We have no record of anyone objecting, of anyone claiming these men were pushing an "invention".

Note that the power given to the apostles by Christ was twofold: to forgive sins or to hold them bound, which means to retain them unforgiven. Several things follow from this. First, the apostles could not know what sins to forgive, what not to forgive, unless they were first told the sins by the sinner. This implies confession. Second, their authority was not merely to proclaim that God had already forgiven sins or that he would forgive sins if there were proper repentance.

Such interpretations do not account for the distinction between forgiving and retaining—nor do they account for the importance given to the utterance in John 20:22–23. If God has already forgiven all a man's sins or will forgive them all, past and future, on a single act of repentance, then it makes little sense to tell the apostles they have been given the power to "retain" sins, since forgiveness would be an all-or-nothing thing and nothing could be "retained". If forgiveness can be partial, how is one to tell which sins have been forgiven, which not, in the absence of a priestly decision? One cannot very well rely on gut feelings. No, the biblical passages make sense, hang together, only if the apostles and their successors were given a real authority.

Still, some people are not convinced. One is Paul Juris, a former priest, now a fundamentalist, who has written a pamphlet

[7] Cyprian, *De lapsis* 28.
[8] Ambrose, *De paenitentia* 1, 2, 7.
[9] Leo I (the Great), *Epistulae* 108, 2.

on this subject.[10] The pamphlet is widely distributed by organizations opposed to Catholicism. The cover describes the work as "a study of John 20:23, a much misunderstood and misused portion of Scripture pertaining to the forgiveness of sins". Juris begins by mentioning "two main schools of thought", the first being the Catholic position, the second the fundamentalist. He puts the fundamentalist position this way: "In this setting and with these words, Jesus was commissioning his disciples, in the power of the Holy Spirit, to go and preach the Gospel to every creature. Those who believed the Gospel, their sins would be forgiven. Those who refused to believe the Gospel, their sins would be retained."

He correctly notes that "among Christians, it is generally agreed that regular confession of one's sins is obviously necessary to remain in good relationship with God. So the issue is not whether we should or should not confess our sins. Rather, the real issue is: How does God say that our sins are forgiven or retained?" Juris says, "Since John 20:23 can be interpreted in more than one way, it will be necessary to examine this portion of Scripture not only in its context, but also in the light of other Scriptures pertaining directly to this subject. And, since we know that God's Word never contradicts itself, what better way could we arrive at the true meaning of this verse of Scripture, than by comparing it with other Scriptures?"

This sounds fine, on the surface, but this apparently reasonable approach masks what really happens next. Juris engages in verse slinging, listing as many verses as he can find that refer to God forgiving sins, in hope the sheer mass of verses will settle the question. Yet none of the verses he lists specifically interprets John 20:23, and none contradicts the Catholic interpretation. For instance, he cites verses such as these: "Be it known therefore to you, brethren, that through him [Christ] forgiveness of sins is proclaimed to you, and in him everyone who believes is acquitted of all the things of which you could not be acquitted by the Law of Moses" (Acts 13:38–39); "And he said to them, Go into the whole

---

[10] *The Forgiveness of Sins.*

world and preach the Gospel to every creature. He who believes and is baptized shall be saved, but he who does not believe shall be condemned" (Mk 16:15–16).

Juris says verses such as these demonstrate that "all that was left for the disciples to do was to 'go' and 'proclaim' this wonderful good news (the Gospel) to all men. As they proclaimed this good news of the Gospel, those who believed the Gospel, their sins would be forgiven. Those who rejected (did not believe) the Gospel, their sins would be retained." This is not a proof; these verses, and the others he lists, do not interpret John 20:23. Juris does nothing more than show the Bible says God will forgive sins, something no one doubts. He does not remotely prove that John 20:23 is equivalent to a command to "go" and to "preach". He sidesteps the evident problems in the fundamentalist interpretation of the verse.

It takes no scholar to see the passage does not say anything about preaching the good news. Jesus tells the apostles that "when you forgive men's sins, they are forgiven". Nothing here about preaching—that is handled elsewhere, such as in Matthew 28:19 and related verses. Instead, Jesus is telling the apostles that they have been empowered to do something. He does not say, "When God forgives men's sins, they are forgiven." It is hardly necessary to say that. He uses the second person plural: "you". He talks about the apostles forgiving, not preaching. When he refers to retaining sins, he uses the same form: "When you hold them bound, they are held bound." There it is again, "you".

What Juris does—his pamphlet is a good example of this—is to select verses, all that he can find, that mention the same general topic, the forgiveness of sins. Since the other verses he gives, about two dozen of them, speak about forgiveness by God, he concludes, improperly, that God could not have appointed men as his agents. The best Juris can do, ultimately, is to assert that John 20:23 means the apostles were given authority only to proclaim the forgivenss of sins—but asserting is not proving.

Granted, his is a technique that works. Many readers get the impression the fundamentalist interpretation has been shown to be true. After all, if one proposes to interpret one verse and accomplishes that by listing irrelevant verses that refer to something other than the specific point in controversy, lazy readers will conclude an impressive array of evidence has been marshaled. All they have to do is count the citations. Here is one for the Catholics, they say, looking at John 20:22–23, but ten or twenty or thirty for the fundamentalists. The fundamentalists must be right! They do not detect that the ten or twenty or thirty verses are a smokescreen.

Juris' technique illustrates that fundamentalists do not really "find" their doctrines through a literal reading of the Bible. They approach the Bible with already-held views, their own tradition, one might say, and they use the Bible to substantiate these views. Some can be substantiated easily, such as the reality of the Resurrection. Others cannot be substantiated by Scripture at all, because they are contrary to Scripture. In these cases, Scripture is either ignored or interpreted in an awkwardly metaphorical sense, as with John 6, where the Eucharist is promised, or as with John 20:22–23, where the sacrament of penance is established.

Another point. Fundamentalist writers often ignore John 20:22–23 since it is troublesome. They shift focus, insisting there is "only one mediator between God and man, Jesus Christ" (1 Tim 2:5). True, but they draw an improper inference. Christ was at liberty to decide how his mediation would be applied to us. It is a question of fact. Naturally enough, the one who is offended does the forgiving. When we sin, we offend God, so it is he to whom we look for forgiveness. But he can arrange his forgiveness either personally and immediately or through an agent. Which did he declare to be the usual (though not exclusive) way to forgive sins: by direct application to him or by means of confessing to a priest? If the first, then John 20:22–23 becomes unintelligible. The words would not remotely mean what they so clearly seem to say.

Is the Catholic who confesses his sins to a priest any better off than the non-Catholic who confesses straight to God? Yes. First, he seeks forgiveness the way Christ intended it to be sought. Second, by confessing to a priest the Catholic learns a lesson in humility, which is conveniently avoided when one confesses only through private prayer—and how we all desire to escape humbling experiences! Third, the Catholic receives sacramental graces the non-Catholic does not get; through the sacrament of penance not only are sins forgiven, but graces are obtained. Fourth, and in some ways the most important, the Catholic is assured that his sins are forgiven; he does not have to rely on a subjective "feeling". Lastly, the Catholic can also obtain sound advice on avoiding sin in the future, while the non-Catholic praying in private remains uninstructed.

True, Christ could have decided that sins would normally be forgiven merely through private prayer, but he knew the world would grow old before his return. With himself gone, he wanted his followers to have every possible consolation, every possible assurance, every possible help, so he instituted the sacrament through which we are reconciled to God. During his lifetime Christ sent out his followers to do his work. Just before he left this world, he gave the apostles special authority, commissioning them to make God's forgiveness present to all lands, to all people, and the whole Christian world accepted this until just a few centuries ago. If there is an "invention" here, it is not the sacrament of penance, but the notion that the priestly forgiveness of sins is not to be found in the Bible or in early Christian history.

Chapter 16

Purgatory

In 1769 James Boswell had this exchange with Samuel Johnson:

> *Boswell*: "What do you think, Sir, of purgatory, as believed by the Roman Catholicks?"
>
> *Johnson*: "Why, Sir, it is a very harmless doctrine. They are of the opinion that the generality of mankind are neither so obstinately wicked as to deserve everlasting punishment, nor so good as to merit being admitted into the society of blessed spirits; and therefore that God is graciously pleased to allow a middle state, where they may be purified by certain degrees of suffering. You see, Sir, there is nothing unreasonable in this."
>
> *Boswell*: "But then, Sir, their Masses for the dead?"
>
> *Johnson*: "Why, Sir, if it be at once established that there are souls in purgatory, it is as proper to pray for them, as for our brethren of mankind who are yet in this life."[1]

Although Johnson was no "Catholick", he recognized that the doctrine of purgatory is not at odds with other tenets of Christianity. In fact, as he may have known, there is considerable scriptural warrant for it, even if the doctrine is not explicitly set out in the Bible.

The doctrine can be stated briefly. Purgatory is a state of purification, where the soul that has fully repented of its sins but has not fully expiated them has removed from itself the last elements of uncleanliness. In purgatory all remaining love of self is transformed into love of God. At death one's soul goes to heaven, if it is completely fit for heaven; to purgatory, if it is not quite fit for heaven, but not worthy of condemnation; or to hell, if it is completely unfit for heaven. Purgatory is a temporary state. Everyone

---

[1] Boswell, *Johnson*, 1:376–77.

who enters it will get to heaven, and, after the last soul leaves purgatory for heaven, purgatory will cease to exist. There will remain only heaven and hell.

When we die, we undergo what is called the particular, or individual, judgment. We are judged instantly and receive our reward, for good or ill. We know at once what our final destiny will be. At the end of time, though, when the last people have died, there will come the general judgment to which the Bible refers. In it all our sins will be revealed. Augustine said, in *The City of God,* that "temporary punishments are suffered by some in this life only, by others after death, by others both now and then; but all of them before that last and strictest judgment".[2] It is between the particular and general judgments, then, that the soul expiates its sins: "I tell you, you will not get out till you have paid the very last penny" (Lk 12:59). If full expiation occurs before the general judgment, the soul is released from purgatory and goes to heaven.

Fundamentalists note that biblical references to the judgment refer only to heaven and hell. Quite true. That is because most of the references are to the general judgment, when all will be judged at once (which means, for those who died earlier and already underwent an individual judgment, a kind of rejudging, but one that is public). It is at the general judgment that the justice and mercy of God will be demonstrated to all. Opponents of the Catholic position are generally silent about what happens to the souls of people who die long before the Last Day. There is no hint from Scripture that these souls remain in suspended animation. No, "men die only once, and after that comes judgment" (Heb 9:27). Judgment is immediate—which, by the way, is one reason why reincarnation is impossible. It is here, between individual judgment and general judgment, that a soul may find itself in purgatory.

Fundamentalists are fond of saying the Catholic Church "invented" the doctrine of purgatory, but they have trouble saying just when. Most professional anti-Catholics—the ones who make their living attacking "Romanism"—seem to place the blame on

---

[2] Augustine, *De civitate Dei* 21, 13.

Pope Gregory the Great, who reigned from 590–604. That hardly accounts for the request of Monica, mother of Augustine, who asked her son, in the fourth century, to remember her soul in his Masses. This would have made no sense if she thought her soul could not be helped by prayers, if she thought there was no possibility of being somewhere other than heaven or hell.

Still less does the ascription of the doctrine to Gregory account for the graffiti in the catacombs, where the earliest Christians, during the persecutions of the first three centuries, recorded prayers for the dead. Indeed, some of the earliest noninspired Christian writings, such as the *Acts of Paul and Thecla* (second century), refer to the Christian custom of praying for the dead. Such prayers would have been made only if Christians believed in purgatory, even if they did not use that name for it.

No, the historical argument breaks down. Whenever a date is set for the "invention" of purgatory, one can point to something to show the doctrine was already old many years before that date. Besides, if at some point the doctrine was pulled out of a clerical hat, why does ecclesiastical history record no protest? A study of the history of doctrines shows Christians in the first centuries were up in arms, sometimes quite literally, if anyone suggested the least change in beliefs. They were extremely conservative people, their test of the truth of a doctrine being the question: Was this believed by our ancestors? Surely belief in purgatory would be considered a great change, if it had not been believed from the first—so where are the records of protests? They do not exist, and they never existed. There is no hint, in the oldest writings available to us (or in later ones, for that matter), that "true believers" in the immediate postapostolic years complained about purgatory as a novel doctrine. They must have understood that the oral teaching of the apostles, what Catholics call Tradition, and the Bible not only did not contradict the doctrine but endorsed it.

It is no wonder, then, that professional anti-Catholics spend little time on the history of the belief. (Who can blame them for avoiding an unpleasant subject?) They prefer to claim, instead, that the Bible speaks only of heaven and hell. Wrong again. It speaks quite plainly of a third place, where Christ went after his death, the place commonly called the Limbo of the Fathers, where the just who died before the Redemption were waiting for heaven to be opened to them (1 Pet 3:19). This place was neither heaven nor hell.

Even if the Limbo of the Fathers was not purgatory, its existence shows that a temporary, intermediate state is not contrary to Scripture. Look at it this way. If the Limbo of the Fathers *was* purgatory, then this one verse directly teaches the existence of purgatory. If the Limbo of the Fathers was a different temporary state, then the Bible at least says such a state can exist. It at least proves there can be more than just heaven and hell.

Fundamentalists also say, "We cannot find the word purgatory in Scripture." True, but that is hardly the point. The words Trinity and Incarnation are not in Scripture either, yet those doctrines are taught in it. Likewise, Scripture teaches that purgatory exists, even if it does not use that word and even if 1 Peter 3:19 refers to a place other than purgatory.

Christ refers to the sinner for whom "there is no forgiveness, either in this world or in the world to come" (Mt 12:32). This implies expiation can occur after death. Paul tells us that at the day of judgment each man's work will be tried. This trial happens after death. What happens if a man's work fails the test? "He will be the loser; and yet he himself will be saved, though only as men are saved by passing through fire" (1 Cor 3:15). Now this loss, this penalty, cannot refer to consignment to hell, since no one is saved there; and heaven cannot be meant, since there is no suffering ("fire") there. Purgatory alone explains this passage. Then there is the Bible's approbation of prayers for the dead: "It is a holy and wholesome thought to pray for the dead, that they might be loosed from their sins" (2 Macc 12:46). Prayers are not needed by those in heaven, and they cannot help those in hell. That means some people must be in a third place, at least temporarily.[3]

---

[3] Fundamentalists do not accept the inspiration of 2 Maccabees, of course, but they must admit it reflects the religious views of Jews shortly before New Testament times.

Why would anyone go to purgatory? To be cleansed. "Nothing unclean shall enter heaven" (Rev 21:27). Anyone who has not completely expiated his sins—that is, not just had them forgiven, but "made up" for them, been punished for them—in this life is, to some extent, "unclean". Through repentance he may have gained the grace needed to qualify for heaven (which is to say his soul is spiritually alive), but that is not enough. He needs to be cleansed completely. By not admitting the doctrine of purgatory, one necessarily implies that even the slightest defilement results in the loss of the soul, yet even here below not every crime is a capital offense: "Not all sin is deadly" (1 Jn 5:17).

Fundamentalists claim, as an article in Jimmy Swaggart's magazine *The Evangelist* put it, that "Scripture clearly reveals that all the demands of divine justice on the sinner have been completely fulfilled in Jesus Christ. It also reveals that Christ has totally redeemed, or purchased back, that which was lost. The advocates of a purgatory (and the necessity of prayer for the dead) say, in effect, that the redemption of Christ was incomplete. . . . It has all been done for us by Jesus Christ, there is nothing to be added or done by man."[4] This presumes there is a contradiction between the Redemption and our suffering in expiation for our sins. There is not, whether that suffering is in this life or in the next. Paul said he rejoiced "in my sufferings for you, and [I] fill up those things that are wanting in the suffering of Christ" (Col 1:24). Ronald Knox explained this passage by noting that "the obvious meaning is that Christ's sufferings, although fully satisfactory on behalf of our sins, leave us under a debt of honour, as it were, to repay them by sufferings of our own."[5] Paul did not imply there was something lacking in the Redemption, that Christ could not pull it off on his own, and no fundamentalist misreads Colossians 1:24 that way. Analogously, it is not contrary to the Redemption to say we must suffer for our sins; it is a matter of justice. We can suffer here, or hereafter, or in both places, as Augustine wrote.

[4] Sandy Carson, "Is Purgatory Real?" *The Evangelist*, July 1984, 33.
[5] See the footnote to Colossians 1:24 in Knox's translation of the New Testament.

Some say, "God does not demand expiation after having for-given sins." Tell that to King David. When David repented, God sent Nathan with a message for him: "The Lord on his part has forgiven your sin: you shall not die. But since you have utterly spurned the Lord by this deed, the child born to you must surely die" (2 Sam 12:14). Even after David's sin was forgiven, he had to undergo expiation. Can we expect less? Fundamentalists think the answer is yes, because Christ obviated the need for any expia-tion on our part, but the Bible nowhere teaches that. Having one's sins forgiven is not the same thing as having the punishment for them wiped out.

The main reason for opposition to purgatory is that it cannot coexist with fundamentalism's notion of salvation. For funda-mentalists, salvation comes by "accepting Christ as one's per-sonal Savior". Aside from that one act of acceptance, no acts—meaning no good deeds and no sins—make any difference with respect to one's salvation. If one is "born again" in fundamental-ism's sense, salvation has already occurred, and nothing can keep one from heaven. If not "born again", one is damned. In funda-mentalism's scheme of things, purgatory would be superfluous, since cleansing before entering heaven would be unnecessary, on the notion that every soul is unclean and God ignores the unclean-liness by "covering" the soul's sinfulness.

Purgatory makes sense only if there is a requirement that a soul not just be *declared* to be clean, but actually *be* clean. After all, if a guilty soul is merely "covered", if its sinful state still exists but is officially ignored, then, for all the protestations that may be given, it is still a guilty soul. It is still unclean. A man who has not bathed in a month is not cleansed merely by putting on clean clothes; clean clothes will not remove the dirt. Likewise, "cover-ing" a soul will not purify it; its dirty state is merely hidden from view. Catholic theology takes literally the notion that "nothing unclean shall enter heaven". From this it is inferred that a dirty soul, even if "covered", remains a dirty soul and is not fit for heaven. It needs to be cleansed or purged of its dirtiness. The purging comes in purgatory.

There is another argument commonly used against purgatory. It is that the Catholic Church makes money from the doctrine. Without purgatory, the claim goes, the Church would go broke. Any number of anti-Catholic books, from the tamest to the most bizarre, claim the Church owes the majority of its wealth to this doctrine. The numbers do not add up.

When a Catholic requests a memorial Mass for the dead—that is, a Mass said for the benefit of someone in purgatory—it is customary to give the parish a stipend, on the principle that the laborer is worth his hire (Lk 10:7) and those who preside at the altar share the altar's offerings (1 Cor 9:13–14). In the United States, a stipend is commonly around five dollars, but the indigent do not have to pay anything, and no parish maintains a "schedule of fees". A few people, of course, freely offer more. On average, though, a parish can expect to receive something less than five dollars by way of stipend for each memorial Mass said. These Masses are usually said on weekdays.

Look at what happens on a Sunday. There are often hundreds of people at Mass. In a crowded parish, there may be thousands. Many families and individuals deposit five dollars or more into the collection basket; others deposit less. A few give much more. A parish might have four or five or six Masses on a Sunday. The total from the Sunday collections far outstrips the paltry amount received from the memorial Masses. The facts are that no Catholic parish gets rich from Mass stipends—or even gets much at all.

In interpreting the Bible, in determining whether the doctrine of purgatory contradicts or confirms what is found in its pages, we come on a recurring question: "Who is to decide?" It hardly suffices to say, "Let the Bible itself decide", since it is the interpretation of the Bible that is in question, and no book, not even the Bible, can be self-interpreting. Either we interpret it ourselves, using our own resources, or we listen to the word of a divinely appointed interpreter, if one has been established. Catholics hold that Christ empowered the Church to give infallible interpretations of the Bible. "I have still much to say to you, but it is beyond your reach as yet. It will be for him, the truth-giving Spirit, when he comes, to guide you in all truth" (Jn 16:12). This Jesus said to the apostles.

This takes us, of course, to the rule of faith—is it to be found in the Bible alone or in the Bible and Tradition, as handed down by the Church? That question was examined in an earlier chapter, and there is no need to repeat the arguments here. The reader just needs to keep in mind that the controversy about purgatory is really a controversy about much more than purgatory. Purgatory has just been a convenient warring ground. The ultimate disagreement concerns the doctrine of *sola scriptura*. If fundamentalists understood why that doctrine will not wash—why, in fact, it is contrary to Scripture—they would have little difficulty in accepting purgatory and other Catholic beliefs, such as the Immaculate Conception and the Assumption, which are not explicitly stated in the Bible.

Chapter 17

Peter and the Papacy

Like other Protestants, fundamentalists say Peter was never appointed by Christ as the earthly head of the Church for the simple reason that the Church has no earthly head and was never meant to have one. Christ is the Church's only foundation, in every sense of that term.

The papacy, they say, is an institution that arose out of third-century politics, both secular and ecclesiastical; it has no connection, other than mythological, with the New Testament. It was not established by Christ, even though supposed "successors" to Peter and their apologists claim it was. At best the papacy is a ruse; at worst, a work of the devil. In any case, it is an institution designed to give the Catholic Church an authority it simply does not have.

Besides, the argument continues, Peter was never in Rome and so could not have been the first Pope, and that puts the lie to talk about his "successors"; the unbroken chain is broken in its first link. How can Catholics talk about the divine origin of the papacy when their claim about Peter's whereabouts is wrong? Let us begin with this last charge.

At first glance, it might seem the question, whether Peter went to Rome and died there, is inconsequential. In a way it is. After all, his being in Rome would not itself prove the existence of the papacy; it would be a false inference to say he must have been the first Pope since he was in Rome and later Popes ruled from Rome. With that logic, Paul would have an equal claim to the title of first Pope, since he was an apostle and went to Rome. On the other hand, even if Peter never made it to the capital, he still could have

198

been the first Pope, since one of his successors could have been the first holder of that office to settle there.

Besides, if Peter did end his days at Rome, that might have something to say about who his legitimate successors would be (and it does, since the man elected Bishop of Rome is automatically the new Pope on the notion that Peter was the first Bishop of Rome and the Pope is merely Peter's successor), but it would say nothing about the status of the papal office. It would not establish that the papacy was instituted by Christ in the first place.

No, somehow the question, while interesting historically, does not seem to be crucial to the real issue, whether the papacy was founded by Christ and, if so, what authority the Pope wields. Still, most anti-Catholic organizations take up the matter and even go to considerable trouble to prove Peter could not have been in Rome. Why? Because they think they can get mileage out of it.

Here is a point on which we can put the lie to Catholic claims, they think. Catholics trace the papacy to Peter, and they say he was martyred in Rome after heading the Church there. If we could show he never went to Rome, that would undermine—psychologically if not logically—their assertion that Peter was the first Pope. If people conclude the Catholic Church is wrong on this historical point, they will conclude it is wrong on the larger one, the supposed existence of the papacy. Such is the reasoning, the real reasoning, of leading anti-Catholics.

The case is stated most succinctly, even if not so bluntly, by Loraine Boettner in *Roman Catholicism*:

The remarkable thing, however, about Peter's alleged bishopric in Rome is that the New Testament has not one word to say about it. The word Rome occurs only nine times in the Bible [actually, ten times in the Old Testament and ten times in the New], and never is Peter mentioned in connection with it. There is no allusion to Rome in either of his epistles. Paul's journey to the city is recorded in great detail (Acts 27 and 28). There is in fact no New Testament evidence, nor any historical proof of any kind, that Peter ever was in Rome. All rests on legend.[1]

Well, what about it? Admittedly the scriptural evidence for Peter being in Rome is weak. Nowhere does the Bible unequivocally say he was there; neither does it say he was not. Just as the New Testament never says, "Peter then went to Rome", it never says, "Peter did not go to Rome". In fact, very little is said about where he, or any of the apostles other than Paul, *did* go in the years after the Ascension. For the most part, we have to rely on books other than the New Testament for information about what happened to the Twelve, Peter included, in later years.

But Boettner is wrong when he claims "there is no allusion to Rome in either of [Peter's] epistles". There is, in the greeting at the end of the first epistle: "The Church here in Babylon, united with you by God's election, sends you her greeting, and so does my son, Mark" (1 Pet 5:13). Babylon is a code word for Rome. It is used that way six times in the last book of the Bible and in extra-biblical works such as *Sibylline Oracles* (5, 159f.), the *Apocalypse of Baruch* (ii, 1), and *4 Esdras* (3:1). Eusebius Pamphilius, writing about 303, noted that "it is said that Peter's first epistle, in which he makes mention of Mark, was composed at Rome itself; and that he himself indicates this, referring to the city figuratively as Babylon."[2]

Consider the other New Testament citations: "A second angel followed, who cried out, Babylon, great Babylon is fallen; she who made all the nations drunk with the maddening wine of her fornication" (Rev 14:8); "The great city broke in three pieces, while the cities of the heathens came down in ruins. And God did not forget to minister a draught of his wine, his avenging anger, to Babylon, the great city" (Rev 16:19); "There was a title written over his forehead, The mystic Babylon, great mother-city of all harlots, and all that is abominable on earth" (Rev 17:5); "And he

---

[1] Boettner, *Catholicism,* 117.
[2] Eusebius Pamphilius, *Historia ecclesiastica* 2, 15, 4.

cried aloud, Babylon, great Babylon is fallen" (Rev 18:2); "Standing at a distance, for fear of sharing her punishment, they will cry out, Alas, Babylon the great, alas, Babylon the strong, in one brief hour judgment has come upon you" (Rev 18:10); "So, with one crash of ruin, will Babylon fall, the great city" (Rev 18:21).

These references cannot be to the onetime capital of the Babylonian Empire. That Babylon had been reduced to an inconsequential status by the march of years, military defeat, and political subjugation; it was no longer a "great city". It played no important part in the recent history of the ancient world. The only truly "great city" in New Testament times was Rome.

"But there is no good reason for saying that 'Babylon' means 'Rome' ",[3] insists Boettner. But there is, and the good reason is persecution. Peter was known to the authorities as a leader of the Church, and the Church, under Roman law, was organized atheism. (The worship of any gods other than the Roman was considered atheism.) Peter would do himself, not to mention those with him, no service by advertising his presence in the capital—after all, mail service from Rome was then even worse than it is today, and letters could be intercepted easily by Roman officials. Peter was a wanted man, as were all Christian leaders. Why encourage a manhunt? In any event, let us be generous and admit that it is easy for an opponent of Catholicism to think, in good faith, that Peter was never in Rome, at least if he bases his conclusion on the Bible alone. But restricting his inquiry to the Bible is something he should not do; external evidence has to be considered, too.

William A. Jurgens, in his three-volume set *The Faith of the Early Fathers*,[4] an easily accessible and masterly compendium that cites at length a great number of works from the *Didache* to John Damascene, includes thirty references to this question, divided, in the index, about evenly between the statements that "Peter came to Rome and died there" and that "Peter established his See

---

[3] Boettner, *Catholicism*, 120.

[4] William A. Jurgens, *The Faith of the Early Fathers* (Collegeville, Minn.: Liturgical Press, 1970), 421.

at Rome and made the Bishop of Rome his successor in the primacy." A few examples must suffice, but they and other early references demonstrate there can be no question that the universal—
and very early—position (one hesitates to use the word
"tradition", since some people read it as "legend") was that Peter
resided and was martyred in the capital of the Empire.

Dionysius of Corinth, writing to Soter, the twelfth Pope,
about 170, said, "You have also, by your very admonition,
brought together the planting that was made by Peter and Paul at
Rome."[5] It was commonly accepted, from the very first, that
both Peter and Paul were martyred at Rome, probably in the Ne-
ronian persecution.

A generation later Tertullian noted, "How happy is that Church
. . . where Peter endured a passion like that of the Lord, where
Paul was crowned in a death like John's" [6] (referring to John the
Baptist, as both he and Paul were beheaded). Fundamentalists admit Paul died in Rome, so the implication from Tertullian is that
Peter also must have been there. In the same work Tertullian said,
"This is the way in which the apostolic Churches transmit their
lists: like the Church of the Smyrnaeans, which records that Polycarp was placed there by John; like the Church of the Romans,
where Clement was ordained by Peter".[7] This Clement, known
as Clement of Rome, later would be the fourth Pope. (Note that
Tertullian did not say Peter consecrated Clement as Pope, which
would have been impossible since a Pope does not name his own
successor; he merely ordained Clement as priest.) Clement wrote
his Letter to the Corinthians perhaps before 70,[8] just a few years
after Peter and Paul were killed; in it he made reference to Peter
ending his life where Paul ended his.

In writing to them around 110, Ignatius of Antioch remarked
he could not command the Roman Christians the way Peter and

---

[5] Fragment in Eusebius Pamphilius, *Historia ecclesiastica* 2, 25, 8.

[6] Tertullian, *De praescriptione haereticorum* 36, 1.

[7] Tertullian, *De praescriptione haereticorum,* 32, 2.

[8] John A. T. Robinson, *Redating the New Testament* (Philadelphia: Westminster, 1976), 327–47 passim.

Paul once did,[9] such a comment making sense only if Peter had been a leader, if not the leader, of the Church in Rome.

Near the end of the second century, Irenaeus mentioned that Matthew wrote his Gospel "while Peter and Paul were evangelizing in Rome and laying the foundation of the Church". He said the two departed Rome, perhaps to attend the Council of Jerusalem, and he noted that Linus was named as Peter's successor—that is, the second Pope—and that next in line were Anacletus (also known as Cletus) and then Clement of Rome.[10]

Clement of Alexandria wrote at the turn of the third century. A fragment of one of his works is preserved in Eusebius of Caesarea's *Ecclesiastical History,* the first history of the Church. Clement wrote, "When Peter preached the Word publicly at Rome, and declared the Gospel by the Spirit, many who were present requested that Mark, who had been for a long time his follower and who remembered his sayings, should write down what had been proclaimed."[11]

Peter of Alexandria was bishop of that city and died around 311. A few years before his death he wrote a treatise on penance. In it he said, "Peter, the first chosen of the apostles, having been apprehended often and thrown into prison and treated with ignominy, at last was crucified in Rome."[12] Seven years later, Lactantius noted that "when Nero was already reigning Peter came to Rome, where, in virtue of the performance of certain miracles which he worked by that power of God which had been given to him, he converted many to righteousness and established a firm and steadfast temple to God."[13] Nero reigned from 54 to 68.

Eusebius Pamphilius gave more precise dates than did Lactantius. He said that in 42 (he actually said the "second year of the two hundredth and fifth olympiad") "the apostle Peter, after he has established the Church in Antioch, is sent to Rome, where he

[9] Ignatius of Antioch, *Epistula ad Romanos* 4, 3.
[10] Irenaeus, *Adversus haereses* 3, 3, 3.
[11] Fragment in Eusebius Pamphilius, *Historia ecclesiastica* 6, 14, 1.
[12] Peter of Alexandria, *De paenitentia* canon 9.
[13] Lactantius, *De mortibus persecutorum* 2, 5.

remains as bishop of that city, preaching the Gospel for twenty-five years." He went on to say that "Nero is the first, in addition to all his other crimes, to make a persecution against the Christians, in which Peter and Paul died gloriously at Rome."[14]

These citations could be multiplied. It should be enough to note that no ancient writer claimed Peter ended his life elsewhere than in Rome. True, many refer to the fact that he was at one point in Antioch, but most go on to say he went on from there to the capital. Remember, these are the works that form the basis of Christian historical writing in the immediate post–New Testament centuries. On the question of Peter's whereabouts they are in agreement, and their cumulative testimony should carry considerable weight.

To sum up, Boettner does not know what he is talking about when he claims there is no "historical proof of any kind" and that "all rests on legend". The truth is that *all* the historical evidence is on the side of the Catholic position.

Continuing, Boettner, like other fundamentalist apologists, claims that "exhaustive research by archaeologists has been made down through the centuries to find some inscription in the Catacombs and other ruins of ancient places in Rome that would indicate Peter at least visited Rome. But the only things found which gave any promise at all were some bones of uncertain origin."[15] Boettner saw *Roman Catholicism* through the presses in 1962. His original book and the revisions to it since have failed to mention the results of the excavations under the high altar of St. Peter's Basilica, excavations that had been under way for decades but that were undertaken in earnest after World War II.

Pope Paul VI was able to announce officially something that had been discussed in archaeological literature and religious publications for years, that the actual tomb of the first Pope had been identified conclusively, that his remains were apparently present, and that in the vicinity of his tomb were inscriptions

---

[14] Eusebius Pamphilius, *Chronicon* ad an. Dom. 42, ad an. Dom. 68.
[15] Boettner, *Catholicism*, 118.

identifying the place as Peter's burial site, meaning early Christians knew that the Prince of the Apostles was there. The story of how all this was determined, with scientific accuracy, is too long to recount here. It is discussed in detail in John Evangelist Walsh's *The Bones of St. Peter*.[16]

It is enough to say that the combination of historical and scientific evidence is such that no one willing to look at the facts with an open mind can doubt that Peter was in Rome. To deny that fact is to let prejudice override reason. Grant, then, that Peter really was in Rome and really died and was buried there. What can be said about him, particularly from Scripture? Fundamentalists say he was just the equal of the other apostles, not their leader. He enjoyed no primacy, and he was granted by Christ no powers not given to the others.

In fact, there is ample evidence in the New Testament that Peter was first in authority among the apostles. When they were named, Peter almost always headed the list (Mt 10:1–4; Mk 3:16–19; Lk 6:14–16; Acts 1:13); sometimes it was only "Peter and his companions" (Lk 9:32). Peter was the one who generally spoke for the apostles (Mt 18:21; Mk 8:29; Lk 12:41; Jn 6:69), and he figured in many of the most dramatic scenes (Mt 14:28–32; 17:24; Mk 10:28). On Pentecost it was he who first preached to the crowds (Acts 2:14–40), and he worked the first healing (Acts 3:6–7). And to Peter came the revelation that Gentiles were to be baptized (Acts 10:46–48).

Peter's preeminent position among the apostles was symbolized at the very beginning of his relationship with Christ, although the implications were only slowly unfolded. At their first meeting, Christ told Simon that his name would thereafter be Peter, which translates as Rock (Jn 1:42). The startling thing was that in the Old Testament only God was called a rock. The word was never used as a proper name for a man. If one were to turn to a companion and say, "From now on your name is Asparagus", people would wonder. Why Asparagus? What is the meaning of

<hr />

[16] Walsh, *Bones*.

it? What does it signify? Indeed, why Peter for Simon the fisherman? Why give him as a name a word only used for God before this moment?

Christ was not given to meaningless gestures, and neither were the Jews as a whole when it came to names. Giving a new name meant that the status of the person was changed, as when Abram was changed to Abraham (Gen 17:5); Jacob to Israel (Gen 32:28); Eliacim to Joakim (2 Kings 23:34); and Daniel, Ananias, Misael, and Azarias to Baltassar, Sidrach, Misach, and Abdenago (Dan 1:6–8). But no Jew had ever been called Rock because that was reserved for God. The Jews would give other names taken from nature, such as Barach (which means lightning; Jos 19:45), Deborah (bee; Gen 35:8), and Rachel (ewe; Gen 29:16), but not Rock. In the New Testament James and John were surnamed Boanerges, Sons of Thunder, by Christ (Mk 3:17), but that was never regularly used in place of their original names. Simon's new name supplanted the old.

Not only was there significance in Simon being given a name that had been used only to describe God, but the place where the renaming occurred was also important. "Then Jesus came into the neighborhood of Caesarea Philippi" (Mt 16:13), a city that Philip the Tetrarch built and named in honor of Caesar Augustus, who had died in A.D. 14. The city lay near cascades in the Jordan River and not far from a gigantic wall of rock two hundred feet high and five hundred feet long, part of the southern foothills of Mount Hermon.[17]

Caesarea Philippi is no more. Near its ruins is the small Arab town of Banias, and at the base of the rock wall may be found what is left of one of the springs that fed the Jordan. It was here that Jesus pointed to Simon and said, "Thou art Peter" (Mt 16:18). The significance of the event must have been clear to the other apostles. As devout Jews they knew at once that the location was meant to emphasize the importance of what was being done.

---

[17] For an account of the locale, see Stanley L. Jaki, *And on This Rock* (Notre Dame, Ind.: Ave Maria, 1978), 21–55 passim.

None complained of Simon being singled out for this honor, and in the rest of the New Testament he is called by his new name, while James and John remain just James and John, not Boanerges.

When he first saw Simon, "Jesus looked at him closely and said, 'Thou art Simon the son of Jonah; thou shalt be called Cephas' (which means the same as Peter)" (Jn 1:42). The word Cephas is merely the transliteration of the Aramaic *Kepha* into Greek. *Kepha* means rock. Later, after Peter and the other disciples had been with Christ for some time, they went to Caesarea Philippi, where Peter made his profession of faith: "Thou art the Christ, the Son of the living God" (Mt 16:17). Jesus told Peter that this truth was revealed to him specially, and then he reiterated: "Thou art Peter" (Mt 16:18). To this was added the promise that the Church that would be founded would, in some way, be founded on Peter (Mt 16:18).

Then two important things were told the apostle. "Whatever thou shalt bind on earth shall be bound in heaven; whatever thou shalt loose on earth shall be loosed in heaven" (Mt 16:19). Here Peter was singled out for the authority that provides for the forgiveness of sins and the making of disciplinary rules. Later the apostles as a whole would be given similar power, but here Peter received it in a special sense; the later grant to them did not diminish the uniqueness of what was granted Peter. Indeed, Peter alone was promised something else. "I will give to thee [singular] the keys to the kingdom of heaven" (Mt 16:19). In ancient times keys were the hallmark of authority. A walled city might have one great gate and that gate one great lock worked by one great key. To be given the key to the city (an honor that exists even today, although its import is largely lost) meant to be given free access to and authority over the city. The city to which Peter was given the keys was the heavenly city itself. This symbolism for authority is used elsewhere in the Bible (Is 22:22; Rev 1:18).

Finally, after the Resurrection, Jesus appeared to his disciples and asked Peter three times, "Dost thou love me?" (Jn 21:15–17). In expiation of his threefold denial, Peter gave a threefold affirmation of love. Then Christ, who is the Good Shepherd (Jn

10:11, 14), gave Peter all the authority he earlier promised: "Feed my sheep" (Jn 21:17). Thus was completed the prediction made just before Jesus and his followers went for the last time to Olivet.

Immediately before his denials were predicted, Peter was told, "Simon, Simon, behold, Satan has claimed power over you all, so that he can sift you like wheat; but I have prayed for thee [singular], that thy faith may not fail; when, after a while, thou hast come back to me [after the denials], it is for thee to be the support of thy brethren" (Lk 22:31–32). Christ prayed that Peter would have faith that would never fail, that he would be a guide for the others, and Christ's prayer, being perfectly efficacious, was sure to be fulfilled. Here we see the roots of papal infallibility and the primacy that is the Bishop of Rome's.

Now take a closer look at the key verse: "Thou art Peter, and upon this rock I will build my Church" (Mt 16:18). Disputes about this line have always concerned the meaning of the term rock. To whom, or to what, does it refer? Since Simon's fresh name of Peter itself means rock, the sentence could be rewritten as: "Thou art Rock and upon this rock I will build my Church." The play on words seems obvious, but commentators wishing to avoid what follows from this—the establishment of the papacy— have suggested that the word rock could not refer to Peter but must refer to his profession of faith or to Christ.

According to the rules of grammar, the phrase "this rock" must relate to the closest noun. Peter's profession of faith ("Thou art the Christ, the Son of the living God") is two verses earlier, while his name, a proper noun, is in the immediately preceding clause. As an analogy, consider this artificial sentence: "I have a car and a truck, and it is blue." Which is blue? The truck, because that is the noun closest to the pronoun "it". This identification would be even clearer if the reference to the car were two sentences earlier, as the reference to Peter's profession is two sentences earlier than the term rock.

The same kind of objection applies to the argument that the rock is Christ himself, since he is mentioned within the profession of faith. The fact that he is elsewhere, by a different metaphor, called the cornerstone (Eph 2:20; 1 Pet 2:4–8) does not disprove that here Peter is the foundation. Christ is naturally the principal and, since he will be returning to heaven, the invisible foundation of the Church that will be established, but Peter is named by him as the secondary and, because he and his successors will remain on earth, the visible foundation. Peter can be a foundation only because first Christ is one.

There is another analogy. At times we ask our friends to pray for us, and we pray for them. Our prayers ask God for special help for one another. When we pray in this way, what are we doing? We are acting as mediators, as go-betweens. We are approaching God on someone else's behalf. Does this contradict Paul's statement that Christ is the one mediator (1 Tim 2:5)? No, because our mediatorship is entirely secondary to and dependent on his. He could have established his mediatorship in any way he chose, and he chose to have us participate when he commanded us to pray for one another (Mt 5:44; 1 Tim 2:1–4; Rom 15:30; Acts 12:5), even for the dead (2 Tim 1:16–18). So, just as there can be secondary mediators and a primary one, there can be a secondary foundation and a primary one.

Opponents of the Catholic interpretation of Matthew 16:18 also note that in the Greek text the name of the apostle is *Petros,* a masculine noun, while rock is rendered as *petra,* which is feminine. The first means a small stone, the second a massive rock. If Peter was meant to be the massive rock, the steady foundation of the Church here below, why is his name not *Petra*? As Loraine Boettner puts it in *Roman Catholicism,* "The Greek *petros* is commonly used of a small, movable stone, a mere pebble, as it were. But *petra* means an immovable foundation, in this instance, the basic truth that Peter had just confessed, the deity of Christ."[18] The Bible is clear on this point: Peter was no sure foundation.

Boettner continues by saying, "Had Christ intended to say that the Church would be founded on Peter, it would have been ridiculous for Him to have shifted to the feminine form of the word in

---

[18] Boettner, *Catholicism,* 106.

the middle of the statement, saying, if we may translate literally and somewhat whimsically, 'And I say unto thee, that thou art Mr. Rock, and upon this, the Miss Rock, I will build my church.'. . . He made two complete, distinct statements. He said, 'Thou art Peter,' and, 'Upon this rock (change of gender, indicating change of subject) I will build my church.' "[19] Boettner's "whimsy" obscures the straightforward solution to this problem.

The first thing to note is that Christ did not speak to the disciples in Greek. (And not Hebrew, either, which was reserved as a sacred language and was not in common use, somewhat analogously to the way Latin, in the recent past, was the sacred language for Catholics, but was not used by them in everyday speech.) Christ spoke Aramaic, the common language of Palestine at the time. In that language the word for rock is *kepha*. What was said was thus: "Thou art *Kepha,* and upon this *kepha* I will build my Church." When Matthew's Gospel was translated from the original Aramaic to Greek,[20] there arose a problem that did not confront the evangelist when he first composed his account of Christ's life in his native tongue.

In Aramaic the word *kepha* has the same ending whether it refers to a rock or is used as a man's name. In Greek, though, the word for rock, *petra,* is feminine in gender. The translator could use it for the second appearance of *kepha* in the sentence, but not for the first, because it would be inappropriate to give a man a feminine name. So he put a masculine ending on it, and there was *Petros,* which happened to be a preexisting word meaning a small stone. Some of the effect of the play on words was lost, but that was the best that could be done in Greek. In English, as in Aramaic, there is no problem with endings, so an English rendering could read: "Thou art Rock, and upon this rock I will build my church." In modern French Bibles, the word *pierre* appears in both places. The real meaning is hard to miss.

[19] Boettner, *Catholicism,* 106.
[20] Papias, *De expositione oraculorum Dominicorum,* fragment in Eusebius Pamphilius, *Historia ecclesiastica* 3, 39, 14.

Another point: If the rock really did refer to Christ, as fundamentalists claim (basing their argument on 1 Corinthians 10:4,
"and the rock was Christ"), why did Matthew leave the passage
as it was? In the original Aramaic, and in the English that is a
closer parallel to it than is the Greek, the passage seems clear
enough. Matthew must have realized that his readers would conclude the obvious from "Rock . . . rock". If he meant Christ to be
understood as the rock, why did he not say so? Why did he con-
struct his sentences so awkwardly that contortions would be required to elicit the fundamentalist interpretation? Why did he take
a chance and leave it up to Paul to write a clarifying text (presuming, of course, that 1 Corinthians was written after Matthew, as
most biblical scholars assert; if it came first, it could not have been
written to clarify it)?

The reason, of course, is that Matthew knew full well that what
the sentence seemed to say was just what it really was saying. It
was Simon—weak, Christ-denying Simon—who was chosen to
be the first link in the chain of the papacy. The scandal, to fundamentalists, is that Christ would choose as his Vicar the weakest of
the apostles, not the strongest. But God seems to enjoy working
through the lowly in order to confound the mighty, and his
choice of Peter was quite in keeping with other selections he had
made, such as deciding to be born in a stable rather than a palace.
In a way, it was Peter's weakness that would manifest the strength
of the papacy. After all, noted G. K. Chesterton when writing of
the succession of popes, a chain is only as strong as its weakest
link.[21]

Still, however apt Chesterton's comment might be, a fundamentalist will not see it as supporting the Catholic position since it
presumes the divine establishment of the papacy. His mind will
turn, instead, to snatches of ecclesiastical history he has imbibed
from visiting preachers or from anti-Catholic literature. What
will stick in his mind is the claim that the papacy has achieved its

---

[21] G. K. Chesterton, *Heretics* (London: Bodley Head, 1910), 67.

position of authority through purely human machinations. Providence, he has been told, had nothing to do with it.

This is the theme of Henry T. Hudson's *Papal Power*,[22] published in an attractive paperback format in England, but printed and distributed in America. This may be the most exhaustive look at the papacy to come from the hands of a fundamentalist in recent years. In five chapters Hudson examines the "origins of papal power", the development of the papacy before the Reformation, Luther's attack on the papacy, the further development of the institution after the Reformation, and papal claims in light of Scripture. (The chapter on Luther really does not focus on the Reformer's analysis of the papacy; it is better described as plain hagiography.)

In the introduction Hudson comments on the 1979 visit of John Paul II to the United States and asks, "Whatever happened to the traditional anti-papal sentiments common in American history?"[23] In a footnote he points out that Loraine Boettner has said that two-thirds of the American population in 1776 was Reformed Protestant. Hudson longs for the good old days.

His appreciations of ecclesiastical history and biblical criticism are not without weaknesses. He believes, for instance, that the papacy was supremely strong during the Middle Ages, when in fact the Popes were at the mercy of princes and were largely ignored by irreformable bishops and persnickety abbots. He thinks Rome was without influence in the earliest ecumenical councils, when in fact the popes sent legates and formally approved the councils' decisions. With respect to Peter's presence in Rome, Hudson thinks Paul's statement that "only Luke is with me" (2 Tim 4:11) settles the matter. "This is conclusive."[24] If it is, it is *too* conclusive. If the line proves Peter was not in Rome, it also proves no Christians, other than Luke and Paul, were there. Yet Paul wrote an epistle to the Christians in Rome, who apparently were numerous. Were

[22] Henry T. Hudson, *Papal Power* (Welwyn, England: Evangelical, 1981).
[23] Hudson, *Power*, 2.
[24] Hudson, *Power*, 21, n. 2.

they all out of town when 2 Timothy was written? If so, why was Luke still around?

When the interpretation of Matthew 16:18 is the question, Hudson is satisfied to say, "A simple, straightforward consideration of the grammatical construction seems to rule out Peter as the *petra*."[25] If he is to be satisfied with simple, straightforward grammatical constructions, why no mention of the Aramaic, which is even simpler than the Greek and which states: "Thou art *Kepha,* and upon this *kepha* I will build my Church"? This seems to say the rock is Peter, but Hudson makes no allusion to the Catholic arguments.

His book's key contention, what distinguishes it from other anti-Catholic works (not because other anti-Catholics would disagree, but because few of them bother to discuss the matter), is that the papacy obtained its exalted position through fraud. Hudson discusses at length forgeries on which the Popes supposedly built their power. It is quite true there were forgeries, and they were used, long after the events they purport to describe, to bolster Rome's position, but commentators of almost all stripes, save the fundamentalist, agree the forgeries had little or no practical effect. The papacy already was established firmly when the forgeries first appeared, and documents such as the Donation of Constantine and the False Decretals added little to the status of the institution. Granted, it was imprudent for any Church official to base an argument on them, and Lorenzo Valla's *Discourse on the Forgery of the Alleged Donation of Constantine,* which appeared in 1440, made many scholars look incompetent, but the fact remains that the papacy would have been what it was with or without the forgeries. They had far less effect on the institution than Parson Weems' biography had on the American public's perception of George Washington.

The curious thing is that, although Hudson decries forgeries used by partisans of Rome, he says nothing against forgeries used by Hudson. The last seventeen pages of the book are nothing less

[25] Hudson, *Power,* 21, n. 3.

than the complete transcript of the speech said to have been given by Bishop Josip Strossmayer at Vatican I in 1870. Hudson does not defend the speech against the charges that it is a forgery; he does not even imply that he knows of such charges. He accepts the speech's bona fides unquestioningly.

In doing so he demonstrates that while fundamentalists can produce tracts, newsletters, and even books in quantity, they rarely make any effort to test their claims against the Catholic version of the facts. They do not seem to know there *is* a Catholic version. How simple it would be to open the *Catholic Encyclopedia* and see, in the article on Strossmayer, that the speech attributed to him is a forgery. No one is obligated to accept the article writer's word for it, but sources are given, and with a little legwork the sources can be checked. But checking is not something professional anti-Catholics are inclined to do. They are not so much interested in accuracy as in effect.

Chapter 18

Infallibility of the Pope

Pretend for a moment a Pope is infallible not only in matters of faith or morals, but in trigonometry. He is presented with an examination consisting of one hundred trigonometry problems. What is the *least* number of problems he will answer correctly?

Someone who says "one hundred" may understand trigonometry, but his understanding of infallibility is no better than the average non-Catholic's. The correct answer is: zero. Although infallible in trigonometry, the Pope might get none of the problems right. Being infallible in trigonometry would mean being prevented from putting down the wrong answers. It would not mean being able to put down the right ones. The answer sheet could be left entirely blank—and would be, if the Pope had not done his homework.

It is the same in real life. Through the guardianship of the Holy Spirit, the Pope is guaranteed not to teach error regarding faith or morals (presuming, of course, he intends to make an *ex cathedra* statement and is not speaking as a private scholar). But he cannot teach what is true unless he first knows what is true, and he learns that the same way we do.

Catholics who fail this quiz may appreciate why nearly all fundamentalists misunderstand infallibility. They do not know what infallibility means. Most of them hear "infallibility" and think "impeccability". They think Catholics believe the Pope cannot sin. Those who do not make that elementary blunder imagine the Pope operates like Joseph Smith, the founder of Mormonism, who claimed to have at one time the Old Testament's Urim and Thummim. Smith repaired to his oracle to translate the Book of Mormon from the golden plates, or so he said, and most non-

Catholics think the Pope relies on some sort of amulet or magical incantation when an infallible definition is due. Given this, it might be too much to expect the average fundamentalist to understand the niceties of infallibility. The first thing he would have to perceive (after being told the subject concerns the absence of error, not of sin) is that infallibility belongs to the body of bishops as a whole, when, in moral unity, they teach a doctrine as true. "He who listens to you, listens to me" (Lk 10:16); "all that you bind on earth shall be bound in heaven" (Mt 18:18).

Vatican II put it this way:

> Although the individual bishops do not enjoy the prerogative of infallibility, they can nevertheless proclaim Christ's doctrine infallibly. This is so, even when they are dispersed around the world, provided that while maintaining the bond of unity among themselves and with Peter's successor, and while teaching authentically on a matter of faith or morals, they concur in a single viewpoint as the one which must be held conclusively. This authority is even more clearly verified when, gathered together in an ecumenical council, they are teachers and judges of faith and morals for the universal Church. Their definitions must then be adhered to with the submission of faith.

Infallibility belongs in a special way to the Pope as the head of the bishops (Mt 16:17–19; Jn 21:15–17) and is something he

> enjoys in virtue of his office, when, as the supreme shepherd and teacher of all the faithful, who confirms his brethren in their faith (cf. Luke 22:32), he proclaims by a definitive act some doctrine of faith or morals. Therefore his definitions, of themselves, and not from the consent of the Church, are justly held irreformable, for they are pronounced with the assistance of the Holy Spirit, an assistance promised to him in blessed Peter.[1]

The infallibility of the Pope is certainly a doctrine that has developed, but it is not one that sprang out of nowhere in 1870. It is implicit in these Petrine texts: John 21:15–17 ("Feed my sheep . . ."); Luke 22:32 ("I have prayed for thee that thy faith may not

---

[1] *Lumen Gentium*, 25.

fail"); Matthew 16:18 ("Thou art Peter . . ."). Christ instructed the Church to preach the good news (Mt 28:19–20) and promised the protection of the Holy Spirit "to guide you into all truth" (Jn 16:13). That mandate and that promise guarantee that the Church will never fall away from his teachings (1 Tim 3:15), even if individual Catholics might. The inability of the Church to teach error is infallibility, and it is a negative protection. It means what is officially taught will not be wrong, not that the official teachers will have the wits about them to stand up and teach what is right when it needs to be taught.

As Christians got clearer and clearer notions of the teaching authority of the whole Church and of the primacy of the Pope, they got clearer notions of the Pope's own infallibility. This happened early on. In 433 Pope Sixtus III declared that to assent to the Bishop of Rome's decision is to assent to Peter, who lives in his successors and whose faith does not fail.[2] Cyprian of Carthage, writing about 256, asked: "Would heretics dare to come to the very seat of Peter whence apostolic faith is derived and whither no errors can come?"[3] Augustine of Hippo summed up the ancient attitude when he remarked, "Rome has spoken; the case is closed."[4]

Leslie Rumble and Charles M. Carty, the famed radio priests of two generations ago, put it this way:

> Before the definition of infallibility in 1870, the Popes did not know they were infallible with the same full certainty of faith as that possessed by later Popes. But they were infallible in fact. The gift of papal infallibility was essential to the Church, not the definition of the gift. You wonder why it was defined only in 1870. But definitions are not given unnecessarily. If no discussion arises on a given point, and no one disputes it, there is no need for a definition. But in the seventeenth century the question of the Pope's doctrinal authority came more and more to the front, until in 1870, the Vatican

[2] Cited in Leslie Rumble and Charles M. Carty, *Radio Replies* (Rockford, Ill.: TAN Books, 1979), 3:95.

[3] Cyprian, *Epistulae* 59 (55), 14.

[4] Augustine, *Sermones* 131, 10.

Council was asked to settle the question once and for all. The time had come for the Church to know herself fully on this point.[5]

An infallible papal pronouncement is made only when some doctrine is called into question. Most have never been doubted by the vast majority of Catholics, although, at any one time, one could find someone to discount nearly any belief. Pick up a catechism and look at the great number of doctrines, most of which have never been formally defined by an *ex cathedra* papal statement. There are, in fact, few topics on which it would be possible for the Pope to make an infallible decision without seconding infallible pronouncements from some other source, such as an ecumenical council or the unanimous teaching of the Fathers.[6]

At least the outline, if not the text references, of the preceding paragraphs should be familiar to literate Catholics, to whom this subject should seem reasonably straightforward. It is a different story for fundamentalists. For them papal infallibility seems a muddle because their idea of what it covers is muddled.

Joseph Zacchello, ordained a priest in Italy and sent to the United States to serve Italian-Americans, converted to "Bible Christianity" in 1944. Four years later he published *Secrets of Romanism*. Because of the resurgence of anti-Catholic sentiment, the book has been reprinted recently. Zacchello argues against papal infallibility on the ground that it "is powerless to prevent divisions. Popes have anathematized other Popes, Councils have contradicted Councils, and doctors of theology have violently opposed other doctors." Besides, he notes, "the Roman Church often had two Popes; and once there were three rival Popes at one time (the Great Western Schism 1378–1417)."[7]

[5] Rumble and Carty, *Replies*, 3:96.

[6] An example would be Pope Paul VI's encyclical *Humanae vitae*. The encyclical may not have met the requirements of Vatican I, but the doctrine it enunciated is nevertheless infallibly taught. An infallible doctrine can be repeated in a document that is not itself infallible.

[7] Joseph Zacchello, *Secrets of Romanism* (Neptune, N.J.: Loizeaux Brothers, 1948), 10–11. There never were three Popes at once, of course. The problem was determining which of three claimants was the real Pope.

This is confusing—and inaccurate. No Catholic ever claimed papal infallibility would "prevent divisions". Yes, some Popes have contradicted other Popes, in their private opinions or with respect to disciplinary rulings, but never has any Pope officially contradicted what an earlier Pope officially taught about faith or morals. The same may be said about ecumenical councils, which also teach infallibly. No ecumenical council has ever contradicted the teaching of an earlier ecumenical council on faith or morals. Have "doctors of theology . . . violently opposed other doctors"? Of course, but Catholics do not hold that theologians are infallible, so disagreement between them is immaterial, and certainly the fact that they may disagree with one another says nothing about the existence of papal infallibility.

Consider Zacchello's misleading comment about the Great Western Schism. What happened was this. In 1378 Urban VI was lawfully elected Pope. Some cardinals thought he was not properly elected, so they elected another man, Clement VII. There were good men on both sides, supporters of each claimant honestly thinking they were backing the real Pope. No one imagined there could be two Popes at once. To settle the dispute, another group of cardinals exceeded their rights and declared both Urban and Clement deposed. They elected still a third claimant, Alexander V. All this time, Urban was the authentic Pope. Eventually he died, as did his rivals. Urban's third successor was Gregory XII. In order to end the confusion, which by this time had lasted nearly forty years, a council was convened, and Gregory resigned. The successors to Clement and Alexander were declared to have been improperly elected, and a new Pope, Martin V, was elected. In all these years there was never any question about there being more than one Pope; there was only a mistake among the faithful regarding who was the legitimate successor to the Prince of the Apostles.

It is at least as bad with Ralph Woodrow, author of *Babylon Mystery Religion*. He says, "People naturally question how infallibility could be linked with the papal office when some of the popes had been very poor examples in morals and integrity." But he at once recognizes that he is confusing infallibility with impeccability, so he covers himself by saying, "And if the infallibility be applied only to doctrines pronounced by the popes, how was it that some popes disagreed with other popes?"[8] He wants to have it both ways; he gets more mileage out of his argument if the reader thinks infallibility and impeccability are identical, but he makes allowances for some readers knowing the difference.

After recounting the admittedly bizarre case of Pope Formosus, whose corpse was disinterred and placed in the dock during a posthumous trial, Woodrow claims "such sharp disagreement between popes certainly argues against the ideal of papal infallibility".[9] This evinces a basic confusion, since the issue must always be phrased this way: Have two popes disagreed when officially teaching on faith or morals? The Formosus case had nothing to do with any such teaching or any such disagreement.

Formosus had been the bishop of Porto, and he was elected Pope at a time when it was considered improper for a bishop to transfer from one see to another. This was merely a disciplinary rule and did not invalidate his election. His second successor, Stephen VII, prompted by the emperor, Lambert, found it politically expedient to declare that Formosus had become Pope improperly and that his ordinations were consequently invalid. Thus the trial. Formosus was found "guilty", and his ordinations were declared null. So, there certainly was a disagreement (if that is the proper word) between Formosus, by then dead, and Stephen, but the posthumous trial, no matter how repugnant, had nothing to do with a definition regarding faith or morals, so the question of papal infallibility simply does not apply.

Woodrow continues by pointing out that "Pope Sixtus V had a version of the Bible prepared which he declared to be authentic. Two years later Pope Clement VIII declared that it was full of errors and ordered another to be made!"[10] And he says, "When we consider the hundreds of times and ways that popes have contra-

---

[8] Woodrow, *Babylon,* 100.
[9] Woodrow, *Babylon,* 101.
[10] Woodrow, *Babylon,* 102.

dicted each other over the centuries, we can understand how the idea of papal infallibility is difficult for many people to accept. While it is true that most papal statements are not made within the narrow confines of the 1870 *ex cathedra* definition, yet if popes have erred in so many other ways, how can we believe they are guaranteed a divine infallibility for a few moments if and when they should indeed decide to speak *ex cathedra*?"[11]

It is unsurprising that Woodrow ends his chapter on papal infallibility with an exercise in numerology, noting that "as early as 1612 it was pointed out, as Andreas Helwig did in his book *Roman Antichrist,* that the title 'Vicar of Christ' has a numerical value of 666." When written as "Vicar of the Son of God", *Vicarius Filii Dei,* the letters sum to 666, if the Roman values are used. "The number reminds us, of course, of Revelation 13:18, 'Let him that hath understanding count the number of the beast: for it is the number of a man; and his number is six hundred threescore and six.' "

There are several things wrong with this argument. *Vicarius Filii Dei* never has been used as a title by any Pope. The Pope's full title is Bishop of Rome, Vicar of Jesus Christ [or, more simply, Vicar of Christ—*Vicarius Christi*], Successor of the Prince of the Apostles, Supreme Pontiff of the Universal Church, Patriarch of the West, Primate of Italy, Archbishop and Metropolitan of the Roman Province, and Sovereign of the City of the Vatican.

Latin, like most other ancient languages, used letters to represent numbers. The letters of *Vicarius Filii Dei* do indeed add up to 666. The letters of *Vicarius Christi* do not. Anti-Catholic pundits, unable to use *Vicarius Christi*—the Pope's real title—to their advantage, turn to a similar-sounding title and claim—voila!—that the Pope is the beast.[12]

In doing this, these opponents of Catholicism overlook an important fact. The last book of the Bible was written in Greek, not Latin. We should expect "the number of the beast" to be under

---

[11] Woodrow, *Babylon,* 102–3.

[12] Martin Luther's name, when written in Latin, also tallies 666, as do hundreds of other names.

stood through Greek numerology, not Latin. The name or title that totals 666 should be based on Greek. But there *is* a way that Latin figures in, although it does not help the anti-Catholics' argument.

By the end of the second century there were in circulation manuscripts that gave "the number of the beast" as 616 instead of 666. Why this discrepancy? Apparently there was confusion on the part of one or more copyists, and that confusion gives credence to the most widely accepted theory about the identity of the beast, that the beast was Nero Caesar.

The Greek form of his name in Hebrew letters is *nrwn qsr*. Each letter stands for a number (n = 50, r = 200, w = 6, q = 100, s = 60). Adding up the letters (50 + 200 + 6 + 50 + 100 + 60 + 200) yields 666. The Latin form of his name, when given in Hebrew letters, is slightly different: *nrw qsr*. Its letters total 616, the alternative reading of the manuscripts. It may have been natural for copyists whose mother tongue was Latin, knowing the reference was to Nero, to presume 666 was an error and that 616 was the true number. They may have "corrected" what they perceived to be an error. So we see the earliest manuscripts giving 666 and some later manuscripts—copied when Latin had become the lingua franca of the Mediterranean—giving 616.

Not only does Nero's name work out arithmetically, and not only does identifying him as the beast account for the manuscript evidence, but he fits the context of Revelation. He was the first emperor to persecute Christians, and he would have been the perfect choice for the beast. So vigorous were his persecutions, in fact, that it was rumored Nero came to life again in one of his successors, Domitian, who was also a persecutor. Domitian was known as *Nero redivivus*.

In any event, whatever the real identity of the beast, Ralph Woodrow gives no good reason for tying the number 666 to the papacy. The best he can do is to use a misrepresentation as a proof. Like other anti-Catholics, he so desperately wants the beast to be identified with the papacy that he does not bother to stick with the facts.

But Woodrow and his arguments are too easy to dismiss. The best attack by a fundamentalist is given, as usual, by Loraine Boettner in his *Roman Catholicism*. As mentioned in a previous chapter, he begins with a error large even by his standard. "Infallibility is not claimed for every statement made by the pope," he says, "but only for those made when he is speaking *ex cathedra,* that is, seated in his papal chair, the chair of St. Peter, and speaking in his official capacity as head of the church."[13] At this point an asterisk leads one to a footnote that states that the chair venerated as Peter's comes from the ninth century and is of French origin. "It is not an antique of the first century", the point being, apparently, that even if papal infallibility were theoretically possible, it is not possible in practice since today's Popes are unable to sit in Peter's actual chair.

Chair or no chair, Popes keep publishing their decisions, and Boettner has to deal with that fact. "It is interesting to notice that the popes, in issuing their decrees or pronouncements, do not label them *ex cathedra* or not *ex cathedra*. We may be sure that if this power were a reality they would not hesitate so to label them, that in fact they would find it very advantageous to do so. Surely it would be of inestimable value to know which deliverances are *ex cathedra* and which are not, which are infallible and authoritative and which are only private observations and therefore as fallible as those of anyone else."[14] Boettner's appreciation of human nature is modest. To insert in all noninfallible pronouncements a note that "this is *not ex cathedra*" would be to invite everyone to commit Boettner's error, which is to think the Pope's noninfallible teachings are "therefore as fallible as those of anyone else". Precisely because the Pope "does his homework", and because of the way he prepares his statements, and because he is who he is, they are far less likely to be fallible—that is, wrong—than those given by others. The Pope speaks not off the top of his head, but from a tradition of right teaching.

---

[13] Boettner, *Catholicism*, 235.
[14] Boettner, *Catholicism*, 236.

The author of *Roman Catholicism* is unable to resist quoting a famous Catholic historian: "How true the words of England's Lord Acton, himself a Roman Catholic, who after visiting Rome and seeing at firsthand the workings of the papacy wrote: 'All power corrupts, and absolute power corrupts absolutely.' "[15] First of all, Boettner gives the standard misquotation. Acton actually said, "Power *tends to* corrupt, and absolute power corrupts absolutely." He wrote this in a letter to Anglican Bishop Mandell Creighton on April 5, 1887, long after Vatican I. Second, Boettner fantasizes that Acton had the same kind of shock Martin Luther supposedly had when the monk first visited Rome, but Acton was long familiar with the place. Besides, his aphorism was in reference not just to Popes, but to kings and all men in positions of authority. To imply he was limiting his comment to the papacy, to suggest he was indicating rejection of papal infallibility, is to give a false impression of what he was saying.

Nevertheless, Boettner is far more accurate than Woodrow: "The doctrine of papal infallibility does not mean that the pope is infallible as a man. It does not relate to his personal habits. It does not mean that he is sinless. Nor does it mean that he is inspired as were the apostles so that he can write Scripture." So far he is correct. But he immediately goes wrong, though not as egregiously as others: "It means rather that in his official capacity as teacher of the church he has the guidance of the Holy Spirit so that he can interpret and state clearly and positively doctrines which allegedly have been a part of the heritage of the church from the beginning."[16] Boettner does not quite grasp what infallibility covers. He does not understand that it is a negative protection and that a Pope too lazy to do his homework would not be able to make an infallible decision on anything. The charism of infallibility does not help a Pope know what is true, nor does it "inspire" him to teach what is true.

Boettner also errs, somewhat more subtly, in saying that "for centuries before the doctrine of papal infallibility was adopted

---

[15] Boettner, *Catholicism,* 238.
[16] Boettner, *Catholicism,* 236.

there was much difference of opinion as to where that infallibility lay. . . . But in 1870 it was declared to reside in the pope alone, and all good Catholics are now compelled to accept that view."[17] Vatican I did not say infallibility resides in the Pope alone, for the very good reason that it resides also in the bishops teaching in union with the Pope.

As a biblical example of the fallibility of Popes, Boettner gives this: "That Peter, the alleged first pope, was not infallible as a teacher of faith and morals is evident from his conduct at Antioch when he refused to eat with Gentile Christians lest he offend certain Jews from Palestine (Gal. 2:11–16). Instead, he would have fastened the ritual requirements of Judaism on the new Christian church. This should have been no problem at all for him if he had the special guidance of the Holy Spirit claimed by the Church of Rome for the pope."[18] Here Boettner imagines infallibility to be something like inspiration, and, like other fundamentalist writers, he never seems to apply to particular cases the standards of Vatican I. It may be because he, like his followers, confuses doctrine and morals with discipline and customs. Peter's conduct at Antioch was not an attempt by him to teach formally on doctrine or morals.

Boettner caps his attack with a commentary on John Henry Newman. "It is well known that Cardinal Newman was strongly opposed to the promulgation of the doctrine of infallibility." That much is true, but with the next sentence Boettner goes awry. "But having left the Church of England in order to join the Roman Church and having given it such fulsome praise, he was powerless to prevent the change and did not have the courage to come back out of it. . . . It was a bitter pill for Newman to swallow, but he submitted and acknowledged papal infallibility."[19] There are two things wrong with this analysis (or psychoanalysis). First, the implication that doctrine was being changed. It was

[17] Boettner, *Catholicism*, 241.

[18] Boettner, *Catholicism*, 239.

[19] Boettner, *Catholicism*, 243.

not; it was just being made explicit. This point one can let slide. The libel of Newman is another thing altogether. Boettner apparently never read, or if he read he quickly forgot, the seventh part of Newman's *Apologia Pro Vita Sua,* the part titled "General Answer to Mr. Kingsley". It is here that Newman examined infallibility. He wrote in 1864—six years before the definition given at Vatican I—about a problem that he wrestled with before his conversion in 1845.

Boettner will have us think Newman had no suspicion that papal infallibility might be a fact and, when it appeared that it would be proclaimed, he found that he had converted for the worse. Even if this were a true account of Newman's thinking, which it is not, why did Newman not leave the Catholic Church if he thought papal infallibility nonexistent? After all, in 1845 he left the secure and socially acceptable established church for what in England was the inconsequential and outcast Roman Catholic Church. Reconverting would have been easy by comparison, particularly if he could refer to some papal usurpation. Why didn't he? Because he not only accepted papal infallibility, he believed in it—and had since before he had become a Catholic. He opposed not the content of the definition given at Vatican I, but the wisdom of promulgating the definition at that time; he thought the promulgation was inopportune, not inaccurate.

Like other anti-Catholic writers, Boettner cites a number of "errors of the popes". With respect to what he identifies as doctrinal matters, he lists a dozen instances, most of which have nothing to do with the question at hand. For instance: "Zozimus (417–418) pronounced Pelagius an orthodox teacher, but later reversed his position at the insistence of Augustine."[20] This demonstrates nothing more than that Augustine provided Zozimus with additional information on Pelagius, so the Pope had a more complete appreciation of the man's doctrines. Besides, declaring a particular individual orthodox or unorthodox is simply not an attempted exercise of infallibility. Continuing, Boettner asks, "How is the

[20] Boettner, *Catholicism,* 248.

decree of Clement XIV (July 21, 1773) suppressing the Jesuits to be harmonized with the contrary decree of Pius VII (August 7, 1814) restoring them?"[21] Again, neither decree had anything to do with teaching faith or morals; each was purely a disciplinary matter.

Boettner's argument is really reduced to three cases, those of Popes Liberius, Vigilius, and Honorius, the three cases to which all opponents of papal infallibility repair because they are the only cases that do not collapse as soon as they are mentioned. None of the instances can be shoehorned into the 1870 definition.

Boettner claims "Liberius, in 358, subscribed to a heretical Arian creed in order to gain the bishopric of Rome under the heretical emperor Constantius."[22] If Liberius did this—which, apparently, he did not—it would prove nothing, since his subscribing to a heresy *before* becoming Pope could have nothing to do with an exercise of papal infallibility. Infallibility is not retroactive. Election to the papacy does not validate a man's earlier teachings.

Most commentators who bring up Liberius, it must be said, make a charge different from Boettner's. They say Liberius subscribed to a heretical formula while he was Pope. In fact what he put his signature to was an ambiguous document that could be understood in either an orthodox or a heretical manner. When he did this he was not a free agent, since he had been forced into exile by the emperor. Even if the document had been strictly heretical, admitting of no orthodox interpretation, and even if Liberius signed it voluntarily, the issue of infallibility still would not have arisen since he signed only as a private theologian and was not signing something that purported to be a teaching that was to be held by all Christians. The requirements for an infallible papal teaching simply were not met.

Vigilius, Boettner says, "refused to condemn certain heretical teachers of the time of the Monophysite controversy and boycotted the fifth Ecumenical Council which met at Constantinople

---

[21] Boettner, *Catholicism*, 250.
[22] Boettner, *Catholicism*, 248.

in 553. When the Council proceeded without him and threatened to excommunicate and anathematize him, he submitted to its opinions, confessing that he had been a tool of Satan."[23] This misses the sense of what really happened. Emperior Justinian published a decree condemning the writings of three men long dead. Their writings were known as the Three Chapters, and the heresy to which they subscribed was Nestorianism, which held that in Christ there are two persons joined together, God the Son and the man Jesus. (The orthodox doctrine is that there is only one Person in Christ, the divine, but two natures.) Justinian's decree was designed to please the Monophysites. Monophysitism was a heresy that arose as a reaction to Nestorianism; it held that in Christ there is only one nature, the divine. The decree was signed by the Eastern patriarchs, but other bishops objected, saying the decree undermined the orthodox position by seeming to favor Monophysitism by default. At first Vigilius refused to condemn the Three Chapters, but in 548 he did, at the same time affirming the orthodox position. Later he retracted his condemnation. He continued to vacillate, and the ecumenical council was called. The council condemned the Three Chapters, and finally Vigilius gave in, joining in the condemnation. Throughout all this, he supported the orthodox position. The controversy concerned the expediency of condemning certain writings and of judging three men who had long since been judged by God. Vigilius intended to condemn only what was condemnable in the Three Chapters, not what was orthodox. The drawn-out incident is certainly confusing, but it gives no support to the anti-infallibility position since Vigilius never asserted that a heretical belief was to be believed as true.

Then comes the last of the three standard cases. According to an authority Boettner cites, "The greatest scandal of this nature is pope Honorius. He specifically taught the Monothelite heresy in two letters to the patriarch of Constantinople."[24] (Monothelitism

---

[23] Boettner, *Catholicism*, 248.
[24] Boettner, *Catholicism*, 249.

arose as a reaction to Monophysitism. It held that in Christ there is only one will, the divine. The orthodox position is that in him there are two wills, the divine and the human, but the two wills are in perfect harmony.)

Actually, Honorius elected to teach nothing at all. Ronald Knox, in a letter to Arnold Lunn reprinted in their book *Difficulties,* put the matter like this: "And Honorius, so far from pronouncing an infallible opinion in the Monothelite controversy, was 'quite extraordinarily not' (as Gore used to say) pronouncing a decision at all. To the best of his human wisdom, he thought the controversy ought to be left unsettled, for the greater peace of the Church. In fact, he was an inopportunist. We, wise after the event, say that he was wrong. But nobody, I think, has ever claimed that the Pope is infallible in *not* defining a doctrine."[25]

Summing up, Knox asked Lunn, "Has it ever occurred to you how few are the alleged 'failures of infallibility'? I mean, if somebody propounded in your presence the thesis that all the kings of England have been impeccable, you would not find yourself murmuring, 'Oh, well, people said rather unpleasant things about Jane Shore . . . and the best historians seem to think that Charles II spent too much of his time with Nell Gwynn.' Here have these Popes been, fulminating anathema after anathema for centuries—certain in all human probability to contradict themselves or one another over again. Instead of which you get this measly crop of two or three alleged failures!"[26] He acknowledged that this does not prove infallibility, but it does make the anti-infallibility argument look weak.

After examining alleged failures relating to definitions of faith, Boettner looks at "infallibility in the moral sphere" and immediately stumbles. He forgets what he quoted from Vatican I a few pages earlier and considers cases that speak not against infallibility, but against impeccability. He cites a few well-worn instances

[25] Ronald Knox and Arnold Lunn, *Difficulties* (London: Eyre & Spottiswoode, 1952), 126–27.
[26] Knox, *Difficulties,* 127.

of papal immorality, naming Popes John XI, John XII, and Alexander VI, but he mentions not one incorrect papal ruling on a question of morals. If a Pope proclaims *ex cathedra* that lying is a sin and then immediately tells a lie, infallibility is not disproved, although that Pope's impeccability certainly is. For infallibility to be disproved, Boettner would have to show an *ex cathedra* definition stating that lying is moral. He offers no such example, or anything parallel, because none exists.

Fundamentalists' rejection of papal infallibility stems from their view of the Church. They do not think Christ established a visible Church, which means they do not believe in a hierarchy of bishops headed by the Pope. This is no place to give an elaborate demonstration of the establishment of a visible Church. It is enough to note that the New Testament shows the apostles setting up, after their Master's instructions, a visible organization, and every Christian writer in the early centuries—in fact, nearly all Christians until the Reformation—took it for granted that Christ set up an ongoing organization.

If he did, he must have provided for its continuation; for its easy identification (that is, it had to be visible so it could be found); and, since he would be gone from Earth, for some method by which it could preserve intact all his teachings. All this was effected through the apostolic succession of bishops, and the preservation of the Christian message, in its fullness, was guaranteed through the gift of infallibility—of the Church as a whole, but mainly as enjoyed by the temporal head of the Church, the Pope.

The Holy Spirit prevents a Pope from officially teaching error, and this charism follows, necessarily, from the existence of the Church itself. If the Church is to do what Christ said it would—and not do what he said it would not do, such as have the gates of hell prevail against it—then it must be able to teach infallibly. It must prove itself to be a perfectly steady guide in matters pertaining to salvation. There is no guarantee that any particular Pope will not let slip by chances to teach the truth, or that he will be sinless, or that mere disciplinary decisions will be intelligently made. It would be convenient if he were omniscient or impeccable, but his not being so will not subvert the Church. But he must be able to teach rightly, for that is the main function of the Church. For men to be saved, they must know what is to be believed. They must have a perfectly steady rock to build on when it comes to official teaching, and that is why papal infallibility exists.

Chapter 19

The Eucharist

Fundamentalist attacks on the Church always come around, as they must, to the Eucharist. Keith Green devoted the first of his *Catholic Chronicles* to what he acknowledged to be the core devotional doctrine of Catholics, and he was smart to do so. Bart Brewer, Donald F. Maconaghie, Jimmy Swaggart—they all zero in on the Eucharist, and in doing so they demonstrate that fundamentalists, contrary to popular belief, are not always literalists. This is shown in their interpretation of the key scriptural passage, the sixth chapter of John's Gospel, in which Christ speaks about the sacrament that will be instituted at the Last Supper.

The narrative opens on the eastern shore of the Sea of Galilee with the feeding of the five thousand, the only miracle recorded by all four evangelists. After the people were fed, Jesus withdrew to the hillside to be alone. Night fell, and the disciples went down to the lake without him and, embarking in the only boat available, sailed for Capharnaum, which was on the western shore. Jesus caught up with them some time later by walking on the water. The multitude, thinking he still must be with them, stayed overnight where the miracle had been performed. The next morning they discovered Jesus was nowhere to be found and, when other boats put in near them, they embarked for Capharnaum, where they found Jesus and asked him when (but not how) he had made his way there, apparently thinking he had set off on foot before dawn for the long walk around the lake. He did not answer directly, but told them to "work to earn food which affords, continually, eternal life" (Jn 6:27). He had provided them their fill of natural bread; now he began to speak of supernatural bread.

With verse 30 begins a colloquy that took place in the synagogue at Capharnaum. The Jews asked him what sign he could perform, and, as a challenge, they noted that "our fathers had manna to eat in the desert" (Jn 6:31). Could Jesus top that? He told them the real bread from heaven comes from the Father. "Give us this bread", they insisted. "But Jesus told them, It is I who am the bread of life" (Jn 6:34–35). He was getting more explicit, and the Jews started to complain, but still understood him to be speaking metaphorically. Jesus repeated what he said before, then summarized: "I myself am the bread that has come down from heaven. If anyone eats of this bread, he shall live forever. And now, what is this bread that I am to give? It is my flesh, given for the life of the world" (Jn 6:51–52). Then the Jews asked, incredulously, "How can this man give us his flesh to eat?" (Jn 6:53).

Hugh Pope, in commenting on this chapter, remarked that at last "they had understood Him literally and were stupefied; but because they had understood Him correctly, He repeats His words with extraordinary emphasis, so much so that only now does He introduce the statement about drinking His blood":[1] "You can have no life in yourselves, unless you eat the flesh of the Son of Man, and drink his blood. The man who eats my flesh and drinks my blood enjoys eternal life, and I will raise him up on the last day. My flesh is real food, my blood is real drink. He who eats my flesh, and drinks my blood, lives continually in me, and I in him" (Jn 6:54–57).

There was no attempt to soften what was said, no attempt to correct "misunderstandings", for there were none. His listeners understood him quite well. No one any longer thought he was speaking metaphorically. If they had, why no correction? On other occasions, whenever there was confusion, Christ explained what he meant. Here, where any misunderstanding would be cat-

[1] Hugh Pope, *The Layman's New Testament* (London: Sheed and Ward, 1934), 333.

astrophic, there was no effort to correct. Instead, he repeated what he had said.

"There were many of his disciples who said, when they heard it, This is strange talk, who can be expected to listen to it?" (Jn 6:61). These were his *disciples,* people who already were used to his remarkable ways. He warned them not to think carnally, but spiritually: "Only the spirit gives life; the flesh is of no avail; and the words I have been speaking to you are spirit, and life" (Jn 6:64). But he knew some did not believe, including the one who was to betray him. (It is here, in the rejection of the Eucharist, that Judas fell away.) "After this, many of his disciples went back to their own ways, and walked no more in his company" (Jn 6:67).

This is the only record we have of any of Christ's followers forsaking him for doctrinal reasons. If they merely had misunderstood him, if they foolishly had taken a metaphor in a literal sense, why did he not call them back and straighten things out? Both the Jews, who were suspicious of him, and his disciples, who had accepted everything up to this point, would have remained had he told them he meant no more than a symbol.

But he did not correct these first protesters, these proto-Protestants. Twelve times he said he was the bread that came down from heaven; four times he said they would have "to eat my flesh and drink my blood". John 6 was an extended promise of what would be instituted at the Last Supper—and it was a promise that could not be more explicit. Or so it would seem to a Catholic. But what do fundamentalists say?

Anti-Catholic writers identify two approaches to use when "disproving" the Real Presence. Jimmy Swaggart summarized them this way: "In all honesty we must repudiate this dogma on two counts: (1) It is opposed to Scripture. (2) It is contradicted by the evidence of the senses."[2]

Fundamentalists concentrate on the first count, the argument from "the evidence of the senses" being weak since even a rudi-

---

[2] Jimmy Swaggart, "The Mass—The Holy Eucharist", *The Evangelist,* October 1985, 35.

mentary understanding of transubstantiation makes one realize that the dogma, by definition, cannot be refuted through an appeal to sensory perception since there is not *supposed* to be any perceptible change to the eucharistic elements. Besides, an argument based on the senses must be an argument based on science or philosophy, and fundamentalists prefer to argue from the Bible.

In arguing from Scripture, every fundamentalist says Christ was speaking metaphorically in John 6 and during the Last Supper. Bart Brewer, head of Mission to Catholics International, says that "if I were to show someone a photograph of my son and say, 'This is my son', they [*sic*] would not take these words literally. The Scripture is written with such common language that it is obvious to any observant reader that the Lord's Supper was intended primarily as a memorial and in no sense a literal sacrifice. In taking Biblical statements literally, we must be sure that doing so is consistent with the context and not in contradiction to other clear teaching." Brewer also argues that "when Jesus said 'this is my body' or 'blood', he did not change the substance, but was explaining that he is the one 'represented' by the passover bread and wine. Jesus did not say *touto gignetai,* this has become or is turned into, but *touto esti,* which can only mean this represents or stands for."[3] Brewer's Greek is deficient here. *Esti* is nothing else than the verb "is". Its usual meaning is the literal, although it can be used figuratively, just as in English. If this crucial term is supposed to be read as "represents", why was it not clearly put so in the Greek?

Brewer continues: "It is perfectly clear in the Gospels that Christ spoke in figurative terms, referring to Himself as 'the door', 'the vine', 'the light', 'the root', 'the rock', 'the bright and morning star', et cetera."[4] In this Brewer is seconded by Donald F. Maconaghie of the Conversion Center: "It is clear that our Lord used a sign or figure which the Council of Trent would have

[3] From his tracts *The Roman Catholic Sacrifice of the Mass* and *The Mystery of the Eucharist.*
[4] Brewer, *Sacrifice* and *Mystery.*

us cursed for believing when He said, 'Except ye eat My flesh and drink My blood ye have no life in you' John 6:53. Was our Lord transubstantiated into a literal door? He said, 'I am the door' John 10:9. Or into a vine? He said, 'I am the true vine' John 15:1. Notice we also read: 'The ten horns are ten kings' Daniel 7:24. 'These great beasts which are four, are four kings' Daniel 7:17. 'The seven kine are seven years' Genesis 41:26."[5]

Leslie Rumble and Charles M. Carty answered this common charge years ago: "There is no logical parallel between the words 'This is My body' and 'I am the vine' or 'I am the door.' For the images of the vine and door can have, of their very nature, a symbolical sense. Christ is like a vine because all the sap of my spiritual life comes from Him. He is like a door since I go to heaven through Him. But a piece of bread is in no way like His flesh. Of its very nature it cannot symbolize the actual body of Christ. And he excludes that Himself by saying, 'The bread that I will give is My flesh for the life of the world, and My flesh is meat indeed.' That is, it is to be actually eaten, not merely commemorated in some symbolical way."[6]

Not surprisingly, Swaggart agrees with Maconaghie and Brewer. He writes, "*This is my body . . . this is my blood,* are accepted literally in Catholic dogma. On the same basis we should accept without thinking that Jesus gives us literal living waters which will produce eternal life (John 4:14), or that Jesus is truly a door (John 10:7–9), that He is a lamb (John 1:29), or that He is a growing vine (John 15:5). If the Catholic hierarchy is to be consistent, they [sic] *should* foster adoration of doors, vines, and lambs. Certainly, these figures of speech are descriptive and colorful, but they are transparently figurative, just as are the terms 'my body,' and 'my blood'. The New Testament Church and the Early Church understood and accepted this just as it was offered, *as a figure of speech.*"[7]

---

[5] From his tract *Transubstantiation.*

[6] Rumble and Carty, *Replies,* 186.

[7] Swaggart, "Mass", 38.

Is that so? Let us see what the Early Church thought.

Writing to the Smyrnaeans around 110 and referring to "those who hold heterodox opinions", Ignatius of Antioch said, "They abstain from the Eucharist and from prayer, because they do not confess that the Eucharist is the flesh of our Savior Jesus Christ, flesh which suffered for our sins and which the Father, in his goodness, raised up again."[8]

Forty years later, Justin Martyr wrote, "We call this food Eucharist, and no one else is permitted to partake of it, except one who believes our teaching to be true and who has been washed in the washing which is for the remission of sins and for regeneration and is thereby living as Christ has enjoined. For not as common bread nor common drink do we receive these; but since Jesus Christ our Savior was made incarnate by the word of God and had both flesh and blood for our salvation, so too, as we have been taught, the food which has been made into the Eucharist by the Eucharistic prayer set down by him, and by the change of which our blood and flesh is nourished, is both the flesh and the blood of that incarnated Jesus."[9]

Irenaeus of Lyons, in his masterwork, *Against Heresies,* written toward the close of the second century, said that Christ "has declared the cup, a part of creation, to be his own Blood, from which he causes our blood to flow; and the bread, a part of creation, he has established as his own Body, from which he gives increase to our bodies". He asks, "If the Lord were from other than the Father, how could he rightly take bread, which is of the same creation as our own, and confess it to be his Body and affirm that the mixture in the cup is his Blood?"[10]

Origen, writing about 244, demonstrated that reverence is given to the smallest particle from the host. "I wish to admonish you with examples from your religion. You are accustomed to take part in the divine mysteries, so you know how, when you

---

[8] Ignatius, *Epistula ad Smyrnaeos* 6, 2.
[9] Justin Martyr, *Apologia prima pro Christianis* 65.
[10] Irenaeus, *Adversus haereses* 5, 2, 2; 4, 33, 7.

have received the Body of the Lord, you reverently exercise every care lest a particle of it fall and lest anything of the consecrated gift perish. You account yourselves guilty, and rightly do you so believe, if any of it be lost through negligence."[11]

Athanasius, bishop of Alexandria, said this in his *Sermon to the Newly Baptized*, delivered in 373: "You shall see the Levites bringing loaves and a cup of wine and placing them on a table. So long as the prayers of supplication and entreaties have not been made, there is only bread and wine. But after the great and wonderful prayers have been completed, then the bread is become the Body, and the wine the Blood, of our Lord Jesus Christ."[12]

As a final example, taken from dozens that could have been used, Cyril of Jerusalem, in his *Catechetical Lectures,* presented in the middle of the fourth century, told his listeners: "Do not, therefore, regard the Bread and Wine as simply that; for they are, according to the Master's declaration, the Body and Blood of Christ. Even though the senses suggest to you the other, let faith make you firm. Do not judge in this matter by taste, but be fully assured by faith, not doubting that you have been deemed worthy of the Body and Blood of Christ."[13]

Whatever else might be said, it is certain that the early Church took John 6 and the accounts of the Last Supper literally. There is no record in the early centuries of any Christian doubting the Catholic interpretation. There exists no document in which the literal interpretation is opposed and only the metaphorical accepted. Brewer persists by saying, "The doctrine of transubstantiation does not date back to the Last Supper as is supposed. . . . The idea of a corporal presence was vaguely held by some, such as Ambrose, but it was not until 831 A.D. that Paschasius Radbertus, a Benedictine monk, published a treatise openly advocating the doctrine of transubstantiation. Even then, for almost another four hundred years, theological war was waged over this teaching by

---

[11] Origen, *In Exodum homiliae* 13, 3.

[12] Athanasius, *Sermo ad nuper baptizatos.*

[13] Cyril of Jerusalem, *Catecheses* 22, 6.

bishops and people alike until at the Fourth Lateran Council in 1215 A.D., it was officially defined and canonized as a dogma."[14]

This is misleading. First of all, the Real Presence was not "vaguely" held by Ambrose. In his treatise *The Sacraments,* composed about 390, he wrote, "You may perhaps say: 'My bread is ordinary.' But that bread is bread before the words of the sacraments; where the consecration has entered in, the bread becomes the flesh of Christ. And let us add this: How can what is bread be the Body of Christ? By the consecration. The consecration takes place by certain words, but whose words? Those of the Lord Jesus. . . . Therefore it is the word of Christ that confects the sacrament."[15] Nothing vague about that.

And what about Paschasius Radbertus? Was he the first to believe in transubstantiation? Radbertus was abbot of Old Corbie Monastery near Amiens. In 831 he composed a treatise that contained this ambiguous expression: "This is precisely the same flesh that was born of Mary, suffered on the Cross, and rose from the tomb."[16] He narrated some eucharistic miracles that gave the impression that Christ must be understood to be sensibly present in the sacrament, and another monk at his abbey, Ratramus, wrote a countertreatise noting that one must distinguish between the appearance of Christ in the Eucharist and the appearance of his body received from Mary, but *he* used language that might suggest Christ is only symbolically present in the Eucharist. Both Radbertus and Ratramus were orthodox; the trouble was that neither was precise in wording.

"The debate between these principals soon became a theological free-for-all", said historian Newman Eberhardt.[17] Others entered the fray, sometimes proposing rectifying language that was even more confusing than what Radbertus and Ratramus wrote.

---

[14] In the tract *The Mystery of the Eucharist.*

[15] Ambrose, *De sacramentis libri sex* 4, 4, 14.

[16] Paschasius Radbertus, *De corpore et sanguine Domini.*

[17] Newman Eberhardt, *A Summary of Catholic History* (St. Louis: Herder, 1961), 1:464.

The dispute ended by 860, with no one denying the Real Presence. What should be noted is that, despite various attempts to phrase the doctrine of the Real Presence accurately, there was no cry from anyone that this was a new doctrine. It was taken as a given. Those who inadvertently implied the Presence might be symbolic only were considered the innovators, not those who presumed it was Real.

In the theological world there was no further controversy on the issue until Berengarius of Tours, who died in 1088. He had studied the dispute that began with Radbertus and Ratramus and concluded that Christ was indeed present only symbolically. He repeatedly signed recantations and then, safe at home, reiterated his original position. This theological seesaw went on for decades, until he finally subscribed to an unambiguous formula. Church historians say he apparently died reconciled.[18] Whether or not he did, he is the first Christian, so far as we can tell from the records, who denied the Real Presence. Paschasius Radbertus and Berengarius of Tours are remembered to history only because the one seemed to doubt the Real Presence and the other actually did. What this tells us is that the accepted belief was the opposite of what they were understood to hold.

Back to the words of the text. Keith Green identified in his *Catholic Chronicles* two biblical passages as the keys to the Catholic position. The first is John 6:55–56: "The man who eats my flesh and drinks my blood enjoys eternal life, and I will raise him up on the last day. My flesh is real food, my blood is real drink." Green said that "with just a little study of the whole passage (verses 27–71), it is clear that Jesus was not talking about physical, but spiritual food and drink." He argued that since Jesus says "he who comes to me will never be hungry" (Jn 6:35), "*to come to Him is to 'eat'!*" Similarly, since Jesus tells us in the same verse that "he who has faith in me will never know thirst", it follows that "*to believe on Him is to 'drink'!*"[19]

---

[18] Eberhardt, *Summary*, I: 610.
[19] From his tract *The Holy Eucharist: Eating the Flesh of Deity*.

Bart Brewer concurs. "These verses actually disprove the dogma of transubstantiation. The ones who took Jesus' words literally were offended. That is why He clarified their misunderstanding by teaching them that what he said was to be understood spiritually (see verse 63). . . . Looking back to verse 47, it is obvious that 'eating' is equivalent to 'believing.' It is certain that what is meant by eating this flesh and drinking this blood is neither more nor less than 'believing' in Christ."[20] In short, the command to eat Christ's flesh and drink his blood must be taken metaphorically.

But there is a problem with that. As John A. O'Brien put it, "the phrase 'to eat the flesh and drink the blood', when used figuratively among the Jews, as among the Arabs of today, meant to inflict upon a person some serious injury, especially by calumny or by false accusation. To interpret the phrase figuratively then would be to make our Lord promise life everlasting to the culprit for slandering and hating Him, which would reduce the whole passage to utter nonsense."[21] Christ would be saying, "He that reviles me has eternal life."

The scriptural argument is capped, by all fundamentalist writers, with an appeal to John 6:64: "Only the spirit gives life; the flesh is of no avail; and the words I have been speaking to you are spirit, and life." This is a verse to which fundamentalists always return, and it was, by the way, the first verse that Jimmy Swaggart threw at Catholic writer Barbara Nauer when they discussed the interpretation of this chapter. She was stunned by his use of the line, for the very good reason that in the context of the narration it can be seen not to relate to the question they were examining, which was: Is the Real Presence real? Swaggart thought this verse more than compensated for the apparent (and literal) meaning of the earlier part of John 6. He interpreted Nauer's pause as a silent acknowledgement of defeat, when in fact she was trying to un-

---

[20] *Challenger*, October/November 1984.
[21] O'Brien, *Faith*, 215.

derstand what this non sequitur had to do with the issue at hand.[22] Did Swaggart think that Christ, who had just commanded his disciples to eat his flesh, now said their doing so would be pointless? Is that what "the flesh is of no avail" means? "Eat my flesh, but you'll find it's a waste of time"—is that how he was to be understood? And were the disciples to understand the line "the words I have been speaking to you are spirit, and life" as nothing but a circumlocution, and a fairly clumsy one at that, for "symbolic"? No one can come up with interpretations like these unless he first holds to the fundamentalist position and thinks it necessary to find some rationale, no matter how tortuous, for discarding the Catholic interpretation.

In John 6:64 the word "flesh" is not used in the same sense as in John 6:53–59. It is being used more in the Pauline sense, in which it is contrasted with "spirit". The contrast is between unaided nature and nature elevated by grace. Compare John 3:6: "What is born by natural birth is a thing of nature, what is born by spiritual birth is a thing of spirit." Christ detects in some of his listeners an unsupernatural attitude that looks for earthly rewards and that turns away from his teaching on the Eucharist. When he says "the flesh is of no avail", he does not mean "my flesh"—that would contradict his immediately prior remarks. He means instead carnal understanding, as distinguished from spiritual.

Return to Keith Green. He examined John 6:55–56, the first of the passages he identified as key, and then turned to the second, Matthew 26:26, 28: "This is my body . . . this is my blood." He noted that

Catholics base their whole religious system on their interpretation of these two verses. They adamantly teach that right here, Jesus is pronouncing the first priestly blessing that mysteriously changes the bread and wine into his body and blood. The absolute folly of such a conclusion is proved by this one observation: *He was literally still there* before, during, and after they had partaken of the bread and cup! He had not changed into some liquid and bread—His flesh

---

[22] Personal correspondence to the author from Barbara Nauer.

was still on His bones, and His blood was still in His veins. He had not vanished away to reappear in the form of a piece of bread or a cup of wine![23]

So here we have the diabolically clever Catholic Church telling us the transformation was real, yet Jesus was still at the table. Catholic exegetes through the centuries missed the fact that he was still present, that he did not disappear in a puff of smoke and end up on the platter and in the cup. How stupid Catholics have been, to miss the obvious! (Perhaps this just shows that *none* of them ever read beyond John 6:28; if any Catholic had, he could have blown the whistle, and the Church would not have made such a fool of itself.) This is the loose thinking fundamentalists end up with if they conclude, as they do, that the answer to the Catholic position is elementary because the Catholic position is so clearly erroneous.

The reply to Green is simple: Christ was present at the Last Supper in two ways. He was present at the table in a natural way, as were the apostles, and he was present in the eucharistic elements in a sacramental way, which is precisely the way he is present in them today, in Catholic churches throughout the world. That Christ can be present in two ways simultaneously is indeed a mystery (a mystery being a religious truth that cannot be comprehended fully by reason), but it is not an impossibility. Something does not become impossible simply because we cannot understand it. After all, God is present everywhere—all Christians acknowledge that—and that is as much a mystery as Christ's presence in the Eucharist. Are we to deny God's omnipresence because we cannot conceive how he pulls it off? If Christ, who was on earth in a natural body and now reigns in heaven in a glorified body, can make the world out of nothing, certainly he can make bread and wine into his own Body and Blood. That should not be hard to accept, no matter how hard it might be to fathom. There is no good reason to limit God's acts to the extent of our understanding.

[23] Green, *Eucharist*.

The fundamentalists' problem is that theirs is a religion almost entirely lacking in the mysterious. More precisely, they readily acknowledge only those mysteries that are purely spiritual, such as the Trinity. They know the doctrine of the Trinity has been revealed, that something about the Trinity can be known, that certain deductions can be drawn from what is known; and they realize the essence of the Trinity lies beyond human comprehension, and they are happy to leave it at that. When it comes to mysteries that involve the mixing of spirit and matter, a kind of Docetism shows.

For fundamentalists the sacraments are out because they necessitate a spiritual reality, grace, being conveyed by means of matter. This seems a violation of the divine plan. Matter is not to be used, but overcome or avoided, and in this lies the unease with which they view the Incarnation. One suspects that, had they been asked by the Creator their opinion of how to effect mankind's salvation, they would have advised him to adopt an approach that would have appealed to Mary Baker Eddy. How much cleaner things would be if spirit never dirtied itself with matter! But God, quite literally, loves matter, and he loves it so much that he comes to us under the appearance of bread and wine. There is no contradiction in Christ being both physically and sacramentally present.

The verses fundamentalists have the hardest time with are 1 Corinthians 11:26–30: "So it is the Lord's death that you are heralding, whenever you eat this bread and drink this cup, until he comes. And therefore, if anyone eats this bread or drinks this cup of the Lord unworthily, he will be held to account for the Lord's body and blood. [Douay-Rheims translation: ". . . shall be guilty of the body and blood of the Lord".] A man must examine himself first, and then eat of that bread and drink of that cup; he is eating and drinking damnation to himself if he eats and drinks unworthily, not recognizing the Lord's body for what it is." And what should it be recognized as? A mere metaphor? Then how can receiving unworthily be equated with being "guilty of the body and blood of the Lord"?

"Plain and simple reason", observed Nicholas Cardinal Wiseman more than a century ago in his *Lectures on the Real Presence*, "seems to tell us that the presence of Christ's body is necessary for an offense committed against it. A man cannot be 'guilty of majesty' unless the majesty exists in the object against which his crime is committed. In like manner, an offender against the Blessed Eucharist cannot be described as guilty of Christ's Body and Blood, if these be not present in the Sacrament."[24]

"How could a person be guilty, if he had merely eaten a little bread and drunk a little wine, as a picture or representation or reminder of the Last Supper?" asked Rumble and Carty more recently. "No one is guilty of homicide if he merely does violence to the picture or statue of a man without touching the man in person. St. Paul's words are meaningless without the dogma of the Real Presence."[25] They may indeed then be meaningless, but fundamentalists would rather live with a meaningless Real Absence than a meaning-full Real Presence.

---

[24] Nicholas Wiseman, *Lectures on the Real Presence,* 319.

[25] Leslie Rumble and Charles M. Carty, *Eucharist Quizzes to a Street Preacher* (Rockford, Ill.: TAN Books, 1976), 7–8.

Chapter 20

The Mass

There is no mistaking it. Fundamentalists do not like the Mass, and they like it even less than they otherwise might because they misunderstand what it is. Jimmy Swaggart says, "The Roman Catholic church teaches that the Holy Mass is an expiatory (sin removing) sacrifice, in which the Son of God is actually sacrificed anew on the cross."[1] Loraine Boettner calls the Mass a "jumble of medieval superstition".[2] Keith Green called the Mass blasphemous because there can be no continuing offering for sin, Christ having died "once for all".[3] One comfortably may assume these men never read an official Catholic explanation of the Mass—or, if they did, that they did not understand it. Each could have turned for help to Vatican II, which put the Catholic position succinctly:

> At the Last Supper, on the night He was betrayed, our Savior instituted the Eucharistic Sacrifice of His Body and Blood. He did this in order to perpetuate the sacrifice of the Cross throughout the centuries until He should come again, and so to entrust to His beloved spouse, the Church, a memorial of His death and resurrection: a sacrament of love, a sign of unity, a bond of charity, a paschal banquet in which Christ is consumed, the mind is filled with grace, and a pledge of future glory is given to us.[4]

One does not need to read the documents of Vatican II to know Catholics say the Mass was instituted at the Last Supper. Any modestly informed Catholic can set an inquirer right on this and

[1] Swaggart, "Mass", 33–34.
[2] Boettner, *Catholicism*, 175.
[3] In his tract *The Sacrifice of the Mass*.
[4] *Sacrosanctum Concilium* 47.

direct him to the biblical accounts of the final night Jesus was with
his disciples. Anyone turning to the text would find these words:
"Then he took bread, and blessed and broke it, and gave it to
them, saying, This is my body, given for you; do this for a commemoration of me" (Lk 22:19). The Greek here and in the parallel
Gospel passages (Mt 26:26; Mk 14:22) reads: *Touto estin to soma
mou*. It is given slightly differently by Paul: *Touto mou estin to soma*
(1 Cor 11:24). They all translate as "This is my body." The verb
estin is the equivalent of the English "is" and can mean "is really"
or "is figuratively". The usual meaning of *estin* is the former, just
as, in English, the verb is usually taken in the real or literal sense.

Fundamentalists, of course, insist Christ, in saying, "This is
my body", spoke only a trope. This interpretation is precluded by
Paul's discussion of the Eucharist in 1 Corinthians 23–24 and by
the whole tenor of John 6, the chapter where the Eucharist is
promised. The Greek word for "body" in John 6 is *sarx*, which
can only mean physical flesh, and the word for "eat" translates as
"gnaws" or "chews". This is not the language of metaphor.

The literal meaning cannot be avoided except through violence
to the text—and through the rejection of the universal understanding of the early Christian centuries. The writings of Paul and
John reflect belief in a Presence that is Real. There is no basis for
forcing anything else out of the lines, and no writer tried to do so
until the early Middle Ages. In short, Christ did not institute a
Figurative Presence.

Sometimes fundamentalists say the use of the word "is" can be
explained by the fact that Aramaic, the language spoken by
Christ, had no word for "represents". Jesus just had to do the best
he could with a restricted vocabulary. Those who make this claim
are behind the times, even for fundamentalists, most of whom
now acknowledge that such an argument is feeble since, as Cardinal Wiseman showed a century ago, Aramaic has about three
dozen words that can mean "represents",[5] so Christ would have
had no difficulty at all in giving an unmistakable equivalent of
"this represents my body."

5 Rumble and Carty, *Quizzes,* 7.

There have been attempts to get around the plain sense of the passage by wishing the words away. James Moffatt produced his second translation of the New Testament in 1913; it gives Matthew 26:26 and parallel passages this way: "Take and eat this, it means my body." With this Moffatt ceased to be a translator and became an interpreter. Present-day fundamentalists do not rely on his version of the New Testament, generally preferring the Authorized Version instead, but Moffatt's lapse from scholarly proprieties (what Arnold Lunn called "a glaring example of the subordination of scholarship to sectarian prejudice")[6] is indicative of the problems the accounts of the Last Supper cause people who refuse to take the words at face value.

As if the Catholic claim about the reality of the Real Presence were not bad enough, the Church insists that the Mass is the continuation and re-presentation of the sacrifice of Calvary. It is *not* a re-Crucifixion of Christ. He does not suffer and die again. On the other hand, it is more than just a memorial service.

John A. O'Brien says:

> The manner in which the sacrifices are offered is alone different: on the Cross Christ really shed His blood and was really slain; in the Mass, however, there is no real shedding of blood, no real death; but the separate consecration of the bread and of the wine symbolizes the separation of the body and blood of Christ and thus symbolizes His death upon the Cross. The Mass is the renewal and perpetuation of the sacrifice of the Cross in the sense that it offers anew to God the Victim of Calvary and thus commemorates the sacrifice of the Cross, reenacts it symbolically and mystically, and applies the fruits of Christ's death upon the Cross to individual human souls. All the efficacy of the Mass is derived, therefore, from the sacrifice of Calvary.[7]

Keith Green would not have bought such an explanation. The second of Green's *Catholic Chronicles* is called *The Sacrifice of the Mass*. The subtitle is *Jesus Dies Again,* which aptly summarizes Green's position. Though Green now presumably knows better,

---

[6] Lunn, *Third Day,* 103.
[7] O'Brien, *Faith,* 304.

having had a chance to obtain the proper interpretation of the Bible from the Author himself, people who rely on his writings apparently do not, so let us take a look at what he thought while here below.

His tract asks:

> Have you ever wondered why in every Catholic church they still have Jesus up on the cross? Every crucifix with Jesus portrayed as nailed to it tells the whole Catholic story—Jesus is still dying for the sins of the world! But that's a lie! We need only look to the Scriptures to see the truth. The Epistle to the Hebrews speaks of the 'once for all' sacrifice of Christ on the cross, not a daily sacrifice on altars. The Bible repeatedly affirms in the clearest and most positive terms that Christ's sacrifice on Calvary was complete in that one offering. And that it was never to be repeated is set forth explicitly in Hebrews, chapters 7, 9, and 10.

Green then quotes Hebrews 7:27; 9:12; 9:25–28; and 10:10–14. (The Catholic reader should review these passages; Hebrews 9:28, for instance, reads: "Christ was offered once for all, to drain the cup of the world's sins.") Green notes that "throughout these verses occurs the statement 'once for all' which shows how perfect, complete, and final Jesus' sacrifice was! . . . Any pretense of a continuous offering for sin is worse than vain, it is blasphemy and true fulfillment of the Scripture, 'Seeing they crucify to themselves the Son of God afresh, and put Him to an open shame' " (Heb 6:6). Green does not mention the context in which Hebrews 6:6 is placed. It has nothing directly to do with the Mass. Instead, the first verses of the chapter deal with those who fall away from the Faith after baptism. Forgiveness of their sins cannot come through a second baptism, since there is only one baptism established by Christ. What do they want? the sacred writer asks. Do they want a new baptism to be given through a second Crucifixion? That is the only way it could happen. "Would they crucify the Son of God a second time, hold him up to mockery a second time, for their own ends?"

This verse simply does not say what Green thought it did. Nor do the others. The Catholic Church specifically says Christ does not die again—his death is indeed once for all—but that does not contradict the doctrine of the Mass. It would be something else if the Church were to claim he *does* die again, but it does not make that claim. A re-presenting of the original sacrifice does not necessitate a new Crucifixion.

Keith Green has not been the only fundamentalist writer, of course, to disapprove of the Mass. "It must not be supposed for a minute", warns Loraine Boettner in *Roman Catholicism,* "that modern Roman Catholics do not literally believe this jumble of medieval superstition. They have been taught it from infancy, and they do believe it. It is the very sternest doctrine of their church. It is one of the chief doctrines, if indeed it is not the chief doctrine, upon which their church rests."[8] Boettner's argument is summarized in one paragraph. It is worth quoting at length. He says:

> This doctrine of the mass, of course, is based on the assumption that the words of Christ, "This is my body" and "This is my blood" (Matt. 26:26–28), must be taken literally. The accounts of the institution of the Lord's Supper, both in the Gospels and in Paul's letter to the Corinthians, make it perfectly clear that He spoke in figurative terms. Jesus said, "This cup is the new covenant in my blood" (Luke 22:20). And Paul quotes Jesus as saying: "This is the new covenant in my blood. . . . For as oft as ye eat this bread, and drink the cup, ye proclaim the Lord's death till he come" (1 Cor. 11:25–26). In these words He used a double figure of speech. The cup is put for the wine, and the wine is called the new covenant. The cup was not literally the new covenant, although it is declared to be so as definitely as the bread is declared to be His body. They did not literally drink the cup, nor did they literally drink the new covenant. How ridiculous to say that they did! Nor was the bread literally His body, or the wine His blood. After giving the wine to the disciples Jesus said: "I shall not drink from henceforth of the fruit of the vine, until the Kingdom of God shall come" (Luke 22:18). So the wine, even as He gave it to them, and after he had given it to them, remained "the fruit of the vine"![9]

[8] Boettner, *Catholicism,* 175.
[9] Boettner, *Catholicism,* 176.

Boettner continues by giving a cleverly incomplete quotation. He writes, "Paul too says that the bread remains bread: 'Wherefore whosoever shall eat the bread and drink the cup of the Lord in an unworthy manner. . . . But let each man prove himself, and so let him eat of the bread, and drink of the cup' " (1 Cor 11:27–28).[10] The part of verse 27 represented by the ellipsis is crucial. It reads: "shall be guilty of the body and blood of the Lord". Why does Boettner omit this? Because to be guilty of someone's body and blood is to revile him, and one can hardly revile baked flour or fermented grape juice. This omitted line makes no sense at all unless it means a profanation of the sacrament is something serious, and it clearly implies the bread and wine become Christ himself.

Boettner is not through. He has to mimic the early pagan opponents to Christianity by saying that "another and more important proof that the bread and wine are not changed into the literal and actual flesh and blood of Christ is this: the literal interpretation makes the sacrament a form of *cannibalism*. For that is precisely what cannibalism is—the eating of human flesh. Rome attempts to deny this, but without much logic."[11] Peter Stravinskas turns this charge on its head and uses it to make an important observation. Allegations of cannibalism actually backfire on fundamentalists because, in bringing the topic up today, they encourage Catholics to note that it was brought up centuries ago. Stravinskas notes that "both Tertullian and Minucius Felix . . . give considerable attention in their second-century writings to the charge of cannibalism being leveled against the Church. A belief in the Real Presence thus clearly existed in the Early Church, for no 'simple memorial supper' would have evoked such specific and violent charges from the general pagan population."[12]

Leslie Rumble and Charles M. Carty also addressed the cannibalism claim.

> When Christ promised that He would give His very flesh to eat, the Jews protested because they imagined a natural and cannibalistic

---

[10] Boettner, *Catholicism,* 176.

[11] Boettner, *Catholicism,* 176.

[12] Stravinskas, *Response,* 91.

eating of Christ's body. Christ refuted this notion of the manner in which His flesh was to be received by saying that He would ascend into heaven, not leaving His body in its human form upon earth. But He did not say that they were not to eat His actual body. He would thus contradict Himself, for a little earlier He had said, "My flesh is meat indeed and My blood is drink indeed" John 6:56. He meant, therefore, "You will not be asked to eat My flesh in the horrible and natural way you think, for My body as you see it with your eyes will be gone from this earth. Yet I shall leave my flesh and blood in another and supernatural way which your natural and carnal minds cannot understand. The carnal or fleshly judgment profits nothing. I ask you, therefore, to have faith in Me. It is the spirit of faith which will enable you to believe, not your natural judgment."[13]

Another fundamentalist dissatisfied with the Mass is Ralph Woodrow. He presents his view in *Babylon Mystery Religion* by giving in full a poem he acknowledges to be crude. The author is listed as anonymous, and with good reason. The poem is called "A Roman Miracle", and in forty lines it tells the story of a Protestant woman who married a Catholic. One day her husband brought his priest to dinner in order to effect her conversion. After the priest gave his counsel, they all agreed to meet again, and he promised to confect the sacrament in her presence if she would prepare the bread. He returned, did as he said, and prepared to eat. At the last moment she warned him that "half an ounce of arsenic was mixed right in the batter, / But since you have its nature changed, it cannot really matter." The priest, of course, ran away, eating nothing, and the contrite husband turned to his wife, saying: "To gulp such mummery and tripe, I'm not for sure, quite able; / I'll go with you and we'll renounce this Roman Catholic fable."[14]

The literary worth of the poem is as modest as Woodrow's understanding of transubstantiation. On Catholic principles, the

---

[13] Rumble and Carty, *Replies,* 1:176.
[14] Woodrow, *Babylon,* 125.

priest was quite right, of course, to refuse to eat, for the simple reason that only the bread, not the poison, could be transubstantiated. Anything mixed with the bread would have remained unaltered (assuming the mixture would not have been unconfectable matter in the first place), and the bread would have retained the appearance and properties of bread. The arsenic would have remained poison. Transubstantiation would not have made the arsenic disappear, but this is something Woodrow seems not to realize. He just wants to poke fun at Catholics who "play" with bread and wine, but a review of Genesis might give him pause.

The Old Testament predicted that Christ would offer a true sacrifice to God in bread and wine—that he would use those elements. Melchisedech, the king of Salem and a priest, offered sacrifice under the form of bread and wine (Gen 14:18). Psalm 110 predicted Christ would be a priest "according to the order of Melchisedech", that is, offering a sacrifice in bread and wine. We must, then, look for some sacrifice other than Calvary, since it was not under the form of bread and wine. The Mass fits the bill.

Joseph Zacchello, revealer of *Secrets of Romanism,* demurs: "Melchisedech brought bread and wine to refresh Abraham and his followers, not to sacrifice. The Roman version is a mistranslation. It translates '*And* he was a priest', as follows: '*For* he was a priest', in order to make it appear that he brought forth bread and wine in his official capacity as a priest to offer sacrifice with them."[15] Zacchello grasps for straws. The conjunction "and" in Greek often has the force of "for", so here "and he was a priest" means the same as "for he was a priest". What is more, "according to the order of Melchisedech" means "in the manner of Melchisedech" ("order" not referring, of course, to the modern notion of a religious order, there being no such thing in Old Testament days). The only "manner" shown by Melchisedech was the use of bread and wine. A priest sacrifices the items offered—that is the main task of all priests, in all cultures, at all times—so the bread and wine must have been what Melchisedech

---

[15] Zacchello, *Secrets,* 69.

sacrificed. He did not bring these elements along just because he thought it might be time for Abraham's lunch.

Fundamentalists sometimes admit Christ followed the example of Melchisedech at the Last Supper, but claim it was a rite that was not to be continued. They undermine their opposition to the Mass in saying this, since such an admission shows, at least, that the Last Supper was truly sacrificial. The key, though, is that they overlook that Christ said, "Do this for a commemoration of me" (Lk 22:19). Clearly, he was not talking about a one-time thing.

It is this command that makes fundamentalists uncomfortable. They think its Catholic interpretation minimizes the salvific work of Christ. Not so. "If all people were saved in that one momentous occasion," asks Stravinskas, "why does the Church continue to offer the sacrifice of the Mass? Because the salvation promised and earned is conditional; because it is contingent upon our acceptance of Jesus, our desire to be saved, and our living of a lifestyle which demonstrates an understanding of what life in Christ means. Since we were not present, we need to be reminded of what God has done for us. Our remembrance and ritual reenactment of the event make it happen again—for us." [16]

One should keep in mind that, after foretelling the rejection of the Jewish priesthood, the prophet Malachi predicted a new sacrifice would be offered in every place. "From the rising of the sun even to the going down, my name is great among the Gentiles; and in every place there is a sacrifice and there is offered to my name a clean oblation" (Malachi 1:10–11). Note that he speaks of one sacrifice, not many sacrifices, but one that is offered everywhere. The sacrifice of Calvary took place in one place only. We must look for a sacrifice apart from Calvary, one that is given under the form of bread and wine. Only the Mass meets the requirements.

As might be expected, fundamentalists put little stock in claims about the antiquity of the sacrificial aspects of the Mass, even if they think the Mass, in the form of a mere commemorative meal,

---

[16] Stravinskas, *Response,* 85.

commenced with the Last Supper. Many say the Mass as a sacrifice was not taught until the Middle Ages, alleging Innocent III was the first Pope to teach the doctrine. He merely insisted on a doctrine that had been held from the first but was being publicly doubted in his time. He formalized, but did not invent, the notion that the Mass is a sacrifice. Jimmy Swaggart, for one, goes further back than do most fundamentalists, claiming, "By the third century the idea of sacrifice had begun to intrude."[17] Still other fundamentalists say Cyprian of Carthage was the first to mention a sacrifice.[18] Irenaeus, writing *Against Heresies* in the second century, was ahead of Cyprian when he wrote of the sacrificial nature of the Mass,[19] and Clement of Rome in his turn was ahead of Irenaeus when he wrote about those "from the episcopate who blamelessly and holily have offered its Sacrifices".[20] It simply is not possible to get closer to New Testament times than this because Clement was writing *during* New Testament times. After all, at least one apostle, John, was still alive.

Fundamentalists are particularly upset about the Catholic notion that the sacrifice on Calvary is somehow continued through the centuries by the Mass. To them it seems Catholics are trying to have it both ways. The Church on the one hand says that Calvary is "perpetuated", which seems to mean the same act of killing, the same letting of blood, is repeated again and again. This violates the "once for all" idea, fundamentalists claim. On the other hand, what Catholics call a sacrifice seems in fact to have no relation to biblical sacrifices since it does not look the same; after all, no splotches of blood are to be found on Catholic altars. "We must, of course, take strong exception to such pretended sacrifice", Boettner instructs.

---

[17] Jimmy Swaggart, *Roman Catholicism* (Baton Rouge: Jimmy Swaggart Ministries, 1986), 60.

[18] For instance, Bartholomew F. Brewer in his tract *Scriptural Truths for Roman Catholics*.

[19] Irenaeus, *Adversus haereses* 4, 17, 5.

[20] Clement of Rome, *Epistula ad Corinthios* 44, 4.

We cannot regard it as anything other than a deception, a mockery, and an abomination before God. The so-called sacrifice of the mass certainly is not identical with that on Calvary, regardless of what the priests may say. There is in the mass no real Christ, no suffering, and no bleeding. And a bloodless sacrifice is ineffectual. The writer of the book of Hebrews says that "apart from shedding of blood there is no remission" of sin (9:22); and John says, "The blood of Jesus his Son cleanseth us from all sin" (1 John 1:7). Since admittedly there is no blood in the mass, it simply cannot be a sacrifice for sin.[21]

Boettner misreads chapter 9 of Hebrews, which begins with an examination of the Old Covenant. Moses is described as taking the blood of calves and goats and using it in the purification of the tabernacle (Heb 9:19–21; see Ex 24:6–8 for the origins of this). "And if such purification was needed for what was but a representation of the heavenly world, the heavenly world itself will need sacrifices more availing still. The sanctuary into which Jesus has entered is not one made by human hands, is not some adumbration of the truth; he has entered heaven itself, where he now appears in God's sight on our behalf. Nor does he make a repeated offering of himself, as the high priest, when he enters the sanctuary, makes a yearly offering of the blood that is not his own" (Heb 9:23–25). So it was under the Old Law that a repeated blood sacrifice was necessary for the remission of sins. Under the Christian dispensation, blood (Christ's) is shed only once, but it is continually offered to the Father.

How can that be? ask fundamentalists. They have to keep in mind that "what Jesus Christ was yesterday, and is today, he remains for ever" (Heb 13:8). What Jesus did in the past is present to God now, and God can make the sacrifice of Calvary present to us at Mass. "So it is the Lord's death you are heralding, whenever you eat this bread and drink this cup, until he comes" (1 Cor 11:26).

In the final analysis, what makes the Mass literally unbelievable for fundamentalists is that they cannot conceive of a single act that

[21] Boettner, *Catholicism*, 174.

is perpetuated through time. For them, what happened on Calvary happened there alone and remains in the dead past. They see Catholic priests conducting a sacrifice today and conclude that today's sacrifice must be distinct from Calvary's. If it really is a sacrifice, it is an attempt to replay Calvary in the most literal way—which, they know, is quite impossible. Christ cannot be killed again. So, for fundamentalists, what priests do at the altar really reduces to a show. Priests may think they are re-presenting the same sacrifice, but fundamentalists know they are only play-acting.

It is fundamentalists' sense of the mysterious, their sense of the supernatural, that is undeveloped. Ask them about the nature of the afterlife. One will receive no enlightening answer, maybe no answer at all. It is as if they have hardly thought about the subject. Just what is the spiritual life like, anyway? It hardly does any good to say people will be happy in heaven. Some people are happy in the Bronx, but heaven must be something other than a superlative version of a New York borough. Having been instructed poorly in the supernatural as such, fundamentalists have not given it much thought, and they have trouble imagining that God is actually beyond time. They usually think of eternity as being nothing but endless years, a time line that disappears into the mists at each end, and they do not think of Calvary being in a perpetual Now.

They could imagine, say, several Jewish priests, all at about the same time, offering what could be termed a single sacrifice in the Temple. First one comes in, then another, and a few minutes later a third. They can see how three separate acts of offering could be considered a single sacrifice, if the three acts are nearly simultaneous. But thousands, millions of Masses through the centuries, each Mass like the others, but each quite different in appearance from Calvary itself? How can we say they are all the re-presentation of that original Sacrifice? If they cannot imagine the continuity being not so much in time, which is marked by days and hours, but outside of time, which is a single Now, they cannot help but think Catholics are trying to pull a fast one. It requires a determined refocusing of the mind to see things from the Catholic perspective, and this is not easy for fundamentalists to accomplish. It is far easier for Catholics to put themselves in fundamentalist shoes than for fundamentalists to step into ours. It is something like the problem that even Catholics have in getting a right appreciation of the Eucharist.

"You see, we are so materialistic", noted Ronald Knox in *The Window in the Wall,*

> our minds are so chained to the things of sense, that we imagine our Lord as instituting the Blessed Sacrament with bread and wine as the remote matter of it because bread and wine reminded him of that grace which he intended the Blessed Sacrament to bestow. But, if you come to think of it, it was just the other way about. When he created the worlds, he gave common bread and wine for our use in order that we might understand what the Blessed Sacrament was when it came to be instituted. He did not design the Sacred Host to be something like bread. He designed bread to be something like the Sacred Host.[22]

One who has trouble grasping this insight will understand how difficult it is for fundamentalists to get a true appreciation of the Catholic doctrine of the Mass. They are so accustomed to reading the relevant biblical verses in a particular way that they cannot see there is far more than initially meets their eyes.

[22] Ronald Knox, *The Window in the Wall* (London: Burns and Oates, 1956), 80.

Chapter 21

Honoring the Saints

A diocesan priest, a man who always seemed to have the right words for the occasion, was celebrating a nuptial Mass. The bride had been raised a Catholic, but the groom had not. He was a recent convert. His entire family and almost all his friends at the wedding were non-Catholics. Since many of the bride's friends were not Catholics either, few people at the Mass understood what was going on. The priest therefore interspersed his liturgical duties with explanations.

It is traditional, at the conclusion of the ceremony, for the bride to take a bouquet to a side altar and lay it at the feet of a statue of the Virgin, at the same time praying that she might emulate Mary as a wife and mother. When the time came for that gesture, the priest commented that the placing of the flowers is done because "we Catholics worship Mary". There was a collective sigh from the few Catholics in the church and a collective gasp from the non-Catholics, who apparently had their worst suspicions confirmed.

Was the priest right or wrong? Well, probably both. He was right in his understanding of the word "worship", although he was using it in what is almost an archaic sense. He was surely wrong in using it in front of people who would misunderstand his meaning. After all, in common speech worship means adoration given to God alone. In this sense Catholics do not worship Mary or any of the other saints. But in an older usage the term worship means not just adoration of God but the honor given to anyone deserving honor.

Begin with the word itself. It comes from the Old English *weorthscipe,* which means the condition of being worthy of honor, respect, or dignity. To worship in the older, larger sense is to ascribe honor, worth, or excellence to someone, whether a sage, a magistrate, or God. But there are different kinds of worship as there are different kinds of honor. The highest honor, and thus the highest worship, is given to God alone, while the honor or worship given to living men or to saints in heaven is of a different sort. Idolatry thus does not simply mean giving worship (in the old sense) to living men or to saints; it means giving them the kind reserved for God.

Nowadays there is a problem with using the word because in the popular mind it refers to God alone. For practical purposes it has come to mean nothing else than adoration. Although it was commonly used in the wider sense as recently as the nineteenth century (when, for instance, Orestes Brownson, perhaps the foremost Catholic intellectual America has produced, wrote *The Worship of Mary*), it is perhaps too confusing to use it that way now, as the example of the priest shows. It is no doubt wise to restrict its use to God and to use for saints and others terms such as honor and veneration.

Is this a distinction without a difference? It would be if the honor given to God were the same as the honor given to a saint. But it is not.

Consider how honor is given. We regularly give it to public officials. In the United States it is customary to address a judge as "Your Honor". (It has been the British custom to address certain magistrates—here it comes—as "Your Worship", but that is another can of worms.) In the marriage ceremony it used to be said that the wife would "love, honor, and obey" her husband. On Mount Sinai there was a command given to "honor thy father and thy mother" (Ex 20:12). Letters to legislators are addressed to "The Hon. So-and-So". And just about anyone, living or dead, who bears an exalted rank is said to be worthy of honor, and that is particularly true of historical figures, as when children are, or at least used to be, instructed to honor the Founding Fathers.

So, if there can be nothing wrong with honoring the living, who still have an opportunity to ruin their lives through sin, or the uncanonized dead, about whose state of spiritual health we can only guess, certainly there can be no argument against giving honor to saints whose lives are done and who ended them in sanctity. If merit deserves to be honored wherever it is found, it surely should be honored among God's special friends.

When we speak of honoring saints and particularly Mary, the greatest of the saints, what do we mean? How is this honor demonstrated? One way is through art. Our regard for the saints is shown through the employment of statues or paintings, just as we honor a deceased relative by keeping his photograph on the mantelpiece. It is said by fundamentalists, of course, that Catholics worship statues. Not only is this untrue, it is even untrue that Catholics honor statues. After all, a statue is nothing but a carved block of marble or a chunk of plaster, and no one gives honor to marble yet unquarried or plaster still in the mixing bowl.

The fact that someone kneels before a statue to pray does not mean that he is praying to the statue, just as the fact that one kneels with a Bible in his hands—as fundamentalists at times do—does not mean that he is worshiping the Bible. Statues or paintings or other artistic devices are used to recall to the mind the person or thing depicted. Just as it is easier to remember one's mother by looking at her photograph, so it is easier to recall the lives of the saints, and thus be edified by their examples, by looking at representations of them.

More important than honor shown to saints through artistic expression is the honor shown through personal communication, through prayer. Catholics honor saints, and particularly Mary, by praying to them and asking them to intercede with God on their behalf. This immediately brings up the question: Can saints in heaven hear us? After all, with extraordinarily rare exceptions, any communication with them seems to be at best a one-way street. True, there have been apparitions of Mary and some saints to a few individuals, but the Church has repeatedly said that no one is obliged to believe that these take place or to place any credence in what is said during them. Private revelations are binding only on the individuals to whom they are made; belief in them is not necessary for salvation. So, if we discount such instances, it seems that prayers go to the saints but that no unmistakable answers are received from them. So how do we know they hear us?

For the Catholic the answer can be almost deceptively simple: We know, because the Church tells us so. However satisfying such an answer may be to those who believe in the Magisterium and think there is a good reason to accept its teachings, it is hardly convincing to fundamentalists, who are unable to find any comfort in hagiographical accounts—or even in historical accounts of such things as Fatima.[1]

The fundamentalists' chief problem in accepting that saints can hear prayers is that their notions of heaven and the afterlife are attenuated. For many of them the afterlife is hardly a life at all. They, like many Christians, draw a blank when they try to explain what heaven is like. Some can imagine nothing other than the stereotypic harps and choirs. Others say heaven is an impenetrable haze and that all we can know is that we will be happy there.

One thing that certainly can be said is that those in heaven are alive to God. "Have you never read in the book of Moses how God spoke to him at the burning bush, and said, 'I am the God of Abraham, and the God of Isaac, and the God of Jacob?' Yet it is of living men, not dead men, that he is the God" (Mk 12:26–27). The saints in heaven are more alive now than we are. In the arms of God, they are more solicitous of us than when they were on earth. Just as Paul asked the other disciples to pray for him (Rom 15:30; Col 4:3; 1 Th 1:11), so now we can ask Paul and the other

---

[1] I once heard a priest recount the Miracle of the Sun, as he saw it as a boy from his home in the Azores. None of his relatives believed him when he explained what he witnessed in the sky. They presumed it was a childish fantasy. Weeks later the accounts from Fatima filtered in, and only then did his family understand that he had been granted a special privilege. This kind of story, when told by the protagonist himself, can be particularly effective in convincing people of the reality of saintly interventions, but few people, particularly outside the Church, ever have a chance to talk with an eyewitness to the supernatural.

saints in heaven to intercede for us with God. We are not cut off from fellow Christians at death, but are, strangely enough and contrary to our unreflecting thoughts, brought closer. We continue in one communion, the communion of saints.

To fundamentalists the term communion of saints and its allied term, the Mystical Body of Christ, mean nothing. They have never heard of them, except for those who once were Catholics, and probably none of *them* ever understood the phrases. It is enough to remind fundamentalists of the image of the vine and its branches (Jn 15:1–8). They accept this as a metaphor of our relation to Christ, he being the vine, we the branches that live through him. They can see that if we are connected to Christ, we are connected to one another, but they tend to forget that those in heaven are not suddenly cut off from the vine. The saints remain as branches, which, if the symbolism means anything, means they remain related to us.

Paul develops Christ's teaching about the Mystical Body, about the vine and branches. He sees Christ as the head, the members of the Church as the body. The acts of any one member are profitable to all the members. "There was to be no want of unity in the body; all the different parts of it were to make each other's welfare their common care. If one part is suffering, all the rest suffer with it; if one part is treated with honor, all the rest find pleasure in it. And you are Christ's body, organs of it depending on each other" (1 Cor 12:25–27). He goes on, saying, "Each of us has one body, with many different parts, and not all these parts have the same function; just so we, though many in number, form one body in Christ, and each acts as the counterpart of another" (Rom 12:4–5).

A natural, even a necessary, inference from this teaching is intercessory prayer, which Paul requests for himself and all the saints: "Only, brethren, I entreat you by our Lord Jesus Christ, and by the love of the Holy Spirit, to give me the help of your prayers to God on my behalf" (Rom 15:30); "offer your supplication for all the saints" (Eph 6:18). Here, of course, Paul is writing about the members of the Church Militant, but his teaching on the Mystical Body implies that prayers unite us with the Church Triumphant, too.

While the Bible does not explicitly refer to the veneration and invocation of saints, there is scriptural warrant for the practice. First there is the veneration offered angels (Jos 5:14; Dan 8:17; Tob 12:16). This veneration is predicated on the angels' supernatural dignity, which comes from their union with God (Mt 18:10). Since the saints are also united with God (1 Cor 13:12; 1 John 3:2), it follows that they are also worthy of veneration.

The ancient Jews believed in the intercession of saints. Judas Maccabaeus saw in a vision "most worthy of credence" how two deceased men, the high priest Onias and the prophet Jeremiah, interceded with God for the Jews (2 Macc 15:11–16). And Jeremiah himself wrote that Moses and Samuel made intercession for the Jews, apparently meaning after their deaths (Jer 15:1). We learn that angels and saints place the prayers of the holy on earth at God's feet (Tob 12:12; Rev 5:8, 8:3), which is to say that they support the prayers with their intercessions. These verses also mean, apparently, that the angels and saints are the ones prayed to and that they then take these prayers to God.

John Henry Newman said that, in Revelation,

> the sacred writer goes so far as to speak of "grace and peace" being sent to us, not only from the Almighty, but "from the seven Spirits that are before His throne", thus associating the Eternal with the ministers of His mercies; and this carries us on to the remarkable passage of St. Justin, one of the earliest Fathers, who, in his Apology, says, "To Him (God), and His Son who came from Him, and taught us these things, and the host of other good Angels who follow and resemble Him, and the Prophetic Spirit, we pay veneration and homage."

Newman then said that "one instance is given us, which testifies to the continuation of so high an office beyond this life. Lazarus, in the parable, is seen in Abraham's bosom. It is usual to pass over this striking passage with the remark that it is a Jewish expression; whereas, Jewish belief or not, it is recognised and sanctioned by our Lord Himself."[2] If Dives could pray to Lazarus (that must have been how he spoke to him) across the unbridgeable abyss, then why should we not be able to pray to saints across an abyss they have successfully crossed and we hope to cross?

But why ask the saints to pray to God on one's behalf? Why not pray to God directly? After all, ask fundamentalists, isn't Christ the one mediator (1 Tim 2:5), and do not the saints become mediators in violation of that if they pray for us? Orestes Brownson answered the first of these questions in a series of articles he wrote for *Ave Maria* magazine in 1865 and 1866. "But still it is asked", Brownson noted,

what need to pray the saints at all, and why not pray directly to God himself, since he is infinitely nearer to us, and more ready and able to help us than any saint is or can be? In reply, I answer that Catholics do pray directly to God, and perhaps even more than they do who reject prayers to the saints; and I might ask, in our turn, why pray even directly to God, since he knows all our wants better than we ourselves know them, knows what we are going to pray for before the prayer is formed in our own heart, and is infinitely more willing to help us than we are to ask his help? The same principle that justifies prayer to God justifies prayers to the saints to intercede for us.[3]

Brownson also answered the charge that saints cannot hear our prayers.

But it is alleged, even by persons who call themselves Christians, that however well disposed the saints might be to intercede for us, they cannot hear our invocations, and therefore our prayers to them are vain and even superstitious. If they cannot hear us, our prayers to them *are* unquestionably superstitious, and not to be tolerated. But wherefore can they not hear us? Are they not living men and women—even more living than when they tabernacled with us? . . . There can be no communion where there is no medium of

[2] John Henry Newman, *Letter to the Rev. E. B. Pusey, D.D., on his Recent Eirenicon* (1866).

[3] Orestes A. Brownson, *Saint Worship* (Paterson, N.J.: St. Anthony Guild Press, 1963), 40.

communication. We who live have a medium of communication with those who have gone to their reward and therefore form one communion with them. This medium is Christ himself, who is the head of every man, and whose life is the life of all who are begotten anew by the Holy Ghost. . . . There is no more mystery in the way the saints hear our invocations than there is in the way we hear one another. Mystery there is, but it is the same mystery in both cases, and it would be absurd to maintain that we do not hear one another because we cannot explain how we do it. There being a medium of communication between us and the saints, and they and we forming only one communion, one body of our Lord, being members of him and members of one another, nothing can be more reasonable, more natural even, than that we should invoke their prayers, and that they should intercede for us. It is in accordance alike with the order of nature and the order of grace.[4]

In response to fundamentalists' other question, about Christ being the one mediator, consider what we do for one another now. We pray for others, and we ask others to pray for us. By doing so we indeed act as mediators since we pray to God on behalf of others, and our friends are mediators for us. (Attend a fundamentalist service and see how Brother This and Sister That ask the congregation to "pray over them"; fundamentalists' theories are often contradicted by their acts.) This prayer for one another does not violate Christ's role as the one mediator, because ours is a secondary mediatorship that is entirely dependent on his. Paul asked his friends to pray for him as he prayed for them, and today Christians do the same, but none of this violates the truth that without Christ our prayers to the Father would be ineffectual.

A common objection to prayer to the saints is stated by Loraine Boettner:

How, then, can a human being such as Mary hear the prayers of millions of Roman Catholics, in many different countries, praying in many different languages, all at the same time? Let any priest or layman try to converse with only three people at the same time and see how impossible that is for a human being. . . . The objections

---

[4] Brownson, *Worship*, 51–54.

against prayers to Mary apply equally against prayers to the saints. For they too are only creatures, infinitely less than God, able to be at only one place at a time and to do only one thing at a time. How, then, can they listen to and answer thousands upon thousands of petitions made simultaneously in many different lands and in many different languages? Many such petitions are expressed, not orally, but only mentally, silently. How can Mary and the saints, without being like God, be present everywhere and know the secrets of all hearts?[5]

Ex-priest Joseph Zacchello quotes at length from John Hunkley's *How I Became a Non-Catholic*. Hunkley took pencil and paper, estimated how many times a day Rosaries are recited around the world, timed how long it takes to say a Hail Mary, and determined that Mary would "have to listen to 46,296 petitions at one and the same time, simultaneously, every second of time from one end of the year to the other". But no one except God can listen to so many petitions at once, he claimed, which means either Mary cannot hear them, or Catholics think she is divine.[6]

If being in heaven were like being in the next room, then such objections would be valid. Someone in the next room would indeed suffer the restrictions posed by space and time. But the saints are not in the next room, and heaven has no space or time. In heaven everything happens in one great Present; there is neither past nor future in our sense of the terms. When God looks at his creation, he sees all of it at once, all that has been, all that now is, all that will be. It is by his sufferance we communicate with one another on earth, and he likewise lets us communicate with the saints in heaven—who, like God, are outside of space and time. To say that they do not have time to listen to many prayers at once is to commit a basic error—they do not have time at all, because they are beyond time. This does not imply that they therefore must be omniscient as is God, for it is only through God's willing it that they can communicate with others in heaven or with us.

[5] Boettner, *Catholicism*, 142–43.
[6] Zacchello, *Secrets*, 129–30.

Chapter 22

Marian Beliefs

The Marian doctrines are, for fundamentalists, among the most annoying of the doctrines people identify as peculiarly Catholic. Fundamentalists disapprove of any talk about Mary as the Mother of God, as the Mediatrix, as the Mother of the Church; they disbelieve in her Immaculate Conception, do not think she was assumed into heaven, and hold that she was not a lifelong virgin. For many fundamentalists, Catholicism is little more than a subordination of basic Christianity (C. S. Lewis' "mere Christianity") to a confusing skein of Marian beliefs; they see these beliefs as interfering with, even canceling, the proper attitude toward Christ. Let us examine the Marian doctrines fundamentalist writers most frequently complain about.

Immaculate Conception

Catholic exegetes, in discussing the Immaculate Conception, begin with the Annunciation. Gabriel greeted Mary by saying "Hail, full of grace, the Lord is with thee" (Lk 1:28). This is the traditional rendering, based on the Vulgate. The phrase "full of grace" is a translation, by way of the Latin, of the Greek *kecharito-mene*, but it is not a transliteration. In Greek, "full of grace" would be *pleres charitos*, which is used for Christ in John 1:14 and for Stephen in Acts 6:8, not *kecharitomene*.

Newer translations, based directly on the Greek, render Luke 1:28 as "Rejoice, you who enjoy God's favor! The Lord is with you" (New Jerusalem Bible) or "Rejoice, O highly favored daughter! The Lord is with you" (New American Bible). These translations are imperfect, since they give the impression that the favor bestowed on Mary was no different from that given other women in the Bible.[1] If she had been merely "highly favored", in the normal connotation of those words (and it is the normal connotation that many people will read here), her status would have been indistinguishable from that of Elizabeth, the mother of John the Baptist; or Sarah, the wife of Abraham; or Anna, the mother of Samuel—all of whom, by the way, were long childless and were "highly favored" because God acceded to their pleas to bear children.

"*Charis* means favor, disinterested benevolence, coming from God", explains René Laurentin. "Does this mean that *kecharitomene* means only the extrinsic favor of God? From two points of view it means much more." Both theologically and philologically, he says, the word indicates "a transformation of the subject". The sense is not just "to look upon with favor, but to transform by this favor or grace".[2] *Kecharitomene,* then, signifies a plenitude of favor or grace.

The newer translations leave out something the Greek conveys, something the older translation conveys, which is that this grace (and the core of the word *kecharitomene* is *charis,* after all) is at once permanent and of a singular kind. The Greek indicates a perfection of grace. A perfection must be perfect not only intensively, but extensively. The grace Mary enjoyed must not only have been as "full" or strong or complete as possible at any given time, but it must have extended over the whole of her life, from conception. That is, she must have been in a state of sanctifying grace from the first moment of her existence to have been called "full of grace" or to have been filled with divine favor in a singular way. This is just what the doctrine of the Immaculate Conception holds: that Mary, "in the first instant of her conception was, by a singular grace and privilege of Almighty God in view of the mer-

---

[1] At least the New Jerusalem Bible, in its footnote to Luke 1:28, says that "you who enjoy God's favour" means "you who have been and remain filled with the divine favour".

[2] René Laurentin, *The Truth of Christmas beyond the Myths* (Petersham, Mass.: St. Bede's Publications, 1986), 18–19.

its of Jesus Christ, the Savior of the human race, preserved exempt from all stain of original sin".[3]

(One should keep in mind what the Immaculate Conception is *not*. Some non-Catholics think the term refers to Christ's conception in Mary's womb without the intervention of a human father; the proper name for that is the Virgin Birth. Others think the Immaculate Conception means Mary herself was conceived "by the power of the Holy Spirit", in the way Jesus was, but it does not. The Immaculate Conception means that Mary, whose conception was brought about the normal way, was conceived in the womb of her mother without the stain of original sin. The essence of original sin consists in the lack of sanctifying grace. Mary was preserved from this defect; from the first instant of her existence she was in the state of sanctifying grace.)

Fundamentalists' chief reason for objecting to the Immaculate Conception and Mary's consequent sinlessness—which is what her lifelong state of sanctifying grace implies—is that Mary was but a creature, and we are told that "all have sinned" (Rom 3:23). Besides, they say, Mary said her "spirit rejoices in God my Savior" (Lk 1:47), and only a sinner needs a Savior. Since Mary was a sinner, she could not have been immaculately conceived.

Take the second citation first. The Church has a simple and sensible answer to this difficulty. It is this: Mary, too, required a Savior. Like all other descendants of Adam, by her nature she was subject to the necessity of contracting original sin. But by a special intervention of God, undertaken at the instant she was conceived, she was preserved from the stain of original sin and certain of its consequences. She was therefore redeemed by the grace of Christ, but in a special way, by anticipation. The doctrine of the Immaculate Conception thus does not contradict Luke 1:47.

What about Romans 3:23, "all have sinned"? Fundamentalists, as a rule, think it means more than that everyone is subject to original sin. They think it means everyone commits actual sins. They conclude it means Mary must have sinned during her life, and that

---

[3] *Ineffabilis Deus* (Denz. 1641).

certainly would speak against an Immaculate Conception. Is the fundamentalists' analysis solid? Not really. Think about a child below the age of reason. By definition he cannot sin, since sinning requires the ability to reason and the ability to intend to sin. If the child dies before ever committing an actual sin, because he is not mature enough to know what he is doing, what act of his brings him under their interpretation of Romans 3:23? None, of course.

Paul's comment to the Christians in Rome thus would seem to have one of two meanings. Despite the phrasing, it might be that it refers not to absolutely everyone, but just to the mass of mankind (which means young children and other special cases, such as Mary, would be excluded without having to be singled out). If not that, then it would mean that everyone, without exception, is subject to original sin, which is true for a young child, for the unborn, even for Mary—but she, although due to be subject to it, was preserved from its stain.

It took a positive act of God to keep her from coming under its effects the way we have. We had the stain of original sin removed through baptism, which brings sanctifying grace to the soul, thus making the soul spiritually alive and capable of enjoying heaven, and makes the recipient a member of the Church. We might say that Mary received a very special kind of "baptism" at her conception, but, because since she never contracted original sin, she enjoyed certain privileges we never can, such as entire avoidance of sin.

On occasion one will hear that the Immaculate Conception cannot be squared with Mary's own description of herself: "He has looked graciously on the lowliness of his handmaid" (Lk 1:48). How could she be lowly if she were, as Catholics say, the highest creature, what the poet Wordsworth called "our tainted nature's solitary boast"?[4] If she understood herself to be lowly, does that not mean she understood herself to have sinned?

---

[4] William Wordsworth, "The Virgin", *Complete Works of William Wordsworth* (Boston: Houghton Mifflin, 1911), 7:316.

The key is that sin is not the only motive for lowliness. Compared to God, any creature, no matter how perfect, is lowly, Mary included. Jesus, referring to his human nature, said, "Learn from me, for I am gentle and humble of heart" (Mt 11:29). Certainly he was without sin, and if he could describe himself as lowly, there can be no argument against Mary describing herself the same way.

The doctrine of the Immaculate Conception was officially defined by Pope Pius IX in 1854. When fundamentalists claim that the doctrine was "invented" at this time, they misunderstand both the history of dogmas and what prompts the Church to issue, from time to time, definitive pronouncements regarding faith or morals. They are under the impression that no dogma is believed until the Pope or an ecumenical council issues a formal statement about it.

Actually, dogmas are defined formally only when there is a controversy that needs to be cleared up or when the Magisterium thinks the faithful can be helped by particular emphasis being drawn to some already-existing belief. The definition of the Immaculate Conception was prompted by the latter motive; it did not come about because there were widespread doubts about the doctrine. Pius IX, who was highly devoted to the Virgin, hoped the definition would inspire others in their devotion to her.

The Assumption

As they reject the Immaculate Conception and Mary's perpetual virginity, so fundamentalists reject the dogma of the Assumption, but they do not worry about it much. What little thought they give to it concerns why Catholics think Mary did not die. That is not the Catholic position, of course, but fundamentalists think it is, and they are concerned about a privilege that finds no warrant in Scripture.

They note that Enoch "walked with God, and he was seen no more because God took him" (Gen 5:24). He was translated so as not to see death (Heb 11:5). Then there was Elijah, who was taken up into heaven in a fiery chariot (2 Kings 2:1–13). The Bible says nothing about what happened to Mary, they note, and does it not seem there would be some mention of her never dying? After all, it would have been truly "remark-able".

There is a certain sense in their argument, and if the doctrine of the Assumption were what they think it is, the argument would carry some weight. But it is beside the point because Catholic commentators, not to mention the Popes, have agreed that Mary died; that belief has long been expressed through the liturgy. (The Church has never formally defined whether she died or not, and the integrity of the doctrine of the Assumption would not be impaired if she did not die, but the almost universal consensus is that she did in fact die.) The Assumption is therefore simpler than fundamentalists fear, although still not acceptable to them. In 1950 Pope Pius XII, in an exercise of papal infallibility, defined that Mary, "after the completion of her earthly life"—note the silence regarding her death—"was assumed body and soul into the glory of Heaven".[5] In short, her body was not allowed to corrupt; it was not allowed to remain in a tomb.

(It is also necessary to keep in mind what the Assumption is *not*. Some people think Catholics believe Mary "ascended" into heaven. That is not correct. Christ, by his own power, ascended into heaven. Mary was assumed or taken up into heaven by God. She did not do it under her own power.)

True, no express scriptural proofs for the doctrine are available. The possibility of a bodily assumption before the Second Coming is not excluded by 1 Corinthians 15:23, and it is even suggested by Matthew 27:52–53: "and the graves were opened, and many bodies arose out of them, bodies of holy men gone to their rest: who, after his rising again, left their graves and went into the holy city, where they were seen by many".

There is also what might be called the negative historical proof. As every fundamentalist knows, from the first Catholics gave homage to saints, including many about whom we now know nothing. Cities vied for the title of the last resting place of the

[5] *Munificentissimus Deus* (Denz. 2333).

most famous saints. Rome, for example, claims the tombs of Peter and Paul, Peter's tomb being under the high altar of the Basilica that bears his name. Other cities claim the mortal remains of
other saints, both famous and obscure. We know the bones of
some saints were distributed to several cities, so more than one,
for example, are able to claim the "head" of this or that saint, even
if the "head" is only a small portion of the skull. With a few exceptions (such as Peter, who was only claimed by Rome, never,
for example, by Antioch, where he worked before moving on to
Rome), the more famous or important the saint, the more cities
wanted his relics.

We know that after the Crucifixion Mary was cared for by the
apostle John (Jn 19:26–27). Early Christian writings say John
went to live at Ephesus and that Mary accompanied him. There is
some dispute about where she ended life; perhaps there, perhaps
back at Jerusalem. Neither those cities nor any other claimed her
remains, although there are claims about possessing her (temporary) tomb. Why did no city claim the bones of Mary? Apparently
because there were no bones to claim and people knew it.

Remember, in the early Christian centuries relics of saints were
jealously guarded, highly prized. The bones of those martyred in
the Colosseum, for instance, were quickly gathered up and preserved; there are many accounts of this in the biographies of those
who gave their lives for the Faith. Yet here was Mary, certainly
the most privileged of all the saints, certainly the most saintly, but
we have no record of her bodily remains being venerated anywhere.

Most arguments in favor of the Assumption, as developed over
the centuries by the Fathers and Doctors of the Church, concern
not so much scriptural references (there are few that speak even
indirectly to the matter), but rather the fittingness of the privilege. The speculative grounds considered include Mary's freedom from sin, her Motherhood of God, her perpetual virginity,
and—the key—her participation in the salvific work of Christ. It
seems most fitting that she should attain the full fruit of the Redemption, which is the glorification of the soul and body.

Yet there is more than just fittingness. Pius XII said the Assumption is really a consequence of the Immaculate Conception. "These two singular privileges bestowed upon the Mother of God stand out in most splendid light at the beginning and the end of her earthly journey. For the greatest possible glorification of her virgin body is the complement, at once appropriate and marvelous, of the absolute innocence of her soul, which was free from all stain. . . . [S]he shared in Christ's glorious triumph over sin and its sad consequences."[6]

"But", ask fundamentalists, "if Mary was immaculately conceived, and if death was a consequence of original sin, why did she die?" Although she was wholly innocent and never committed a sin, she died in order to be in union with Jesus. Keep in mind that he did not have to die to effect our redemption; he could have just willed it, and that would have been sufficient. But he *chose* to die. Mary identified herself with his work, her whole life being a co-operation with God's plan of salvation, certainly from her saying, "Let it be done to me according to thy word" (Lk 1:38), but really from the very start of her life. She accepted death as Jesus accepted death, and she suffered (Lk 2:35) in union with his suffering. Just as she shared in his work, she shared in his glorification. She shared in his Resurrection by having her glorified body taken into heaven, the way the glorified bodies of all the saved will be taken into heaven on the Last Day.

Still, fundamentalists ask, where is the proof from Scripture? Strictly, there is none. It was the Catholic Church that was commissioned by Christ to teach all nations and to teach them infallibly. The mere fact that the Church teaches the doctrine of the Assumption as something definitely true is a guarantee that it *is* true. Here, of course, we get into an entirely separate matter, the question of *sola scriptura,* which is considered elsewhere. It is enough to say there is no problem with an infallible Church officially defining a doctrine that, although not in contradiction to Scripture, cannot be found on its face. After all, the Bible says

---

[6] *Fulgens Corona* 21.

nothing against the Assumption; silence is not the same as rejection, although, to be sure, silence is not the same as affirmation either. Silence is just—silence.

The Mother of God

Frank Sheed said that Louisa Cozens, "who earned her daily bread scrubbing floors", "had as gifted a theological mind as I have met",[7] although she had only a primary school education. In 1928 she spent many evenings, after work, at the apartment where Sheed and his wife, Maisie Ward, lived because it was the only quiet place she could write. There, without reference books, she composed *A Handbook of Heresies,* probably the best small-compass account of departures from the Faith. It covers everything from Ebionism to modernism.

Cozens had a knack for getting right to the pith. In her discussion of Nestorianism, named after the bishop of Constantinople who, around 429, declared that Mary was the Mother of Christ, but not the Mother of God, thereby denying the hypostatic union, Cozens noted that "Protestants, if asked to declare their belief in the Incarnation, nearly always define it in terms which prove their underlying Nestorianism. Even when they are willing to say that Jesus Christ is God, they shrink from the Catholic statement, that God was born of Mary; that God shed his blood for us on Calvary; that God died. Today as in the fifth century, in London as at Ephesus, the honour of Mary is the safeguard, the outpost of the adoration of her son. To acknowledge the *Theotokos* ["God-bearer"] is to believe in God the Son made man."[8]

Little wonder, then, that fundamentalists, who are in so many ways archetypal Protestants, cringe when they hear Catholics refer to the Virgin as the Mother of God. How can God have a Mother, they ask, since that would imply she is older than God? The question is laughable for Catholics, but fundamentalists take

<hr>

[7] Frank Sheed, *The Church and I* (Garden City, N.Y.: Doubleday, 1974), 46.
[8] M. L. Cozens, *A Handbook of Heresies* (London: Sheed and Ward, 1974), 45.

it seriously. It is not the real reason, of course, that they disapprove of the idea of *Theotokos*. They do not say to themselves that they would call Mary the Mother of God if only this question of chronology could be answered to their satisfaction.

Their real objection is that the phrase "Mother of God" elevates Mary too much. Sure, they say, she was Christ's mother, Jesus' mother, and no doubt a good woman, but otherwise undistinguished. They perceive God as being so "wholly other" that there is a real, if unperceived, difficulty in their accepting the Incarnation in its fullest sense. It is easy for them to fall into Nestorius' position; he held that the union of the two natures in Christ was little more than a moral union of two distinct persons, the divine Son and the human Jesus. So very often, when fundamentalists discuss the matter privately and at length, they end up saying the same thing, all because of their effort to escape honoring Mary.

The answer to difficulties regarding Mary's status as the Mother of God can be explained only by noting the distinction between personhood and nature. Fundamentalists say Mary was the mother of Christ's human nature, not the mother of his divine nature, but with a little effort they can be brought to see that this is wrong. After all, was your mother the mother of your human nature? No, she was the mother of *you*. It is a *person* who is conceived and born, not a *nature*. What person was born of Mary? A divine Person only, not a human person—but a divine Person who took on a human nature. The one born of Mary "shall be called the son of God" (Lk 1:35), and "God sent his son, made of a woman" (Gal 4:4).

To say that Christ was a human person is to deny the hypostatic union. Most fundamentalists do not know that term—they are confused, too, about the distinction between person and nature—but they can perceive the contradiction inherent in their position if someone shows it to them. They can see that if Mary was not the Mother of God, then she was the mother only of Christ as a human person. They can see that if *that* was the case, then Christ was two distinct persons, a human person and a divine Person. But this is something fundamentalists do not believe; they acknowledge one Person in two natures, even if they have trouble stating the belief as such.

So there is a logical, but not psychological, contradiction here. If thought through, they would see that their position on the *Theotokos* leads to an impossible conclusion, but they have not thought it through because fundamentalism's spirit is antitheological, antispeculative. It holds theorizing on religious matters to be an invitation to heterodoxy, a view that stems from its insistence that Christian truth is ultimately experienced, not known, that will is higher than intellect. This makes for endless difficulties when Catholics and fundamentalists sit down to talk, since the latter are suspicious of syllogisms. The difficulties can be overcome with patience and an awareness that there are often unmentioned presuppositions that have to be handled first if a discussion is to get anywhere.

Mary as Mediatrix

Fundamentalists think Catholics put Mary on a par with her Son. After all, what is the word mediatrix but the feminine of mediator? Do not Catholics go even further, calling Mary the Mediatrix of all graces? Does this not deny Christ's role as the one Mediator?

The contradiction here is illusory. As Thomas Aquinas said in reference to 2 Corinthians 5:19, "Christ alone is the perfect mediator of God and men, inasmuch as, by his death, he reconciled the human race to God. . . . However, nothing hinders certain others from being called mediators, in some respect, between God and man, forasmuch as they cooperate in uniting men to God, dispositively or ministerially."[9] After all, we mediate for others when we pray to God on their behalf, which, of course, is something fundamentalists themselves do. This does not argue against Christ being the sole Mediator, because our modest efforts are entirely dependent on him. In a far more perfect way, Mary shares in his mediation. Her status as Mediatrix of all graces exists in a double sense.

---

[9] *Summa theologiae* III, 26, 1.

First, she gave the world its Redeemer, the source of all graces, and in this sense she is the channel of all graces. She freely cooperated with God's plan (Lk 1:38: "Be it done to me according to thy word"), and, as St. Thomas wrote, at the Annunciation, at the key moment for our race, she represented the whole of humanity.[10] The Fathers of the Church contrast Mary's obedience, which was perfectly free, with Eve's disobedience.

Second, Mary is the Mediatrix of all graces because of her intercession for us in heaven. What this means is that no grace accrues to us without her intercession. We are not to suppose that we are obliged to ask for all graces through her or that her intercession is intrinsically necessary for the application of graces. Instead, through God's will, grace is not conferred on anyone without Mary's cooperation.

True, scriptural proofs for this are lacking. Theologians refer to a mystical interpretation of John 19:26 ("Woman behold thy son, son behold thy mother"), an interpretation that sees John as the representative of the human race, Mary thus becoming the spiritual mother. They note the doctrine is reasonable because it is fitting.

This is little consolation to fundamentalists, of course, who see little fitting about it and who put little stock in speculative theology and even less in mystical theology. As a practical matter, this kind of doctrine is one of the last accepted by someone approaching the Church, particularly someone coming to the Church from fundamentalism, and it is accepted, ultimately, on the authority of the Church rather than on the authority of clear scriptural references. Fundamentalists, always looking for a biblical citation, can see no reason to accept a belief in Mary as Mediatrix of all graces, but they can, if they take the effort, come to see that there is, at least, nothing in the doctrine that contradicts Christ's role as the one Mediator. His role as Mediator is not lessened because she has been allowed to assist him.

---

[10] *Summa theologiae* III, 30, 1.

The Veneration of Mary

To fundamentalists, the veneration of Mary is nothing other than the worship of Mary, as shown by their use of the term Mariolatry. They really believe Catholics put Mary on the same level as God. Some of their complaints seem ridiculous to Catholics. The most common, perhaps, is that in the Rosary ten prayers are said to Mary for every one said to the Father.[11] The implication is usually left unspoken, but one is supposed to conclude, apparently, that Catholics prefer Mary ten to one over God. Looked at this way, the Rosary becomes a medieval Gallup poll.

Bill Jackson writes about Mary in his *Christian's Guide to Roman Catholicism*. He explains that "the rise in devotion to her came when a backslidden church, having lost the reality of Christ, was presented with the pagan concept of a female deity and she was deemed able to mediate between them and a God Who was too far away".[12] One of the problems with this argument is timing. Paganism effectively disappeared by the end of the sixth century, but devotion to Mary of a sort seen today was not common until the Middle Ages, by which time paganism was not even a distant memory.

Granted, there is a certain logic in claiming Catholicism adopted pagan ways when paganism was still vibrant. In fact, this is exactly what fundamentalists claim when they say Catholicism, as distinguished from Christianity, arose at the beginning of the fourth century, when Christianity was legalized in the Roman Empire. Most Romans were still pagans, they note, so it made sense for the Catholic authorities to curry favor with adher-

---

[11] This is an example of fundamentalists' curious penchant for proof by (misapplied) statistics. Some of them base their belief in the inspiration of Scripture on the mathematical unlikelihood of a long series of Old Testament prophecies coming true. Unfortunately for them, such an argument has nothing to say about the inspiration of biblical books that do not contain prophecies.

[12] Bill Jackson, *A Christian's Guide to Roman Catholicism* (Manteca, Calif.: Christians Evangelizing Catholics, n.d.), sec. 36.

ents of the majority religion. They do not realize their argument undercuts any claim that the Church appealed to paganism in promoting the veneration of the Virgin. There were no pagans left in the former Roman territory as the Middle Ages opened, so what could be gained by taking on a devotion designed to appeal to them?

One of the favorite tactics of fundamentalists, in disparaging the honors given to Mary, is to quote from some Marian devotional works. Chief among them is Alphonsus Liguori's *The Glories of Mary*, which is still popular and still in print. Liguori's book is a source of one-liners that, taken out of context (and his context is often a page or more, or even a whole chapter), seem to put Mary not just on a par with her Son, but above him. It is not easy dealing with a writer, even a saint, whose style is full of literary conceits and hyperbolic statements. *The Glories of Mary* is precisely the kind of book one should not press into the hands of a non-Catholic who has no appreciation of the Church's position on Mary—not because it is wrong and not because it reveals "secrets" reserved for the initiated, but because it is not easy to understand.

It is a matter of sequence, a matter of the groundwork that needs to be done first. There is no question that Liguori is orthodox, of course, and that his writings are enlightening, but they are simply too much for a fundamentalist to absorb. In reading Liguori, all the fundamentalist's fears seem confirmed, and that is only to be expected, since he has no appreciation of what the Catholic position on Mary really is and—what is just as bad—no appreciation of the style of religious writing that was popular in the eighteenth century, when Liguori wrote. It is remarkably easy for a fundamentalist to be frightened away from the Church. He needs to be shown Catholicism slowly, much the way the Faith was revealed only in increments to the catechumens of the early centuries. The fundamentalist feels real revulsion at doctrines he understands poorly, such as the Marian doctrines, but he can be brought to understand and even to adhere to them if the proper foundation is laid.

Mary's Perpetual Virginity

When Catholics call Mary the Virgin, they mean she remained a virgin throughout her life. When Protestants use the term, they mean she was a virgin only until the birth of Jesus; they believe that she and Joseph later had children, all those called "the brethren of the Lord". What gives rise to the disagreement are biblical verses that use the terms "brethren", "brother", or "sister".

These are representative verses: "While he was still speaking to the multitude, it chanced that his mother and his brethren were standing without, desiring speech with him" (Mt 12:46); "Is this not the carpenter, the son of Mary, the brother of James and Joseph and Judas and Simon? Do not his sisters live here near us?" (Mk 6:3); "For even his brethren were without faith in him" (Jn 7:5); "All these, with one mind, gave themselves up to prayer, together with Mary the mother of Jesus, and the rest of the women and his brethren" (Acts 1:14); "Have we not the right to travel about with a woman who is a sister, as the other apostles do, as the Lord's brethren do, and Cephas?" (1 Cor 9:5).

The first thing to note, when trying to understand such verses, is that the term "brother" has a wide meaning in the Bible. It is not restricted to brothers german or half brothers. The same goes for "sister" and the plural "brethren". Lot is described as Abraham's "brother" (Gen 14:14), but Lot was the son of Aran, Abraham's deceased brother (Gen 11:26–28); this means Lot was really Abraham's nephew. Jacob is called the "brother" of his uncle Laban (Gen 29:15). Cis and Eleazar were the sons of Moholi; Cis had sons of his own, but Eleazar had no sons, only daughters, who married their "brethren", the sons of Cis. These "brethren" were really their cousins (1 Chron 23:21–22).

The terms "brethren", "brother", and "sister" did not refer only to close relatives, as in the above examples. Sometimes they meant only a kinsman (Dt 23:7; 2 Esd 5:7; Jer 34:9), as in the reference to the forty-two "brethren" of king Ochozias (2 Kings 10:13–14). The words could mean even people apparently unrelated, such as a friend (2 Sam 1:26; 1 Kings 9:13, 20:32), or just an ally (Amos 1:9).

Why this ambiguous usage? Because neither Hebrew nor Aramaic, the language spoken by Christ and his disciples, had a special word meaning "cousin". Speakers of those languages used either the word for "brother" or a circumlocution, such as "the son of the sister of my father". Using a circumlocution was a clumsy way to speak, so they naturally fell to using the word "brother".

The writers of the New Testament were brought up to use the Aramaic equivalent of "brethren" to mean both cousins and sons of the same father—plus other relatives and even nonrelatives. When they wrote in Greek, they did the same thing the translators of the Septuagint did. In the Septuagint the Hebrew word that includes both true brothers and cousins was translated as *adelphos,* which in Greek has the (usually) narrow meaning that the English "brother" has. Unlike Hebrew or Aramaic, Greek has a separate word for cousin, *anepsios,* but the translators of the Septuagint favored *adelphos,* even for true cousins.

One might say they transliterated instead of translated. They took an exact equivalent of the Hebrew word for "brother" and did not use *adelphos* here (for sons of the same parents), *anepsios* there (for cousins). This same usage was employed by the writers of the New Testament and passed into English translations of the Bible. To determine just what "brethren" or "brother" or "sister" means in any one verse, we must look at the context. When we do that, we see insuperable problems arise if we assume that Mary had children other than Jesus.

At the Annunciation, when the angel Gabriel appeared to Mary, she asked, "How can that be, since I have no knowledge of man?" (Lk 1:34). From the earliest interpretations of the Bible we see that this was taken to mean that she had made a vow of lifelong virginity, even in marriage. If she had taken no such vow, the question would make no sense at all.

There is no reason to assume Mary was wholly ignorant of the rudiments of biology. She presumably knew the normal way in which children are conceived. If she anticipated having children and did not intend to maintain a vow of virginity, she would hardly have to ask "how" she was to have a child, since having a child the normal way would be expected by a newlywed. No, her question makes sense only if there was an apparent, but not a real, conflict between keeping a vow of virginity and acceding to the angel's request. A careful look at the New Testament shows Mary kept her vow and never had any children other than Jesus.

In the story of his being found in the Temple, Jesus, at age twelve, is mentioned as evidently the only Son of Mary (Lk 2:41–51); there is no hint of other children in the family. The people of Nazareth, where he grew up, refer to him as "the son of Mary" (Mk 6:3), not as "a son of Mary". The Greek expression implies he is her only son. In fact, others in the Gospels are never referred to as Mary's sons, not even when they are called Jesus' "brethren". If they were in fact her sons, this would be strange usage.

There is another point, perhaps a little harder for moderns, or at least Westerners, to grasp. It is that the attitude taken by the "brethren of the Lord" implies they are his elders. In ancient and, particularly, in Eastern societies (remember, the Holy Land is in Asia), older sons gave advice to younger, but younger never gave advice to older—it was considered disrespectful to do so. But we find Jesus' "brethren" saying to him that Galilee was no place for him and that he should go to Judaea so his disciples could see his doings, so he could make a name for himself (Jn 7:3–4). Another time, they sought to restrain him for his own benefit, saying, "He must be mad" (Mk 3:21). This kind of behavior could make sense for ancient Jews only if the "brethren" were older than Jesus, but that alone eliminates them as his brothers german, since Jesus, we know, was Mary's "first-born".

Consider what happened at the foot of the Cross. When he was dying, Jesus entrusted his Mother to the apostle John: "Jesus, seeing his mother there, and the disciple, too, whom he loved, standing by, said to his mother, Woman, this is thy son. Then he said to the disciple, this is thy mother. And from that hour the disciple took her into his own keeping" (Jn 19:26–27). The Gospels mention four "brethren", James, Joseph, Simon, and Jude. It is hard to imagine why Jesus would have disregarded family ties and made this provision for his Mother if these four were also her sons.

Fundamentalists are insistent nevertheless that "brethren of the Lord" must be interpreted in the strict sense. They most commonly make two arguments based on this verse: "And he knew her not till she brought forth her first-born son" (Mt 1:25). They first argue that the natural inference from "till" is that Joseph and Mary afterward lived together as husband and wife, in the usual sense, and had several children. Otherwise, they ask, bringing up their second point, why would Jesus be called "first-born"? Does that not mean there must have been at least a "second-born", perhaps a "third-born" and "fourth-born", and so on?

The problem for them is that they are trying to use the modern meaning of "till" (or "until") instead of the meaning it had when the Bible was written. In the Bible, it means only that some action did not happen up to a certain point; it does not imply that the action did happen later, which is the modern sense of the term. In fact, if the modern sense is forced on the Bible, some ridiculous meanings result.

Consider this line: "Michal the daughter of Saul had no children until the day of her death" (2 Sam 6:23). Are we to assume she had children after her death? How about the raven that Noah released from the ark? The bird "went forth and did not return till the waters were dried up upon the earth" (Gen 8:7). In fact, we know the raven never returned at all. Then there was the burial of Moses. About the location of his grave it was said that no man knows "until this present day" (Dt 34:6)—but we know that no one has known since that day either. Or how about this: "And they went up to mount Sion with joy and gladness, and offered holocausts, because not one of them was slain till they had returned in peace" (1 Macc 5:54). Does this mean the soldiers were slain after they returned from battle?

The examples could be multiplied, but there should be no need. It should be clear that nothing at all can be proved from the use of the word "till" in Matthew 1:25. Recent translations give a better sense of the verse: "He had no relations with her at any time before she bore a son" (New American Bible); "he had not known her when she bore a son" (Knox translation).

The other argument used by fundamentalists concerns the term "first-born". They say Jesus could not be called Mary's "first-born" unless there were other children that followed him. This is a misunderstanding of the way the ancient Jews used the term. For them it meant the child that opened the womb (Ex 13:2; Nb 3:12). Under the Mosaic law, it was the "first-born" son that was to be sanctified (Ex 34:20). Did this mean the parents had to wait until a second son was born before they could call their first the "first-born"? Hardly. The first male child of a marriage was termed the "first-born" even if he turned out to be the only child of the marriage. This usage is illustrated by a funerary inscription discovered in Egypt. The inscription refers to a woman who died during the birth of her "first-born".

Fundamentalists also say it would have been repugnant for Mary and Joseph to enter a marriage and yet remain virgins. They call married virginity an "unnatural" arrangement. Certainly it is unusual, but not as unusual as having the Son of God in one's family, not as unusual as having a true virgin give birth to a child. The Holy Family was neither an average family nor even one suited to be chosen as "family of the year" from among a large number of similarly situated families. We should not expect its members to act as we would. The Holy Family is the ideal family, but not because it is like "regular" families in all major respects, only better. In major respects it is totally unlike any other family. The circumstances demanded that, just as they demanded the utmost in sacrifice on the part of Mary and Joseph. This was a special family, set aside for the nurture of the Son of God. No greater dignity could be given to marriage than that.

Backing up the testimony of Scripture regarding Mary's perpetual virginity is the testimony of early Christian writings. Consider the controversy between Jerome and Helvidius. It was Helvidius, writing around 380, who first brought up the notion that the "brethren of the Lord" were children born to Mary and Joseph after Jesus' birth. Jerome first declined to comment on Helvidius' remarks because they were a "novel, wicked, and a daring affront to the faith of the whole world".[13] This was an entirely new interpretation, one nobody had ventured before, and it was beneath contempt.

At length, however, Jerome's friends convinced him to write a reply, which turned out to be his treatise called *On the Perpetual Virginity of the Blessed Mary*. He used not only the scriptural arguments given above, but cited earlier Christian writers, such as Ignatius, Polycarp, Irenaeus, and Justin Martyr. Helvidius claimed the support of two writers, Tertullian and Victorinus, but Jerome showed this was no support at all, since Tertullian was a heretic (a Montanist) and the passage from Victorinus had been misinterpreted. Helvidius was unable to come up with a reply, and his theory was not employed again until modern times.

So, if it is established that the "brethren of the Lord" were not Jesus' brothers german or half brothers, who were they? That they were Jesus' cousins has been the accepted view at least from the time of Jerome until recent centuries. (Before Jerome the consensus was that they definitely were not Mary's sons, but not necessarily that they were her nephews.)

Of the four "brethren" who are named in the Gospels, consider, for the sake of argument, only James. Similar reasoning can be used for the other three. We know that James' mother was named Mary. Look at the descriptions of the women standing beneath the Cross: "Among them were Mary Magdalen, and Mary the mother of James and Joseph, and the mother of the sons of Zebedee" (Mt 27:56); "Among them were Mary Magdalen, and Mary the mother of James the less and of Joseph, and Salome" (Mk 15:40). Then look at what John says: "And meanwhile his [Jesus'] mother, Mary the wife of Cleophas, and Mary Magdalen had taken their stand beside the cross of Jesus" (Jn 19:25). If we compare these parallel accounts of the scene of the Crucifixion, we see that the mother of James and Joseph must be the wife of Cleophas. So far so good.

---

[13] Jerome, *De perpetua virginitatae Beatae Mariae adversus Helvidium*.

An argument against this, though, is that James is elsewhere (Mt 10:3) described as the son of Alphaeus, which would mean this Mary, whoever she was, was the wife of both Cleophas and Alphaeus. One solution is that she was widowed once, then remarried. More probably Alphaeus and Cleophas (Clopas in Greek) are the same person, since the Aramaic name for Alphaeus could be rendered in Greek in different ways, either as Alphaeus or Clopas. Another possibility is that Alphaeus took a Greek name similar to his Jewish name, the way that Saul took the name Paul.

So it is probable, anyway, that James is the son of this other Mary and Cleophas. If the testimony of Hegesippus, a second-century historian, is believed, Cleophas was the brother of Joseph, the foster father of Jesus.[14] James would thus be Joseph's nephew and a cousin of Jesus, who was Joseph's putative son. This identification of the "brethren of the Lord" as Jesus' cousins is open to legitimate question—they might even be relatives more distantly removed—and our inability to know certainly their status says nothing about the main point, which is that the Bible demonstrates that they were not, anyway, the Virgin Mary's children.

Why are fundamentalists, particularly those most opposed to Catholicism, so insistent that Mary was not perpetually a virgin? There seem to be two reasons.

One is dislike of celibacy for priests and nuns. They are aware that it is Catholic teaching that celibacy is to be highly prized, that there is much virtue and much common sense in priests and nuns giving up the privilege of marriage in order to serve Christ better. They know Catholics refer to the example of Mary when praising consecrated virginity. So, by undermining her status, they hope to undermine that of priests and nuns. By claiming Mary did not live her life as a virgin, they hope to make religious celibacy seem contrary to the gospel.

---

[14] Fragment in Eusebius Pamphilius, *Historia ecclesiastica* 4, 22, 4; 3, 11, 1.

The other reason concerns Mary herself. In the Catholic scheme of things, she is certainly different from other women, so much so that she is considered worthy of special devotion (not of course of worship, *latria*, but of a level of honor, *hyperdulia*, higher than other saints receive). Her status accounts for the attention paid her. Fundamentalists think that what she gets, by way of devotion, is necessarily taken from Christ.

This is neither true nor logical, but they nevertheless think devotion to Mary must be discouraged if proper devotion to our Lord is to be maintained. One way to diminish her status is to show she was just like other women, more or less, and that can be done in part by showing she had other children. Their desire to do this tends to make impossible fundamentalists' accurate weighing of the facts. Their presuppositions do not allow them to see what the Bible really implies about the "brethren of the Lord".

Chapter 23

The Inquisition

Sooner or later, any exchange of views with fundamentalists will come around to the Inquisition. The topic can hardly be avoided. To non-Catholics the Inquisition is a scandal; to Catholics, an embarrassment; to both, a confusion. At the least, it is a handy stick with which to engage in Catholic-bashing, because most Catholics are at a loss for a sensible reply. The topic is so vast, its history so intricate, they do not know how to begin to respond to fundamentalists, even though few of the latter know the first thing about the Inquisition. What little they do know comes from tendentious little pamphlets written by people whose main interest is not historical accuracy.

The Inquisition was spread over six centuries and half a continent. It appeared first in southern France in response to Catharism and the civil discord that accompanied that religious and ideological plague, and later it was working, in fits and starts and in quite different formats, in Italy and the Holy Roman Empire, where it functioned for only a few decades in the thirteenth century. In between it was established in Spain, and there it became a creature of the state and was effectively out of the control of Church authorities.

Technically, five forms of the Inquisition may be distinguished. First came the episcopal, established in 1184 and operating mainly in France. Individual bishops ran the show, but not entirely well. Innocent III sought more control and established the legatine Inquisition, which was under the authority of the Cistercians. That was in 1198. Procedures were further formalized in 1231, when Gregory IX set up the monastic Inquisition, with the Dominicans in control. Commentators usually speak of these

three forms as one institution, the Medieval Inquisition. It died
out as Catharism disappeared.

Quite separate was the Roman Inquisition, begun in 1542 under Paul III. This was the one under which Galileo was tried, and
it was the least active and most benign of the three main variations. Separate again was the Spanish Inquisition, begun in 1478,
a state institution used to ferret out Jews and Moors who converted to Christianity not out of conviction but for purposes of
political or social advantage. It was the Spanish Inquisition that
had the worst record.[1]

Surprisingly enough, Loraine Boettner, the intellectual godfather of modern fundamentalist anti-Catholicism, has little to say
about the Inquisition in his *Roman Catholicism*. One would think
he would make more extensive use of the issue since it is such a
fine weapon against the Church. He looks only at the Spanish
Inquisition and then only briefly, relying mainly on an article appearing in *Christian Heritage* magazine in 1959. The author, Walter M. Montano, wrote that "it has been shown by [Juan
Antonio] Llorente, who carefully examined the records of the
Tribunal, and whose statements are drawn from the most authoritative sources, that 105,285 victims fell under the inquisitor general Torquemada; 51,167 under Cisneros; and 34,952 fell under
Diego Perez. It is further reckoned that 31,912 were burned alive!
Half that number, 15,659, suffered the punishment of the statute,
and 291,450 were sent to penitentiaries. Half a million families
were destroyed by the Inquisition, and it cost Spain two million
children!"[2]

This quotation illustrates the reliability of sources used by fundamentalists such as Boettner, who does not inform the reader
that Llorente, who had been appointed a secretary to the Inquisition in 1789, was hardly a responsible historian. In 1801 he was
dismissed for alleged embezzlement. Although a Spaniard, he

---

[1] For a dispassionate account, see Fernand Hayward, *The Inquisition* (Staten Island, N.Y.: Alba House, 1965).

[2] Boettner, *Catholicism*, 433.

sided with the French when they invaded Spain in 1808. After the return of the Spanish king, Llorente retired to Paris, where in 1817 he published *The Critical History of the Spanish Inquisition*. He claimed to make use of official documents to which he said he had access, and it was from these documents he calculated the number of executions. When challenged on the figures, he said he had burned the papers on which he had relied.[3] Critics have asked whether one can trust a man who says he destroyed original documents deliberately.

In any event, there is considerable dispute, even among honest historians, regarding how many deaths occurred under the Spanish Inquisition, and this is no place to settle that squabble. It is enough to note that responsible estimates vary, some historians asserting fewer than three thousand death sentences were handed down during three centuries, others putting the figure higher. As a point of comparison, Sir James Stephens, in his *History of English Criminal Law*, notes there were eight hundred executions a year during the early post-Reformation period in England, where the Inquisition never operated.[4] One could also refer to the burning of alleged witches, a practice almost unknown in Catholic countries. (Goethe, in his *Italienische Reise*, attributed the lack of belief in witches to Catholics' use of the confessional.)[5] In Britain thirty thousand went to the stake for witchcraft; in Protestant Germany the figure was one hundred thousand.[6] Such statistics do not make the Spanish executions right, but they perhaps indicate that severity in punishment was not due to Catholicism as such, but must be attributed to the general character of the times.

Most fundamentalists who write about the Inquisition rely on the books of Henry C. Lea (1825–1909), who published a massive

---

[3] Kevin Long, "The Spanish Inquisition: A Second Look", *Faith & Reason*, Summer 1982, 59–60.

[4] Rumble and Carty, *Replies*, 1:218.

[5] *Goethes Werke* (Stuttgart: Cotta, 1867), 20:245.

[6] William Thomas Walsh, *Isabella of Spain* (New York: Robert M. McBride, 1930), 275; R. Trevor Davies, *The Golden Century of Spain: 1501–1621* (London: Macmillan, 1937), 14.

three-volume account. His *History of the Inquisition in the Middle Ages*[7] was called, in a priest's introduction to the French edition, "the most thorough history of the Inquisition which we possess".

Remarkably enough, it is probably *still* the most thorough (at sixteen hundred pages, certainly the longest) history in English, for there have been few scholars willing to grapple with the all-encompassing historical analysis the institution demands.

It is unfortunate that it has been Lea's work that has molded public opinion in English-speaking countries, because, although it contains a great amount of data, it is marred by an unrelenting bias. "Honest he may be," said Elphège Vacandard, himself an authority on the Inquisition, "but impartial never. His pen too often gives way to his prejudices and his hatred of the Catholic Church. His critical judgment is sometimes gravely at fault."[8] But his faults are virtues in the eyes of fundamentalists.

Lea was an American. His counterpart in England was Cambridge historian G. G. Coulton (1858–1947), an ardent foe of the Catholic Church and well known for his love of controversy. When the subject was Rome, the Cambridge don had difficulty containing himself. He might be known best for an exchange of letters he had with Arnold Lunn, the letters appearing as *Is the Catholic Church Anti-Social?* Lunn scolded Coulton for eating up an entire third of the book with a single letter that largely strayed from the agreed topic and focused instead on his pet anti-Catholic attacks.[9] Coulton, too, is a favorite of literate fundamentalists.

Considering himself the English Lea, Coulton took pains to protect his mentor's reputation. Herbert Thurston, an English Jesuit who remarked that Lea's "work abounded in reckless deductions from inadequate evidence", said one could find ten palpable blunders on any ten consecutive pages of Lea's books.[10] Coulton,

---

[7] Henry C. Lea, *A History of the Inquisition in the Middle Ages* (New York: Harper, 1887).

[8] Elphège Vacandard, *L'Inquisition* (Paris, 1907), viii.

[9] G. G. Coulton and Arnold Lunn, *Is the Catholic Church Anti-Social?* (London: Burns Oates & Washbourne, 1946), 127.

[10] Coulton and Lunn, *Anti-Social?* 104–12, 128, 132.

incensed, challenged him to prove it, had an associate select ten pages from Lea at random, and, in an act of magnanimity, threw in two pages extra. To his consternation Thurston pointed out fifteen blunders in the twelve pages. Coulton acknowledged to Lunn that Lea "had stumbled badly" and admitted his own "mistaken credulity".[11]

One cannot conclude from this anecdote that all Lea and Coulton wrote about the Inquisition was wrong. They made real progress in basic research. Proper credit should not be denied them. The problem is that they could not weigh the facts properly because they were burdened with fierce animosity toward the Church—animosity that had nothing to do with the Inquisition as such. Their prejudices hindered them in separating reliable information from unreliable. They were too quick to accept statements unfavorable to the Church, too slow to dismiss statements inspired by malice similar to their own.

Of course, the contrary problem has not been unknown. Some Catholic writers, particularly those less interested in digging for truth than in giving a quick excuse, have glossed over incontrovertible facts and done what they could to whitewash the Inquisition, reminding one of hagiographers who reduce saints from human beings to porcelain dolls by ignoring awkward facts in their lives. This is as much a disservice to the truth as exaggerating the Inquisition's bad points. These well-intentioned but misguided Catholic apologists are, in one respect at least, much like Lea, Coulton, and the present strain of anti-Catholic fundamentalists. They fear, as the others hope, that the facts about the Inquisition will demonstrate the illegitimacy of the Catholic Church. But the facts will not do that at all. The Church has nothing to fear from the truth or a right appreciation of it. No account of foolishness, misguided zeal, or cruelty by Catholics can undo the divine foundation of the Church, although admittedly such things are stumbling blocks to Catholic and non-Catholic alike. What must be

[11] Coulton and Lunn, *Anti-Social?* 110.

grasped is that the Church contains within itself all sorts of sinners and knaves, and some of them reach high rank. The wheat and chaff coexist in the Kingdom until the end, and that was how the Founder intended it.

The problem for fundamentalists is that they perceive the Church to contain only the elect. For them, sinners are outside the doors. Locate sinners, and one locates another place where the Church is not. It is easy to demonstrate sin operating through the Inquisition, at least to the extent dry records allow us to perceive sin at the remove of centuries, and for the fundamentalist this proves the Inquisition, if it was the arm of a church, was the arm of a false church. Catholics, thinking fundamentalists might have a point, tend to be defensive. That is the wrong attitude. The right attitude for Catholics is to discover what really happened and to understand the Inquisition *in situ*—and then to explain to anti-Catholics, hard although this may be, why the sorry tale does not prove what they think it proves.

There can be no Catholic who would not wish that the Inquisition—or at least its bad elements, which were not coextensive with it—had never happened. In many respects, it was a logical consequence of the times and, for all its gore, not easily distinguishable from civil courts in its procedures and punishments, but the fact that cruelty can be found elsewhere in old records does not justify the cruelty that operated through the inquisitorial process.

How should a Catholic answer charges about the Inquisition? He should not attempt to deny the undeniable; history cannot be wished away. On the other hand, he should not, out of embarrassment, acquiesce in every fundamentalist slander. What he should try to do is give his questioner a little perspective. If he is able, the Catholic should learn enough about the Inquisition to give his opponent some sort of overview and to demonstrate that while much of what he knows about the Inquisition is true in quality, it is wrong in quantity. If understood, this may help the fundamentalist see that the mere existence of the Inquisition does not disprove the Church's credentials.

Many fundamentalists believe that more people died under the Inquisition than in any war or plague, but in this they rely on ridiculous "statistics" generated by one-upmanship among anti-Catholics, each of whom, it seems, tries to come up with the largest number of casualties. Trying to straighten out such historical confusions can take one only so far, of course, and one should not put undue emphasis on numbers. As Ronald Knox said, we should be cautious, "lest we should wander interminably in a wilderness of comparative atrocity statistics".[12] In fact, no one knows how many people perished through the Inquisition. We happen to live in a century of statistics. Everything is quantified, and we save records the way squirrels save acorns, but often with far less reason. It is difficult for us to appreciate that in earlier centuries statistical abstracts were not drawn up because people saw no need for them. We do, indeed, have some records of how many people were executed, but they are spotty. No doubt most such records just disappeared over the centuries, and there were probably few to begin with. We can make at best rough estimates of the number of deaths.

We can determine for certain, though, two things about the numbers given by most fundamentalists: they are exaggerated or, worse, fabrications. It would be one thing to err in extrapolations or calculations. An error of 100 or even 500 percent would not be large in piecing together what facts are available. But an error of 2.5 million percent? If you take the conservative figure that some Catholic scholars accept (around four thousand executions total, throughout the history of the Inquisition, in all countries where it operated), that is roughly the size of the error in the figure given in *The Mystery of Babylon Revealed,* a book that states that 95 million people were killed during the Inquisition.[13]

---

[12] Ronald Knox and Arnold Lunn, *Difficulties* (London: Eyre and Spottiswoode, 1952), 40.

[13] Only slightly less preposterous, Jimmy Swaggart claims "the Roman Catholic church murdered some *twenty million* people during the existence of the Inquisition." *Catholicism,* 31.

The figure of 95 million deaths is so grotesquely off that one immediately doubts the writer's sanity or at least his grasp of the elementary facts of demographics. Not until modern times did the population of the whole of Europe approach 95 million.[14] The Inquisition did not operate in England, Scandinavia, Northern Europe, or Eastern Europe. Although on paper its extent was wide, in practice it was confined almost entirely to southern France, Italy, Spain, and a few parts of the Holy Roman Empire. The Black Death, which killed about a third of Europe's population, is credited by historians with major changes in the social structure. The Inquisition is credited with few, precisely because the number of its victims was by comparison small.

Far better than wasting time arguing about statistics that can only be roughly approximated or about numbers taken out of a magician's hat, the Catholic should ask the fundamentalist what he thinks the existence of the Inquisition demonstrates. After all, no fundamentalist will bring up the subject unless he thinks it proves something about the Catholic Church. What is that something? That the Church contains sinners? Guilty as charged. That at times sinners have reached positions of authority? Ditto. That even otherwise good Catholics, afire with zeal, sometimes lose their balance? True, all true, but such charges could be made and verified even if the Inquisition never existed.

Fundamentalist writers claim the Inquisition reveals the Catholic Church could not be the Church founded by Christ. They use the Inquisition as a good—perhaps their best—bad example. Yet to call an institution into question is not to prove it false, and the Church has not been false to its commission. Individual Catholics, yes—it has always been that way, since the denials of Peter, and it will continue that way until the end—but no degree of unsaintliness on the part of Catholics proves the Church to be other than what it claims to be, even though that unsaintliness puts grave obstacles in the path of people outside and inside the Church. As a practical matter, there is only so much mileage in

[14] The present-day population of France, Spain, and Italy is about 150 million.

the anti-Catholics' argument, and they recognize it; most people perceive at once its weakness, how it can apply equally against Reformation Christianity. If the Inquisition establishes the falsity of Catholicism, the witch trials establish the falsity of Protestantism.

Perhaps a more compelling, if often unstated, reason fundamentalists bring up the Inquisition is that they think it was begun to "liquidate" fundamentalists. They identify themselves with Catharists (also known as Albigensians), or perhaps it is better to say they identify Catharists with themselves. They think Catharists were twelfth-century fundamentalists and that the Catholic Church did to them just what it would do to fundamentalists today if it had the means. This is a fantasy. Fundamentalist writers take one point—that Catharists used a vernacular version of the Bible—and conclude that these people were "Bible Christians". The truth is that they were hardly Christians at all. Theirs was a curious heresy that perhaps (no one knows for sure) came to France from what is now Bulgaria. Catharism was a mixture of Gnosticism, which claimed a secret source of religious knowledge, and Manichaeanism, which said matter is evil, and it had serious, civilization-destroying, social consequences.

Marriage was scorned because it legitimized sexual relations, which Catharists identified as the original sin. Concubinage was permitted because it was temporary and secret and was not given formal approval, while marriage was permanent, open, and publicly sanctioned. The consequences from such theories are not hard to imagine.

There was one key sacrament, the *consolamentum*, which could be received only once and which was absolutely necessary for salvation. Any sin committed after receiving the *consolamentum* deprived one of heaven. The Catharist thus waited until he was on his deathbed to receive his "baptism". What followed next, for those who did not die promptly of natural causes, was the *endura*, which was not readily distinguishable from euthanasia. If the Catharist wanted to die as a "martyr", he was suffocated with a pillow. If he wanted to go out as a "confessor", he was starved to death. Religious authorities would reside in the home of the dying Catharist to ensure his family did not sneak food in.

There was also a political angle to the heresy. Feudal society was based on the oath of fealty, much as ours is based on contract. Catharists denied the lawfulness of oaths, and that threatened to undermine the social fabric; imagine what would happen today if all contractual obligations, no matter how old or well established, were suddenly eliminated. Catharists interpreted Christ's words to Peter concerning tribute money ("then the children are free"; Mt 17:25) as authorizing them to withhold taxes and to refuse allegiance to secular rulers. Catharism was both a moral and a political evil. Even Lea admitted "the cause of orthodoxy was the cause of progress and civilization. Had Catharism become dominant, or even had it been allowed to exist on equal terms, its influence could not have failed to become disastrous." Whatever else might be said about Catharism, it was certainly not the same as modern fundamentalism, and fundamentalists' sympathy with the heresy is sadly misplaced.

What is needed by all disputants is perspective. Catholics in particular, if they want to see a discussion of the Inquisition result in understanding rather than fisticuffs, need to appreciate what is really in question. At one time Catholic apologists tried to justify all aspects of the Inquisition. That was foolish. There has never been any need for a whitewash. Today many Catholics fail to understand what fundamentalists are driving at, and they restrict themselves to secondary matters. Instead, they should discover what fundamentalists are trying to prove with their talk about hecatombs.

Granted, there is a certain utility, but a decidedly limited one, in demonstrating that the kinds and degrees of punishments inflicted by the Inquisition were similar to or even lighter than those generally meted out by secular courts. It is equally true that, despite what we consider the Inquisition's lamentable procedures, many people preferred to have their cases tried by ecclesiastical courts because the secular courts had fewer safeguards; indeed, when the Inquisition was abolished in Spain, people rioted in favor of its return. The *Catholic Encyclopedia* remarks accurately that "it is well known that belief in the justice of punishing heresy with death was so common among the sixteenth-century reformers— Luther, Zwingli, Calvin, and their adherents—that we may say their toleration began where their power ended".[15] Jean Guitton has noted that "we must measure the horror of the remedy by the horror of the disease".[16] And, as some have pointed out, we should keep in mind that as recently as fifty years ago, torture ("the third degree") was routinely used even by American police.

Such arguments are better suited to discussions with reasonably informed people than with fundamentalists who think they can injure Catholicism by talking about judicial practices that are universally acknowledged, now, to be unjust. "The Inquisition was punctilious in its adherence to law," wrote Donald Attwater, "but after full allowance has been made for 'other times, other manners', some of its procedure[s] and punishments must be set down as utterly unreasonable and in consequence cruel."[17] One should not seek to justify them, but to explain them and, most importantly, to explain how they could have been associated with a divinely established Church and how, from their existence, it is not proper to conclude that the Church of Rome is not the Church of Christ. This is where any discussion should focus.

[15] *Catholic Encyclopedia*, s.v. "Inquisition", 8:35.

[16] Jean Guitton, *Great Heresies and Church Councils* (New York: Harper and Row, 1963), 130.

[17] Donald Attwater, ed., *A Catholic Dictionary* (New York: Macmillan, 1949), 256.

Chapter 24

Practical Apologetics

Almost everyone has been through it. There is a knock at the door, usually at some inconvenient hour, and outside is a man with a wide smile, an open Bible, and awkward questions, beginning with, "Have you been saved, friend?" When he discovers you are a Catholic, which you volunteer in hope it will frighten him away, he reaches into his valise and brings out several Catholic Bibles. "Which would you prefer we use—New American Bible, Jerusalem Bible, maybe the old Douay-Rheims?" You talk with him for what seems like hours, and finally he goes away with an air of triumph, while you retire with a sore throat.

Or the altercation—somehow it always ends up being an altercation—starts after Mass. You exit church to find people distributing leaflets opposing Catholic beliefs. If you so much as look one of them in the eye, he rushes over, and you cannot wriggle your way through the crowd fast enough to get away. "Here's the truth about the idolatry of the Mass", you are told in an insistent voice as a tract is pressed into your hands. "Read it."

"No, thanks; not interested", you say, so he tells you, word for word, just what you would have read and keeps backing you toward the curb until you engage him in talk or step into whizzing traffic. You try being brusque, but even that does not discourage him.

Perhaps it starts in a social setting. At your prolife meeting, once the business session is over and everyone settles back for a little conviviality and a spot of tea, fundamentalists search out the Catholics. You sit in the corner, trying to be unobtrusive, but one sidles up to you anyway and, before you can ask her opinion about the first nonreligious topic that comes to mind, she leans over and asks, "Wouldn't you like to have an absolute assurance of salvation?"

"Sure," you say, "but . . ." You are interrupted as she motions you to wait while she flips heavily underlined pages of the New Testament to find just the right rebuttal to the comment you had no chance to make, and from there it is a long evening and all downhill.

These discussions, whether with the fellow at your door, the pamphleteer outside church, or the woman at the meeting, seem to go nowhere. You know things are being taken out of context, but you do not remember what the context is. There are snappy rejoinders edging toward the tip of your tongue, but they fail to pass through your teeth. (Later you will kick yourself for not being quick-witted.) If you put Catholic beliefs into your own, unconsidered words, you find instead you have put your foot in your mouth and confirmed your adversary's worst suspicions. For some questions you do not have the vaguest hint of an answer; in fact, you have the nagging suspicion that maybe, just maybe, your opponent is on to something, God forbid.

You end up dissatisfied, and no one—least of all you—seems at all convinced by what you have said. Quite the contrary. Your interlocutor appears more set in anti-Catholic prejudices than ever, and people around you, if there are any left by the time you are through, seem to be muttering under their breath, presumably about your descent from Caspar Milquetoast. You did not handle the situation well, and you know it.

If there is a moral to this, it is that knowing *how* to argue is just as important as knowing *what* to argue. If you have no appreciation of technique, all the knowledge in the world will not help since you will not be able to pass it along. You can be a walking theological treatise (which, Lord knows, you are not), but if you antagonize opponents or talk past them, you have wasted your time and theirs. It is not enough to be a good conversationalist. That will not make up for doctrinal or historical ignorance. Style without substance is worthless. To be an effective apologist, you must marry delivery and content.

In the earlier chapters of this book you learned about the anti-Catholic movement among fundamentalists, its origins, its arguments, and what can be said to counter its charges. In the next chapter you will learn what to read to deepen your understanding of Catholicism and fundamentalism. That done, you naturally will want to know how to put your newfound knowledge to work. You will begin by recalling the motto of the Benedictine monks, *ora et labora*. You will begin your apologetics work with prayer. You will accomplish nothing—not merely a little, mind you, but nothing at all—without a serious prayer life. Even good works, such as "instructing the ignorant", will go nowhere unless you put everything into God's hands—and not just at the outset, but daily, in your studies, in your discussions, in your frustrations. Yes, especially in your frustrations, which will be many because your successes will seem so meager, so few. They will be there, but many of them you will never see. Fundamentalists did not become what they are overnight, particularly those who converted from Catholicism, and most of them, even if they ultimately find rest at Rome, will not move toward the Church with any speed you can detect. In most cases you plant a seed and let it germinate on its own. If a few people ask for more assistance, you give it, but for every fundamentalist whose opinion of the Church seems to be mellowing, there will be ten who seem as firmly anti-Catholic as ever. You have to let grace take its course.

How should you pray for this kind of apostolate? One way that makes sense is to meditate on scriptural passages. Why? Because it does double duty. It is at once prayer and work, the work being the inescapable reading you must do in the Bible. No matter how fine your religious training, no matter how well you think you know doctrines or Church history, you need to be at home with Scripture if you intend to make an impression on fundamentalists. Of course, you should be conversant with the Bible anyway, not solely in preparation for controversy, but for its own sake—for *your* own sake.

If the only thing that gets you to open the Bible is umbrage at the latest anti-Catholic slander, that will do for starters. You might say it is like contrition versus attrition. Perfect contrition, sorrow arising out of love of God, is the ideal in confession, but you will have your sins forgiven if the best you can manage is attrition, fear of punishment. Reading the Bible because it is the word of God is better than reading it because you need to find replies to fundamentalists' accusations—but any port in a storm. The important thing is to start reading; once you do, it will be easy to make a habit of turning to the sacred text.

Concentrate on the New Testament, but not to the exclusion of the Old. It is more important to go through the New Testament a dozen times than to go through the Old twice. There is no need to memorize great chunks of the Bible, the way some fundamentalists do. You should be especially familiar, though, with the Gospels. If you are not at ease with the details of Christ's life, you are in trouble. Frank Sheed, the great street-corner apologist, put it this way: "A Catholic apologist who is not soaked in the Gospels is an anomaly in himself, and his work is doomed to aridity."[1]

The New Testament is short enough to be read in the evenings of a single week. Spend several weeks with it before doing anything else, paying particular attention to the Gospels, but not ignoring the Epistles. Work in the Old Testament gradually. Not all of the Old Testament is needed for your work, so do not worry if you take a year or two to get to parts of it, but do make an effort to read the historical and the major prophetical books as soon as possible. You should not, of course, read the Bible to the exclusion of other works because, if you do, you will end up lacking perspective, like many fundamentalists. Still, the Bible has to be the ground of your other reading.

But which Bible? It does little good to purchase the "best" version, whichever that may be objectively, if you will not read it. You are not interested in an ornament for the coffee table, but in a book you can pick up as comfortably as your favorite novel. The best version for you will be the version you will read. If the one you choose is what most people regard as an inferior edition, you can graduate to a superior one later. The first thing is to get in the

---

[1] Sheed and Ward, *Evidence*, 20.

habit of Bible reading. Once you do, it will be easy to take up a superior translation.

It might be wise to purchase several translations even if you know which you will use for your regular reading. The reason? To compare renderings. If you know no Greek, Hebrew, or Latin, the best way to get a feel for the meaning of a verse is to see how different translations phrase it. Particularly useful will be a cheap copy of the King James Version of the New Testament. Most fundamentalists use that translation—some not even knowing it *is* a translation but believing it is the original—and discussions are often made easier if their wording can be compared with yours, particularly since a number of their confusions arise from misunderstanding seventeenth-century diction.

You have heard the adage that "the exception proves the rule". Of course, the exception *disproves* the rule, if you think about it, but that is using prove in the modern sense of substantiate. When the adage was not an adage but a current idiom, the word prove (coming from the Latin *probare,* from which we get our word probate) did not mean substantiate, but test. An exception was said to test, to bend, even to snap a rule, and in that sense the saying is quite true. When prove is used in the modern sense, the saying is flat-out wrong. It is this kind of confusion that afflicts some fundamentalists who insist on using the King James Version. They use twentieth-century instead of seventeenth-century definitions, and that puts them on the wrong track. This can be demonstrated if you show them one or more modern translations alongside the King James.

Familiarize yourself with anti-Catholic literature. See what topics are emphasized: the Bible as the sole rule of faith, justification by faith alone, the "idolatry of the Mass", "worship" of Mary and the saints, "Catholic inventions", and much more. See how the arguments, weak as they are, are handled. You will perceive at once, if you have not already noticed, that anti-Catholic materials are skewed, but if you cannot think of complete and ready rejoinders, make notes and study up. It will hardly do to say, "I can't remember why that's wrong, but it is, and you'll just have to take my word for it." The Appendix gives addresses of some of the anti-Catholic organizations mentioned in this book; write for samples of their literature. Once you have understood their arguments and have learned more about your own faith, you will be ready to engage in friendly arguments.

There are two preliminary points to keep in mind when arguing with fundamentalists. The first is that there is nothing wrong, in itself, with arguing. Some people have the mistaken notion that all argumentation is uncharitable, but that tells more about their own arguing skills, or lack of them, than anything else. After all, people who find their own arguments resulting in fisticuffs do not really know how to argue and cannot be expected to think arguments can be profitable. The second point is that most fundamentalists welcome a good argument; they want to be challenged, and they want to see if their position "works". Many of them have been trained to argue with Catholics whom they seek to evangelize, though, to be sure, they do not expect Catholics to argue back.

You will discover that most fundamentalists have a surprisingly limited repertoire of accusations. (Do not confuse them with the professional anti-Catholics, whose accusations are seemingly endless, which is to be expected of people who make their livings attacking Rome.) Most fundamentalists, even those trained for small-scale anti-Catholic work, have done far less reading in Catholicism than you already have done in fundamentalism, if you have read the previous chapters. They are told Catholics not only know nothing about the Bible, but little about their own Faith, so they expect to accost people who are pushovers. It is disturbing enough to them to find Catholics answering their questions instead of standing openmouthed; it is worse to be put on the defensive and to be forced to answer pointed questions about fundamentalism. This few of them are trained to do, and in short order they take refuge in the plea that they need to check with their pastors. Do not gloat when you see them forced to make a strategic retreat. You soon might be "advancing toward the rear" yourself.

When arguing, do not argue to win. You can "win" yet drive people further from the Church. Argue to explain. Your task is to show fundamentalists the Catholic position from the inside, not to make cheap debater's points. You must scrupulously avoid striving for quick victories with which to impress onlookers, and you must realize that each time you sink to the *ad hominem,* you alienate another listener and the Church loses another present or prospective member. People who interpret "argument" to mean raised voices, large gesticulations, and cutting remarks are not suited to apologetics. All these are out. The skills of a good apologist are not the same as the skills of a good orator or a good debater, much less of a second-class orator or debater. Instead, strive for the skills of a good missionary, because that is what an apologist is.

This work is not for people with thin skins or short fuses. Losing your temper, or being thrown off balance by someone who loses his, means you have lost an opportunity for clearing away mental cobwebs. If you take offense at being called pagan or blasphemous or stupid when explaining Catholic doctrines, if you flaunt your annoyance and cannot help shaking your head when confronted with unthinking comments, find some other way to occupy your spare time.

If you stick with apologetics, you will discover soon enough the lure of verbal combat, which, although an unbloody warfare, can leave wounds every bit as lethal as those inflicted with regular munitions. It must be done right or not at all. Remember, you are not opposing fundamentalism so much as explaining Catholicism; your work is essentially positive and constructive, not negative and destructive. To the extent you do oppose fundamentalism (after all, error should be countered, even when mixed with truth), make sure you oppose fundamentalism and not fundamentalists.

Not everyone opposing the Catholic religion is a loon or is working in bad faith, and, if you cannot appreciate that, you will do more harm than good. Few fundamentalists, even those who are actively anti-Catholic, do what they do out of spite. They are working with clear consciences, but they have been misinformed. Perhaps they should have done more homework, but the fault is not entirely theirs. They trust the sources they have had, but now they should be shown there is more to consider. You will not get them to open their minds by encouraging them to close their hearts. Hatred directed against the Church cannot be offset by hatred on behalf of the Church. You must approach fundamentalists in charity.

When you do enter discussions, avoid verse-slinging. It accomplishes little. A barrage of biblical citations overwhelms only those ignorant of the Bible. The first time fundamentalists cornered you with verses that were unfamiliar, you did not know what to say. You had not even heard some of the lines before, and the rest, in an odd translation, sounded not quite right. True, you were unconvinced by this tactic, but you *were* thrown for a loop. Later, you did your homework and learned there was nothing to fear. The verses, if read in context, really supported the Catholic Faith. Just as this way of arguing no longer impresses you, if it ever did, it does not impress fundamentalists who find Catholics using it in return. They already have a fixed interpretation of each line of the Bible, and their interpretations cannot be overcome by your quoting the text and stopping there. Mere quotation is not enough. You have to go step by step, explaining what each verse means, but before you do that, you have to give an overview of the subject under discussion. Tossing quotations left and right is a waste of time.

Do not go to the other extreme and fail to use biblical citations. They are absolutely necessary if you want to make your points effectively. What is to be avoided is the carefree tossing around of verses that only seem to be related, usually because they have a word in common. For example, to refute the Catholic notion that "rock" in Matthew 16:18 refers to Peter, fundamentalists list as many verses as they can find in which "rock" refers to God. They do not bother to look at Matthew 16:18 in itself, and they forget that the whole point of the verse is precisely that Peter was being given a title usually reserved to God—and what did *that* signify?

Your goal is to reorient your listeners, giving them a new perspective. Remember, they think they take their beliefs straight from the Bible. In fact, the Bible is used to substantiate already-held beliefs. They begin with their own "tradition", which is generally their pastor's interpretation of the Bible. For many fundamentalists, their pastor is their pope. They accept his every word. When confronted with hard questions, they do not turn to the Bible to discover the answers; they say instead, "Let us ask our pastor." What is more, their faith is largely colored by the church they attend. Some denominations emphasize one aspect of belief; others emphasize others. The assurance of salvation is the subject of the majority of sermons at some churches, the Second Coming at others, and baptism by immersion at still others. Congregants will be especially familiar with scriptural passages relating to their pastor's favorite doctrines, will be less familiar with passages relating to other fundamentalist doctrines, and might be quite unfamiliar with the rest of the Bible.

You must enter discussions with a plan. Know what the main points should be, and then stick with them. All anti-Catholics concentrate on a few scriptural passages that seem damaging to Catholicism. Take the initiative. Address their points, but do not allow them to ask all the questions. Ask your own. You of course must know how to respond to their standard charges, but be prepared to bring up issues they conveniently skip. Put them on the spot and point out the weaknesses of fundamentalism. Do this not to demonstrate how smart you were for choosing the Catholic Church, but to emphasize that although much of what they hold is true, some is not, and for the fullness of truth they need to look to Rome.

One of the most annoying things in getting into a conversation with evangelistic fundamentalists (that is not redundant: not all of them are evangelistic) is that you do not seem to get a word in edgewise. You do not seem to be able to steer the conversation your way. The less well versed you are in Catholicism, the worse the problem. The discussion may start with the most common question, "Are you saved?" Or it may start with any of several standard openings. It seems as though you hardly start to form a reply when more questions are thrown at you, each leading you further into uncharted areas. You feel adrift, unable to turn to a topic on which you have done your homework. By the time your interlocutor decamps, you feel stymied, having given no good answers and having posed no good questions.

You need to learn a few techniques for taking charge. Here is one, and it is simple: sidestep the first question and pose your own, so you can turn the conversation to your favorite topic. It is not at all rude to do this; you are under no obligation to let yourself be led around by the nose. Until you are at ease with all the major issues, so that you can handle any likely opening by fundamentalists, you may *have* to do this if you want to get anywhere in your apologetics work.

The way to do it is to use Jesus' ploy (though of course he did not do this for the reasons you would). Recall how he responded when the chief priests and elders approached him and asked, "What authority have you for acting like this? And who gave you this authority?" Jesus said, "I will ask you a question, just one; if you tell me the answer to it, then I will tell you my authority for acting like this" (Mt 21:23–24). He took charge of the discussion by bringing up the point he wanted to discuss, by setting aside his questioners' topic.

Do the same kind of thing yourself. Let us assume you are asked, "Where does the Bible mention purgatory?" And let us assume you are not up to discussing purgatory, having not done your homework, but are up to discussing the notion of *sola scriptura*. You can use this approach: "I'd be happy to talk about that if we can first talk about why you think the Bible is the sole rule of faith. After all, your question implies we should look to the Bible alone. I want you to substantiate your belief, since, so far as I understand it, the Bible nowhere says it is the sole rule of faith." Then take it from there. Follow up with more questions. You may or may not get back to purgatory—if you do, you will just have to wing it—but you will steer the conversation (mainly) to topics on which you are prepared.

Now of course this is an expedient, not an ideal. In point of fact you should be able to explain purgatory, but you have to operate based on how things are, not on how they ought to be. You cannot become a theological whiz overnight. You can discuss only what you know, and, until you can handle most topics with facility, you will have to be able to turn conversations to topics with which you are at ease. It would be nice to wait until you had every issue, major and minor, down pat, but are you going to want to start engaging in apologetics as a nonagenarian? Work with what you have, and learn what more you can, but do not keep the bench warm waiting for a revelation.

Keep in mind that your fundamentalist opponents are not really any more knowledgeable than you are today—quite possibly less. They seem more knowledgeable because they pose the first question and usually steer the conversation, yet they can get flustered easily. Their success, like the aura of invincibility they exude, depends entirely on your ignorance. As likely as not, they would not know what to say if you made intelligent responses or posed tough questions of your own. They have been trained much like the newspaper boy who comes to the door with a memorized patter. You have seen it often enough. If the boy recalls his lines, and if you keep your mouth shut, everything goes well, and he might have a new subscriber. If you ask him anything about the paper other than the price, he does not know what to say. His delivery depends on your allowing him to stick with his canned talk.

It is the same with most fundamentalists. They undergo a short course in "soul winning" and are trained to recite a fixed patter on the assumption that people they talk to, including virtually all Catholics, do not know enough about Christianity to ask tough questions of their own. The fundamentalists' instructors are mostly right in training them this way. The technique works well, which is why it is used. They expect to have doors slammed in their faces, but they do not expect to be talked back to—at least not intelligently. When you throw out a question of your own and take charge of the conversation, as often as not they do not know what to say. They have been told how to go about "soul winning", but they receive little training in being on the defensive. Why prepare for the statistically improbable? By taking charge of the discussion, you not only keep yourself from getting frustrated, you get to evangelize the evangelist. The discussion over, retire to your study and bone up on one of the topics you are still unsure about.

By the way, never be afraid to acknowledge ignorance. If you do not know the answer to a question, say so. You will survive, and so will your ego. The answers you give on other points will be taken more seriously if people you speak with see you are not trying to bluster your way through a conversation. There is nothing easier to spot than a fake.

You must be absolutely honest. Never pretend doctrines or facts are other than they really are. Do not avoid the hard cases, but do not pander to your listeners either. Never succumb to the temptation to tell them what they want to hear or, more commonly, not to tell them what they do not want to hear. Christ informed the people of his day that there would be many things difficult to accept in his teaching. Acceptance has gotten no easier. Whether doctrinal or moral, there is no need to try to make hard truths palatable. Just state them as they are, but first know what they are. Admit your ignorance (to yourself at least), then do your homework. An embarrassment today can result in fuller understanding—and better apologetics—tomorrow.

Early on, discuss the history of the Bible. You need to make plain it was the Church that formed the Bible, not the Bible that formed the Church. Note, too, that the New Testament was not designed as a catechism. Its various parts were written to people who already were Christians, so it could not have been intended as the sole source of religious teaching. In the beginning, teaching was oral and was under the authority of the Church, which eventually decided what books belonged to the Bible and what did not.

Fundamentalists say, "Let us start by admitting that the Bible is the sole rule of faith." Translation: "Let us admit the Church has no authoritative role; all answers to religious questions are to be found on the face of Scripture only." Do not agree to it. It just begs the question, and it is untrue. As a counter, ask your opponents to try to prove that the Bible was intended to be the sole rule of faith. The Bible itself makes no such claim (it calls itself "profit-able" for salvation, not the sole rule of faith), but you have to know which verses to cite to prove that.

Fundamentalists also say that if a doctrine is not clearly in the Bible, it is not a doctrine to be held by Christians. This ignores what the Bible really is and what it is not. As Frank Sheed put it in one of his last books, *Death into Life,* "The Gospels give a selection of what Christ did and said, with each writer choosing the elements needed for the portrait he was drawing. The Epistles were for the most part written as the occasion arose—some point of doctrine was being misinterpreted, perhaps. Thus one cannot argue from the silence of the New Testament that any particular doctrine was not being taught. Purgatory for instance!"[2]

No matter how well they have memorized it, fundamentalists know little other than the Bible, which they know only selec-tively. They know little Church history, little formal theology. They may never have seen a catechism. You must provide the larger picture. If the topic is an interpretation of a scriptural pas-sage, go to a good commentary and study up, but also go straight to the Fathers of the Church to learn what they wrote about the subject and to books dealing with the history of doctrines and Catholic customs. Appeals to early Christian writers are often useful. Explain to your listeners that finding out what the first Christians understood the apostles to teach is crucial. Make them see it is unlikely that people who were writing when the Church was young and memories of Christ were vivid would errone-ously report what beliefs the early Church started with or how it interpreted Scripture. If early Christian writers took it for granted that a sacrificial priesthood was established by Christ (which they did), that fact is a powerful argument in support of the priest-hood. If writers living a few generations after Christ mentioned the Real Presence (which they did), that argues in favor of the Catholic interpretation of John 6. Try to show a doctrine in rela-tion to other doctrines, a custom in relation to other customs,

---

[2] Frank Sheed, *Death into Life* (New York: Arena Lettres, 1977), 74.

New Testament times in relation to the immediately following centuries. It is important for fundamentalists to see the Church and Church history as a totality. You will have to show them how everything fits together.

Ecclesiastical history is a messy discipline. It is not nearly as well formed as dogmatic or moral theology. Even if you never are inclined to misrepresent teachings of the Church, you might be tempted to put an unwarrantedly good face on some event or person in its history. There is a tendency to want every Catholic to look good in everything he does, to have him make the right decisions at all times, as though he had been blessed with preternatural prescience. Conversely, there is a temptation to think someone outside the Church is always working in bad faith.

It is a mistake to paint historical characters in white and black only, each Catholic being angelic, each Protestant devilish. If you approach history that way, you either will make no progress in understanding it, or your first impressions soon will be discarded as you discover the humanity of the people behind the events. We begin our reading or writing, naturally enough, with certain predispositions, but these need to be refined as we progress—or we are not progressing at all.

In the preface to his masterwork, *Enthusiasm,* Ronald Knox noted he had been writing the book "for thirty years and a little more; no year has passed but I have added to it, patched it, rewritten it, in the time that could be spared from other occupations". It did not turn out as he first thought it would.

To be sure, when the plan of the Book was first conceived, all those years ago, it was to have been a broadside, a trumpet-blast, an end of controversy. . . . [H]ere, I would say, is what happens inevitably, if once the principle of Catholic unity is lost! All this confusion, this priggishness, this pedantry, this eccentricity and worse, follows directly from the rash step that takes you outside the fold of Peter! All my historical figures, Wesley himself included, were to be a kind of rogues' gallery, an awful warning against illuminism. But somehow, in the writing, my whole treatment of the subject became different; the more you got to know the men, the more human did they become, for better or worse.[3]

In a way, Knox ended up admiring John Wesley, "a man so far in reaction from the tendencies of his age that he seems a living commentary on them, yet so much a child of his age that you cannot think of him fitting in with any other".[4] Knox could write about the plain goodness of the man and still remark that his message and that of his followers "was simple only in so far as they left nine-tenths of Christian doctrine out of consideration, and concentrated on the remaining tenth—soteriology",[5] a comment that applies perfectly to today's fundamentalists, in so many ways the heirs of Wesley, although they may not realize it. To be sure, no modern fundamentalists, overtly anti-Catholic or otherwise, can be put on Wesley's plane, but the point Knox was making applies to them still: these are, in the main, good people, and grace has not passed them by.

Just as you should not presume the worst on the part of Protestants, do not get into the habit of swallowing everything said or done by Catholics. It may astonish some to learn that on occasion individual Catholics have been wrong, their Protestant opponents right—the Catholics having missed the truly Catholic position on an issue, the Protestants having stumbled across it. What is more, the number of canonized saints is small, and with good reason. Even with all the spiritual wellsprings found in the Church, many of its members fare poorly, at least in comparison to their hopes and everyone else's expectations. We are consistently off the mark—but we would be lost entirely if it were not for the Church.

When talk turns to awkward points of Church history, do not misrepresent them. Do not hide blemishes. There is no need to. Put things in context, and remind your listeners that the King-

---

[3] Ronald Knox, *Enthusiasm* (London: Oxford University Press, 1950), v–vi.

[4] Knox, *Enthusiasm*, 422.

[5] Knox, *Enthusiasm*, 515.

dom of God (a term that, in the Bible, usually refers to the Church rather than heaven) contains wheat and chaff, saints and sinners. But be careful how you phrase rebuttals. Here is a cautionary example.

Fundamentalists with a little knowledge of the papacy will inquire about the "bad Popes". A few decades ago, among Catholic apologists it was considered clever to answer in this vein: "Yes, there have been some 'bad Popes', perhaps six or seven men being truly unworthy of the office. Given the large number of Popes, this is a proportion of about one in forty. On the other hand, one in twelve of the men Christ himself chose turned out bad." True, but not convincing by itself. No, you have to approach the problem in a different way. Mere cleverness will not do.

Sarcasm will not do either. Sarcasm always backfires. Avoid it even when your opponents stoop to it. When they do, their consciences will annoy them later; if their consciences are dormant, things will eventually catch up with them anyway. Do not allow them to justify their rudeness by exchanging wisecrack for wisecrack. Keep clear of name-calling. If you see a fundamentalist thumping a Bible (and some do so, quite literally), do not refer to him as a Bible thumper, even if he sneeringly calls you a papist or Romanist or something worse. Allow him the title of Christian, even if he will not return the favor.

Granted, at times the temptation to give as one has received will be overpowering; make a resolution not to repeat the offense, then continue with your work. Ignoring rudeness is usually easier to accomplish when it comes to you in a letter rather than straight to your face. A letter you can put aside until your temper cools, but an oral insult seems to call for an instant and thus unreflecting response. Make a real effort to keep your tongue in check.

To argue effectively, you not only will have to control your temper; you also will have to know what fundamentalists mean by particular terms. You can waste much time by discussing two different things while using the same terminology. Consider faith. For Catholics, faith is the acceptance of revealed truths, doctrines, on God's word alone. This is called theological or confessional faith. For fundamentalists, faith is trust in Christ's promises, not belief in a set of dogmas. This is called fiducial faith. Tradition is another confusing term. In the New Testament are injunctions not to adhere to the "traditions of men". When fundamentalists hear Catholics say the twin sources of revealed truth are Scripture and Tradition, they equate Tradition with "traditions of men", and they conclude the Catholic Church is contradicting the Bible directly. Terms you might think can be taken only univocally, such as inspiration and heaven, can mean something quite different to fundamentalists.

Avoid technical words unless a thorough grounding has been laid. Even Catholics misunderstand what is meant by transubstantiation, Immaculate Conception, and hypostatic union. On the other hand, do not be monosyllabic. To oversimplify is to sidestep fine points, which is equally bad. Do not presume a question means what it seems to mean. Find out what your inquirers really are talking about. Take time. If the question refers to the Virgin Birth, make sure they do not mean the birth of the Virgin. Take up a single topic at a time; look at it leisurely, from several angles, and never presume fundamentalists know what you mean by apparently simple terms such as soul, revelation, Mass. If they did, they would not have such odd ideas of what the Church stands for. You have to speak with them the way you would speak with uninstructed Catholics.

Keep your expectations modest. Do not expect conversions, because they are not overnight things. Count yourself successful if your opponents leave with the feeling that there is a sensible, even if not acceptable, Catholic response to each of their charges. It would be a great triumph just to have an active anti-Catholic withdraw from the fray and mull things over. You have to give things time.

After all, no one is born anti-Catholic. There are not even any "cradle anti-Catholics" to parallel "cradle Catholics". Often the most vituperative foes of the Church, both within and without fundamentalism, are former Catholics who left the Church as adults. Their leaving was a slow process of unperceived difficulties turning into doubts, of doubts turning into denials, of denials turning into affirmations of new doctrines. To expect a sudden reconversion is to ignore human nature.

Fundamentalists think Catholics have no answers at all to the usual charges and believe a few snappy questions are all it takes to transfix a Catholic, to leave him dumbfounded, groping helplessly for answers that are not there. They forget that while their "born-again" experience may have been of a moment's duration, it came only after a long leave-taking of the Catholic religion. They did not fall away from their old Faith in an instant, as though struck down on the Damascus Road.

Similarly, their return, if there is to be one, will not be quick. It will take months, even years, before they begin to see the Church as it really is and begin to shed their prejudices, each prejudice acquired with difficulty and let go with even more. So, if an active anti-Catholic sits things out for a while, that is as much as can be expected. If he at length gets a few things straight about Catholicism, there likely will follow an avalanche of understanding. Perhaps he will come all the way home, either with your help or on his own, or he may remain a fundamentalist while ceasing to be an anti-Catholic. Although you would wish more for him personally, defusing an agent of anti-Catholic bigotry would be a success in itself, because that would mean fewer Catholics would be enticed out of the Church before they could be authentically catechized (or recatechized, as the case may be) and fewer fundamentalists would have their prejudices reinforced.

From the beginning you must make those outside see what the Church's positions really *are*. Do not start by justifying Catholic doctrines through apposite Bible passages or appeals to syllogistic reasoning. Those can be effective techniques, and at some point they will be necessary, but at the very beginning they invite digressions. First you need to show your listeners what the Church really teaches. They almost always will have preconceived and quite wrong notions.

Your first task, then, and often your hardest, is to get terminology straight and to be able to explain, in your own words, what

Catholics hold. Only once the doctrines are understood in themselves should you turn to their justifications, but showing what doctrines mean is the principal task you have. Until you do that, you cannot move forward. Once you have the definitions clear, fundamentalists, like other non-Catholics who have gone through similar instruction, will want to learn more because they will have been introduced to something fresh, something whole, something fulfilling. They will have glimpsed the unity of Christianity for the first time.

Chapter 25

Food for the Mind

The prospective apologist needs thorough preparation, both in answering specific questions and in preparing a stronger general foundation for his own faith. The books discussed in this chapter will transform an average Catholic whose gut feelings are right into one who not only knows the answers to the questions that used to stump him, but now can pass on his newfound learning in a way that others, far more confused than he ever was, can understand. These books are not the only ones worthy of study, of course, but they have proved particularly useful in the specialized task of dealing with fundamentalist attacks on the Catholic religion.[1]

In what order these books will be read will depend largely on one's predispositions. Some can be taken up and put down at leisure; reading in snatches is quite sufficient. Others need to be read in a more sustained fashion—not in one evening necessarily, assuming that is even possible for people not afflicted with insomnia, but over a short period of time. One needs to set aside time daily so the first chapter is not forgotten by the time the last is reached. Just as the story line can be lost if one puts down a novel for any length of time, so the overall picture some of these books

---

[1] Not every apologetics book is useful in dealing with fundamentalists. Some are written more for the inquiring agnostic than for the believing Protestant, and even those that are not usually neglect fundamentalism's specific charges. Since these charges are often identical to ones leveled against the Church two generations ago, many of the most useful apologetics works are old. Distressingly few recent works about the Faith discuss problems in Church history or argue the foundation of doctrines—apparently because the authors think history is unimportant and doctrines are mutable.

were designed to give will not be apprehended if one dallies in reading them.

Some of the material will have to be gone over more than once—you will want to read some things several times, just for your own enjoyment—and even then, after all this work, you will still need access to other, more detailed works, such as the *Catholic Encyclopedia* (the preferred 1914 edition, available through Catholic used-book dealers) or the *New Catholic Encyclopedia* (1967 edition, inferior in coverage but adequate).

The Catholic unsure of his intellectual stamina should not be scared off. He does not have to try to devour the whole pie. Much good can be done, both for oneself and for non-Catholics, by getting the basics, by reading only the key works. (Anyone who would read the whole of an encyclopedia is an undiscriminating pedant and would never make it as an apologist!)[2]

Keep in mind that it is not enough to have absorbed general overviews of Catholicism, however good they might be. That will not prepare you to withstand a barrage of criticism. You will wilt under the onslaught of specific and often surprising questions, each of which needs to be handled if people confused about the Faith are to have their doubts cleared up. The trouble is that writers of surveys of Catholicism do not ask tough questions or put you on the spot. That is not their purpose. They presume you are predisposed to the Faith and are seeking to broaden your knowledge generally. That is admirable and necessary, but you can have a general grasp yet be unable to say anything sensible to fundamentalists when they question you, because their questions throw you for a loop. You will rarely guess correctly how they will phrase their accusations, because your presuppositions are different. It takes a Catholic considerable training and a long tenure in the school of hard knocks to begin to think like a fundamentalist, to pose the kinds of questions fundamentalists pose.

To get a feel for what you would be up against, particularly if you want to do apologetics work on a serious basis, you need to

---

[2] Editors of encyclopedias excepted, of course.

see just what fundamentalists say about the Church—and in their own words. Write to anti-Catholic organizations (see the Appendix for addresses) and request sample literature. Some Catholics hesitate doing this. They cannot bear giving professional anti-Catholics a penny. They think doing so is almost treasonous. The feeling is understandable, but it is a matter of false scruples. If you were a military commander and your counterpart on the other side had written a book outlining his tactical theories, you would be wise to let him have the royalties and get a copy of his book into your hands as soon as possible. You would owe it to your cause.

So write away for anti-Catholic literature, study it, and learn on which topics you need help, but do not limit yourself to acquiring tracts. No collection of anti-Catholic material would be complete without a copy of Loraine Boettner's *Roman Catholicism*.[3] Many Protestant bookstores carry it; if it cannot be found on the shelves, it can be ordered through them or through any other bookstore. Although a fat hardback, it is cheap, and some fundamentalist and evangelical bookstores carry it at a good discount over the already-low cover price, perhaps a prime reason it has been disseminated so widely.

The core of many arguments, historical or otherwise, will be the Bible, and the apologist needs to be at ease with it. Fundamentalists often work on the principle that the Bible is such a straightforward book that any literate person can pick it up and, without much trouble, find the correct interpretation of any passage, presuming he has been "born again". Those not reborn, in the fundamentalists' sense of the term, have no guarantee they will arrive at the right understanding.

Fundamentalists think the intervening centuries have not made the Bible any more confusing for us than it was for people who lived in New Testament times, and they think that way (although they do not realize it) because they begin, not with the Bible, but

---

[3] Loraine Boettner, *Roman Catholicism* (Philadelphia: Presbyterian and Reformed, 1962).

with an accepted set of beliefs, which they then substantiate by "searching the Scriptures".

The truth is that the Bible is both an easy and a difficult book. It is easy in its language—no jargon or bureaucratese here—but it is difficult in that it is not really one book, but six dozen books composed over centuries for a variety of reasons and audiences. No sacred writer thought, as he sat down with pen and papyrus, that he was adding the *nth* chapter to a single book in the way that, some years ago, there was a fad among writers of detective stories to compose books each chapter of which was by a different author and was built directly on the chapters preceding.[4] No, the Bible is better thought of as a miscellany. The New Testament alone has several kinds of writings: four partially overlapping biographies, something at once a history and a travelogue, private letters written to individuals and open ones written to small communities, and an example of a peculiar kind of literature, the apocalyptic. The same goes for the Old Testament, which contains still other kinds of works: law codes, prophetic utterances, poetry, even an extended love song.

The Catholic needs to read the Bible, of course, and to read it regularly, but that is hardly enough. He needs also works that will make up for time lost, that will give him insights that he might reach only after decades of assiduous and prayerful reading of the sacred text, and he needs an appreciation of the background of the Bible, of the kinds of works it contains, and of methods and theories of interpretation. Only when he has this will his Bible reading turn truly fruitful.

The first thing, then, after securing one or more translations of the Bible itself, to buy is a commentary. Still available from used-book dealers is *A Catholic Commentary on Holy Scripture*,[5] published in Britain in 1953 and using the Douay-Rheims translation.

---

[4] An example is *The Floating Admiral* (New York: Doubleday, Doran, 1931), contributors including Agatha Christie, Dorothy Sayers, G. K. Chesterton, and Ronald Knox.

[5] Bernard Orchard et al., eds., *A Catholic Commentary on Holy Scripture* (New York: Thomas Nelson, 1953).

The editorial committee was headed by Bernard Orchard, and contributors included such men as B. C. Butler, Thomas Corbishley, C. C. Martindale, E. C. Messenger, and Hugh Pope.[6] In addition to commentaries on individual books of the Bible, this work includes thirty-five articles introducing the Old and New Testaments and examining such topics as the synoptic problem, the various texts and versions of the Bible, proper interpretation, inspiration and inerrancy, and the geography and history of Israel.

In 1969 appeared *A New Catholic Commentary on Holy Scripture,*[7] using the Revised Standard Version instead of the Douay-Rheims. About a fifth of the original edition was carried over, as were several of the original contributors. The new edition is superior in some ways (for example, it takes into account real advances in biblical scholarship), but it may not appeal to everyone in other ways.

As a substitute or supplement one should consider *The Jerome Biblical Commentary,*[8] first published in 1968 and since updated and stocked by most Catholic bookstores. Although this American commentary is not as trustworthy as its British counterparts, it is still worth having, and the orthodox Catholic can skip the more tendentious essays. After all, when it comes to comments on individual books of the Bible, as distinguished from articles giving overviews of the Pentateuch or the life of Christ, there is little room for foolery. In any event, do not be put off by being unable to locate an ideal commentary, since there is no such thing.

Newer than the latest commentaries is William G. Most's *Free from All Error.*[9] Most, known for his orthodoxy and willingness

---

[6] Author of *The Layman's New Testament* (London: Sheed and Ward), 1934, which is particularly helpful in replying to verse-slinging.

[7] Reginald C. Fuller et al., eds., *A New Catholic Commentary on Holy Scripture* (London: Nelson, 1969).

[8] Raymond E. Brown et al., eds., *The Jerome Biblical Commentary* (Englewood Cliffs, N.J.: Prentice-Hall, 1968).

[9] William G. Most, *Free from All Error* (Libertyville, Ill.: Franciscan Marytown Press, 1985).

to engage modernists in verbal combat, examines the authorship, inerrancy, and historicity of Scripture. In this book, which is not a replacement for but a fine addition to a commentary, he devotes separate chapters to Genesis, the infancy narratives, apocalyptic books, and wisdom literature. He examines the historical-critical method of scriptural interpretation, the prejudices of form and redaction critics, and how we determine which books are inspired and belong in the Bible and which are not and do not.

Also worth having are two books by John Steinmueller, the three-volume *Companion to Scripture Studies*[10] and *The Sword of the Spirit*.[11] The first volume of the *Companion* discusses inspiration, the canon of the Bible, texts and versions, and hermeneutics. It considers the history of exegesis in the ancient, medieval, and modern periods and biblical antiquities, which include sacred places (such as the temples of Solomon, Zorobabel, and Herod), sacred persons, sacred rituals, and even sacred seasons, and it closes with a chapter on the geography of the Holy Land.

The second volume covers the Old Testament, while the third covers the New. Each book of the Bible is considered, but not in the manner of a commentary. Steinmueller does not use a verse-by-verse approach. Typically, after giving a bibliography, he presents an outline of a book, then devotes a few paragraphs to its author, origin, intended audience, and special aims. In the third volume each book of the New Testament is given more space than could be given in the second volume to each of the Old, and there is a fine analysis of the synoptic problem and a useful, if unhappily too short, life of Christ.

The Sword of the Spirit covers the meaning, inspiration, authors, and canon of the Bible, biblical theology, the history of the Bible, and conflicting views in modern biblical scholarship. It might be read before turning to a commentary or the more daunting *Companion*.

---

[10] John Steinmueller, *A Companion to Scripture Studies* (New York: Joseph F. Wagner, 1969).

[11] John Steinmueller, *The Sword of the Spirit* (Waco, Tex.: Stella Maris, 1978).

Steinmueller's pages on early English versions of the Bible will be a disappointment to fundamentalists who pick up *The Sword of the Spirit*, most of them having a sense that the King James Version was the first in English (and some of them believing it was in fact the *original* version), because he shows English translations long predated the Reformation. Catholics new to the history of the Bible will benefit from this discussion, although for the full story one needs to turn to Hugh Pope's *English Versions of the Bible*,[12] which examines at greater length than one might think possible all the translations to the twentieth century.

Another handy work is Henri Daniel-Rops' *Daily Life in the Time of Jesus*.[13] This supplement to the commentaries is an extended and readable examination of the society of first-century Palestine. Discussed are the class structure, personal cleanliness, arts and science, occupations, the Jewish family, the city of Jerusalem, and much more, in a text the cover blurb rightly calls "a masterful synthesis of the complex array of the economic, political, and cultural currents of the pivotal era of human history". It is the kind of book the apologist will want to reach for when his discussions with fundamentalists involve interpreting Scripture in light of its own time.

Fundamentalists do not argue against the Church merely from Scripture, limiting themselves to events of the first century. They also decry later Catholic "inventions" and what they consider to be the universally sorry history of the universal Church. The more knowledgeable among them bring up specific historical points—the Inquisition, the "bad Popes", abuses leading up to the Reformation—and expect Catholics to be able to explain how such enormities could proceed from the Church Christ established.

There are two problems here. First, most of the ecclesiastical history fundamentalists know is wrong, being little more than vague prejudices mixed with scraps of pseudolearning. Few of

---

[12] Hugh Pope, *English Versions*.

[13] Henri Daniel-Rops, *Daily Life in the Time of Jesus* (Ann Arbor, Mich.: Servant Books, 1980).

them, though, have any reason to doubt that what has been handed down to them (part of their "tradition", in a way) is the real story of the Catholic Church.

The second problem is that, although some of the history they have is accurate, at least in the bare sense of dates and names, they have no grasp of what that history *means*. Their basic problem, of course, is that their own religion is frozen in apostolic times. They fail to see that the true Faith may alter its appearance, although not its content, as the centuries pass, and that later events can shed light on earlier, just as the New Testament allows a deeper appreciation of the Old; and they forget, it seems, that Christianity, although not *of* the world, is certainly *in* it. From decades of refusing to examine events with a critical mind, their instincts have become antihistorical.

Fundamentalists rightly note that priestly celibacy became mandatory only in the Middle Ages, but they have no feel for the process leading up to the rule and so conclude it was instituted out of the blue. They know Constantine legalized Christianity in 313, and they have been told his Edict of Milan precipitated the rise of the Catholic Church, but they know little of the shape of Christianity in the years immediately preceding or following Constantine's rule. They envision distinctively Catholic practices, such as auricular confession and the use of Latin, as popping up out of nowhere, and this bothers them no end—as it should, if their historical outlook were true.

The only way to overcome these stumbling blocks—and that is just what so much of Catholicism is when not understood in itself—is for the Catholic apologist to be able to take each historical question and find an answer, putting the issue in context, first showing what really happened, then integrating the facts with what his fundamentalist questioner already knows, thus giving him the broad picture. This can cause endless headaches, of course, and sometimes it is either impossible or not worth trying to accomplish, but often it is crucial.

Most fundamentalists embrace only one or two historical squabbles with gusto, and, if their confusions about them can be cleared up—and it may take very little effort to do that—they will be open to learning about the Faith. They will then be receptive to talk about the other historical complaints they have, the ones on which they do not stake their reputations. A few fundamentalists have so many questions and know so much that is not so, that one cannot hope to satisfy them, no matter how much homework is done, no matter how many citations are given, no matter how many pages from history texts are photocopied and sent off with explanatory cover letters. A hundred matters can be settled to their grudging satisfaction, but, hydralike, two hundred more will arise. These people can be touched only by grace, not by anything the Catholic apologist can do. They revel in their confusion and would be lost if they did not have a full bag of complaints concerning the history of the Church.

Yet they are a small minority of fundamentalists, most of whom can be approached on the level of history, most of whom would welcome serious historical discussions (which is not to say, by any means, that one needs to be a certified historian to speak with them). To enter such discussions, whether on the lecture platform, in a Bible-study class, or around the cracker barrel, the Catholic needs, in addition to a thick skin, a good grounding in Church history. He does not need to have on the tip of his tongue an answer to every question, although there are a few standard complaints for which he indeed will have set replies. He needs to be able to look up answers in handy reference works, ones that are really useful for his purposes. When he tells a fundamentalist that he will get back with the answer in a few days, he needs to be able to do just that. Not to get back with an answer because one does not have on hand the right books means, to a suspicious interlocutor, that there is no answer to his charge.

Some of the best historical works are no longer in print, such as Newman Eberhardt's *A Summary of Catholic History*,[14] Fernand Mourret's *A History of the Catholic Church*,[15] and Henri Daniel-Rops' *History of the Church of Christ*.[16] An especially promising

---

[14] Eberhardt, *Summary*.

[15] Fernand Mourret, *A History of the Catholic Church* (St. Louis: Herder, 1946).

[16] Henri Daniel-Rops, *A History of the Church of Christ* (New York: Dutton, 1960).

venture is Warren Carroll's six-volume project titled *A History of Christendom*.[17] At this writing incomplete, the series can be highly recommended as orthodox, temperate, detailed, and accurate. Another fine history is Philip Hughes' *History of the Church*.[18] This three-volume set takes the story to the time of Luther. Hughes was unable to finish the planned fourth volume, but that does not matter much, since most questions fundamentalists have about Catholic history concern matters in the early centuries and in the Middle Ages.

Published concurrently with Hughes' three-volume set was a one-volume abridgment, *A Popular History of the Catholic Church*.[19] It carries the story to 1946, and, although pre-Reformation topics are handled more concisely than in the larger work, the book gives the reader new to Church history a surprisingly satisfying overview of events. For the first time there is a real connection between the history of the first years of the Church, as found in the New Testament, and the history one has lived through. The first century is tied to the twentieth, the intervening years no longer being a void.

Not to be overlooked is the first major historical work by a Christian, the fourth-century *Ecclesiastical History*[20] of Eusebius. Available with Greek and English on facing pages, it will impress on the reader better than any other ancient writing that the Catholic Church and its distinguishing elements existed from the first.

A history book deals mainly with people and actions and not so much with ideas and their development, although that necessarily plays a substantial part in any history of Catholicism. It is hard to trace doctrinal developments, no matter how many straight history texts one has access to. What is needed is an account of the

---

[17] Warren Carroll, *A History of Christendom* (Front Royal, Va.: Christendom College Press, 1985).

[18] Philip Hughes, *A History of the Church* (London: Sheed and Ward, 1934, 1948).

[19] Hughes, *A Popular History of the Catholic Church* (New York: Macmillan, 1947).

[20] Eusebius Pamphilius, *The Ecclesiastical History* (Cambridge, Mass.: Harvard, 1975), cited in this book as *Historia ecclesiastica*.

history of beliefs themselves. The premier work of that kind is Joseph Tixeront's *History of Dogmas*,[21] a three-volume set that is prime reading for the apologist. As John A. Hardon explains on the cover, Tixeront takes the basic truths of the Faith and "analyzes these truths in their historical context from the New Testament through the last of the Fathers in the eighth century. Three crucial concepts are especially demonstrated: (1) that the Catholic faith has remained essentially unchanged since the time of Christ to the present day, (2) that there nevertheless has been a marvelous development of doctrine fulfilling Christ's prophecy, 'when the spirit of truth comes He will lead you to the complete truth' (John 16:13), and (3) that this continuity and development of Christian doctrine has been possible only because of the Roman Catholic Church, of which the Bishop of Rome is the visible head."

An invaluable companion series is Johannes Quasten's *Patrology*.[22] This standard reference work, in four volumes, is an introduction to the Christian authors of the early centuries. (Patrology, the study of the Fathers of the Church, of their contemporaries—both orthodox and heterodox—and of the authenticity of the works attributed to them, should be distinguished from patristics, the study of their thought, which is more the kind of thing found in Tixeront's books.) *Patrology* will give the reader a good grasp of how Christian literature developed in the early centuries, and that in turn shows the continuity of the Church and its doctrines.

William A. Jurgens' *The Faith of the Early Fathers*[23] is another three-volume set that covers the same years as does Tixeront's and somewhat more than does Quasten's—that is, from the first

---

[21] Joseph Tixeront, *History of Dogmas* (Westminster, Md.: Christian Classics, 1984).

[22] Johannes Quasten, *Patrology* (Westminster, Md.: Christian Classics, 1983, 1986).

[23] William A. Jurgens, *The Faith of the Early Fathers* (Collegeville, Minn.: Liturgical Press, 1970, 1979).

century through the eighth. It is a work of remarkable compression and utility and cannot be recommended highly enough.

There are available, for hundreds of dollars, English translations of early Christian literature, not just the writings of the Fathers, but also of other orthodox commentators and of heretics. These shelf-long sets are for libraries and for bookish apologists with fat wallets. Until Jurgens' anthology appeared, there was nothing convenient in size that could be had at a convenient price. The value of *The Faith of the Early Fathers* is not to be found, though, in how much shelf space or how many dollars it saves, but in its doctrinal index, which lets the reader locate at once references to the sorts of issues fundamentalists bring up. There are 2,390 quotations in the three volumes, some a few lines long, some several paragraphs, and they are cross-referenced under 1,046 doctrinal headings, which are organized much like a catechism.

For example, headings 849 through 899 deal with the Eucharist. Headings 849 through 867, which include 88 citations (some of the headings having more than a dozen), are restricted to the topic of the Real Presence, and numbers 868 through 899 cover Communion, the Mass, and liturgy and law. Heading 851, for instance, is the proposition that "Christ is really present in the Eucharist under the appearance of bread and wine". Twenty citations are given. Number 852 is that "the truth of the Real Presence is evident from the words of institution", and for that there are seven citations.

In addition to the doctrinal index there are an index of scriptural references and a detailed alphabetical index. What is more, each writer and his works are introduced in a few well-turned paragraphs. Jurgens includes helpful footnotes, covering all the hard or controverted points, and gives suggestions for further reading.

As a final handbook on doctrines, consider Ludwig Ott's *Fundamentals of Catholic Dogma*.[24] This is a true tome, but one worth

---

[24] Ludwig Ott, *Fundamentals of Catholic Dogma* (Rockford, Ill.: TAN Books, 1974).

obtaining. It is invaluable for the research an apologist promises to do on short notice, and ex-Catholics who are returning to the Faith through a program of good reading have said Ott's work, though intimidating at first sight, is helpful because it presents so much between two covers. Ott discusses the whole of Catholic dogma, and the value of his work lies not just in his precision and compact explanations, but in his references. How can Catholics claim the Church was established as a visible institution? What is the basis for that? Ott covers the issue, giving references to and quotations from papal encyclicals (somewhat useful, but of course not authoritative in fundamentalists' eyes), the Bible (here is what they want), the Fathers and Doctors of the Church, and Church councils. He also gives heretical views, referring to the theories of the Spiritualist sects of the Middle Ages, to Hus, Calvin, and Luther. So it goes, with every topic.

Ott does not present a complete answer in the form fundamentalists will understand or find convincing, at least not usually, and his is certainly not the first book one would recommend to a fundamentalist beginning to learn about the Faith or to an uninstructed Catholic. But it can put the Catholic apologist on the right track, ensuring he will find all the right biblical references and enough other leads so he can build firm arguments.

Not exactly a handbook on doctrines, but an extended commentary on their growth, is the premier theological work in English, John Henry Newman's *Essay on the Development of Christian Doctrine*.[25] While not the first book the apologist will want for his library, it is one he should read early on so he can understand how an examination of the history of doctrines can lead one to the Church. Newman was an Anglican with strong Catholic sympathies when he began writing this book, and as he finished it he converted. One might say he wrote himself into the Church. What his research demonstrated to him was that the Catholic Church, contrary to what he had been brought up to believe, had not added dogmas at random; there were no Catholic "inventions", but maturations of the original deposit of faith.

[25] Newman, *Essay*.

If one were to select a single book as a guide to the art of apologetics, it would be Frank Sheed's *Catholic Evidence Training Outlines*.[26] This marvelous work was used to train members of the Catholic Evidence Guild, which Sheed and his wife, Maisie Ward, guided more than half a century ago. At one time the Guild had six hundred street-corner preachers in England alone. Street-corner preaching, of course, is now passé: anyone talking religion from a soapbox in the park is presumed to be a bit off—and usually is. Besides, the audiences have changed.

In the twenties, thirties, and forties, one could stand up in Hyde Park, announce that papal infallibility was the topic, and be sure of gathering a crowd that included, along with the usual assortment of cranks and habitual hecklers, a large number of intelligent listeners. However popular street-corner preaching once was in England, its popularity here was never great, and in both places it has nearly disappeared. But no matter. The lessons that Sheed taught his Guild members two generations ago are just the lessons serious Catholic apologists need to learn today, and they can be used effectively in one-on-one talks or in group discussions.

Catholic Evidence Training Outlines went through several editions, rapidly improving with age and experience. The book began as a collection of short lesson plans used in the weekly courses Guild members had to take (and pass, after rigorous tests) before being allowed to speak publicly. Opposite the title page is a boxed warning that "the speakers are again reminded that these are not street-corner outlines but class outlines to prepare them for the street corner", and that is just what the bulk of the book is.

The first forty pages are devoted to the theory of street-corner apologetics (perfectly applicable still, even if the discussion takes place in the home, on the steps outside of church, or in print, rather than on a lecture platform) and to how Guild training should be organized. Sheed had it down to a science, and it shows in his writing.

Then come two dozen short chapters, if they can be called

[26] Sheed and Ward, *Evidence*.

chapters—the course for junior speakers, people who were allowed to speak on only the basics. Twice as many chapters cover topics for senior speakers. Each chapter consists of a narrowly drawn topic, the key points schematically described; recommended readings; and true-to-life sample questions. The student who could not answer each question with aplomb (and they are tough) could not graduate from one subject to the next. It was common to find hundreds of Guild members who were allowed to talk on only a handful of topics. It took years of regular training to become a senior speaker or, higher still, a chairman, the person who acted as moderator on the platform and who was considered competent to handle any question the audience might pose.

As a rule, several people would speak, taking turns. A senior speaker might start off, to get the crowd warmed up. Then a junior speaker or two would give ten-minute talks on some of the basics of the Faith. Then, perhaps, another senior speaker would have as his topic a particularly sticky or confusing issue, such as the Inquisition or the Mystical Body of Christ. Questions could come from the crowd at any time, and heckling was common. It was the chairman's job to get the speakers up and (just as important) down in a timely manner, and he would take over if a speaker was getting in over his head or was losing control of the crowd.

All in all, it was a thorough, militarylike system, one that worked remarkably well in bringing converts to the Church and in developing the faith of the Catholics who participated. The scheme of operation can be appreciated by reading the nine "technical lectures" that are sandwiched between the junior and senior courses. They are on such things as "Relating to the Mind of the Listeners", "How to Handle a Crowd", and dealing with "Questions and Interjections". At the end of the book, in addition to an appendix comprised of six specialized lectures, is a general survey of key points.[27]

---

[27] In writing *Catholic Evidence Training Outlines*, Frank Sheed was assisted by his wife, Maisie Ward. The portions cited in this book seem to have been written by Sheed.

If *Catholic Evidence Training Outlines* is the best source book to have, a good runner-up, and one that is easily obtained, is *Radio Replies*,[28] Leslie Rumble and Charles M. Carty's three-volume set. The books contain 4,374 questions posed to the "Radio Priests" during their many years on the air in the United States and Australia. The questions are tough because they are authentic. Rumble and Carty took the questions as they were sent in and prepared complete, readable, and pointed responses. Virtually every question a fundamentalist could ask will be found in *Radio Replies*. What is more, virtually every question a nonreligious skeptic or a confused Catholic could ask will be found there.

True, these books are old, the last appearing in 1942, but it is uncanny how useful they are now. Only a handful of the hundreds of topics considered are truly dated, and of course some of the terminology has changed. Those are minor points. Anyone not prejudiced against what was written the day before yesterday will profit immensely from *Radio Replies*. These might well be the most-thumbed books on an apologist's shelf, the ones he turns to first when he promises to find an answer to a question that is puzzling a prospective convert to (or from) Catholicism.

Fulton Sheen began his preface to *Radio Replies* by noting that "there are not over a hundred people in the United States who hate the Catholic Church. There are millions, however, who hate what they wrongly believe to be the Catholic Church—which is quite a different thing. . . . If, then, the hatred of the Church is founded on erroneous beliefs, it follows that [the] basic need of the day is instruction."[29] And *Radio Replies* is certainly a gem of an instructional aid. Sometimes Rumble and Carty cover a topic completely, giving the reader far more than he needs to satisfy his curiosity. At other times they give, if not a full treatment, at least enough that the reader knows where to look for detailed information.

There are other works by Frank Sheed that deserve mention, because he probably had a firmer grasp of practical apologetics

---

[28] Rumble and Carty, *Replies*.
[29] Rumble and Carty, *Replies*, 1:ix.

than any other recent Catholic writer. His *Theology and Sanity*[30] was originally published in 1946; the revised paperback edition features a fascinating preface in which Sheed gives some history of his street-corner apostolate and pokes fun at people who siphon the reality out of the Resurrection and Ascension, "leaving for our nourishment only the spiritual meaning of incidents all the truer for never having happened!" He explains:

> When I wrote *Theology and Sanity*, I had been teaching the Faith under the open sky for a quarter of a century. . . . Every paragraph had been tried out on forty or fifty outdoor audiences before I got it down on paper. Listeners were free to walk away the moment they were bored—I tried to learn from their boredom. If they stayed, they could utter their reactions—anything from agreement to intelligent criticism to mockery to blasphemy—with a freedom which speakers who knew only the ivory tower of pulpit or lecture hall found unnerving. It was unbelievably educative. I doubt if there was any objection against the Faith in all the centuries that was not hurled at us. And, unlike the great theologians whose writings had helped to form our minds, we could not go off and think about the objection for a year or two, then write an article. We had to cope—somehow—there and then. The crowd was truly co-author of the book: not a sentence that has not been reshaped by them. This really is aggiornamento—doctrines restated, not to be made more acceptable but more comprehensible, related to the questions people were actually asking, to the needs they were actually feeling, in the language they actually spoke.[31]

This book presents to the reader a fully rounded and accurate representation of the Catholic view of reality, a view remarkably unlike that held by fundamentalists. Even most Catholics have a weak appreciation of it, and it is something that needs to be well comprehended by anyone wanting to pass along the Faith. The title *Theology and Sanity* comes from Sheed's notion that to be truly sane is to take into account the whole of reality as it really is.

[30] Frank Sheed, *Theology and Sanity* (Huntington, Ind.: Our Sunday Visitor, 1978).

[31] Sheed, *Sanity*, ix.

To disbelieve in the supernatural (as even many Catholics, *in practice,* seem to do), is to live other than sanely, much as a physician who disbelieves in bacteria lives other than sanely.

Sheed begins with a fine explanation of the Trinity, which is usually thought of as a dry topic but which his outdoor crowds found the most captivating. The next section looks at angels and men, the Fall, the Redemption, and the Mystical Body of Christ, and it gives perhaps the best popular account of life after death to be found anywhere. The last section explains why we need to be habituated to reality, how our insufficiencies are made up for by the sufficiencies of the Church, and how "sanity points toward sanctity".[32]

It is not enough to have the Faith firmly in hand and to be able to answer questions with a glib tongue. There is a tendency for religion to seem dry, Scholastic in the bad sense. This is easily overcome if one has a deep appreciation of the life of Christ. The New Testament, of course, is the place to turn, but reading it alone is insufficient unless one is graced with considerable powers of synthesis. Help is needed to see the larger picture, and there are several books that do a fine job in that.

Again, one is by Sheed. It is *To Know Christ Jesus*.[33] The opening line of the foreword says, "This book is not a Life of Christ." Sheed means there is too much we do not know about Jesus, at least regarding his everyday activities (we know, for instance, only one event between his infancy and the start of his ministry), for this to be a regular biography. What Sheed proposes to do, and what he does admirably, is introduce us to Someone through the Gospels. His book is really a preparation for reading the Gospels. Things are put in the right sequence, in the right perspective, and then, when one turns back to the sacred writings, there is a new and deeper understanding. The Gospels

---

[32] Sheed, *Sanity*, 324–26. Also to be recommended is Sheed's *Theology for Beginners* (New York: Sheed and Ward, 1957), which covers much of the same ground from a different perspective.

[33] Frank Sheed, *To Know Christ Jesus* (Ann Arbor, Mich.: Servant Books, 1980).

are in many ways so haphazard in organization, so confusing in terminology, that we need a road map to get around them and to know what we have seen. It is a bit like visiting a large city. You can drive around all day and still have no feel for it; but study a map, see where the main buildings are and how the highways intersect, and you can get back in the car and, for the first time, really appreciate what is there.

Similar to Sheed's book is Fulton Sheen's *Life of Christ*,[34] his most famous work. Written in response to an unnamed trial that afflicted him for years, it centers on what struck him as the main point of Christ's life, that Christ did not come into the world to live but to die. "Unless there is a Good Friday in our lives there will never be an Easter Sunday. The Cross is the condition of the empty tomb, and the crown of thorns is the preface to the halo of light."[35] Sheen takes the reader through our Lord's life chronologically, as might be expected, and he punctuates his recounting of what we think should be a familiar tale with astonishing insights. This book is every bit as good as Sheed's in giving the prospective apologist the indispensable overview.

Not to be overlooked is Romano Guardini's *The Lord*,[36] which may be the epitome of the genre. Guardini begins by noting that neither a psychology nor a biography of Jesus is possible—the divine is not to be comprehended by finite minds.

> All we can do is ponder such words as: "And Jesus advanced in wisdom and age and grace before God and men" (Luke 2:52), or the passage in the Epistle to the Galatians which describes him as one "in the fullness of time," ripening to maturity deeply conscious of the history about him. . . . We can only reverently pause before this or that word or act, ready to learn, adore, obey.

Guardini offers "the spiritual commentaries of some four years of Sunday services undertaken with the sole purpose of obeying as well as possible the Lord's command to proclaim him, his mes-

---

[34] Fulton Sheen, *Life of Christ* (Garden City, N.Y.: Doubleday, 1977).
[35] Sheen, *Life*, 9.
[36] Romano Guardini, *The Lord* (Chicago: Regnery, 1954).

sage, and his works".[37] It is generally agreed that Guardini fulfilled his task well.

Gathering the books mentioned in this chapter will be neither convenient nor inexpensive. While only someone wanting to go into apologetics on a more or less formal basis (or a bookworm) will acquire all the books, any Catholic who wants to develop his own faith so he can speak effectively with fundamentalists will get most of them. The fundamentalist problem is not a small one, and the problems fundamentalists have with Catholicism are not few. There is no one book that will arm Catholics adequately for the task, and it will take months to read what *must* be read. But the homework needs to be done—for oneself, for one's family and friends who might be tempted toward fundamentalism, and for fundamentalists, both ex-Catholic and never-Catholic, who are thinking of coming home to Rome or who, if they find their questions answered, might start thinking that way.

[37] Guardini, *Lord*, vi.

Chapter 26

Afterword

"There is something very gallant about these Literalists", wrote Hilaire Belloc nearly a lifetime ago. The people known today as fundamentalists

> never retreated, they never surrendered, they were incapable of maneuver, and the few that remain will die where they stand rather give way a foot. Their simplicity sometimes has a holy quality about it. . . . Most of us, asked to make a guess, would say that in fifty years no odd Literalist could still be found crawling on the earth. Do not be too sure. Our children may live to see a revival of this type in some strange land.[1]

Writing only five years after the Scopes Trial, Belloc naturally emphasized fundamentalism's attitude toward the first eleven chapters of Genesis. Perhaps that was all he knew about this brand of Christianity. Besides, it was mainly an American phenomenon, and the real battles were being fought elsewhere. Still, he perceived fundamentalists' tenacity. Whatever they stood for, they stood for it solidly, and he was right to imagine a revival of fundamentalism "in some strange land", such as the one across the Atlantic from England. He had no way of knowing, of course, of the travails the Catholic Church would undergo during the next half century. He could not imagine a resurgence of modernism, which seemed quite dead in 1930, or how, in two generations, Catholics would be woefully uninstructed in their religion, easy marks for sects that offered simple answers for the spiritual problems of an age that had ceased to be Christian in any real sense. He could not

---

[1] Hilaire Belloc, *Survivals and New Arrivals* (New York: Macmillan, 1930), 20, 56.

know of the hollowness so many Catholics would feel—good people who one day woke to realize that their bonds to the Church were tenuous and that they might happily go wherever the Bible, as interpreted by fundamentalists, seemed to lead them. Someone who understands all this is Joseph Cardinal Ratzinger. The Prefect of the Congregation for the Doctrine of the Faith has said that

[o]ur catechesis . . . must unmask the point on which these new "missionaries" harp: the impression, namely, that Scripture is to be read in a "literal" sense, while Catholics assertedly have weakened or forgotten it. This *literalness* often signifies a betrayal of *fidelity*. The isolation of single sentences and verses is misleading and loses sight of the whole. Read as a whole, the Bible is really "Catholic". But this must first be shown through a catechetical instruction that would rehabilitate the faithful to a reading of sacred Scripture in and with the Church.[2]

The key, then, is instruction—and not just in the proper approach to the Bible, but to all aspects of the Faith. Almost without exception, Catholics returning to the Church from fundamentalism report they never would have left had they been well catechized. Had they known what the Catholic religion really was, they would have been able to deal with awkward questions thrown their way. Fundamentalist neighborliness, however freely accepted, would not have resulted in the acceptance of fundamentalist doctrines.

Many Catholics think people are attracted to fundamentalism only for social and emotional reasons; since such suasions cannot be overcome by syllogisms, they see no point in discussing doctrines. Catholics who have returned to the Church from fundamentalism put the emphasis differently. They admit that frustration with the Church and its officials and members may have played a part in their conversion to fundamentalism, and they acknowledge that personal problems, such as loneliness, may have made fundamentalism (or at least fundamentalists) look attractive

---

[2] Joseph Ratzinger, *The Ratzinger Report* (San Francisco: Ignatius, 1985), 118.

at the beginning. Yet they almost universally declare that what kept them out of the Catholic Church was doctrine. Whatever their initial reasons for examining fundamentalism, they stayed away from Catholicism because they decided its teachings were untrue.

They also reconverted for doctrinal reasons. They came to understand that fundamentalism contains much religious truth, but also much error, and the fullness of religious truth, they learned, can only be found at Rome. They came to believe in the Catholic religion again because someone took the time to tell them what the Church really stands for or because, fortuitously, they stumbled on the facts for themselves.

The committed fundamentalist, who is often a former Catholic, *knows* the Catholic religion is wrong and thinks he can prove it from the Bible. The first step is to demonstrate to him that much of what he knows simply is not so. Emotional barriers will be overcome later, and they will fall as he realizes he has not been told the whole story. Glad-handing alone will not suffice; in fact, it is often counterproductive. The fundamentalist *wants* Catholics to discuss doctrines, and when they do not—when they deliberately shy away from even trying—he concludes their doctrinal beliefs are groundless, and the indictment against Rome seems rock solid.

Although it is essential to treat fundamentalists with respect and love (especially difficult for those too quick with jabs, whether verbal or pugilistic), that is hardly sufficient and will resolve no confusions and produce no converts. Fundamentalists must be approached on the level of doctrine, which means making biblical (but also historical and other) arguments. It has been on the level of doctrine that the fundamentalist challenge to the Church has found its power. This power lies not in the objective truth of the fundamentalist position, which is a mixture of truth and error, but in fundamentalism's insistence that truth really matters, that one's salvation depends on accepting God's truth in its entirety, in all its consequences. People find this intellectually challenging and immensely attractive—and not just attractive, but compelling, for who says A must say B.

If Catholics expect to answer fundamentalism, they will have to answer it not just with charity—necessary, although hardly sufficient—but with doctrine. They will have to appeal not just to the heart but to the intellect. After all, it is the truth that sets us free.

Appendix

Materials explaining and defending Catholic beliefs, history, and practices may be obtained from Catholic Answers, Inc., a nonprofit, tax-exempt organization run by Catholic laymen. Its director is the author of this book. Available are a monthly publication titled *Catholic Answers,* tracts (in English or Spanish) on a wide variety of topics, and audiocassette tapes of debates and lectures. Write for a catalogue, sending a self-addressed, stamped envelope to:

> Catholic Answers
> P. O. Box 17181
> San Diego, California 92117

Anti-Catholic literature may be obtained on request or for a small donation from the following organizations. When writing, ask for a catalogue and samples of literature.

1. Chick Publications
   P. O. Box 662
   Chino, California 91710
2. Christians Evangelizing Catholics
   P. O. Box 24758
   San Jose, California 95154
3. The Conversion Center
   Drawer V
   Havertown, Pennsylvania 19083
4. Mission to Catholics International
   P. O. Box 19280
   San Diego, California 92119

5. Radio Bible Class
   Grand Rapids, Michigan 49555-0001
6. Jimmy Swaggart Ministries
   P. O. Box 2550
   Baton Rouge, Louisiana 70821-2550

Bibliography

James Barr, *Fundamentalism* (Philadelphia: Westminster, 1977).

Loraine Boettner, *Roman Catholicism* (Philadelphia: Presbyterian and Reformed, 1962).

Batholomew F. Brewer, *Pilgrimage from Rome* (Greenville, S.C.: Bob Jones University Press, 1982).

Raymond Brown et al., eds., *The Jerome Biblical Commentary* (Englewood Cliffs, N.J.: Prentice-Hall, 1968).

Orestes Brownson, *Saint Worship* (Paterson, N.J.: St. Anthony Guild Press, 1963).

Warren Carroll, *A History of Christendom* (Front Royal, Va.: Christendom College Press, 1985).

Jack Chick, *Smokescreens* (Chino, Calif.: Chick Publications, 1983).

G. G. Coulton and Arnold Lunn, *Is the Catholic Church Anti-Social?* (London: Burns Oates and Washburn, 1946).

Henri Daniel-Rops, *Daily Life in the Time of Jesus* (Ann Arbor, Mich.: Servant Books, 1980).

A. C. Dixon, et al., eds., *The Fundamentals* (Los Angeles: Bible Institute of Los Angeles, 1909).

Newman Eberhardt, *A Summary of Catholic History* (St. Louis: Herder, 1961).

Eusebius Pamphilius, *The Ecclesiastical History* (Cambridge, Mass.: Harvard, 1975).

Jerry Falwell, *The Fundamentalist Phenomenon* (New York: Doubleday, 1981).

Reginald Fuller et al., eds., *A New Catholic Commentary on Holy Scripture* (London: Thomas Nelson, 1969).

Romano Guardini, *The Lord* (Chicago: Regnery, 1954).

Fernand Hayward, *The Inquisition* (Staten Island, N.Y.: Alba House, 1965).

Gabriel Hebert, *Fundamentalism and the Church* (Philadelphia: Westminster, 1957).

Henry T. Hudson, *Papal Power* (Welwyn, England: Evangelical, 1981).

Philip Hughes, *A History of the Church* (London: Sheed and Ward, 1934).

—— *A Popular History of the Catholic Church* (Garden City, N.Y.: Doubleday, 1949).

Bill Jackson, *A Christian's Guide to Roman Catholicism* (Manteca, Calif.: Christians Evangelizing Catholics, n.d.).

Stanley L. Jaki, *And on This Rock* (Notre Dame, Ind.: Ave Maria, 1978).

William A. Jurgens, *The Faith of the Early Fathers* (Collegeville, Minn.: Liturgical Press, 1970).

Ronald Knox, *Enthusiasm* (London: Oxford University Press, 1950).

—— and Arnold Lunn, *Difficulties* (London: Eyre and Spottiswoode, 1952).

Henry C. Lea, *A History of the Inquisition of the Middle Ages* (New York: Harper, 1887).

Arnold Lunn, *The Third Day* (London: Burns and Oates, 1945).

George Marsden, ed., *Evangelicalism and Modern America* (Grand Rapids: Eerdmans, 1984).

William G. Most, *Free from All Error* (Libertyville, Ill.: Franciscan Marytown Press, 1985).

John Henry Newman, *An Essay on the Development of Christian Doctrine* (Baltimore: Penguin, 1974).

—— *On the Inspiration of Scripture,* eds., J. Derek Holmes and Robert Murray (Washington: Corpus Books, 1967).

Bernard Orchard et al., eds. *A Catholic Commentary on Holy Scripture* (New York: Thomas Nelson, 1953).

Ludwid Ott, *Fundamentals of Catholic Dogma* (Rockford, Ill.: TAN Books, 1974).

Hugh Pope, *English Versions of the Bible* (St. Louis: Herder, 1952).

—— *The Layman's New Testament* (London: Sheed and Ward, 1934).

Johannes Quasten, *Patrology* (Westminster, Md.: Christian Classics, 1983).

Leslie Rumble and Charles M. Carty, *Radio Replies* (Rockford, Ill.: TAN Books, 1979).

Ernest R. Sandeen, *The Roots of Fundamentalism* (Chicago: University of Chicago Press, 1970).

Frank Sheed, *Theology and Sanity* (Huntington, Ind.: Our Sunday Visitor, 1978).

———— *To Know Christ Jesus* (Ann Arbor, Mich.: Servant Books, 1980).

———— and Maisie Ward, *Catholic Evidence Training Outlines* (London, Sheed and Ward, 1948).

John Steinmueller, *A Companion to Scripture Studies* (New York: Joseph F. Wagner, 1969).

———— *The Sword of the Spirit* (Waco, Tex.: Stella Maris Books, 1978).

Jimmy Swaggart, *Catholicism & Christianity* (Baton Rouge: Jimmy Swaggart Ministries, 1986).

Joseph Tixeront, *History of Dogmas* (Westminster, Md.: Christian Classics, 1984).

John Evangelist Walsh, *The Bones of St. Peter* (Garden City, N.Y.: Doubleday, 1982).

Ralph Woodrow, *Babylon Mystery Religion* (Riverside, Calif.: Ralph Woodrow Evangelistic Association, 1966).

Joseph Zacchello, *Secrets of Romanism* (Neptune, N.J.: Loizeaux Brothers, 1948).

Index

Acton, Lord, 224
Acts of Paul and Thecla, 192
Albigensianism, 45. *See also* Catharism
Alamo, Elizabeth, 117
Alamo, Susan, 115–116
Alamo, Tony, 53, 93, 113n, 115–117, 119
Alexander V, Anti-Pope, 219
Alexander VI, Pope, 229–230
All Souls' Day, 47
Ambrose, 185, 238–239
Anabaptists, 178
Anacletus (Cletus), Pope, 203
Angels, veneration of, 264
Anglicanism, 18, 82
Annunciation, 268, 279, 283
Anti-Catholicism: growth of, 118–120; difficulty of answering, 75
Anti-Catholic literature, what to read, 321–322, 344–345
Aphraates, 43–44, 184
Apocryphal books, 46, 132
Apologetics: and argumentation, 306–319; based on Bible reading, 303; Bibles to use, 304–305; necessity of prayer, 303; theory and practice, 301–319; street-corner preaching, 333–334. *See also* argumentation
Apostles, powers granted to, 183
Apostolic succession, 198, 199

Aquinas, Thomas, 144, 147, 278–279
Argumentation: goals, 308–309; techniques, 306–319; value of, 306. *See also* apologetics
Arianism, 145, 227
Ascension, 336
Assumption, 83, 147, 152, 154, 197, 272–276; distinguished from Ascension, 273; fundamentalist objections to, 272–273; historical proof of, 273–274; Jimmy Swaggart on, 94
Athanasius, 238
Attwater, Donald, 300
Augustus Caesar, 206
Augustine, 126, 147, 191, 192, 217, 226

Babylon: and history of Catholicism, 157, 158, 160–163; meaning city of Rome, 199–201
Baptism, 175, 182, 271, 309; of bells, 41; in Catholic theology, 177; in fundamentalist theology, 177; of infants, 84, 177–181
Belloc, Hilaire, 76, 340
Berengarius of Tours, 43, 145, 240
Berenson, Bernard, 57–58
Bible: and apologetics, 323; canon

351

of, 130–132; deutero-canonical books, 46, 132; fundamentalism's reliance on, 23; fundamentalism's acceptance of, 20; as history, 124–127; inspiration 121–123; interpretation, 26, 82, 128–130, 196; manuscripts, 124; origin, 312; restrictions on reading, 44–46; versions, 304–305. *See also* Index of Forbidden Books

Birth control, 60

Blanshard, Paul, 32, 59

Bob Jones University Press, 54, 96

Boettner, Loraine, 104, 199–200, 204, 209, 210, 212; career, 28; on Catholic cultures, 25; on confession, 184; on infallibility, 35–37; on Inquisition, 291; on "inventions", 37–47; on Mass, 246, 250–251, 255–256; on John Henry Newman, 225–226; on papacy, 223–230; on Peter, 199–201; reliance on ex-Catholics, 31–33; on rise of Catholicism, 156; *Roman Catholicism*, 28–50, 65, 69, 82, 92–94, 322; on Josip Strossmayer, 34–35; on veneration of saints, 266–267

Born-again experience, 195

Boswell, James, 44, 190

Brethren, of Christ, 282–289

Brewer, Bartholomew F. (Bart), 51–67; 82, 100, 232, 235, 236, 238, 240; on celibacy, 54–55; and Jack Chick, 113; and Conversion Center, 70; *Conversion of a Catholic Priest*, 54; misuse of Greek, 63–65; *Pilgrimage from Rome*, 53, 54, 59, 62, 96; radio program, 62–63; *Scriptural Truths for Roman Catholics*, 62, 63–66. *See also* Mission to Catholics International

Brewer, Ruth, 51, 56

Brownson, Orestes, 260, 265–266

Butler, B. C., 324

Butterfield, Clark, 96, 111

Calvin, John, 14, 112, 300, 332; on canon, 131

Cameron, J. M., 151

Cana, miracle at, 76

Cannibalism and Mass, 251–252

Carroll, Warren, 329

Carthage, Council of (397), 130, 180

Carty, Charles M., 217, 236, 245, 251, 335

Catharism, 178, 291, 298; and feudal society, 299. *See also* Albigensianism

Catholic Answers, Inc., 344

Catholic Chronicles. See Green, Keith

Catholic Encyclopedia, 321

Catholic Evidence Guild, 333–334

Catholicism, fundamentalist histories of, 154–163

Catholic League for Religious and Civil Rights, 110, 114

Cave, William, 30

Celibacy, 41–42, 54–55; and

popes, 91; objections to, 92–93, 288

Chambers, Whittaker, 102–103

Chesterton, G. K., 211

Chick, Jack, 53, 54, 93, 96, 119, 107–115, 344; influence of, 107–109; *Smokescreens*, 111–115

Chiniquy, Charles, 32, 49, 58–59, 63, 68, 111, 115; on Abraham Lincoln, 76

Christ, accepting as one's Savior, 165, 167, 177, 195; deity of, 21; lives of 337–339; as sole mediator, 278–279

Christianity Today, 107, 110, 112

Christian Science, 123

Christians Evangelizing Catholics, 54, 78–85, 97, 334; on charismatic Catholics, 83–84; newsletter, 78–80; and pro-life movement, 80–81; tracts, 80–85. *See also* Jackson, Bill

Christmas, 149, 150

Circumcision, 178

Clement of Alexandria, 203

Clement of Rome (Clement I, Pope), 202, 203

Clement VII, Anti-Pope, 219

Clement VIII, Pope, 220

Clement XIV, Pope, 227

Commentaries, 313, 323–325

Communion of saints, 263

Communion under one kind, 46

Confession, 43–44, 84, 95, 183, 186, 188; advantages of, 188–189. *See also* Forgiveness of sins

Constance, Council of (1414), 46

Constantine, 154, 155, 156, 157, 327

Constantine, Donation of, 213

Constantinople, Fifth Council of (553), 227

Constantius, 227

Conversion Center, 54, 83, 109, 344; literature, 68–69; newsletter, 69–74; operation, 68–77

Corbishley, Thomas, 324

Cornerstone, 112

Coulton, G. G., 293–294

Cozens, Louisa, 276

Creighton, Mandell, 224

Cross, sign of the, 38, 155

Cult: Catholicism as, 81–82; Egyptian, 70

Cyprian, 43, 184, 185, 217, 255

Cyril of Jerusalem, 70, 238

Daniel-Rops, Henri, 326, 328

Darby, John Nelson, 19

Darwinism, 15

Deutero-canonical books, 46, 132

Development of doctrine. *See* Doctrine, development of

Didache, 184, 201

Dionysius of Corinth, 202

Diriam, Joanne, 60

Dispensationalism, 13, 18–19

Divine Comedy, 58

Dobson, Edward, 16–17

Doctrine: definition of, 154; development of, 66–67, 142–153; and practices, 66

Domitian, 222

Dunlap, Alex O., 69

Eastern Orthodoxy, 82

Eberhardt, Newman, 239, 328
Eddy, Mary Baker, 83, 123, 244
Eerdman, W. J., 16
Eliot, T. S., 75
Encyclopedias, 321
Eucharist, 145, 188, 232–245,
    331; Fathers of Church on,
    237–238; Keith Green on, 99–
    100; promise of, 232–234. See
    also Mass; Real Presence
Eusebius, 30, 92, 200, 203, 329
Evangelicalism, 11, 14, 18
Evangelist, The, 86–94
Extreme unction, 39
Ewin, Wilson, 169–171

Faith, definition of, 316–317
False Decretals, 213
Falwell, Jerry, 86, 87n
Father, as title for priests, 74
Fatima, 262
First-born, definition of, 284–286
Formosus, Pope, 220
Fosdick, Harry Emerson, 17
Foxe, John, 83n
Fundamentalism: attraction of,
    25–26; and Bible, 26, 101–102;
    Catholic attitude toward, 10,
    24–25; converts to, 13–14;
    definition, 11; and evangelical-
    ism, 11; growth of, 13; his-
    tory, 13–26; and inspiration,
    121–124; and religious mys-
    teries, 244; origin of name, 17;
    and paganism, 162; tenets, 17;
    training in, 311
Fundamentals, The, 15, 16, 21

Galileo, 291

Gnosticism, 298
Goethe, Johann Wolfgang von,
    292
Grace: and Mary, 268–270, 278–
    279; sanctifying, 166, 270, 271
Gray, James M., 16
Great Awakening, 18
Greek, 90, 100
Green, Keith, 170–171, 242–243,
    246; Catholic Chronicles, 99–
    104; on Eucharist, 232, 240; on
    Mass 248–50
Green Melody, 99n
Gregory I (the Great), Pope, 32n,
    39, 142, 192
Gregory VII (Hildebrand), Pope,
    211
Gregory IX, Pope, 290
Gregory XII, Pope, 219
Guadalupe, Our Lady of, 47–48
Guardini, Romano, 338–339
Guitton, Jean, 300

Hagin, Kenneth E., 165–166
Hardon, John, 330
Heaven, 17, 19, 21, 40, 61, 74, 75,
    79, 94, 158, 164–169, 177, 178,
    183, 190–195, 207, 209, 216,
    233, 234, 236, 243, 252, 256,
    257, 260–263, 267, 268, 271–
    273, 275, 279, 317
Hell, 17, 21, 23, 52, 87, 95, 139,
    190–193, 230
Helvidius, 286–287
Helwig, Andreas, 221
Hierarchy, 157
Hippo, Council of (393), 130
Hislop, Alexander, 68–69, 160

History: of dogmas, 330; of
    Church, 314–316, 326–329
Hodge, Charles, 16
Holiness Churches, 18
Holmes, J. Derek, 128
Holy Family, 286
Honor, types of, 260
Honorius I, Pope, 227–229
Honorius III, Pope, 44
Howard, Thomas, 60
Hudson, Henry T., 212–214
Hughes, Philip, 32, 329
Humanae vitae, 218n
Hunkley, John, 267
Hus, John, 71, 332
Hypostatic union, 276, 277, 317

Iconoclastic heresy, 41
Ignatius of Antioch, 202, 237, 287
Images, 40–41
Immaculate Conception, 84, 144,
    147, 152, 154, 197, 268–272,
    275, 317; defined formally,
    272; objections to, 270. See also
    Mary
Incarnation, 193
Index of Forbidden Books, 44–
    45, 82, 95
Indulgences, 95
Inerrancy, 20
Infallibility: of Church, 125–126,
    139, 230, 275; episcopal, 216;
    papal, 146–147, 152, 208, 215–
    231, 273, 333; definition, 217–
    218; doctrinal development,
    216–218; ex cathedra state-
    ments, 36; and impeccability,
    215, 219–20; misunderstand-
    ings, 218; Pastor Aeternus, 35–

36; rejection of, 230; Vatican I
    on, 217–218; Vatican II on,
    216
Innocent III, Pope, 42, 43, 255,
    290
Inquisition, 95, 290–300, 326,
    334; Catholic whitewashing,
    294–295, 299; deaths under,
    291–292, 296–297; establish-
    ment, 290; executions in En-
    gland compared, 293; forms,
    290–291; geographical extent,
    290, 297; how to discuss, 295;
    why fundamentalists discuss,
    297
Inspiration, biblical, 19–20, 121–
    133, 317; Bible's claim to, 122–
    123; Catholic basis for, 124–
    127; inadequate reasons to
    believe in, 121–124
Ireland, 48–49, 76
Irenaeus, 143, 184, 203, 237, 255,
    287

Jackson, Bill, 78, 150, 280; Jack
    Chick against, 113; and devel-
    opment of doctrine, 147–148.
    See also Christians Evangeliz-
    ing Catholics
Jerome, 286–287
Jimmy Swaggart Ministries, 54,
    88, 345. See also Swaggart,
    Jimmy
Joad, C. E. M., 126
John Chrysostom, 180
John Damascene, 201
John Paul II, Pope, 212
John XI, Pope, 229
John XII, Pope, 229

John XIII, Pope, 41
John XXIII, Pope, 85
Johnson, Samuel, 44, 190
Jonah, 129–130
Jones, Bob, 57, 58
Judgment: general, 190; particular, 191
Jurgens, William A., 201, 330–331
Juris, Paul, 185–188
Justification: in Bible, 167–168; Reformation theory, 167
Justinian, 228
Justin Martyr, 237, 264, 287

Kempis, Thomas à, 131
Keys. See Peter
King James Version, 83, 305, 326
Knox, John, 72, 112
Knox, Ronald, 129, 172, 194, 229, 258, 314–315
Koran, 121, 122, 123

Lactantius, 203
Lambert, 220
Last Days, 114, 191, 275
Last Days Ministries, 99
Last Supper, 76, 145, 232, 234, 235, 238, 246, 254
Lateran, Fourth Council of (1215), 43, 44, 145, 155, 184, 239
Latin, 39–40
Laurentin, Rene, 269
Law, Curtis Lee, 17
Lea, Henry C., 292–294
Lehmann, L. H., 32, 57, 58
Leo I, Pope, 185
Lewis, C. S., 58, 268
Liberius, Pope, 227

Liguori, Alphonsus, 85, 281
Limbo of the Fathers, 193
Lincoln, Abraham, 39, 76–77, 111
Lindsey, Hal, 19, 61
Linus, Pope, 92, 203
Llorente, Juan Antonio, 291–292
Lloyd-Jones, D. Martyn, 150–151
Lunn, Arnold, 21, 60, 126, 229, 248, 293–294
Luther, Martin, 14, 33, 71, 72, 111, 131–132, 212, 224, 300, 329, 332

McLoughlin, Emmett, 32
Maconaghie, Donald F., 69–74, 149, 232, 235, 236
Manhattan, Avro, 111, 115
Manichaeanism, 298
Marriage, 42, 288; and Catharism, 45, 298; and paganism, 150, 156. See also Celibacy
Martin V, Pope, 219
Martindale, C. C., 324
Mary, 48, 152–153, 239; in Catholic theology, 268–289; death, 272–273; mediatrix, 278–279; Mother of God, 69–70, 268, 274, 276–278; sinlessness, 270–271; veneration, 75, 160, 259–267, 280–281; virginity, 93, 274, 282–289
Mass, 38, 40, 44, 64, 93, 246–258, 317, 331; Keith Green on, 100–101; memorial, 196. See also Eucharist; Real Presence
Mediator, 61, 90, 188, 209, 265, 266, 278, 279
Mediatrix. See Mary

Melchisedech, 253–254
Messenger, E. C., 324
Methodism, 18
Milan, Edict of (313), 155, 156, 327
Millennialism, 13, 18, 19, 22
Minucius Felix, 251
Mission to Catholics International, 69, 82, 83, 109, 344; and Conversion Center, 70; operations, 51–67; history, 52, 58; newsletter 53, 58–63
Modernism, 276, 340
Moffatt, James, 248
Monasticism, 48
Monica, 192
Monk, Maria, 54
Monophysitism, 227–228
Monothelitism, 228–229
Montano, Walter, M., 291
Moody, Dwight L., 112
Morals, strictures on drinking, etc., 23–24, 47
Mormon, Book of, 123
Mormonism, 215
Most, William G., 131–132, 324–325
Mother of God. See Mary
Moule, H. C. G., 16
Mourret, Fernand, 328
Mystery, fundamentalism and, 257–258
Mystery religions, 158–159
Mystical Body of Christ, 263, 334, 337

Name, significance of change in Bible, 206
National Catholic Register, 113–114

Nauer, Barbara, 97, 241–242
Nero, 202, 203, 204, 222
Nestorius, 70
Nestorianism, 228, 276
New Catholic Encyclopedia, 321
Newman, John Henry, 60, 140, 153, 155–156, 264–265, 332; Apologia Pro Vita Sua, 33, 226; An Essay on the Development of Christian Doctrine, 71–73; on inspiration, 127–128; Donald F. Maconaghie on, 71–73; on paganism, 149–150; on papal infallibility, 225–226; on sola scriptura, 135–136, 151–152
Nicaea, First Council of (325), 145
Nichols, Norman, 61

O'Brien, John A., 241, 248
Omnipresence, 243
Orchard, Bernard, 324
Orders, Holy, 47
Origen, 43, 180, 184, 237
Ott, Ludwig, 331–332
Our Sunday Visitor, 112, 114

Paganism: and Catholicism, 154–163, 280–281; and fundamentalism, 162; tenets, 158–159
Papacy, 64, 90, 160, 198–214; and forgeries, 213–214; history, 212–214. See also Peter; Popes
Paris, Edmond, 115
Paul III, Pope, 291
Paul VI, Pope, 36, 57, 204, 281n
Pelagius, 226
Pena, Mark, 57
Penance. See Confession
Peter, 198–214; first Pope, 90;

foundation of Church, 207–
211; leader of apostles, 205;
keys granted to, 207; married,
41, 91; martyred, 199; name
change, 205–206; powers
granted to, 207; as rock, 209–
211; in Rome, 30, 74–75, 91–
92, 198, 199–205; tomb, 274.
See also Papacy; Popes
Peter of Alexandria, 203
Pezzotta, Anthony, 57
Philip the Tetrarch, 206
Phillips, John, 66
Pius VII, Pope, 227
Pius IX, Pope, 272
Pius XII, Pope, 85, 273, 275
Polycarp, 287
Pope, Hugh, 233, 324, 326
Popes: "bad", 316, 326; as
"beast", 221–222; as Bishop of
Rome, 199; married, 91; titles,
221. *See also* Papacy; Peter
Practices, 154
Prayers: for dead, 157, 193; inter-
cessory, 263–264
Presbyterianism, 82
Primacy, papal, 208
Presumption, 164
Priesthood, 41, 64, 74, 85, 93,
125, 157, 183, 254, 313; and
title "father", 93
Purgatory, 75, 132, 147, 154, 160,
166, 190–197, 310, 313; defini-
tion, 190–191; invention, 192;
and money, 196; purpose, 190,
191, 193, 194
Puritanism, 24

Quasten, Johannes, 30, 330

Radbertus, Paschasius, 95, 238–
239, 240
Radio Bible Class, 123, 174, 345
Rapture, 19, 22
Ratramus, 239, 240
Ratzinger, Joseph 70, 341
Real Presence, 44, 46, 64, 145,
155, 234, 240, 245, 247, 250–
251, 313, 331; and cannibal-
ism, 48. *See also* Eucharist;
Mass
Reconciliation. *See* Confession
Redemption, 166, 194, 273, 275,
337
Reformation, 14–15, 17, 212, 326
Relics, 40, 274
Religion, derogatory sense, 89
Resurrection, 22, 125–126, 275,
336
Revelation: general, 142, 151;
private, 261–262
Rivera, Alberto, 96, 107–116,119
Roberts, Oral, 86
Rock. *See* Peter; Papacy
Rome: Bishop of, 199, 202; in
Bible 199–200
Rosary, 95, 280
Rumble, Leslie, 217, 236, 245,
251, 335

St. Peter's Basilica, 161–162, 204,
274
St. Peter's Chair, 162
Saints: in Bible, 171–172; intercessions, 160; veneration, 157,
259–267
Salvation, 164–176, 195, 275;
assurance of, 23, 101, 164–166,
168–172, 174–175, 309; and

born-again experience, 23; in Catholic theology, 166–167; in fundamentalist theology, 181; Keith Green on, 101

Schism, Great Western (1378–1417), 218–219

Schuller, Robert, 86

Scofield, C. I., 16, 19

Scopes Trial, 13, 340

Second Coming, 17, 18, 22, 273, 309

Septuagint, 283

Seventh-Day Adventism, 56

Sheed, Frank, 148, 276, 304, 313, 333–338

Sheen, Fulton, 32, 49, 55–56, 60, 335, 338

Shriver, Peggy L., 25

Sin: actual, 177, 182; forgiveness, 182–189; mortal and venial, 101; original, 177, 182, 184, 270, 275. See also Confession

Sixtus III, Pope, 217

Sixtus V, Pope, 220

Smith, Gerald Birney, 131–132

Smith, Joseph, 215

Social Gospel, 15, 16, 22

Sola scriptura, 23, 121, 134, 135, 162, 188, 197, 275, 310, 312, 313; Bible denies, 136; Newman on, 135–136, 151–152; origin of doctrine, 141

Solid Rock Ministries, 104–106

Soter, Pope, 212

Spitz, Donald, 104–106

Spurgeon, Charles, 112

Steinmueller, John, 325–326

Stephen VII, Pope, 220

Stephens, James, 292

Stewart, Lyman and Milton, 16

Stipends, for Mass, 196

Stravinskas, Peter, 251, 254

Strossmayer, Josip, 34, 35, 214

Swaggart, Frances, 87, 88, 97

Swaggart, Jimmy, 86–98, 109, 194, 232, 234, 236, 241–242, 246, 255; Catholicism and Christianity, 87, 93–96; influence, 97–98

Sunday worship, 38

Teresa, Mother, 167

Tertullian, 38, 143, 202, 251, 287

Theophilus of Antioch, 43, 144

Theotokos. See Mary

Thurston, Herbert, 293–294

Tixeront, Joseph, 30, 148, 330

Toulouse, Council of (1229), 45

Tradition, 89–90, 95, 134–141, 180, 317

Transubstantiation, 42–43, 94, 145, 154, 155, 235, 238, 241, 252–253, 317

Trent, Council of (1545–1563), 46, 130, 235

Tribulation, 19, 22

Trinity, 43, 144–145, 148, 193, 244, 337

Unitarianism, 82

Urban VI, Pope, 219

Vacandard, Elphege, 293

Valencia, supposed Council of (1229), 44–45

Valla, Lorenzo, 213

Vanauken, Sheldon, 60

Van Impe, Jack, 61

Vatican, First Council of (1870), 34, 36, 214, 217, 218, 224, 225, 229
Vatican, Second Council of (1962–1965), 103, 143–144, 246
Vernacular, 40
Vestments, 39
Victorinus, 287
Vigilius, 287
Vigilius, Pope, 227–228
Vincent of Lerins, 143
Virgin Birth, 21, 23, 317; confused with Immaculate Conception, 270
Virginity, Mary's, 282–289. See also Mary

Waldenses, 178
Walsh, John Evangelist, 205
Ward, Maisie, 276, 333
Warfield, Benjamin B., 16, 19, 21

Washington, George, 213
Weems, Parson, 213
Wesley, John, 72, 314–315
White, Ellen G., 56
Wine, 47, 75–76
Wise, Larry, 61
Wiseman, Nicholas, 245, 247
Witch trials, 292
Woodrow, Ralph, 100, 157, 159–163, 219–224, 252
Wordsworth, William, 271
Worship, definition, 259–260; types, 260. See also Saints, veneration of
Wycliffe, John, 82, 83

Young, E. J., 20

Zacchello, Joseph, 32, 218–219, 253, 267
Zozimus, Pope, 226
Zwingli, Ulrich, 300